CU00607063

Springer Series on Epidemiology and Public Health

Series Editors

Wolfgang Ahrens, Leibniz Institute for Prevention Research and
Epidemiology—BIPS, Bremen, Germany
Iris Pigeot, Leibniz Institute for Prevention Research and
Epidemiology—BIPS, Bremen, Germany

The series has two main aims. First, it publishes textbooks and monographs addressing recent advances in specific research areas. Second, it provides comprehensive overviews of the methods and results of key epidemiological studies marking cornerstones of epidemiological practice, which are otherwise scattered across numerous narrow-focused publications. Thus the series offers in-depth knowledge on a variety of topics, in particular, on epidemiological concepts and methods, statistical tools, applications, epidemiological practice and public health. It also covers innovative areas such as molecular and genetic epidemiology, statistical principles in epidemiology, modern study designs, data management, quality assurance and other recent methodological developments. Written by the key experts and leaders in corresponding fields, the books in the series offer both broad overviews and insights into specific areas and topics. The series serves as an in-depth reference source that can be used complementarily to the "The Handbook of Epidemiology," which provides a starting point of orientation for interested readers (2nd edition published in 2014 http://www.springer.com/public+health/book/978-0-387-09835-7). The series is intended for researchers and professionals involved in health research, health reporting, health promotion, health system administration and related aspects. It is also of interest for public health specialists and researchers, epidemiologists, physicians, biostatisticians, health educators, and students worldwide.

More information about this series at http://www.springer.com/series/7251

Katsunori Kondo
Editor

Social Determinants of Health in Non-communicable Diseases

Case Studies from Japan

 Springer

Editor
Katsunori Kondo M. D., Ph. D.
Professor of Social Epidemiology and Health Policy, Department of Social Preventive
Medical Sciences, Center for Preventive Medical Sciences, Chiba University, Chiba, Japan

Head of Department of Gerontological Evaluation, Center for Gerontology and
Social Science, National Center for Geriatrics and Gerontology, Obu City, Aichi, Japan

ISSN 1869-7933 ISSN 1869-7941 (electronic)
Springer Series on Epidemiology and Public Health
ISBN 978-981-15-1830-0 ISBN 978-981-15-1831-7 (eBook)
https://doi.org/10.1007/978-981-15-1831-7

This book is an open access publication.

© The Editor(s) (if applicable) and The Author(s) 2020
Open Access This book is licensed under the terms of the Creative Commons Attribution-
NonCommercial-NoDerivatives 4.0 International License (http://creativecommons.org/licenses/by-nc-
nd/4.0/), which permits any noncommercial use, sharing, distribution and reproduction in any medium or
format, as long as you give appropriate credit to the original author(s) and the source, provide a link to
the Creative Commons licence and indicate if you modified the licensed material. You do not have
permission under this licence to share adapted material derived from this book or parts of it.
The images or other third party material in this book are included in the book's Creative Commons
licence, unless indicated otherwise in a credit line to the material. If material is not included in the book's
Creative Commons licence and your intended use is not permitted by statutory regulation or exceeds the
permitted use, you will need to obtain permission directly from the copyright holder.
This work is subject to copyright. All commercial rights are reserved by the author(s), whether the whole
or part of the material is concerned, specifically the rights of translation, reprinting, reuse of illustrations,
recitation, broadcasting, reproduction on microfilms or in any other physical way, and transmission or
information storage and retrieval, electronic adaptation, computer software, or by similar or dissimilar
methodology now known or hereafter developed. Regarding these commercial rights a non-exclusive
license has been granted to the publisher.
The use of general descriptive names, registered names, trademarks, service marks, etc. in this publication
does not imply, even in the absence of a specific statement, that such names are exempt from the relevant
protective laws and regulations and therefore free for general use.
The publisher, the authors, and the editors are safe to assume that the advice and information in this book
are believed to be true and accurate at the date of publication. Neither the publisher nor the authors or the
editors give a warranty, expressed or implied, with respect to the material contained herein or for any
errors or omissions that may have been made. The publisher remains neutral with regard to jurisdictional
claims in published maps and institutional affiliations.

This Springer imprint is published by the registered company Springer Nature Singapore Pte Ltd.
The registered company address is: 152 Beach Road, #21-01/04 Gateway East, Singapore 189721,
Singapore

Preface

The health of a population is determined not only by individual lifestyles and genes but also by social factors such as the socioeconomic position and social relationships of each individual. This edited volume focuses on noncommunicable diseases (NCDs) and healthy aging from the perspective of social epidemiology, which is concerned with how social structures, institutions, and relationships influence health. This book reviews the social determinants of health (SDH) that are widely addressed in the field of social epidemiology, with a particular focus on health disparity that is associated with socioeconomic status.

NCDs and healthy aging are becoming public health challenges the world over, including in developing countries. Japan has the highest life expectancy and the largest older population in the world. This means that Japanese society needs evidence concerning the social determinants of NCDs to build a healthy aging society. A serial paper "Social Determinants of Health," which was originally published in Japanese in the *Japanese Journal of Public Health* (*Nihon-Koshu-Eisei-Zasshi*) from 2010 to 2011, forms the basis of this book. The Japanese version of this book was published in 2013 with the aim of introducing evidence in the English literature to a broader cross section of readers.

After the importance of these health disparities and SDH was recognized in Japan, a growing body of knowledge in the fields of social epidemiology and health disparities in Japan began to be published in both English and Japanese. The Science Council of Japan published recommendations for policymakers, who responded to the issue of health disparity and SDH in Japan accordingly. The second term (2013–2023) of the National Health Promotion Movement in the twenty-first century (Health Japan 21) began shortly after the publication of the Japanese version. It included "the reduction of health disparity" as one of its basic goals, and "improvement in the quality of the social environment" was also emphasized.

After publishing the Japanese version of this book, we have added new evidence and experiences into this English version. A reader encountering a literature review on SDH for the first time may be surprised to see how many factors play significant roles in health challenges, such as lifestyles, NCDs, healthy aging, and health promotion. Therefore, this book should help to understand why policy changes in Japan were introduced in the second term of Health Japan 21.

The first half of this volume reviews the available evidence on major NCDs, such as different types of cancer, heart and kidney diseases, diabetes, stroke, and metabolic syndrome. The second half explores various SDH related to healthy aging or functional declines and response, such as dementia, falls, life course, social capital, and health impact assessment. Readers, especially public health researchers and policymakers, will be able to understand the multifaceted measures that are necessary to address health disparity and SDH in the coming era of global aging. We hope that this book will contribute toward the promotion of deeper research, policy development, and practice throughout the world.

Chiba, Japan   Katsunori Kondo M. D., Ph. D.
Obu City, Aichi, Japan
October 2019

Acknowledgments

This work was supported by a Health and Labour Sciences Research Grant (H30-Junkankitou-Ippan-004, H29-Chikyu-Kibo-Ippan-001, H24-Chikyu-Kibo-Ippan-009, H22-Chouju-Sitei-008, 19FA1012), the MEXT-Supported Program for the Strategic Research Foundation at Private Universities, Nihon Fukushi University ("Social epidemiology research for the purpose of creating a society focused on well-being"), Grants-in-Aid for Scientific Research (19530490, 21530585, 17K04306, 18H03062, 16H05556, 18H04071, 19H03860), Japan Agency for Medical Research and Development (19dk0110037), and a grant from the National Center for Gerontology and Geriatrics (#30-31). We received assistance from a Grant-in-Aid for the Publication of Scientific Research Results (Gakujutsu Tosho Shuppan 245263) for the publication of the Japanese version of this work.

Contents

About the Editor

Katsunori Kondo is Professor of Social Epidemiology and Health Policy, Center for Preventive Medical Sciences and the Graduate School of Medicine, Chiba University, Japan. He is also the Head of Department of Gerontological Evaluation at the Center for Gerontology and Social Science, National Center for Geriatrics and Gerontology. He is the Principal Investigator of the Japan Gerontological Evaluation Study (JAGES) Project, which is one of the first prospective cohort studies to investigate the influence of social determinants of health and community social capital on health outcomes among older people. He is the author of the bestselling book, *Health Gap Society—What is Undermining Mind and Health*? Igaku-Shoin, 2005, which was awarded in 2006 by The Society for the Study of Social Policy. Dr. Kondo also wrote *Beyond 'Healthcare Crisis'—Future of Health and Long-Term Care in the UK and Japan*, Igaku-Shoin, 2012; *Prescriptions for Health Gap Society*, Igaku-Shoin, 2017; and edited and wrote *Health Inequalities in Japan: An Empirical Study of the Older People*, Trans Pacific Press, Melbourne, 2010; and *Social Determinants of Health—Reviews of 'Health Disparities' in Non-Communicable Diseases*, Japan Public Health Association, 2013.

Chapter 1
The Social Determinants of Health and Trends Concerning Health Disparity

Katsunori Kondo

1 Introduction

A society's health is determined not only by genes and lifestyle but also by social factors such as individuals' socioeconomic position and social relationships. A large number of social epidemiology studies have revealed a branch of epidemiology concerned with the way that social structures, institutions, and relationships influence health [1]. This was followed by policy responses and practical efforts, such as the recommendations in the final report of the Commission on Social Determinants of Health (WHO) [2] and similar responses from the European Union (EU) [3]. The WHO adopted resolution 62.14—"Reducing health inequities through action on the social determinants of health"—in the World Health Assembly.

The Japanese Ministry of Health, Labour, and Welfare (MHLW) have also indicated one of the basic goals of Health Japan 21 (second term: 2013–2023, see appendices of this book) to be "the reduction of health disparities" along with "the extension of a healthy life expectancy," as shown in Fig. 1.1. By definition, health disparities refer to a gap in health status between groups created by a difference in community or socioeconomic status [1]. Health Japan 21 (first term: 2000–2010) was a 10-year plan that addressed the "comprehensive implementation of national health promotion" and was created with a focus on the lifestyles of individuals. However, this focus took away from other aspects such as its perspective on the social environment. The experience of the first term proved that individual health and improvement of an individual's social environment are inextricably linked and

K. Kondo (✉)
Professor of Social Epidemiology and Health Policy, Department of Social Preventive Medical Sciences, Center for Preventive Medical Sciences, Chiba University, Chiba, Japan

Head of Department of Gerontological Evaluation, Center for Gerontology and Social Science, National Center for Geriatrics and Gerontology, Obu City, Aichi, Japan
e-mail: kkondo@chiba-u.jp

© The Author(s) 2020
K. Kondo (ed.), *Social Determinants of Health in Non-communicable Diseases*,
Springer Series on Epidemiology and Public Health,
https://doi.org/10.1007/978-981-15-1831-7_1

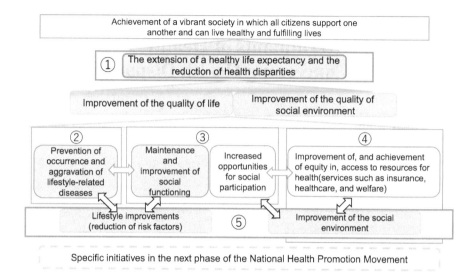

Fig. 1.1 Conceptual diagram of Health Japan 21 (the second term) [1]

both are necessary. Therefore, the improvement of social environments should be given priority [4]. In the second term, the importance of the improvement of social environment quality was stressed. Factors that determine the quality of a social environment are indeed the social determinants of health.

This book reviews studies on social determinants of health (SDH) in noncommunicable diseases (NCDs) and healthy aging. The issues of NCDs and healthy aging are becoming global public health challenges, particularly in developing countries. Chapter 1 describes the background and objectives of this book as well as the importance of the social determinants of NCDs and healthy aging. It also provides an overview of policy responses, including that of the WHO and Health Japan 21.

2 Policy Responses to SDH from the WHO and Europe

Since the 1980 release of the Black Report in the United Kingdom, SDH and the problems concerning health disparities to which they give rise have piqued the interest of researchers in developed countries, particularly in Europe. Since the truth has come to light, society's interest in this issue has been growing and the policy response has begun [3, 5, 6].

In 1991, the WHO Regional Committee for Europe had already set a goal of a 25% reduction in health disparities. The committee stated that it was the duty of governments to mobilize resources—taxation, pensions, employment, education, and state finances—and to eliminate poverty and inequality. In 1998, the United Kingdom's Acheson Inquiry reported that health inequalities had in fact grown, rather than diminished [5]. The inquiry's report argued that social environmental

Table 1.1 Policy areas that affect health

Democratic policies
Human rights
Media policies
Employment policies
Gender equality policies
Child and youth policies
Policies concerning the elderly
Urban development policy
Guarantees of income for the elderly
The sick and the disabled
Housing policies
Labor market policies
Insurance and healthcare policies
Environmental policies
Transportation and transportation safety policies
Accident prevention and emergency healthcare policies
Infectious disease control policies
Education policies
Crime prevention policies
Sports policies
Food and nutrition policies
Taxation
The judicial system

factors, such as poverty, food environment, and employment, had affected individuals' health. The government took responsibility for these findings and announced an action plan in the same year in which the report was published [6]. Five years later, in 2003, the government again released a plan of action to deal with the problem [7]. This program announced measures that included the participation of the Prime Minister's Office, the Cabinet Office, the Treasury, and the Department of Trade and Industry—in addition to that of the Department of Health—as well as numerical targets to be reached by 2010.

In Sweden, numerous policy responses, such as those shown in Table 1.1, were discussed. Furthermore, the 2003 revision to the law on Public Health Objectives explicitly stated the importance of "economic and social security." [8]

In 2005, the WHO implemented the Commission on Social Determinants of Health, and in October of the same year, the United Kingdom, who held the EU presidency at the time, organized an EU summit with the theme of overcoming health inequalities. Ministers, politicians, and senior government officials from 36 countries and numbering 570 officials attended the summit and agreed to redouble their efforts to reduce health inequality and its related problems. Numerical targets for eliminating health inequalities were established in several countries, including the Netherlands, Finland, the United Kingdom, and Ireland, and these countries started implementing their respective policy responses.

In 2008, the WHO Commission on Social Determinants of Health released its final report. This document presented three recommendations: first, it recommended improving the daily living conditions of all people, from childhood throughout their entire lives. The background of this recommendation was the accumulation of research into life course epidemiology (see Chap. 15), which demonstrates a clear link between factors in the childhood environment—including birth weight and pre-school education—and health conditions in later life. Second, the report recommended that inequitable distributions of power, money, and resources need to be addressed. One factor giving rise to health inequalities is differences in lifestyle. However, this factor alone can only explain approximately 20–30% of the gap. In other words, it has become clear that it is important to correct or lessen inequalities in themselves. The third recommendation stated that it is crucial to measure health inequalities, to have a more in-depth understanding of them, and to evaluate (esti-mate) the impact of policies when designing measures such as those suggested by the WHO report. In summary, the report suggested the following steps: recognition that health inequalities are a problem and the measurement of these inequalities is a priority; creation of surveillance systems to monitor health inequalities and the social determinants of health; evaluation (estimation) of the effects of policies and other factors on health inequalities; promotion of the understanding of the social determinants of health among policymakers, health practitioners, and the public; and a stronger emphasis on the SDH within existing public health research.

These developments demonstrate that, in Europe, health inequalities and the SDH are not subjects for only a small segment of researchers to study. Rather, national governments, the EU, and the WHO have all launched policies to address these issues and numerous individuals involved with public health and other practi-tioners have started initiatives that span different government departments and pro-fessions to solve these problems. This is—at least in part—the result of a growing body of empirical research in social epidemiology. The subtitle of the WHO report on the social determinants of health summarizes it as "The Solid Facts." [9] In addi-tion, a second edition of this report [10] was published in 2003, demonstrating its relevance and the growth in this field.

The purposes of this book include presenting relevant sections of these studies and, following the WHO's third recommendation, to "promote understanding of the social determinants of health among policymakers, health practitioners, and the public."

3   Interests and Responses to SDH in Japan

While still more preliminary than the developments in Europe discussed above, Japan is also showing increased interest in the relationship between social inequali-ties and health, of which the body of research is currently growing [11, 12].

In terms of basic literature that can be read in Japanese, the Tokyo Medical and Dental University's WHO Collaborating Centre for Healthy Cities and Urban Policy Research has published a translation of the WHO report on the social determinants of health [10]. *Kenko Kakusa Syakai* [Health Gap Society] written by Professor Katsunori Kondo was published in 2005 and *Shakai Kakusa to Kenkō* [Social Inequalities and Health] was published in 2006 with major contributions from members of the Social Epidemiology Research Group (chaired by Professor Norito Kawakami). In 2007, the *Journal of the National Institute of Public Health* (known as *Hoken Iryō Kagaku* in Japanese) published a special feature (vol. 56, no. 2) entitled "Health Inequality and Health Policy: What's Implied?" [13] More translated works available in Japanese include *The Health of Nations: Why Inequality is Harmful to Your Health* [14], *The Status Syndrome: How Social Standing Affects Our Health and Longevity* [15], *Social Capital and Health* [16], and *The Impact of Inequality: How to Make Sick Societies Healthier* [17]. The authors of the current book have also published a series of articles [18] and books [19–21] concerning societies with health disparities.

Leading figures in social epidemiological research, such as Professors Kawachi (Harvard School of Public Health) and Marmot (University College London), have been invited to academic meetings of the Japanese Society of Public Health. In 2009, the 68th meeting of the society addressed the issue of social inequality and health via a main symposium, a symposium held in conjunction with the Science Council of Japan, and other venues. Furthermore, in the same year, the society established a working group to address the social determinants of health under its monitoring and reporting committee. Reports on suicide, children, nonregular employment, and the older people were published and the Science Council of Japan submitted their recommendations (see the appendices).

At its workshop for the fiscal year 2007 (held in February 2008), the Japanese Association of Public Health Center Directors chose "Health Disparities and What Is Required of Health Centers" as one of the themes for the workshop, and the Japanese Society of Oral Health chose "Thinking about Health Disparities" as the main theme of its 58th general meeting in October 2009.

Although progress has been slow, developments concerning health disparities have become more widespread in Japan, partly because poverty and social disparities have become highly visible social issues during the 2000s in Japan. In response to health disparity problems, questions are being asked in the National Diet, as well as at the Council for the Reform of Healthcare Services for Older People.

4 The Importance of the Issue in Public Health

The effects of SDH and that of health disparities are greater than was generally thought in the past. Research conducted in Japan showed that health disparities can be seen in health-impacting behaviors [22]—notably smoking [23] and exercise [24, 25]—as well as in numerous lifestyle diseases, including risk factors for coronary artery disease [26], stroke [27, 28], high blood pressure [28], and cancer [29]. Health disparities according to social class have also been reported in mental health areas such as depression [20, 21, 30] and sleep disorders [20], in occupational health areas such as work-related stress [31–34], and in dental health [35]. These areas have all been considered in the Health Japan 21 initiative. These disparities are also major contributing factors in trauma-related deaths [36] and suicides [37], for which the incidence in Japan is higher than most developed countries. SDH are crucial when considering measures to deal with these health issues. As the effects of factors before birth and during early childhood on diseases during adulthood became known, it has become apparent that support for maternal and child health, child-rearing support, and the provision of preschool education are also vital. The Japanese Society of Public Health has made proposals [38] that focus on the social determinants of health, including suicide prevention measures and improving measures aimed at the unemployed. Those of lower social classes and who have numerous health problems are particularly unlikely to see doctors [20, 21, 39]. It can be said that this is an important reason why care prevention, preventing functional decline, use of long-term care, and measures to fight metabolic syndrome have not performed as well as was expected [19]. Furthermore, there have been suggestions that the effect of increased co-payments for patient medical fees after reforms to the healthcare system will be to inhibit patients from seeing their doctors [28, 40].

In other words, SDH are closely related to numerous public health, healthcare, and administrative issues, including NCDs and healthy aging, maternal and child health, support for child-rearing, suicide prevention measures, mental health, and reforms of the healthcare system and Health Japan 21. To make these policies, initiatives, and projects more effective, increasing knowledge and understanding of SDH and formulating policies based on this increased appreciation is crucial.

5 Summary

This book discusses various diseases and health problems, focusing on NCDs (see Table 1.2) and healthy aging, and presents the achievements of social epidemiology.

By doing so, the authors of this book clarify and emphasize the importance of health disparities and the SDH in the many public health problems that Japan and other countries are currently facing. The book also addresses both the importance of a life course perspective and the significant relationship between the state of the social environment—including social capital—and health. The authors wish to demonstrate the possibility of measures that may contribute to addressing health issues. This includes health impact assessments, which provide a concrete form to population strategies based on the social realities mentioned above.

The hope of the authors is that those interested in health disparities and SDH will grow in number and that this influence will spill over into other areas and eventually spread across the globe.

Table 1.2 Topics in this book

Problematic behavior in children
Metabolic syndrome
Cancer
Coronary artery disease
Stroke
Chronic kidney disease
Diabetes
Suicide
Depression
Dementia
Falls and broken bones
Malnutrition among the elderly
Dental problems
Life course epidemiology
Social capital and health
Access to healthcare and health disparity
Initiatives concerning health disparity and health impact assessment
What measures can be taken against health disparity
Focus on the actions of the WHO

References

1. Jiki Kokumin Kenkōzukuri Undō Puran Sakutei Senmon Iinkai. "Kenkō Nippon 21 (Dai 2-ji) no Suishin ni Kan Suru Sankō Shiryō" Kōsei Kagaku Shingikai Chiiki Hoken Kenkō Zōshin Eiyō Bukai. 2012. http://www.mhlw.go.jp/bunya/kenkou/dl/kenkounippon21_02.pdf.
2. Commission on Social Determinants of Health. Closing the gap in a generation: health equity through action on the social determinants of health. World Health Organisation; 2008.
3. Whitehead M. Diffusion of ideas on social inequalities in health: a European perspective. Milbank Q. 1988;76(3):469–92.
4. Berkman LF, Kawachi I. Social epidemiology. New York: Oxford University Press; 2000.
5. Department of Health. Independent inquiry into inequalities in health: Report (Chairman: Sir Donald Acheson). London: The Stationary Office; 1998.
6. Department of Health. Reducing health inequalities: an action report. London: DoH; 1999.
7. Department of Health. Tackling health inequalities: a programme for action. London: Department of Health; 2003.
8. Hogstedt C, Lundgren B, Moberg H, Pettersson B, Ågren G. Background to the new Swedish public health policy. Scan J Public Health. 2004;32(Supplement 64):6–17.
9. Wilkinson RG, Marmot M, editors. Social determinants of health: the solid facts. Geneva: World Health Organization; 1998.
10. Wilkinson RG, Marmot M, editors. Social determinants of health: the solid facts. 2nd ed. Geneva: World Health Organization; 2003.. http://www.tmd.ac.jp/med/hlth/whocc/pdf/solid-facts2nd.pdf

11. Fukuda Y, Nakamura K, Takano T. Higher mortality in areas of lower socioeconomic position measured by a single index of deprivation in Japan. Public Health. 2007;121:163–73.
12. Kagamimori S, Gaina A, Nasermoaddeli A. Socioeconomic status and health in the Japanese population. Soc Sci Med. 2009;68(12):2152–60.
13. Kokuritsu Hoken Iryō Kagakuin. Kenkō Kakusa to Hoken Iryō Seisaku. Hoken Iryō Kagaku. 2007; 56(2).
14. Kawachi I, Kennedy B. The health of nations: why inequality is harmful to your health. New York: The New Press; 2002.
15. Marmot M. The status syndrome: how social standing affects our health and longevity. New York: Times Books; 2004.
16. Kawachi I, Subramanian S, Kim D, editors. Social capital and health. New York: Springer Science + Business Media, LLC; 2008.
17. Wilkinson R. The impact of inequality: how to make sick societies healthier. New York: The New Press; 2005.
18. Kondo K. 'Kenkō Kakusa Shakai' e no Shohōsen: Shohō no Tame ni Nani ga Hitsuyō ka. Hokenshi Jānaru. 2006;62(10):854–9.
19. Kondo K. Kenkō Kakusa Shakai: Nani ga Kokoro to Kenkō wo Mushibamu no ka. Tokyo: Igaku Shoin; 2005.
20. Kondo K, editor. Kenshō "Kenkō Kakusa Shakai": Kaigo Yobō ni Muketa Shakai Ekigakuteki Daikibo Chōsa. Tokyo: Igaku Shoin; 2007.
21. Kondo K. "Kenkō Kakusa Shakai" wo Ikinuku. Tokyo: Asahi Shimbun Shuppan; 2010.
22. Fukuda Y, Nakamura K, Takano T. Accumulation of health risk behaviours is associated with lower socioeconomic status and women's urban residence: a multilevel analysis in Japan. BMC Public Health. 2005;5(1):53.
23. Fukuda Y, Nakamura K, Takano T. Socioeconomic pattern of smoking in Japan: income inequality and gender and age differences. Ann Epidemiol. 2005;15(5):365–72.
24. Takao S, Kawakami N, Ohtsu T. Occupational class and physical activity among Japanese employees. Soc Sci Med. 2003;57(12):2281–9.
25. Kondo K. Karei Suteeji to Undō: Kenkō wo Kettei Suru Yōin: Shakaiteki Yōin to Raifukōsu. Taiiku no Kagaku. 2008;58(12):842–6.
26. Nishi N, Makino K, Fukuda H, Tatara K. Effects of socioeconomic indicators on coronary risk factors, self-rated health and psychologoical well-being among urban Japanese civil servants. Soc Sci Med. 2004;58(6):1159–70.
27. Ichimura H, Hashimoto H, Shimizutani S. Japanese study of aging and retirement: JSTAR first results 2009 report. Tokyo: Research Institute of Economy, Trade and Industry; 2009.
28. Murata C, Yamada T, Chen C-C, Ojima T, Hirai H, Kondo K. Barriers to health care among the elderly in Japan. Int J Environ Res Public Health. 2010;7(4):1330–41.
29. Nishi N, Sugiyama H, Hsu WL, et al. Differences in mortality and incidence for major sites of cancer by education level in a Japanese population. Ann Epidemiol. 2008;18(7):584–91.
30. Murata C, Kondo K, Hirai H, Ichida Y, Ojima T. Association between depression and socio-economic status among community-dwelling elderly in Japan: the Aichi Gerentological Evaluation Study (AGES). Health Place. 2008;14(3):406–14.
31. Kawakami N, Kobayashi Y, Hashimoto H, editors. Shakai Kakusa to Kenkō Shakai Ekigaku kara no Apurōchi. Tokyo: Tokyo Daigaku Shuppan Kai; 2006.
32. Sekine M, Tatsuse T, Kagamimori S. Nihon, Eikoku, Finrando no Kōmuin ni Okeru Shakaikeizaiteki Jōkyō to Kenkō: Shinrishakaiteki Sutoresu to Kenkō Risuku Kōdō no Yakuwari. Kōsei no Shihyō. 2008;55(11):13–21.
33. Sekine M, Chandola T, Martikainen P, Marmot M, Kagamimori S. Socioeconomic inequalities in physical and mental functioning of British, Finnish, and Japanese civil servants: role of job demand, control, and work hours. Soc Sci Med. 2009;69(10):1417–25.
34. Kawakami N, Haratani T, Kobayashi F, et al. Occupational class and exposure to job stressors among employed men and women in Japan. J Epidemiol. 2004;14(6):204–11.

35. Aida J, Kondo K. Rensai 'Kenkō Kakusa Shakai' e no Shohōsen Bangaihen Shika Shikkan ni Okeru Kenkō Kakusa to Sono Taisaku. Hokenshi Jānaru. 2007;63(11):1038–43.
36. Fujino Y, Tamakoshi A, Iso H, et al. A nationwide cohort study of educational background and major causes of death among the elderly population in Japan. Prev Med. 2005;40(4):444–51.
37. Tanaka T, Kondo K. Jisatsu ni Okeru Shakaikeizai Yōin to Sono Taisaku. Kōshū Eisei. 2010;74(1):78–85.
38. Nihon Kōshū Eisei Gakkai, Kōshū Eisei Monitaringu Repōto Iinkai. Keizai Hendōki no Jisatsu Taisaku no Arikata ni Tsuite. Nihon Kōshū Eisei Zasshi. 2010;57(2):415–8.
39. Hiramatsu M, Kondo K, Hirai H. Kaigo Yobō Shisaku no Taishōsha ga Kenshin wo Jushin Shinai Haikei Yōin: Shakaikeizaiteki Inshi ni Chakumoku Shite. Kōsei no Shihyō. 2009;56(3):1–8.
40. Babazono A, Miyazaki M, Imatoh T, et al. Effects of the increase in co-payments from 20 to 30 percent on the compliance rate of patients with hypertension or diabetes mellitus in the employed health insurance system. Int J Technol Assess Health Care. 2005;21(2):228–33.

Open Access This chapter is licensed under the terms of the Creative Commons Attribution-NonCommercial-NoDerivatives 4.0 International License (http://creativecommons.org/licenses/by-nc-nd/4.0/), which permits any noncommercial use, sharing, distribution and reproduction in any medium or format, as long as you give appropriate credit to the original author(s) and the source, provide a link to the Creative Commons licence and indicate if you modified the licensed material. You do not have permission under this licence to share adapted material derived from this chapter or parts of it.

The images or other third party material in this chapter are included in the chapter's Creative Commons licence, unless indicated otherwise in a credit line to the material. If material is not included in the chapter's Creative Commons licence and your intended use is not permitted by statutory regulation or exceeds the permitted use, you will need to obtain permission directly from the copyright holder.

Chapter 2
Behavioral Problems in Children

Chiyoe Murata

1 Introduction

Mental health problems in childhood are often categorized into two broad categories of symptoms. The first involves externalizing behavioral problems (conduct disorder and oppositional defiant disorder); the second involves internalizing behavioral problems (emotional disorder) [1] that manifest as depression, anxiety, withdrawal, and psychosomatic diseases. Behavioral problems include repeated deviant behavior or aggression among children. Such conduct problems often lead to criminal behavior or substance abuse and place the society as a whole under substantial financial burden and distress. Thus, these conditions are serious public health concerns. Such mental health problems in children may be caused by developmental disorders such as autism spectrum disorders (ASD) and attention deficit/hyperactivity disorders (also known as ADHD), and mental disorders such as schizophrenia. Externalization and internalization may occasionally coexist, as seen in individuals who withdraw from society and subsequently engage in domestic violence.

This chapter focuses on externalizing behavioral problems in children. Behavioral problems in children are believed to be caused not only by mental and physical problems but also other issues, such as family poverty and/or breakdown, poor academic performance, and parental unemployment [2]. We examine whether chil-

---

Chiyoe Murata revised and added new findings to the original manuscript written in Japanese.

C. Murata (✉)
School of Health and Nutrition, Tokaigakuen University, Nagoya, Japan

Department of Social Science, Center for Gerontology and Social Science, National Center for Geriatrics and Gerontology, Obu, Aichi, Japan
e-mail: murata-c@tokaigakuen-u.ac.jp

© The Author(s) 2020
K. Kondo (ed.), *Social Determinants of Health in Non-communicable Diseases*,
Springer Series on Epidemiology and Public Health,
https://doi.org/10.1007/978-981-15-1831-7_2

dren's behavioral problems are associated with a parent's number of years of education and income, and, if so, what sort of countermeasures can be taken.

According to a Japanese survey [3] designed to gain information for use in teacher guidance on behavioral problems in students, conducted by the Ministry of Education, Culture, Sports, Science, and Technology in 2017, a total of 63,325 acts of violence (toward teachers, between students, and toward other people, and property damage) occurred, with 28,315 incidents in elementary schools, 28,702 in middle schools, and 6308 in high schools; overall, 4.8 cases per 1000 students were reported. However, incidents in middle schools or high schools are decreasing, while those in elementary schools have been on the rise, thus suggesting that early intervention is required. Behavioral problems in children lead to poor academic performance (the reverse is also possible) and influence subsequent job opportunities [1]. Childhood is a period when the brain and physical functions are developing, and diverse lifestyle habits and sets of values are formed. Ensuring the safety of the surrounding environment is essential for a child's healthy growth and development. Abuse and developmental disorders underlie many behavioral problems in children: if the necessary assistance is provided early on, it may help to reduce subsequent difficulties among them.

2   Behavioral Problems in Children and Socioeconomic Status

Very few studies have been carried out in Japan to investigate the relationship between socioeconomic status and children's behavioral problems. The findings of one study indicated that 38% of junior high school students held in youth detention centers for delinquency come from households with low income, including those covered under welfare services [4]. As risk factors for delinquency, the author cited male gender, family poverty, parental criminal record, inappropriate child rearing (abuse as per the broad definition), poor academic performance, and developmental disorders [4]. Recently, a series of studies assessed the impact of adverse childhood experiences (ACEs) on health in later life. Older persons with two or more ACEs (parental death, parental divorce, parental mental illness, family violence, physical abuse, psychological neglect, and psychological abuse) before the age of 18 years had more difficulties in handling financial issues or interacting with peers [5]. Another study demonstrated that people with lower socioeconomic status in childhood were more likely to be depressed in their old age [6]. These studies suggest a long-latency effect of ACEs on health status in old age.

Overseas, research by Tremblay et al. [7], who traced 572 newborns in Canada up to 42 months after birth and observed them longitudinally to investigate how physical aggression develops in childhood, confirmed that if the mother had engaged in antisocial behaviors as a student, began raising children at a young age, and continued to smoke during pregnancy; both parents earned low incomes; and the parents did not get along well, the child was less likely to be able to control his or her physical aggressive impulses. An interview survey of young individuals aged

9–17 years in North Carolina also showed that depression and delinquency occurred more often in low-income families [8]. Marmot [9] reported that aggression among children is more common in families with low socioeconomic status, such as those with low incomes and poor educational history.

Moreover, even after considering personal factors such as the parents' educational history or income, numerous studies indicate that behavioral problems in children are related to a neighborhood's socioeconomic factors. For example, a study [10] targeting 734 children aged 5–7 years in Maastricht, the Netherlands, found that parents' low educational history and lower-level job positions were associated with the problem behavior scores of their children based on the Child Behavior Checklist (CBCL; a measure of evaluations to assess a child's psychological state and behavioral problems) [11]. In this particular study, the parents evaluated their children. Multilevel analyses revealed that not parental characteristics per se, but the neighborhood socioeconomic status (such as high unemployment rates and high rates of receiving public welfare benefits) had a significant influence on behavioral problems in children. A Canadian study [12] targeting 3528 children aged 4–5 years suggested that a weak sense of community in a neighborhood is more likely to cause maternal depression and family dysfunction, resulting in a greater risk of inappropriate child rearing, which is likely to lead to behavioral problems in children.

3 Background of Inequalities

Behavioral problems in children tend to be found in families with lower socioeconomic status because of social causation and social selection. Social causation implies that various stressors, such as economic anxiety associated with lower socioeconomic status, lead to depression in parents and inappropriate child rearing, and tend to cause behavioral problems in children. Social selection refers to the hypothesis that children's inclination to violent behavior, owing to the family genetic vulnerability (i.e., antisocial characteristics, including violent tendencies inherited from parents), results in behavioral problems in children that may lead to lower socioeconomic status for the family or for themselves later in life [8].

Thus far, many studies have reported findings that support the social causation theory. A study in New Zealand [13] that included 1093 high school students from poor families in the urban area found that during the 2-year observation period, depression, drug dependence, and delinquency occurred more frequently in the students who were brought up in inappropriate environments that involved abuse and neglect. In particular, delinquency was frequently observed in male high school students. Tremblay [14] reviewed studies performed in Europe, the USA, and Canada, and reported that aggressive behaviors develop within 1–2 years after birth and reach a peak at 3–4 years. Children then seem to learn to control their aggressive impulses through subsequent nurturing. Tremblay [14] concluded that persons raised in an environment where violence was accepted might grow to express aggressive impulse through violence.

The Twin Study of Child and Adolescent Development [15] was a retrospective cohort study performed to examine the association of hereditary effects and environmental impacts on problem behaviors among 1133 pairs of Swedish twins aged 16–17 years. This study reported the association between self-reported delinquency experience, parents' socioeconomic status, and local socioeconomic factors (e.g., unemployment rate). The results revealed that compared to hereditary effects, environmental impacts on child delinquency such as exposure to shoplifting, breaking and entering, drug use, theft, arson, and robbery were higher in the areas where the crime rate and the unemployment rate were higher, and there were few persons with superior education [15]. In other words, children living in socioeconomically advantaged areas are less likely to become delinquent even if they had a genetic predisposition.

In Japan, the results of the survey [16] on ACEs performed in three juvenile training schools were published in the Youth Advisor Program 2007 by the Cabinet Office. The percentages of youth who grew up experiencing physical abuse (19.5–25%), domestic violence (14.1–20.5%), and those who were exposed to people who abused drugs and/or alcohol (20.5–22.2%), were obviously higher in the juvenile training schools than in general high schools (1–2%). According to a study on juvenile views on violence and juvenile delinquency conducted by the Ministry of Internal Affairs and Communications in 1999 [17], the childhood experience of violence by parents in male individuals who engaged in delinquent behavior was as high as 42.3%, while their junior and senior high school counterparts reported levels of 17.4–22.7%. Similarly, in female individuals who engaged in delinquent behavior, this proportion was higher (45.6%) than that in general junior and senior high school students (11.8–13.3%).

In the field of genetics, behavioral problems are believed to be caused by not only genetic factors but also by interaction with the environment in which the individual is raised [18, 19]. For example, children with low-activity monoamine oxidase A (MAOA) gene are likely to engage in violence after growing up. However, when they are abused during childhood, their risk of delinquency is much higher [18]. Frequent behavioral problems often occur because of the combination of genetic vulnerability and exposure to environmental triggers.

In this sense, prenatal, neonatal, and infancy phases are important. In a longitudinal study, 665 children of pregnant women who underwent medical examination in a university hospital were followed from 1986. The children with prenatal alcohol exposure were more likely to score within the clinical range for behavioral problems in the CBCL at 6 years of age [20]. Postnatal depression occurs within around 1 month after giving birth. In a review of 109 research articles, the authors estimated that the rate of mothers' depression during pregnancy and the first postpartum year was between 6.5% and 12.9% [21]. Some of the studies indicated that prenatal depression was associated with mothers' economic anxiety and unstable employment. The prevalence was also as high as 17% in mothers with 3-month-old infants in Japan [22]. Moreover, the mental development of children whose mothers had developed depression was significantly poorer than that of children whose mothers had not developed depression [23]. These findings show that children who exhibit behavioral problems do not necessarily come from lower socioeconomic status. In interviews with children aged 9–17 years in North Carolina, in the USA, delinquency was frequently found in children from poorer families. However, further analysis revealed that behavioral problems were not associated with poverty itself, but lack of love, physical punishment, inappropriate child rearing such as neglect, family history of psychiatric disorders, and repeated relocation. It was also found that the children's odds of developing behavioral problems such as delinquency would be 1.5–1.7 times higher as the number of risk factors increased [24].

Studies have repeatedly found that frequent behavioral problems found in children from a family with low socioeconomic status were the result of gene–environment interaction and that social circumstances surrounding children were important. The life course approach focuses on the impact of the environment in childhood on health, and therefore suggests interventions in early life [14]. This approach is based on the knowledge from epigenetics, which examines whether gene expression varies according to the influence of the environment. A study in this field showed that a rat pup that was brought up by the mother rat with behaviors, including licking and grooming (LG behavior) showed good response to stress (resilient against stress), whereas the rat pup raised without such experience was less resilient [14]. Considering the environment as exposures that the parent gives the child, the child-rearing attitude may influence children's behavior. Suomi [25] reported a series of interesting experiments with primates. Even in the world of primates, there are shy and unsociable monkeys (high-reactor monkeys). They comprise 15–20% of all monkeys. When a monkey with such high-reactor genetic vulnerability is brought up by its own mother monkey with similar characteristics, it becomes a shy and unsociable monkey. However, when such a monkey is brought up by a "super-mum monkey" (a monkey version of high LG rat in the above-mentioned study), it becomes a sociable monkey without behavior problems and its development is actually faster than that of normal monkeys. These experimental findings [14, 25, 26] indicate that appropriate support may prevent problem behavior in humans even if genetic vulnerability is observed.

4   Countermeasures to Behavioral Problems in Children

What can we do to address such issues? There are various novel approaches to support children at risk of behavioral problems. According to a review [27] of 67 studies, including randomized controlled trials in the USA, interventions addressing violent behavior, including delinquency, which consisted of social training such as conflict resolution, were equally effective for not only delinquency in children but also high-risk children (those from families with a low socioeconomic status or with low academic ability). The Positive Opportunities Obvious Change with Hounds (www.pooch.org) is a correction program using animals, which was initiated in 1993 in a juvenile corrective institution in Oregon, in the USA. The project aimed to look for new owners for dogs while the residents in the institution (aged 14–25 years) formed a team with specialists looking after abandoned dogs. Most of the residents in such institutions grow up in families with difficulties such as low income, alcoholism, and different forms of abuse. However, contact with animals and a sense of responsibility for care had a good influence on them. As of 2003, the number of the participants in this project reached 100, and most of them were rehabilitated to their normal life [28]. There is also the case of a psychotherapeutic institution, Green Chimneys (http://www.greenchimneys.org/), for children of the suburbs of New York. In this institution, children's mental health problems such as violent inclinations are treated through care for wild animals [29].

Measures to avoid educational disadvantage are also necessary. The Brookline Early Education Project was an educational program undertaken between the 1960s and 1970s in New York for children at 3 months before birth until entering kindergarten. In this program, in addition to home visits by specialists, parent group activities and activities outside school including reading and recreation were performed. Researchers conducted a follow-up study with 120 participants 25 years after the education program. When compared with individuals who did not receive the intervention, the program participants had achieved higher educational levels and enjoyed higher incomes. Their health conditions were also better [30]. As a part of the Chicago Longitudinal Study [31] in 25 districts in Chicago, 989 children aged 3–4 years and 6–9 years from disadvantaged families participated in an early education program. They showed a higher academic ability 15 years later. The crime rate among them was also lower than that among the children who did not receive such intervention. Detailed cost–benefit analysis using outcome data by the age of 26 years reported benefits such as savings for child welfare and related education cost and tax revenues from increased earnings. Furthermore, a lower crime rate among the program participants (compared to nonparticipants) was reported [32].

As an intervention that included parents, a social experiment called "Moving to Opportunity" [8] was performed in a disadvantaged area with Native American Indians (Indian Reservation), in northern North Carolina, in the USA. In this project, 1420 children aged 9–13 years were followed for 8 years after the opening of casinos that resulted in increased employment opportunities for their parents. The findings revealed that the creation of new jobs for parents contributed to the improvement of behavioral problems among children. According to another research paper [22], unstable employment (e.g., part-time work) and anxiety over financial concerns were associated with depression of mothers in the child's infancy. Childcare support based on policies, including improvement of the employment system seems to be important. One such example is Nobody's Perfect, a program that provides consultation for parents and self-reliance support such as job assistance for single parents [33]. This program was initiated in Canada in the early 1980s. Coordinated by the Public Health Agency of Canada, it is delivered across the country through provincial and territorial organizations. Currently, this program has expanded to places beyond Canada and was initiated in Japan in 2004 by Nobody's Perfect Japan (http://ccc-npnc.org/npnc/) [34].

5 Summary

Behavioral problems such as violence are commonly observed in children from families with a lower socioeconomic status. However, such problems are not inherited. Delinquency and violence are found even in families in higher socioeconomic positions. It appears that the child-rearing environment, local social environment, and support by surrounding people are indispensable for the development of children. A series of studies have shown that appropriate educational interventions and support for parents can reduce the occurrence of problems even if they had susceptibility to stress and a risk of abuse [8, 31]. Problems may be reduced through early detection of risk in children and supportive interventions for both children and their parents.

References

1. Xue Y, Leventhal T, Brooks-Gunn J, Earls FJ. Neighborhood residence and mental health problems of 5- to 11-year-olds. Arch Gen Psychiatry. 2005;62(5):554–63.
2. Blair RJ, Leibenluft E, Pine DS. Conduct disorder and callous-unemotional traits in youth. N Engl J Med. 2014;371:2207–16.
3. The Ministry of Education, Culture, Sports, Science, and Technology. Results of "Surveys about problems in guidance of health such as behavioral problems (violence, bullying, etc.) in children and students." 2017; in Japanese. http://www.mext.go.jp/a_menu/shotou/seitoshi-dou/1302902.htm. Accessed 4 Feb 2019.
4. Oguri M. Adult's eye and child's eye, juvenile delinquency: risk factors of delinquency (commentary). The Japanese Journal of Child Nursing. 2006;29(4):4.
5. Amemiya A, Fujiwara T, Murayama H, Tani Y, Kondo K. Adverse childhood experiences and higher-level functional limitations among older Japanese people: results from the JAGES study. J Gerontol A Biol Sci Med Sci. 2018;73(2):261–6.
6. Tani Y, Fujiwara T, Kondo N, Noma H, Sasaki Y, Kondo K. Childhood socioeconomic status and onset of depression among Japanese older adults: the JAGES prospective cohort study. Am J Geriatr Psychiatry. 2016;24(9):717–26.
7. Tremblay RE, Nagin DS, Seguin JR, et al. Physical aggression during early childhood: trajectories and predictors. Can Child Adolesc Psychiatr Rev. 2005;14(1):3–9.
8. Costello EJ, Compton SN, Keeler G, Angold A. Relationships between poverty and psychopathology: a natural experiment. JAMA. 2003;290(15):2023–9.
9. Marmot MG. Status syndrome: how your social standing directly affects your health. London: Bloomsbury; 2005.
10. Kalff AC, Kroes M, Vles JSH, et al. Neighbourhood level and individual level SES effects on child problem behaviour: a multilevel analysis. J Epidemiol Community Health. 2001;55(4):246–50.
11. Achenbach TM. Manual for the child behavior checklist/4-18 and 1991 profile. Burlington: University of Vermont Department of Psychiatry; 1991.
12. Kohen DE, Leventhal T, Dahinten VS, McIntosh CN. Neighborhood disadvantage: pathways of effects for young children. Child Dev. 2008;79(1):156–69.
13. Schilling EA, Aseltine RH Jr, Gore S. Adverse childhood experiences and mental health in young adults: a longitudinal survey. BMC Public Health. 2007;7:30.

14. Tremblay RE. Understanding development and prevention of chronic physical aggression: towards experimental epigenetic studies. Philos Trans R Soc B Biol Sci. 2008;363(1503):2613–22.
15. Tuvblad C, Grann M, Lichtenstein P. Heritability for adolescent antisocial behavior differs with socioeconomic status: gene-environment interaction. J Child Psychol Psychiatry. 2006;47(7):734–43.
16. Cabinet Office. Youth adviser training program 2007 (revised); in Japanese. https://www8.cao.go.jp/youth/kenkyu/h19-2/html/ua_mkj_pdf.html. Accessed 6 Feb 2019.
17. Ministry of Internal Affairs and Communications. A study on juvenile views on violence and on juvenile delinquency. 2000; in Japanese. https://www8.cao.go.jp/youth/kenkyu/hikoug/hikoug.htm. Accessed 6 Feb 2019.
18. Rutter M, Moffitt TE, Caspi A. Gene-environment interplay and psychopathology: multiple varieties but real effects. J Child Psychol Psychiatry. 2006;47(3–4):226–61.
19. Ridley M. Nature via nurture: genes, experience and what makes us human. New York: Harper Perennial; 2004.
20. Sood B, Delaney-Black V, Covington C, et al. Prenatal alcohol exposure and childhood behavior at age 6 to 7 years: I. dose-response effect. Pediatrics. 2001;108(2):E34.
21. Gavin NI, Gaynes BN, Lohr KN, Meltzer-Brody S, Gartlehner G, Swinson T. Perinatal depression: a systematic review of prevalence and incidence. Obstet Gynecol. 2005;106(5 Pt 1):1071–83.
22. Yamashita H, Yoshida K, Nakano H, Tashiro N. Postnatal depression in Japanese women: detecting the early onset of postnatal depression by closely monitoring the postpartum mood. J Affect Disord. 2000;58(2):145–54.
23. Grigoriadis S, VonderPorten EH, Mamisashvili L, et al. The impact of maternal depression during pregnancy on perinatal outcomes: a systematic review and meta-analysis. J Clin Psychiatry. 2013;74(4):e321–41.
24. Costello EJ, Keeler GP, Angold A. Poverty, race/ethnicity, and psychiatric disorder: a study of rural children. Am J Public Health. 2001;91(9):1494–8.
25. Suomi SJ. Early determinants of behaviour: evidence from primate studies. Br Med Bull. 1997;53(1):170–84.
26. Niedzwiedz CL, Katikireddi SV, Pell JP, Mitchell R. Life course socio-economic position and quality of life in adulthood: a systematic review of life course models. BMC Public Health. 2012;12:628.
27. Limbos MA, Chan LS, Warf C, et al. Effectiveness of interventions to prevent youth violence: A systematic review. Am J Prev Med. 2007;33(1):65–74.
28. Strimple EO. A history of prison inmate-animal interaction programs. Am Behav Sci. 2003;47(1):70–8.
29. Green Chimneys. 2018. https://www.greenchimneys.org/. Accessed 14 June 2018.
30. Palfrey JS, Hauser-Cram P, Bronson MB, Warfield ME, Sirin S, Chan E. The Brookline early education project: a 25-year follow-up study of a family-centered early health and development intervention. Pediatrics. 2005;116(1):144–52.
31. Reynolds AJ, Temple JA, Robertson DL, Mann EA. Long-term effects of an early childhood intervention on educational achievement and juvenile arrest: a 15-year follow-up of low-income children in public schools. JAMA. 2001;285(18):2339–46.
32. Reynolds AJ, Temple JA, White BAB, Ou SR, Robertson DL. Age 26 cost-benefit analysis of the child-parent center early education program. Child Dev. 2011;82(1):379–404.
33. Nobody's Perfect. https://www.canada.ca/en/public-health/services/health-promotion/childhood-adolescence/parent/nobody-perfect.html. Accessed 8 Feb 2019.
34. Nobody's Perfect Japan. In Japanese. http://ccc-npnc.org/program/nobodysperfect.html. Accessed 8 Feb 2019.

Open Access This chapter is licensed under the terms of the Creative Commons Attribution-NonCommercial-NoDerivatives 4.0 International License (http://creativecommons.org/licenses/by-nc-nd/4.0/), which permits any noncommercial use, sharing, distribution and reproduction in any medium or format, as long as you give appropriate credit to the original author(s) and the source, provide a link to the Creative Commons licence and indicate if you modified the licensed material. You do not have permission under this licence to share adapted material derived from this chapter or parts of it.

The images or other third party material in this chapter are included in the chapter's Creative Commons licence, unless indicated otherwise in a credit line to the material. If material is not included in the chapter's Creative Commons licence and your intended use is not permitted by statutory regulation or exceeds the permitted use, you will need to obtain permission directly from the copyright holder.

Chapter 3
Metabolic Syndrome

Yuiko Nagamine and Kiyoko Yoshii

1 Introduction

Since 1958, the leading causes of death in Japan have been malignant neoplasms, heart disease, and cerebrovascular disease. Given that these conditions are linked to lifestyle habits such as diet and exercise, interventions have previously entailed primary prevention in the general population through lifestyle coaching, and secondary prevention in high-risk populations through regular checkups. However, midterm and final assessments for Health Japan 21 (First Term) indicated that these approaches have failed to achieve targets. Accordingly, revised and specific screening protocols and health guidance were formulated in 2008 [1], with metabolic syndrome (hereafter MetS) introduced as a new diagnostic criterion.

MetS is a compendium of abdominal obesity, glucose intolerance, dyslipidemia, hypertension, and others, each of which is a well-known risk factor for cardiovascular disease and type 2 diabetes. Clustering of these conditions in the same patient as a risk factor has also become a focus of research activity. Moreover, visceral adiposity, insulin resistance, and inflammation have attracted attention as underlying states [2, 3]. The World Health Organization (WHO) defined MetS for the first time in 1998, and it has since been variously labeled as Syndrome X and Deadly Quartet. Diagnostic criteria for MetS have also been formulated by the WHO and by other competent authorities, and are now used for clinical and research purposes.

We acknowledge Dr. Kiyoko Yoshii as an author of this chapter in the Japanese version of this book.

Y. Nagamine (✉)
Tokyo Medical and Dental University, Bunkyo-ku, Tokyo, Japan

Chiba University, Chiba, Chiba, Japan

K. Yoshii
Nihon Fukushi University, Mihama, Aichi, Japan

© The Author(s) 2020
K. Kondo (ed.), *Social Determinants of Health in Non-communicable Diseases*,
Springer Series on Epidemiology and Public Health,
https://doi.org/10.1007/978-981-15-1831-7_3

Based on data from the Japan National Health and Nutrition Survey 2007, 30.3% of men and 11.0% of women aged 40–74 years are suspected to have MetS, with another 25.9% and 8.2%, respectively, suspected to have pre-MetS (i.e., one in two men and one in five women) [4]. These individuals receive special health checkups, specific health guidance, and intensive coaching from physicians, nutritionists, and public health nurses to prevent the onset of lifestyle-related illnesses and to lower the attendant medical costs. However, MetS was found to be driven not only by individual lifestyle factors but also by psychosocial factors such as depression and work environment [5, 6]. Hence, intensified individual health coaching alone is likely to be insufficient.

This chapter reviews the prevalence and incidence of MetS in the context of socioeconomic measures such as education, income, occupational class and childhood socioeconomic environments.

2 Socioeconomic Indices and MetS

Studies conducted in the United Kingdom [7–9], the United States [10–15], France [16], Sweden [17, 18], Finland [19], Denmark [20], Portugal [21], Netherlands, Poland [22], Tunis [23], Suriname [24], Iran [25, 26], Brazil [27–29], Mesoamerican countries [30], China [31, 32], Taiwan, and South Korea [33–36] showed that MetS prevalence decreases with better education [10–12, 17–21, 34, 35, 37], occupational class [7, 8, 16, 21], income [11–13, 16, 33, 35, 38], and wealth [9]. For example, a survey of 7013 civil servants in London who were stratified by salary into six grades found that the prevalence of MetS among men and women in the lowest grade was 2.2 and 2.8 times higher, respectively, than in the highest grade [7]. Similarly, a Finnish cohort of 1909 participants showed that the age-adjusted prevalence of MetS was significantly lower among those with ≥16 years of education (21% in men, 14% in women) than among those with ≤9 years of education (41% in men, 27% in women) [19]. Longitudinal analysis also demonstrated that the probability of MetS onset increases as the level of education decreases [14, 15, 39, 40]. However, opposing trends were observed in Nigeria, Saudi Arabia, and India; that is, individuals with high socioeconomic status were more likely to have MetS [41–43].

In addition, MetS prevalence was reported to be associated not only with socioeconomic status of the individual, but also with that of the neighborhood socioeconomic status. Indeed, a US study of 12,709 subjects aged 45–64 years revealed a significant correlation between neighborhood-level indices (income, education, occupation, home ownership, etc.) and MetS prevalence in women, independently of individual socioeconomic indices. For example, white women living in medium- or low-status neighborhoods were 1.14 and 1.17 times more likely, respectively, to develop MetS (after adjusting for age, lifestyle habits, and individual socioeconomic status) than white women in high-status neighborhoods [44]. Likewise, an Australian study of 1877 men and women aged 18 years and over found that the proportion of individuals with university education was inversely and significantly associated with the incidence of metabolic syndrome, as measured over 3.6 years of follow-up. This association persisted even after adjustment for individual-level educational attainment [45].

3   Mechanisms Driving the Negative Relationship Between Socioeconomic Status and MetS

Why is MetS more likely to occur as socioeconomic status declines? One possibility is that persons of lower socioeconomic status tend to more easily acquire undesirable lifestyle habits; for example, smoking, drinking, poor diet, and low physical activity. Another reason is that lower socioeconomic status is associated with greater susceptibility to psychosocial stress; for example, workplace stress, depression, fatigue, tension, low social support, and low self-respect [12]. Nevertheless, analyses of lifestyle habits and psychosocial factors yielded only partial explanations for the significant negative relationship between socioeconomic status and MetS [8, 9, 11, 14–16, 18–20, 33–35, 46].

For example, a Danish study [20] of 6038 men and women stratified into five educational levels found that the odds ratio for MetS in the group with the highest educational attainment was significantly lower (0.32 after adjusting for age and gender) than in the group with the lowest educational attainment. The number of smokers also decreased as education rose, while the number of subjects who exercised in their free time increased. However, the percentage of subjects who drank alcohol also increased. On the other hand, the percentage of subjects who felt depression, fatigue, and stress decreased as education rose, as did the percentage of subjects with poor social networks. These lifestyle habits and psychosocial factors were associated with MetS prevalence as expected. However, the relationship remained significant and nearly unchanged at an odds ratio of 0.40, even after controlling for lifestyle habits and psychosocial factors. Furthermore, a survey [8] of 2197 civil servants in London indicated that both lifestyle habits (smoking, exercise, alcohol, diet) and psychosocial factors (job control) explained approximately 50% of the difference in MetS prevalence due to occupational class.

Taken together, these studies confirm that poor lifestyle habits and psychosocial factors contribute to the socioeconomic gap in MetS prevalence, but only to some extent. Additional variables that may explain this gap include the possibility that relatively fewer persons of low socioeconomic status receive health checks and continue treatment following MetS onset, as well as the possibility that such persons are susceptible to harmful neighborhood environments [12, 47] or prevailing environments such as those around fast food [48]. In any case, the studies also show that MetS prevalence is boosted by complex interactions of various factors.

4   Sex Differences

Sex differences are frequently detected in studies of the relationship between socioeconomic status and MetS. In some studies, the socioeconomic gap in MetS is smaller among men than among women, while in others, such a gap is observed among women, but not men. Gender comparisons were possible in 19 of the 24 studies included in this review. "A relationship or strong relationship was observed only among women" [11–14, 21, 34, 35, 40, 49, 50] in 10 of these studies, while "a stronger relationship was observed among men" [7] in 1 study. "Results were mixed" in 5 studies; that is, depending on the socioeconomic indicator tested, relationships were observed among both men and women, or only among women [9, 16, 38, 42, 51]. Finally, "no sex differences were observed" [10, 19, 20] in 3 studies.

In a French study [16] of 3359 men and women, the odds ratios of MetS among participants who paid ≥€2300 in income tax, in comparison to low-income subjects who paid no income tax, were significantly lower only among women: 0.82 for men and 0.38 for women. In a Korean study [35] of 8541 men and women, the likelihood of MetS among women decreased as education or income increased, but tended to increase as education or income increased among men.

In studies of socioeconomic status against laboratory indices of MetS (body mass index, fasting blood glucose, blood pressure), expected relationships between disease and nearly all laboratory indices were observed only among women. Among men, no relationship or reversed relationships were observed [11, 13, 16, 35, 52]. This difference may mask the relationship between MetS and socioeconomic status among men. An identical pattern was reported in the relationship between obesity and socioeconomic status, in which women demonstrated a more consistent negative relationship; that is, susceptibility to obesity increases as socioeconomic status declines [49, 53]. Of note, these sex differences may have some biological basis. For example, men are more susceptible to poor serum lipid status from a young age than women, while childbearing and menopause are more significant drivers of body weight and serum lipid status in women. Another possibility of biological explanation of the sex difference is menopause in women. Indeed, a survey in Korea showed that part-time or full-time employment significantly lowers the odds ratio for MetS (0.67 and 0.66, respectively) only among postmenopausal women, but not among premenopausal women [54]. On the other hand, women face greater societal pressure to be thin (which also affects employment and marriage prospects), while men of low socioeconomic status tend to have jobs that require physical activity; these and other social sex differences may also play a role [11–13, 16, 35, 55].

5 Childhood Socioeconomic Environment and MetS in Adulthood

Protections against adult diseases are said to begin in childhood (or, in some cases, possibly before birth). Similarly, factors that predispose an individual to MetS are believed to form as early as childhood. The syndrome gradually progresses as a result of the complex effects of genetic factors [56], the uterine environment [57], lifestyle habits in childhood, the home environment [58], and other factors [59, 60].

In studies on the relationship between childhood socioeconomic status and MetS, indicators of childhood socioeconomic status, including the father's occupation during childhood [9, 10, 21, 55, 61, 62], the education level of both parents [63], birth weight [62], age at menarche [21], and height [21], were previously surveyed to assess potential links to MetS in adulthood, controlling for adulthood socioeconomic status (due to the strong correlation between childhood and adulthood socioeconomic status). However, the results of these studies were contradictory, with significant association observed in some [9, 55, 62, 63], but not in others [10, 21, 61]. Nevertheless, we note that even in studies that found no association between childhood socioeconomic status and MetS, associations were often observed with individual laboratory indices of MetS.

In two British studies [9, 55], a significant relationship between childhood socioeconomic status and adulthood MetS was observed only among women. For example, tracking a group of participants born in 1946 revealed that, among women, the father's occupation during childhood, as well as the participant's own occupation and education, are significantly and independently related to MetS. Among men, however, only the participant's education was relevant [55]. Another British survey [62] also showed that birth weight, postnatal weight gain, living environment, and the father's occupation during childhood explain about 11.9% and 4.6% of adulthood MetS in men and women, respectively [62].

Why then is childhood socioeconomic status linked to MetS in adulthood? First of all, it was demonstrated that low birth weight and a subsequent growth spurt, which reflect poor nutrition before birth, elicit insulin resistance and other factors that predispose individuals to adult diseases in adulthood. Low parental socioeconomic status at birth is also considered as a risk factor. In addition, low socioeconomic status in childhood may have harmful consequences on lifestyle habits in adulthood. For example, one study showed that, independent of a person's own socioeconomic status, low socioeconomic status in the father is significantly associated with smoking in adulthood [46]. In addition, low parental socioeconomic status is associated with poor childhood home environment that may include child abuse, among other factors. Another pathway has been suggested in which poor childhood home environment is associated with MetS through poor psychosocial status in adulthood (depression and poor social support) [63]. Thus, childhood experiences associated with low socioeconomic status may adversely affect psychosocial functioning in adulthood, and may easily cause MetS because of factors such as low stress tolerance. Furthermore, a survey of adolescents found that MetS was more prevalent in less reputable high schools than in well-regarded high schools [64], implying that socioeconomic status may begin to influence MetS onset prior to adulthood.

6 Summary

As noted, individual interventions such as special health checks and lifestyle coaching are aimed at reducing MetS, heart disease, and type 2 diabetes. Lifestyle habits such as diet and exercise are unquestionably important. However, the link between

MetS and social factors such as socioeconomic status is poorly understood, as demonstrated here, and is, perhaps for this reason, not investigated often.

Lifestyle coaching alone may not reduce MetS as expected. However, overall reduction of MetS could potentially be achieved with, for example, concurrent measures that target psychological issues often faced by persons of low socioeconomic status, such as economic uncertainty, work stress, depression, and low self-esteem. This reduction may also be achieved by programs tailored to the needs of persons in lower socioeconomic classes whose lifestyle habits and living conditions are otherwise difficult to change. Other social interventions, including in infrastructure and social capital, may also enhance reduction of MetS, although further research is needed.

The independent effect of childhood socioeconomic status on MetS suggests that factors in childhood and adolescence may predispose individuals to MetS in adulthood. For example, persons born to parents of low socioeconomic status are more likely to stay in a similar status as adults, regardless of one's own efforts or intentions, thus increasing the risk of MetS. Therefore, measures against MetS require not only an emphasis on individual effort and personal responsibility, but also multigenerational insight into one's life course.

Up to 2009, most studies focused on social disparities in MetS prevalence in Europe and North America. After 2010, more and more studies emerged from the Middle-East, Asia, Africa, Mesoamerica, and Latin America. Also, studies investigating mechanisms related to life course have dramatically increased recently, along with studies of genetic and contextual or built environments. Accordingly, frameworks and implementation programs to improve MetS are evolving.

References

1. Yamamoto H. Special health checks, special health instruction, and lifestyle-related illness measures conducted by medical insurers (in Japanese). Diabetes Front. 2007;18(NN):621–30.
2. Ford ES. Risks for all-cause mortality, cardiovascular disease, and diabetes associated with the metabolic syndrome: a summary of the evidence. Diabetes Care. 2005;28(7):1769–78.
3. Saitoh S. Epidemiology of metabolic syndrome (in Japanese). J Blood Pressure. 2004;11(NN):537–42.
4. Health, Labour and Welfare Statistics Association. J Health and Welfare Stat 2009 (in Japanese). 2010.4.
5. Stewart-Knox BJ. Psychological underpinnings of metabolic syndrome. Proc Nutr Soc. 2005;64(3):363–9.
6. Raikkonen K, Matthews KA, Kuller LH. Depressive symptoms and stressful life events predict metabolic syndrome among middle-aged women: a comparison of World Health Organization, Adult Treatment Panel III, and International Diabetes Foundation definitions. Diabetes Care. 2007;30(4):872–7.
7. Brunner EJ, Marmot MG, Nanchahal K, et al. Social inequality in coronary risk: central obesity and the metabolic syndrome. Evidence from the Whitehall II study. Diabetologia. 1997;40(11):1341–9.

8. Hemingway H, Shipley M, Brunner E, Britton A, Malik M, Marmot M. Does autonomic function link social position to coronary risk? The Whitehall II study. Circulation. 2005;111(23):3071–7.
9. Perel P, Langenberg C, Ferrie J, Moser K, Brunner E, Marmot M. Household wealth and the metabolic syndrome in the Whitehall II study. Diabetes Care. 2006;29(12):2694–700.
10. Lucove JC, Kaufman JS, James SA. Association between adult and childhood socioeconomic status and prevalence of the metabolic syndrome in African Americans: the Pitt County study. Am J Public Health. 2007;97(2):234–6.
11. Loucks EB, Rehkopf DH, Thurston RC, Kawachi I. Socioeconomic disparities in metabolic syndrome differ by gender: evidence from NHANES III. Ann Epidemiol. 2007;17(1):19–26.
12. Loucks EB, Magnusson KT, Cook S, Rehkopf DH, Ford ES, Berkman LF. Socioeconomic position and the metabolic syndrome in early, middle, and late life: evidence from NHANES 1999-2002. Ann Epidemiol. 2007;17(10):782–90.
13. Salsberry PJ, Corwin E, Reagan PB. A complex web of risks for metabolic syndrome: race/ethnicity, economics, and gender. Am J Prev Med. 2007;33(2):114–20.
14. Carnethon MR, Loria CM, Hill JO, Sidney S, Savage PJ, Liu K. Risk factors for the metabolic syndrome: the coronary artery risk development in young adults (CARDIA) study, 1985-2001. Diabetes Care. 2004;27(11):2707–15.
15. Matthews KA, Räikkönen K, Gallo L, Kuller LH. Association between socioeconomic status and metabolic syndrome in women: testing the reserve capacity model. Health Psychol. 2008;27(5):576–83.
16. Dallongeville J, Cottel D, Ferrières J, et al. Household income is associated with the risk of metabolic syndrome in a sex-specific manner. Diabetes Care. 2005;28(2):409–15.
17. Qader SS, Shakir YA, Nyberg P, Samsioe G. Sociodemographic risk factors of metabolic syndrome in middle-aged women: results from a population-based study of Swedish women, the Women's Health in the Lund Area (WHILA) study. Climacteric. 2008;11(6):475–82.
18. Wamala SP, Lynch J, Horsten M, Mittleman MA, Schenck-Gustafsson K, Orth-Gomér K. Education and the metabolic syndrome in women. Diabetes Care. 1999;22(12):1999–2003.
19. Silventoinen K, Pankow J, Jousilahti P, Hu G, Tuomilehto J. Educational inequalities in the metabolic syndrome and coronary heart disease among middle-aged men and women. Int J Epidemiol. 2005;34(2):327–34.
20. Prescott E, Godtfredsen N, Osler M, Schnohr P, Barefoot J. Social gradient in the metabolic syndrome not explained by psychosocial and behavioural factors: evidence from the Copenhagen City heart study. Eur J Cardiovasc Prev Rehabil. 2007;14(3):405–12.
21. Santos AC, Ebrahim S, Barros H. Gender, socio-economic status and metabolic syndrome in middle-aged and old adults. BMC Public Health. 2008;8:62.
22. Bolanowski J, Bronowicz J, Bolanowska B, Szklarska A, Lipowicz A, Skalik R. Impact of education and place of residence on the risk of metabolic syndrome in polish men and women. Int J Cardiol. 2010;145(3):542–4.
23. Allal-Elasmi M, Haj Taieb S, Hsairi M, et al. The metabolic syndrome: prevalence, main characteristics and association with socio-economic status in adults living in Great Tunis. Diabetes Metab. 2010;36(3):204–8.
24. Krishnadath IS, Toelsie JR, Hofman A, Jaddoe VW. Ethnic disparities in the prevalence of metabolic syndrome and its risk factors in the Suriname Health study: a cross-sectional population study. BMJ Open. 2016;6(12):e013183.
25. Ebrahimi H, Emamian MH, Shariati M, Hashemi H, Fotouhi A. Metabolic syndrome and its risk factors among middle aged population of Iran, a population based study. Diabetes Metab Syndr. 2016;10(1):19–22.
26. Gharipour M, Sadeghi M, Nouri F, et al. Socioeconomic determinants and metabolic syndrome: results from the Isfahan healthy heart program. Acta Biomed. 2017;87(3):291–8.
27. Gronner MF, Bosi PL, Carvalho AM, et al. Prevalence of metabolic syndrome and its association with educational inequalities among Brazilian adults: a population-based study. Braz J Med Biol Res. 2011;44(7):713–9.

28. Schmitt AC, Cardoso MR, Lopes H, et al. Prevalence of metabolic syndrome and associated factors in women aged 35 to 65 years who were enrolled in a family health program in Brazil. Menopause. 2013;20(4):470–6.

29. Moreira GC, Cipullo JP, Ciorlia LA, Cesarino CB, Vilela-Martin JF. Prevalence of metabolic syndrome: association with risk factors and cardiovascular complications in an urban population. PLoS One. 2014;9(9):e105056.

30. Villamor E, Finan CC, Ramirez-Zea M, Roman AV. Prevalence and sociodemographic correlates of metabolic syndrome in school-aged children and their parents in nine Mesoamerican countries. Public Health Nutr. 2017;20(2):255–65.

31. Zhan Y, Yu J, Chen R, et al. Socioeconomic status and metabolic syndrome in the general population of China: a cross-sectional study. BMC Public Health. 2012;12:921.

32. Li YQ, Zhao LQ, Liu XY, et al. Prevalence and distribution of metabolic syndrome in a southern Chinese population. Relation to exercise, smoking, and educational level. Saudi Med J. 2013;34(9):929–36.

33. Paek KW, Chun KH, Jin KN, Lee KS. Do health behaviors moderate the effect of socioeconomic status on metabolic syndrome? Ann Epidemiol. 2006;16(10):756–62.

34. Kim MH, Kim MK, Choi BY, Shin YJ. Educational disparities in the metabolic syndrome in a rapidly changing society—the case of South Korea. Int J Epidemiol. 2005;34(6):1266–73.

35. Park MJ, Yun KE, Lee GE, Cho HJ, Park HS. A cross-sectional study of socioeconomic status and the metabolic syndrome in Korean adults. Ann Epidemiol. 2007;17(4):320–6.

36. Lim H, Nguyen T, Choue R, Wang Y. Sociodemographic disparities in the composition of metabolic syndrome components among adults in South Korea. Diabetes Care. 2012;35(10):2028–35.

37. Paek KW, Chun KH. Moderating effects of interactions between dietary intake and socioeconomic status on the prevalence of metabolic syndrome. Ann Epidemiol. 2011;21(12):877–83.

38. Park YW, Zhu S, Palaniappan L, Heshka S, Carnethon MR, Heymsfield SB. The metabolic syndrome: prevalence and associated risk factor findings in the US population from the third National Health and nutrition examination survey, 1988-1994. Arch Intern Med. 2003;163(4):427–36.

39. Yang X, Tao Q, Sun F, Zhan S. The impact of socioeconomic status on the incidence of metabolic syndrome in a Taiwanese health screening population. Int J Public Health. 2012;57(3):551–9.

40. Wu HF, Tam T, Jin L, et al. Age, gender, and socioeconomic gradients in metabolic syndrome: biomarker evidence from a large sample in Taiwan, 2005–2013. Annals of Epidemiology. 2017;27(5):315–322.e2.

41. Adedoyin RA, Afolabi A, Adegoke OO, Akintomide AO, Awotidebe TO. Relationship between socioeconomic status and metabolic syndrome among Nigerian adults. Diabetes Metab Syndr. 2013;7(2):91–4.

42. Al-Daghri NM, Alkharfy KM, Al-Attas OS, et al. Gender-dependent associations between socioeconomic status and metabolic syndrome: a cross-sectional study in the adult Saudi population. BMC Cardiovasc Disord. 2014;14:51.

43. Deedwania PC, Gupta R, Sharma KK, et al. High prevalence of metabolic syndrome among urban subjects in India: a multisite study. Diabetes Metab Syndr. 2014;8(3):156–61.

44. Chichlowska KL, Rose KM, Diez-Roux AV, Golden SH, McNeill AM, Heiss G. Individual and neighborhood socioeconomic status characteristics and prevalence of metabolic syndrome: the atherosclerosis risk in communities (ARIC) study. Psychosom Med. 2008;70(9):986–92.

45. Ngo AD, Paquet C, Howard NJ, et al. Area-level socioeconomic characteristics and incidence of metabolic syndrome: a prospective cohort study. BMC Public Health. 2013;13:681.

46. Brunner E, Shipley MJ, Blane D, Smith GD, Marmot MG. When does cardiovascular risk start? Past and present socioeconomic circumstances and risk factors in adulthood. J Epidemiol Community Health. 1999;53(12):757–64.

47. Keita AD, Judd SE, Howard VJ, Carson AP, Ard JD, Fernandez JR. Associations of neighborhood area level deprivation with the metabolic syndrome and inflammation among middle- and older- age adults. BMC Public Health. 2014;14:1319.

48. Paquet C, Dubé L, Gauvin L, Kestens Y, Daniel M. Sense of mastery and metabolic risk: moderating role of the local fast-food environment. Psychosom Med. 2010;72(3):324–31.
49. Ko KD, Cho B, Lee WC, Lee HW, Lee HK, Oh BJ. Obesity explains gender differences in the association between education level and metabolic syndrome in South Korea: the results from the Korean National Health and nutrition examination survey 2010. Asia Pac J Public Health. 2015;27(2):NP630–9.
50. Cho KI, Kim BH, Je HG, Jang JS, Park YH. Gender-specific associations between socioeconomic status and psychological factors and metabolic syndrome in the Korean population: findings from the 2013 Korean National Health and nutrition examination survey. Biomed Res Int. 2016;2016:3973197.
51. Ni LF, Dai YT, Su TC, Hu WY. Substance use, gender, socioeconomic status and metabolic syndrome among adults in Taiwan. Public Health Nurs. 2013;30(1):18–28.
52. Nagamine Y, Kondo N, Yokobayashi K, et al. Socioeconomic disparity in the prevalence of objectively evaluated diabetes among older Japanese adults: JAGES cross-sectional data in 2010. J Epidemiol. 2019;29:295–301. https://doi.org/10.2188/jea.JE20170206.
53. McLaren L. Socioeconomic status and obesity. Epidemiol Rev. 2007;29:29–48.
54. Kang HT, Kim HY, Kim JK, Linton JA, Lee YJ. Employment is associated with a lower prevalence of metabolic syndrome in postmenopausal women based on the 2007-2009 Korean National Health Examination and nutrition survey. Menopause. 2014;21(3):221–6.
55. Langenberg C, Kuh D, Wadsworth ME, Brunner E, Hardy R. Social circumstances and education: life course origins of social inequalities in metabolic risk in a prospective national birth cohort. Am J Public Health. 2006;96(12):2216–21.
56. Vermeiren AP, Bosma H, Gielen M, et al. Do genetic factors contribute to the relation between education and metabolic risk factors in young adults? A twin study. Eur J Pub Health. 2013;23(6):986–91.
57. Delpierre C, Fantin R, Barboza-Solis C, Lepage B, Darnaudéry M, Kelly-Irving M. The early life nutritional environment and early life stress as potential pathways towards the metabolic syndrome in mid-life? A lifecourse analysis using the 1958 British birth cohort. BMC Public Health. 2016;16(1):815.
58. Hostinar CE, Ross KM, Chen E, Miller GE. Early-life socioeconomic disadvantage and metabolic health disparities. Psychosom Med. 2017;79(5):514–23.
59. Saland JM. Update on the metabolic syndrome in children. Curr Opin Pediatr. 2007;19(2):183–91.
60. Fukuoka H. Prevention of lifestyle-related illnesses from the fetal stage (in Japanese). Health Care. 2007;49:376–81.
61. Kivimäki M, Smith GD, Juonala M, et al. Socioeconomic position in childhood and adult cardiovascular risk factors, vascular structure, and function: cardiovascular risk in young Finns study. Heart. 2006;92(4):474–80.
62. Parker L, Lamont DW, Unwin N, et al. A lifecourse study of risk for hyperinsulinaemia, dyslipidaemia and obesity (the central metabolic syndrome) at age 49-51 years. Diabet Med. 2003;20(5):406–15.
63. Lehman BJ, Taylor SE, Kiefe CI, Seeman TE. Relation of childhood socioeconomic status and family environment to adult metabolic functioning in the CARDIA study. Psychosom Med. 2005;67(6):846–54.
64. Ozaki R, Qiao Q, Wong GW, et al. Overweight, family history of diabetes and attending schools of lower academic grading are independent predictors for metabolic syndrome in Hong Kong Chinese adolescents. Arch Dis Child. 2007;92(3):224–8.

Open Access This chapter is licensed under the terms of the Creative Commons Attribution-NonCommercial-NoDerivatives 4.0 International License (http://creativecommons.org/licenses/by-nc-nd/4.0/), which permits any noncommercial use, sharing, distribution and reproduction in any medium or format, as long as you give appropriate credit to the original author(s) and the source, provide a link to the Creative Commons licence and indicate if you modified the licensed material. You do not have permission under this licence to share adapted material derived from this chapter or parts of it.

The images or other third party material in this chapter are included in the chapter's Creative Commons licence, unless indicated otherwise in a credit line to the material. If material is not included in the chapter's Creative Commons licence and your intended use is not permitted by statutory regulation or exceeds the permitted use, you will need to obtain permission directly from the copyright holder.

Chapter 4
Cancer and Socioeconomic Status

Takahiro Tabuchi

1 Introduction

A topic of "cancer and socioecomic status (SES)" has been and remains a crucial public health issue. Cancer is the second-leading cause of death worldwide. In 2016, there were 17.2 million incident cases, and over 8.9 million deaths worldwide [1]. In Japan, cancer has been the leading cause of death since 1981. In 2013, there were 0.86 million incident cases, and more than 300,000 deaths [2].

Socioeconomic differences in cancer outcomes have been observed worldwide: persons with lower socioeconomic status were likely to have higher cancer mortality rates. The reduction of this difference has become a political public health goal [3, 4]. A report published by the International Agency for Research on Cancer (IARC) in 1997 called "Social Inequalities and Cancer" indicated that lower SES tends to have higher cancer incidence and poorer cancer survival than higher SES in both developed and less-developed countries [5]. The American Healthy People 2010 initiative is striving to eliminate the socioeconomic gap in cancer [6].

In Japan, equal accessibility was incorporated into the Cancer Control Act to reduce differences in cancer treatment outcomes across facilities and regions. However, to date, discussions and supporting data related to socioeconomic disparities in the cancer continuum are insufficient.

This chapter provides an overview of the socioeconomic difference in cancer, focusing on the Japanese situation: SES includes individual-level factors such as income, education and occupation, and neighborhood-level deprivation; while

---

We acknowledge Dr. Kiyoko Yoshii as an author of this chapter in the Japanese version of this book.

T. Tabuchi (✉)
Osaka International Cancer Institute, Osaka, Osaka, Japan

© The Author(s) 2020
K. Kondo (ed.), *Social Determinants of Health in Non-communicable Diseases*,
Springer Series on Epidemiology and Public Health,
https://doi.org/10.1007/978-981-15-1831-7_4

cancer-related variables include prevention (primary and secondary prevention for cancer) to outcomes (incidence, mortality, survival, and so on).

2 Socioeconomic Disparity in Cancer

Socioeconomic disparities exist across the cancer continuum including mortality, incidence, survival, prevention of risk factors, early detection, treatment, and palliative care [7].

2.1 Cancer Mortality and Incidence

A recent study in the USA reported that individuals in more deprived areas or in lower education and income groups had higher mortality and incidence rates than their more affluent counterparts, with excess risk being particularly marked for lung, colorectal, cervical, stomach, and liver cancer [8]. Education and income disparities in cancer mortality have continued over time. Because mortality in lower socioeconomic groups/areas has decreased more slowly, socioeconomic disparities in cancer mortality have widened.

A previous study that analyzed American mortality data (ages 25–64 years) in 2001 showed that lower education was associated with higher cancer mortality rates: compared with individuals with ≥ 12 years of education, the relative risk of cancer mortality for individuals with <12 years of education was 2.24 for white men, 2.38 for black men, 1.76 for white women, and 1.43 for black women [9]. These results were consistent with other review articles and studies [5, 7].

An epidemiological study of 11,464 American men and women reported that cancer incidence was higher among subjects of lower SES in terms of education and household income [10]. Compared with individuals with ≥ 16 years of education, the cancer incidence ratio for individuals with ≤ 11 years of education was 1.17 (1.22 for men, 1.08 for women).

These associations had been examined across cancer sites. Here are just a few examples. A review of studies conducted in 21 countries between 1966 and 1994 reported relationships between SES and cancer mortality rates in various cancer sites [5]. Cancer sites for which the incidence and mortality rates were higher when SES was lower included lung (men), laryngeal (men), oral (men), pharyngeal (men), esophageal, gastric, and cervical. However, similar association was not found in colon, melanoma, breast, or ovarian cancer. For breast cancer, a review paper reported that women with higher SES show higher breast cancer incidence, which may be explained by reproductive factors, mammography screening, hormone replacement therapy, and lifestyle factors [11].

2.2   Survival in Cancer Patients

Survival rate was lower in cancer patients with lower SES, regardless of cancer site. A review of 42 studies on the association between cancer patient survival rates and SES found that most studies consistently reported that patients of lower SES had poorer survival rates than patients of high SES [12]. A study in the USA [13] also found that 5-year survival for lung, liver, kidney, colorectal, prostate, and breast cancers increased from low to high SES, with the smallest difference between the lowest and the highest SES (quintile) occurring for prostate cancer (−4.8%) and the largest difference for breast cancer (−9.8%) and liver cancer (−10.4%). These differences by SES in the survival may reflect the socioeconomic disparity in examinations and access to medical care for cancer.

2.3   Primary Prevention

The onset of cancer is known to be associated with the following: lifestyle habit factors (smoking, low intake of fruit and vegetables, infrequent exercise, obesity); human papillomavirus, hepatitis C and B virus, and *Helicobacter pylori* infections; and occupational exposure to asbestos [14–16]. The SES differences in cancer incidence may reflect inequalities in smoking, obesity, physical inactivity, diet, alcohol use, screening, and treatment [8].

In many developed countries, smoking rates are observed to increase as SES declines, particularly among men [4, 15]. Smoking is an established risk factor for cancers such as lung, oral, pharyngeal, gastric, liver, colorectal, and bladder cancers [17]. In an analysis of approximately 400,000 persons in ten European countries, approximately 50% of the negative relationship between lung cancer incidence and SES (years of education) was explained by SES differences in smoking [18]. In addition, people in jobs with higher alcohol consumption and smoking rates (sales jobs, journalists, sailors) were reported to have higher rates of liver cancer and gallbladder cancer [19]. Meanwhile, differences in gastric cancer rates according to education are explained by differences in *Helicobacter pylori* infection (i.e., infection rates rise as education decreases) [20].

2.4   Secondary Prevention

The SES differences in secondary prevention (early detection and treatment for cancer) will also be observed in the SES difference in prognosis following cancer diagnosis.

Many reports have stated that cancer screening rates decrease as income and education decrease [4, 21]. For example, in an American survey conducted in 2000,

56.8% of women with <11 years of education and 80.1% of women with ≥16 years of education (aged ≥40 years) had had a mammogram within the past 2 years, while 12.1% of women with <11 years of education and 23.0% of women with ≥16 years of education (aged ≥50 years) had had a mammogram within the past year [4]. The SES differences in cancer screening attendance rates may be caused by the following reasons: low priority on cancer prevention because of the pressures of daily life; difficulty in obtaining accurate information on prevention and screening; not having a regular care physician who would recommend screening; and poor access to screening facilities because of neighborhood conditions [22].

Persons of lower SES have a higher chance of having advanced-stage cancer when diagnosed, as well as a lower chance of early detection [4]. For example, an analysis [10] of 15,357 American men and women found that subjects with ≤11 years of education were 1.48 times more likely than subjects with ≥16 years of education to have advanced-stage colon cancer at the time of diagnosis. Similarly, subjects with a household income of ≤$12,500 were 1.38 times more likely than subjects with a household income of ≥$50,000 to have advanced-stage colon cancer when diagnosed. For women, those with ≤11 years of education were 1.77 times more likely than women with ≥16 years of education to have advanced-stage breast cancer at the time of diagnosis; while women with a household income of ≤$12,500 were 2.30 times more likely than women with a household income of ≥$50,000 to have advanced-stage breast cancer when diagnosed. Another study in the USA [23] showed that low SES was associated with more advanced disease stage and with less aggressive treatment for breast, prostate and colorectal cancers.

Cancer is often diagnosed not only through screenings, but also in examinations that patients seek due to an awareness of their own symptoms. According to reviews of studies on the period of time from awareness of symptoms to cancer diagnosis, this interval is longer at lower SES [24, 25].

2.5 Cancer Treatment and Care

Socioeconomically disadvantaged cancer patients have been shown to present with more advanced disease, receive appropriate therapy less often, and suffer higher rates of mortality than those with no disadvantage [23, 26–28]. An American study of breast, prostate, and colon cancers [23] reported that the percentage of patients who failed to receive appropriate cancer treatment (as demonstrated in guidelines) was higher in the low SES neighborhood. Ward et al. [4] suggested the following causes of the SES differences in cancer treatments: (1) structural obstacles (lack of health insurance or other financial support, geographical distance to treatment facilities); (2) factors relating to physician input (recommending different treatment because of the patient's SES); and (3) factors relating to the patient's response (mistrust of medical care, fatalism, lack of trust in medical personnel).

SES differences may also exist in the quality of palliative care, such as pain management. In a review of previous studies, McNeill et al. stated that disparities in pain management result from the association of factors such as SES, race/ethnicity, enrollment in health insurance, and one's neighborhood of residence [29]. Another study in New York [30] found that 72% of pharmacies in predominantly white neighborhoods stocked morphine for cancer pain, versus only 25% of pharmacies in predominantly nonwhite neighborhoods.

3 International Comparisons

As we have demonstrated, the socioeconomic disparity of rising cancer incidence and mortality rates associated with declining SES has been observed in many countries. However, countries also differ in terms of SES differences in tobacco and alcohol consumption, as well as in terms of screening and medical care systems. Therefore, the socioeconomic disparity in cancer differs by country and region.

According to a study that compared the association between years of education and cancer mortality rates in ten populations in Europe [31], men with lower education had higher lung cancer mortality rates in all populations. However, individual populations differed in terms of lung cancer mortality risk among lowly educated subjects in relation to highly educated subjects: whereas this relative risk was high in Austria (1.97) and the United Kingdom (1.95), it was low in Madrid (1.13). Among women, lower education was associated with higher lung cancer mortality rates in five of the ten countries (UK, Norway, Denmark, Finland and Belgium). Conversely, in Madrid, higher education was associated with higher lung cancer mortality rates. This variance across countries in SES differences in lung cancer mortality rates reflected the pattern of SES differences in smoking rates. Similarly, differences in mortality rates of alcohol-related cancers (oral, laryngeal, pharyngeal, esophageal, liver) by education were particularly large in France and Switzerland [32]. Another review paper has reported that SES differences in cervical cancer incidence are larger in North America and developing countries (South America, Asia, Africa) than in Europe [33]. Yet another review article reported that lower SES is associated with higher incidence of colon cancer in the United States and Canada, but with lower incidence of colon cancer in Europe [28].

4 Findings in Japan

This section demonstrates the link between cancer and socioeconomic status in Japan.

4.1   Risk Factors for Cancer

Similar to tobacco smoking, alcohol intake, and less exercise, higher prevalence of cancer risk factors among low SES individuals has been observed in Japan [34, 35]. Tobacco smoking is the greatest risk factor for cancer incidence and adult mortality in Japan [36, 37]. Given the first priority, we focus on smoking inequality here. Previous systematic reviews of population-level tobacco control interventions and their effects on smoking inequality by socioeconomic status concluded that tobacco taxation reduces smoking inequality by income (although this is not consistent for other socioeconomic factors, such as education) [38]. However, similar results on smoking inequality by tobacco taxation were not observed in Japanese studies [39, 40]. The taxation in 2010 did not decrease smoking inequality by income in Japan [40]. This might be a result of an excessively low tobacco price in Japan, according to the affordability index [41]. To reduce socioeconomic inequality in smoking, a dramatic increase in tobacco price would be necessary, especially in Japan where the tobacco price is very low [42].

4.2   Cancer Screening

Previous studies that have analyzed data from the Comprehensive Survey of Living Conditions, a nationally representative survey in Japan, reported that attendance rates of cancer screening were lower among lower SES populations, such as blue-collar workers, or persons with low income and no health insurance, than their high SES counterparts [43, 44].

To increase participation in Pap smear testing (cervical cancer screening), mammography (breast cancer screening), and fecal occult blood testing (colorectal cancer screening), the Japanese government implemented out-of-pocket costs removal intervention since 2009 (since 2012 for the fecal test) [45, 46]. The changes of multiple inequality indices before and after the intervention suggested that this intervention increased income-based inequality in Pap smear attendance but decreased the inequality in mammography attendance [46]. A differential effect across socioeconomic groups was observed for the fecal test: current smokers and education achievement below high school level were identified as hard-to-reach populations that may be less sensitive to the cost-removal intervention, irrespective of gender [45].

4.3   Incidence, Survival and Mortality

In an ecological study of 67 municipalities in Osaka Prefecture, lower SES areas (municipality level) had higher age-adjusted mortalities and incidences of cancer, as well as lower rates of early diagnosis and 5-year survival [47]. In an analysis using data from the Osaka Cancer Registry, cervical and corpus cancer patients living in higher SES areas (municipality level) had higher rates of early diagnosis and 5-year survival [48]. A study used a small area-based deprivation index ("Cho-Aza" level with average population 3000) in Osaka, and reported that cancer patients living in the deprived area were likely to have lower survival at 5 years, but no association at 1-year survival for patients in the least deprived area [49].

A previous study of approximately 40,000 Japanese individuals found that lower education was associated with higher cancer mortality rates (relative risk: 1.17) [50]. However, another population-based cohort study to assess neighborhood deprivation and risk of cancer incidence, mortality, and survival reported that the neighborhood deprivation index has no substantial overall association with the risk of incidence, mortality, and survival from cancer [51]. The results of these studies may have differed because the direction of the association may differ by cancer site. While inverse association between SES and cancer outcomes was observed in most sites [5], a previous study in Japan found that women with a higher educational level are a high risk group for breast cancer [52].

5   Summary

SES differences in cancer are observed across various levels, including individual SES indicators such as income, education and occupation, and neighborhood-level SES (municipality level and small area level) worldwide and in Japan. Therefore, the socioeconomic inequality in cancer cannot be eliminated solely by efforts at the individual level. Combined efforts at various levels, such as governmental health care policies, efforts by medical institutions, and local initiatives, are necessary [4]. Although technological developments in cancer screening and treatment methods have improved mortality rates, some data show that SES differences are either unchanged or expanding [28, 46, 53, 54]. This situation has resulted in the creation of programs tailored to the needs of individuals with low SES [4, 55].

In Japan, the number of epidemiological studies focusing on SES disparities in cancer has increased in the past decade. However, this research topic includes many perspectives and aspects at various levels; results will differ across specific cancer site, country, area and outcome type (incidence, mortality, survival, and so on) [5]. Although this chapter only captured a few aspects of the evidence about "cancer and SES" (we can only focus on all cancer and some selected cancer sites; SES only included major individual-level socioeconomic factors of income, education, and occupation, and area-level deprivation), further deeper understanding of the socioeconomic disparity in cancer and discussions of the proper roles of government policy and various institutions are also necessary.

Acknowledgements We thank Ms. Taniyama for the valuable support. The study is supported by Health Labour Sciences Research Grants (H28-junkankitou-ippan-002 and H28-junkankitou-ippan-008) and the Japan Society for the Promotion of Science (JSPS) KAKENHI Grants (18H03062).

References

1. Global Burden of Disease Cancer Collaboration, Fitzmaurice C, Akinyemiju TF, et al. Global, regional, and National Cancer Incidence, mortality, years of life lost, years lived with disability, and disability-adjusted life-years for 29 Cancer groups, 1990 to 2016: a systematic analysis for the global burden of disease study. JAMA Oncol. 2018;4:1553–68.
2. National Cancer Center, Center for Cancer Control and Information Services. Monitoring of cancer incidence in Japan: MCIJ2013. Tokyo: Japan National Cancer Center; 2017.
3. Freeman HP. Poverty, culture, and social injustice: determinants of cancer disparities. CA Cancer J Clin. 2004;54:72–7.
4. Ward E, Jemal A, Cokkinides V, et al. Cancer disparities by race/ethnicity and socioeconomic status. CA Cancer J Clin. 2004;54:78–93.
5. Faggiano F, Partanen T, Kogevinas M, Boffetta P. Socioeconomic differences in cancer incidence and mortality. IARC Sci Publ. 1997;(138):65–176.
6. Harper S, Lynch J. Methods for measuring cancer disparities: using data relevant to healthy people 2010 cancer-related objectives. Bethesda, MD: National Cancer Institute; 2005.
7. Kogevinas N, Pearce N, Susser M, Boffetta P. Social inequalities and cancer: IARC Scientific Publications No. 138. Lyon: The International Agency for Research on Cancer; 1997.
8. Singh GK, Jemal A. Socioeconomic and racial/ethnic disparities in cancer mortality, incidence, and survival in the United States, 1950-2014: over six decades of changing patterns and widening inequalities. J Environ Public Health. 2017;2017:2819372.
9. Albano JD, Ward E, Jemal A, et al. Cancer mortality in the United States by education level and race. J Natl Cancer Inst. 2007;99:1384–94.
10. Clegg LX, Reichman ME, Miller BA, et al. Impact of socioeconomic status on cancer incidence and stage at diagnosis: selected findings from the surveillance, epidemiology, and end results: National Longitudinal Mortality Study. Cancer Causes Control. 2009;20:417–35.
11. Lundqvist A, Andersson E, Ahlberg I, et al. Socioeconomic inequalities in breast cancer incidence and mortality in Europe-a systematic review and meta-analysis. Eur J Pub Health. 2016;26:804–13.
12. Kogevinas M, Porta M. Socioeconomic differences in cancer survival: a review of the evidence. IARC Sci Publ. 1997;(138):177–206.
13. Kish JK, Yu M, Percy-Laurry A, Altekruse SF. Racial and ethnic disparities in cancer survival by neighborhood socioeconomic status in surveillance, epidemiology, and end results (SEER) registries. J Natl Cancer Inst Monogr. 2014;2014:236–43.
14. International Agency for Research on Cancer. A review of human carcinogens. Part E: personal habits and indoor combustions. Lyon, France; 2012.
15. Ministry of Health, Labour and Welfare. The study group on health effects of smoking. Smoking and health: a report of the study group on health effects of smoking; 2016.
16. Jemal A, Torre L, Soerjomataram I, Bray F, editors. The cancer atlas. 3rd ed. Atlanta, GA: American Cancer Society; 2019. www.cancer.org/canceratlas.
17. U.S. Department of Health and Human Services, Centers for Disease Control, Office on Smoking and Health. The health consequences of smoking - 50 years of progress. A report of the surgeon General. Rockville, USA; 2014.
18. Menvielle G, Boshuizen H, Kunst AE, et al. The role of smoking and diet in explaining educational inequalities in lung cancer incidence. J Natl Cancer Inst. 2009;101:321–30.
19. Ji J, Hemminki K. Variation in the risk for liver and gallbladder cancers in socioeconomic and occupational groups in Sweden with etiological implications. Int Arch Occup Environ Health. 2005;78:641–9.
20. Nagel G, Linseisen J, Boshuizen HC, et al. Socioeconomic position and the risk of gastric and oesophageal cancer in the European prospective investigation into Cancer and nutrition (EPIC-EURGAST). Int J Epidemiol. 2007;36:66–76.
21. Segnan N. Socioeconomic status and cancer screening. IARC Sci Publ. 1997;(138):369–76.

22. Gerend MA, Pai M. Social determinants of black-white disparities in breast cancer mortality: a review. Cancer Epidemiol Biomark Prev. 2008;17:2913–23.
23. Byers TE, Wolf HJ, Bauer KR, et al. The impact of socioeconomic status on survival after cancer in the United States: findings from the National Program of Cancer registries patterns of care study. Cancer. 2008;113:582–91.
24. Macleod U, Mitchell ED, Burgess C, et al. Risk factors for delayed presentation and referral of symptomatic cancer: evidence for common cancers. Br J Cancer. 2009;101(Suppl 2):S92–S101.
25. Macdonald S, Macleod U, Campbell NC, et al. Systematic review of factors influencing patient and practitioner delay in diagnosis of upper gastrointestinal cancer. Br J Cancer. 2006;94:1272–80.
26. Hall SE, Holman CD, Wisniewski ZS, Semmens J. Prostate cancer: socio-economic, geographical and private-health insurance effects on care and survival. BJU Int. 2005;95:51–8.
27. Mandelblatt J, Andrews H, Kao R, et al. The late-stage diagnosis of colorectal cancer: demographic and socioeconomic factors. Am J Public Health. 1996;86:1794–7.
28. Aarts MJ, Lemmens VE, Louwman MW, et al. Socioeconomic status and changing inequalities in colorectal cancer? A review of the associations with risk, treatment and outcome. Eur J Cancer. 2010;46:2681–95.
29. McNeill JA, Reynolds J, Ney ML. Unequal quality of cancer pain management: disparity in perceived control and proposed solutions. Oncol Nurs Forum. 2007;34:1121–8.
30. Morrison RS, Wallenstein S, Natale DK, et al. "we don't carry that"—failure of pharmacies in predominantly nonwhite neighborhoods to stock opioid analgesics. N Engl J Med. 2000;342:1023–6.
31. Mackenbach JP, Huisman M, Andersen O, et al. Inequalities in lung cancer mortality by the educational level in 10 European populations. Eur J Cancer. 2004;40:126–35.
32. Menvielle G, Kunst AE, Stirbu I, et al. Socioeconomic inequalities in alcohol related cancer mortality among men: to what extent do they differ between Western European populations? Int J Cancer. 2007;121:649–55.
33. Parikh S, Brennan P, Boffetta P. Meta-analysis of social inequality and the risk of cervical cancer. Int J Cancer. 2003;105:687–91.
34. Fukuda Y, Nakamura K, Takano T. Accumulation of health risk behaviours is associated with lower socioeconomic status and women's urban residence: a multilevel analysis in Japan. BMC Public Health. 2005;5:53.
35. Tabuchi T, Kondo N. Educational inequalities in smoking among Japanese adults aged 25-94 years: nationally representative sex- and age-specific statistics. J Epidemiol. 2017;27:186–92.
36. Inoue M, Sawada N, Matsuda T, et al. Attributable causes of cancer in Japan in 2005—systematic assessment to estimate current burden of cancer attributable to known preventable risk factors in Japan. Ann Oncol. 2012;23:1362–9.
37. Ikeda N, Inoue M, Iso H, et al. Adult mortality attributable to preventable risk factors for non-communicable diseases and injuries in Japan: a comparative risk assessment. PLoS Med. 2012;9:e1001160.
38. Thomas S, Fayter D, Misso K, et al. Population tobacco control interventions and their effects on social inequalities in smoking: systematic review. Tob Control. 2008;17:230–7.
39. Tabuchi T, Fujiwara T, Shinozaki T. Tobacco price increase and smoking behaviour changes in various subgroups: a nationwide longitudinal 7-year follow-up study among a middle-aged Japanese population. Tob Control. 2017;26:69–77.
40. Tabuchi T, Nakamura M, Nakayama T, et al. Tobacco Price increase and smoking cessation in Japan, a developed country with affordable tobacco: a National Population-Based Observational Study. J Epidemiol. 2016;26:14–21.
41. Eriksen M, Mackay J, Ross H. The tobacco atlas. 4th ed. Atlanta, GA: American Cancer Society; 2012.
42. Tabuchi T, Iso H, Brunner E. Tobacco control measures to reduce socioeconomic inequality in smoking: the necessity, time-course perspective, and future implications. J Epidemiol. 2018;28:170–5.

43. Fukuda Y, Nakamura K, Takano T. Reduced likelihood of cancer screening among women in urban areas and with low socio-economic status: a multilevel analysis in Japan. Public Health. 2005;119:875–84.

44. Tabuchi T, Nakayama T, Tsukuma H. Disparity of cancer screening attendance rate in Japan. The impact of health insurance. Nihon Iji Shinpo. 2012;4605:84–8.

45. Tabuchi T, Murayama H, Hoshino T, Nakayama T. An out-of-pocket cost removal intervention on fecal occult blood test attendance. Am J Prev Med. 2017;53:e51–62.

46. Tabuchi T, Hoshino T, Nakayama T, et al. Does removal of out-of-pocket costs for cervical and breast cancer screening work? A quasi-experimental study to evaluate the impact on attendance, attendance inequality and average cost per uptake of a Japanese government intervention. Int J Cancer. 2013;133:972–83.

47. Ueda K, Tsukuma H, Ajiki W, Oshima A. Socioeconomic factors and cancer incidence, mortality, and survival in a metropolitan area of Japan: a cross-sectional ecological study. Cancer Sci. 2005;96:684–8.

48. Ueda K, Kawachi I, Tsukuma H. Cervical and corpus cancer survival disparities by socioeconomic status in a metropolitan area of Japan. Cancer Sci. 2006;97:283–91.

49. Ito Y, Nakaya T, Nakayama T, et al. Socioeconomic inequalities in cancer survival: a population-based study of adult patients diagnosed in Osaka, Japan, during the period 1993-2004. Acta Oncol. 2014;53(10):1423–33.

50. Fujino Y, Tamakoshi A, Iso H, et al. A nationwide cohort study of educational background and major causes of death among the elderly population in Japan. Prev Med. 2005;40:444–51.

51. Miki Y, Inoue M, Ikeda A, et al. Neighborhood deprivation and risk of cancer incidence, mortality and survival: results from a population-based cohort study in Japan. PLoS One. 2014;9:e106729.

52. Fujino Y, Mori M, Tamakoshi A, et al. A prospective study of educational background and breast cancer among Japanese women. Cancer Causes Control. 2008;19:931–7.

53. Harper S, Lynch J, Meersman SC, et al. Trends in area-socioeconomic and race-ethnic disparities in breast cancer incidence, stage at diagnosis, screening, mortality, and survival among women ages 50 years and over (1987-2005). Cancer Epidemiol Biomarkers Prev. 2009;18:121–31.

54. Harper S, Lynch J. Selected comparisons of measures of health disparities. Bethesda, MD: National Cancer Institute; 2007, NIH publication no. 07-6281.

55. Bailey TM, Delva J, Gretebeck K, et al. A systematic review of mammography educational interventions for low-income women. Am J Health Promot. 2005;20:96–107.

Open Access This chapter is licensed under the terms of the Creative Commons Attribution-NonCommercial-NoDerivatives 4.0 International License (http://creativecommons.org/licenses/by-nc-nd/4.0/), which permits any noncommercial use, sharing, distribution and reproduction in any medium or format, as long as you give appropriate credit to the original author(s) and the source, provide a link to the Creative Commons licence and indicate if you modified the licensed material. You do not have permission under this licence to share adapted material derived from this chapter or parts of it.

The images or other third party material in this chapter are included in the chapter's Creative Commons licence, unless indicated otherwise in a credit line to the material. If material is not included in the chapter's Creative Commons licence and your intended use is not permitted by statutory regulation or exceeds the permitted use, you will need to obtain permission directly from the copyright holder.

Chapter 5
Coronary Heart Disease

Hirohito Tsuboi, Katsunori Kondo, Hiroshi Kaneko, and Hiroko Yamamoto

1 Introduction

Social determinants of health are factors that are primarily responsible for health inequities. This chapter discusses social determinants of health from the perspectives of socioeconomic status (SES) and coronary heart disease (CHD). We are particularly concerned with the pathways through which socioeconomic inequalities are translated into CHD and the strategy for preventing CHD.

Hiroko Yamamoto was deceased at the time of publication.

H. Tsuboi (✉)
Pharmaceutical and Health Sciences, Institute of Medical, Kanazawa University, Kanazawa, Ishikawa, Japan
e-mail: tsuboih@p.kanazawa-uac.jp

K. Kondo
Professor of Social Epidemiology and Health Policy, Department of Social Preventive Medical Sciences, Center for Preventive Medical Sciences, Chiba University, Chiba, Japan

Head of Department of Gerontological Evaluation, Center for Gerontology and Social Science, National Center for Geriatrics and Gerontology, Obu City, Aichi, Japan

H. Kaneko
Hoshigaoka Maternity Hospital, Nagoya, Aichi, Japan

© The Author(s) 2020
K. Kondo (ed.), *Social Determinants of Health in Non-communicable Diseases*,
Springer Series on Epidemiology and Public Health,
https://doi.org/10.1007/978-981-15-1831-7_5

2 Overview of SES and Coronary Heart Disease

CHD is a broad disease category and consists of several conditions, the most prevalent being myocardial infarction and angina pectoris. CHD affects the vascular system supplying the heart muscle and is attributed to build-up of atheromatous plaques that cover the lining of the coronary arteries. CHD is the leading cause of death over the long term in highly developed and industrialized Western countries, and many studies have been conducted on its causes and prevention. In Japan, CHD is the second-leading cause of death behind malignant neoplasm and has accounted for many cases of heart disease in recent years. In addition, acute myocardial infarction was one of four diseases targeted by regional medical care plans of Japan in fiscal year 2008. Risk factors for CHD are shown in Table 5.1. In addition to these risk factors, SES is also an important factor in CHD.

SES comprises factors such as income, education, and occupation (which includes being employed or unemployed and position at work). Low SES is associated with large increases in CHD risk in high-income countries [1]. For example, in countries like the USA and the UK, which are presumably at a more advanced stage of the cardiovascular disease (CVD) epidemic, there is an inverse relationship between SES and CVD mortality rates [2]. As the prevalence of CHD increases in industrialized and developing countries, it affects the more affluent classes initially and then percolates through the social classes [2]. Although the data are somewhat old, in developing countries like India and Hong Kong, this phenomenon is at the growing stage, and there is a higher CVD prevalence associated mainly with the high-income classes [2]. In Japan, whose population does not have distinctly large economic differentials, the "CHD epidemic percolation" postulation is less evident [2]. In a study on civil servants in Toyama Prefecture, no direct association between CHD and SES was observed [3]. In addition, in a Jichi Medical School Study, educational background was shown to be unrelated to CHD [4]. In Japan, with a

Table 5.1 Risk factors for coronary heart disease	
	• Hypertension
	• Hyperlipidemia
	• Diabetes
	• Smoking
	• Excessive alcohol intake
	• Being physically inactive
	• Unhealthy diet
	• Being overweight or obese (accumulation of visceral fat)
	• Excessive stress
	• Aging
	• Being male (for women, post-menopause)
	• Genetics

continuous and a marked rise in total cholesterol, in sharp contrast to a constant fall in total cholesterol in other developed countries, age-adjusted CHD mortality declined between 1980 and 2008 [5]. Although there may be some protective factors unique to Japan, it is better to describe the relationship between SES and CHD.

CHD is caused by atherosclerosis through luminal narrowing or precipitating thrombi in the coronary artery walls that obstruct blood flow to the heart. Atherosclerosis is a lipoprotein-driven disease that leads to plaque formation at specific sites of the arterial tree through intimal inflammation, necrosis, fibrosis, and calcification. Although most plaques remain asymptomatic (subclinical disease), some become obstructive (stable angina), and others elicit acute thrombosis and may lead to an acute coronary syndrome. Rupture of thin-cap fibroatheroma and subsequent thrombosis may occur spontaneously, but, in some cases, a temporary increase in emotional or physical stress provides the final trigger for the event [6].

Although a direct association between SES and CHD has not been demonstrated in Japan [7], associations between some risk factors for CHD and some aspects of SES were reported in the Jichi Medical School Study. Namely, the study found that male white-collar workers have lower plasma fibrinogen concentrations than male blue-collar workers [8]. Many foreign studies have demonstrated not only a direct association between CHD and SES but also an association between CHD risk factors and SES; in particular, these studies have demonstrated that hypertension, hyperlipidemia, and diabetes mellitus are frequently observed among low-SES classes [9]. Lower SES is also reported to be associated with higher blood pressure, higher waist circumference, higher triglyceride levels in blood, and lower concentration of high-density lipoprotein cholesterol [10].

Thus, SES is considered to affect CHD under certain conditions. One reason for the unclear association between the two in Japan may be the lack of factors related to low-income and unemployed individuals in surveys [7]. Although the prevention of lifestyle-related diseases at the individual level is already one of the initiatives of Health Japan 21, prevention based on social aspects remains almost completely unexplored. Therefore, our objective in this chapter is to demonstrate hints for efficiently preventing CHD based on social aspects. We also discuss the mechanism of the link between SES and CHD as well as the possibility of preventing CHD based on aspects of SES. Using PubMed for literature searches, we referred to Western studies in which the association between CHD and SES was relatively clear. We searched for literature using the terms "{(cardiovascular heart disease) or (coronary heart disease) or (ischemic heart disease)} and {(socioeconomic) or (socioeconomic)}." We referred to reviews for general outlines and to original publications for individual research results.

3   Pathway of the Effect of SES on CHD

This chapter concerns the pathways through which SES is translated into CHD, highlighting the likely role of psychosocial processes. Figure 5.1 shows the possible pathways.

3.1   Health Behaviors and Access to Health Promotion Resources and Medical Care

Studies in the UK and Sweden indicated that low-SES classes are generally characterized by undesirable health behaviors, such as a high prevalence of smoking, unhealthy diet, obesity, and lack of physical activity [11, 12]. Low-SES classes also seldom use health-promotion resources such as health information and health checkups[13] and tend to have an insufficient primary care [14]. Low-SES classes tend to delay hospitalization following cardiovascular events after CHD onset [14]. These behaviors are easily linked to exacerbation of symptoms and death. Thus, among low-SES classes, the multitude of risk factors and insufficient access to medical care and health resources are considered to have negative effects on the onset and prognosis of CHD.

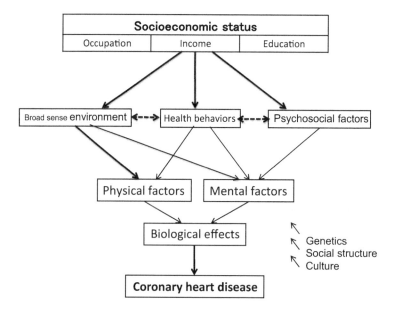

Fig. 5.1   Pathways of the effect of socioeconomic status on coronary heart disease

3.2 Psychosocial and Biological Pathways

Psychosocial factors related to SES can influence CHD risk via stimulation of neu-roendocrine, autonomic, and immune processes. Psychosocial characteristics observed in low-SES individuals include chronic stress, large numbers of life events, depression, anger, hostility, and social isolation; these characteristics are risk factors for CHD through this psychosocial pathway [15]. Conversely, in high-SES indi-viduals, the effect of stress is alleviated by greater senses of control, mastery, and perceived control [15].

The stress reaction is mainly regulated by an axial system consisting of two neu-roendocrine systems: the hypothalamic–pituitary–adrenocortical (HPA) system and the sympathetic adrenomedullary (SAM) system. In response to physiological and psychogenic stressors, the HPA axis orchestrates the systemic release of glucocorti-coids while the SAM system operates through adrenaline (Adr) and noradrenalin (NA) signals. Although these substances possess an anti-stress effect, chronically increased secretion causes damage to organisms. Prolonged high levels of cortisol (Cort), a representative glucocorticoid, result in the onset of diabetes mellitus because of its gluconeogenic effect. Chronically high levels of Cort increase vis-ceral fat, thereby increasing blood pressure [16]. Cort also increases oxidative stress [17], thereby increasing the risk of CHD. Cort has an anti-inflammatory effect, which normally works to prevent CHD. However, because chronically high levels of Cort result in low resistance, Cort ceases to exert a sufficient effect on target organs. This may, in turn, stimulate the immune system and cause inflammation [18]. Enhancement of the SAM system, on the other hand, causes Adr and NA to increase blood pressure, blood glucose, and inflammatory response [19]. Therefore, prolonged, chronically high levels of Adr and NA increase the risk of CHD.

We now discuss evidence for how differences in psychosocial characteristics caused by SES affect CHD. We discuss the psychological aspects, first followed by social aspects.

3.2.1 Depression

Prospective cohort studies provide strong evidence that depression is an indepen-dent etiological and prognostic factor for CHD [20]. The high prevalence of depres-sion in patients with CHD supports a strategy of screening for depressive symptoms in CHD patients [21].

Dysregulation of the HPA axis function is frequent in major depression, and hypercortisolemia can be a mediating factor in the relationship between depression and CHD development [22]. In addition, patients with major depression have been found to exhibit increased biomarkers of inflammation in both the periphery and the brain [18]. Patients with major depression exhibit higher plasma interleukin-6 levels following exposure to a psychological stressor than nondepressed, healthy control participants [18], thus explaining depressed individuals' susceptibility to CHD onset.

Inflammatory cytokine levels are also increased in individuals with metabolic syndrome [23]. Therefore, inflammatory cytokines may have a synergistic effect on CHD. Furthermore, depression has been associated with heightened blood pressure and NA to behavioral tasks [24, 25]. This result suggests that the SAM system is also a factor contributing to CHD.

3.2.2   Hostility and Anger

Well-established associations have been documented between elevated levels of hostility/anger and CHD. Hostility increases blood pressure, catecholamines, platelet activation, and daily Cort secretion [26, 27]. Thus, both HPA and SAM systems are pathways for exacerbation of CHD. In addition, anger has been reported to promote oxidation in the body [28], indicating that oxidation may be associated with the pathway through which anger affects CHD.

3.2.3   Work Environment

The Job Demand Control (JDC) model is a well-known theoretical perspective regarding workload and work-related stress [29]. The JDC model emphasizes job demand and job control (decision latitude) with four working conditions: high-strain jobs (high demands and low controls), low-strain jobs (low demands and high controls), active jobs (high demands and high controls), and passive jobs (low demands and low controls). According to this model, individuals in lower positions experience higher strain [29].

The high strain group is reported to possess characteristics associated with CHD risk factors, such as enhancement of the SAM system [30] and higher levels of Cort in the blood [31]. Although many reports have demonstrated a relationship between high strain and blood pressure, there is also counterevidence that hypertension is not the link between high strain and CHD [32]. Therefore, there is some uncertainty regarding the mechanism of the link between high strain and CHD.

In mental stress-testing studies, which demonstrate the effect of a sense of control, participants demonstrate a positive relationship between strain and systolic blood pressure when exposed to uncontrollable stress; however, no such association is observed for controllable stress [33]. These findings demonstrate that uncontrollable stress exerts a more harmful effect on CHD, even when the nature of the stress is identical.

3.2.4   Social Support

Social support is a factor that can exert a beneficial effect on CHD. Support in the workplace reduces the risk of CHD by decreasing heart rate during sleep, work, and leisure [15]. In a three-factor model in which "support" is added to the (two-factor) JDC model, CHD prevalence and mortality are high among the high-demand/low-control/low-support group [23]. Social support is also a buffer factor against stress and depressive mood outside the workplace [34]. Therefore, social support should indirectly reduce CHD risk factors.

3.2.5   Summary of Psychosocial Pathway

Psychosocial factors can affect CHD through the effects of SES, as described above. As one's chronic psychosocial state affects responses to acute stress, different responses to the same acute stress are observed for different SES. For example, in acute stress tests, participants with low SES exhibit larger responses in terms of biological indicators (blood pressure, heart rate, etc.) than do participants with high SES [15].

3.3   Parents and Childhood

Some studies have indicated that one's parents' and one's own SES during childhood will affect CHD in the future. For example, Swedish and American epidemiological studies demonstrated an association between childhood SES and CHD in late middle age and onward [35, 36]. On the contrary, this association has been denied in Finnish and British studies [37, 38]. A separate British epidemiological study concluded that while SES has a major direct effect on CHD beginning in adulthood, childhood social environment affects CHD through employment and social status [39].

Thus, although the relationship between CHD and childhood SES appears not to be strong, childhood experiences can influence adulthood behavioral and psychosocial factors (smoking, lack of exercise, hostility, occupational strain, unhealthy mental state, etc.), thereby becoming a factor for CHD [1]. In addition, infants with low birth weight are reported to be predisposed to CHD because of the effect of birth weight on subsequent biological indicators such as a blood coagulation system, cholesterol levels, blood pressure, insulin resistance, and abnormal glucose tolerance [40]. Considering that mothers with low SES experience higher rates of babies with low birth weight, there may be a pathway through which birth weight is indirectly associated with CHD risk. Furthermore, stressful environments during pregnancy and in childhood diminish the functioning of the HPA and SAM systems, which may result in a subsequent predisposition for CHD [41].

3.4   Genetic Factors

CHD has a strong hereditary component. MCP-1, MCP-4, MIP-1, RANTES, and other genes associated with atherosclerosis have been identified as risk factors [42]. Although there has been no verification in relation to accumulation of higher-risk genes according to the social gradient, and, thus, genetic involvement in the association between SES and CHD is unknown, it is possible that exposure to exacerbating factors for low SES is involved in gene expression or epigenetic processes.

4 Hints on CHD Prevention

Socioeconomic inequalities in CHD occur in most Western countries and are of major concern to public health authorities. This may become a crucial problem in Japan as well. The World Health Organization cites "social and economic environment," "physical environment," and "individual characteristics and behaviors" as determinants of health. Specific examples are shown below [43].

- Income and social status: Higher income and social status are linked to better health. The magnitude of the gap between the richest and poorest people tends to reflect the differences in health.
- Education: Low education levels are linked with poor health, more stress, and lower self-confidence.
- Physical environment: Safe water and clean air; healthy workplaces; and safe houses, communities, and roads all contribute to good health.
- Employment and working conditions: People who are employed are healthier, particularly those who have more control over their working conditions.
- Social support networks: Greater support from families, friends, and communities are linked to better health.
- Culture: Customs and traditions and the beliefs of the family and community all affect health.
- Genetics: Inheritance plays a part in determining lifespan, healthiness, and the likelihood of developing certain illnesses.
- Personal behavior and coping skills: Balanced eating, keeping active, smoking, drinking, and how we deal with life's stresses and challenges all affect health.
- Health services: Access to and use of services that prevent and treat disease influence health.
- Gender: Men and women experience different types of diseases at different ages.

These determinants of health can be applied in the prevention of CHD and the improvement of health [9].

Many of the above items are associated with social and economic conditions. This suggests that we should introduce CHD-prevention strategies that have seldom been conducted in Japan, focusing on socioeconomic factors.

4.1 Intervention Through Education

Educational programs for the prevention of CHD have been carried out in the USA, Finland, Australia, Switzerland, South Africa, and Germany. These educational programs, which aim to reduce CHD risk factors, included local publicity campaigns, the establishment of designated smoking areas, and the use of mass media; these various programs have all generally achieved favorable results [9]. Although factors such as the spread of statin-based medicine and the improvement of social supports through intervention may be effective, broad education can also improve SES (in which education is a crucial factor).

4.2 Social Security Systems

Material wealth is strongly related to CHD throughout life, while poverty has harmful effects not only on CHD but on overall health. Thus, social security systems take on major significance. In fact, societies with well-developed social security systems are considered to be healthier than market-oriented ones. Specifically, countries in the former group (Austria, Sweden, Norway, Denmark, and Finland) boast lower infant mortality rates and lower percentages of poor children than countries in the latter group (Belgium, Germany, the Netherlands, France, Italy, Switzerland, the UK, Ireland, the USA, and Canada) [44]. This finding demonstrates that given country health policies affect health and disease, including CHD. Therefore, such policies are an important factor in disease prevention. Considering that childhood SES affects health in adulthood [45], the improvement of SES through the development of social security systems is a highly viable candidate for CHD prevention.

4.3 Support for Critical Periods in Life

Thirteen critical periods of the life course have been identified during which people are especially vulnerable to social disadvantage: fetal development; birth; nutrition, growth, and health in childhood educational career; leaving the parental home; entering labor market; establishing social and sexual relationships; job loss or insecurity; parenthood; episodes of illness; labor market exit; and chronic sickness [13]. During such adverse times, adequate support must be provided to maintain health and prevent illness. In addition to providing support on an individual level, providing support to the whole society may also be effective.

5 Summary

In developed Western countries, CHD is generally prevalent among low-SES classes. As we have introduced, the mechanism of this association is affected by many factors, such as a life course from birth to old age, lifestyle habits, and psychosocial stress. In Japan, there are still few empirical studies on the association between SES and CHD; therefore, this relationship is not properly understood. Lifelong studies are necessary to devise strategies for improving SES and preventing CHD [46]. Socio-epidemiological studies will be needed to advance plans for evidence-based medical care in Japan.

References

1. Clark AM, DesMeules M, Luo W, Duncan AS, Wielgosz A. Socioeconomic status and cardiovascular disease: risks and implications for care. Nat Rev Cardiol. 2009;6:712–22.
2. Khor GL. Cardiovascular epidemiology in the Asia-Pacific region. Asia Pac J Clin Nutr. 2001;10:76–80.
3. Sekine M, Chandola T, Martikainen P, Marmot M, Kagamimori S. Socioeconomic inequalities in physical and mental functioning of British, Finnish, and Japanese civil servants: role of job demand, control, and work hours. Soc Sci Med. 2009;69:1417–25.
4. Honjo K, Tsutsumi A, Kayaba K, Jichi Medical School Cohort Study Group. Socioeconomic indicators and cardiovascular disease incidence among Japanese community residents: the Jichi Medical School Cohort Study. Int J Behav Med. 2010;17:58–66.
5. Sekikawa A, Miyamoto Y, Miura K, et al. Continuous decline in mortality from coronary heart disease in Japan despite a continuous and marked rise in total cholesterol: Japanese experience after the Seven Countries Study. Int J Epidemiol. 2015;44:1614–24.
6. Bentzon JF, Otsuka F, Virmani R, Falk E. Mechanisms of plaque formation and rupture. Circ Res. 2014;114:1852–66.
7. Kagamimori S, Gaina A, Nasermoaddeli A. Socioeconomic status and health in the Japanese population. Soc Sci Med. 2009;68:2152–60.
8. Hirokawa K, Tsutsumi A, Kayaba K, Jichi Medical School Cohort Group. Occupation and plasma fibrinogen in Japanese male and female workers: the Jichi Medical School Cohort study. Soc Sci Med. 2009;68:1091–7.
9. Kaplan GA, Keil JE. Socioeconomic factors and cardiovascular disease: a review of the literature. Circulation. 1993;88:1973–98.
10. Manuck SB, Phillips JE, Gianaros PJ, Flory JD, Muldoon MF. Subjective socioeconomic status and presence of the metabolic syndrome in midlife community volunteers. Psychosom Med. 2010;72:35–45.
11. Rosengren A, Orth-Gomér K, Wilhelmsen L. Socioeconomic differences in health indices, social networks and mortality among Swedish men. A study of men born in 1933. Scand J Soc Med. 1998;26:272–80.
12. Marmot MG, Smith GD, Stansfeld S, et al. Health inequalities among British civil servants: the Whitehall II study. Lancet. 1991;337:1387–93.
13. Raphael D. Social exclusion—including processes of material deprivation, lack of participation in common societal activities, and exclusion from decision-making and civic participation—is the means by which low income causes cardiovascular disease. In: Raphael D, editor. Social justice is good for our hearts. Toronto: CSJ Foundation for Research and Education; 2002. p. 21–34.

14. Morrison C, Woodward M, Leslie W, Tunstall-Pedoe H. Effect of socioeconomic group on incidence of, management of, and survival after myocardial infarction and coronary death: analysis of community coronary event register. BMJ. 1997;314:541–6.
15. Steptoe A, Marmot M. The role of psychobiological pathways in socio-economic inequalities in cardiovascular disease risk. Eur Heart J. 2002;23:13–25.
16. Dhabhar FS, McEwen BS. Bidirectional effects of stress and glucocorticoid hormones on immune function: possible explanations for paradoxical observations. In: Ader R, Felten DL, Cohen N, editors. Psychoneuroimmunology, vol. 2. 3rd ed. San Diego, CA: Academic; 2001. p. 301–29.
17. Yamaji M, Tsutamoto T, Kawahara C, et al. Serum cortisol as a useful predictor of cardiac events in patients with chronic heart failure: the impact of oxidative stress. Circ Heart Fail. 2009;2:608–15.
18. Pace TW, Miller AH. Cytokines and glucocorticoid receptor signaling. Ann N Y Acad Sci. 2009;1179:86–105.
19. Flierl MA, Rittirsch D, Nadeau BA, Chen AJ, Sarma JV, Zetoune FS, McGuire SR, List RP, Day DE, Hoesel LM, Gao H, Van Rooijen N, Huber-Lang MS, Neubig RR, Ward PA. Phagocyte-derived catecholamines enhance acute inflammatory injury. Nature. 2007;449:721–5.
20. Hemingway H, Marmot M. Evidence based cardiology: psychosocial factors in the aetiology and prognosis of coronary heart disease. Systematic review of prospective cohort studies. BMJ. 1999;318:1460–7.
21. Lichtman JH, Bigger JT Jr, Blumenthal JA, et al. Depression and coronary heart disease: recommendations for screening, referral, and treatment: a science advisory from the American Heart Association Prevention Committee of the Council on Cardiovascular Nursing, Council on Clinical Cardiology, Council on Epidemiology and Prevention, and Interdisciplinary Council on Quality of Care and Outcomes Research: endorsed by the American Psychiatric Association. Circulation. 2008;118:1768–75.
22. Jokinen J, Nordström P. HPA axis hyperactivity and cardiovascular mortality in mood disorder inpatients. J Affect Disord. 2009;116:88–92.
23. Grippo AJ, Johnson AK. Stress, depression and cardiovascular dysregulation: a review of neurobiological mechanisms and the integration of research from preclinical disease models. Stress. 2009;12:1–21.
24. Light KC, Kothandapani RV, Allen MT. Enhanced cardiovascular and catecholamine responses in women with depressive symptoms. Int J Psychophysiol. 1998;28:157–66.
25. Kirschbaum C, Prussner JC, Stone AA, et al. Persistent high cortisol responses to repeated psychological stress in a subpopulation of healthy men. Psychosom Med. 1995;57:468–74.
26. Suarez EC, Kuhn CM, Schanberg SM, et al. Neuroendocrine, cardiovascular, and emotional responses of hostile men: the role of interpersonal challenge. Psychosom Med. 1998;60:78–88.
27. Shimbo D, Chaplin W, Kuruvilla S, Wasson LT, Abraham D, Burg MM. Hostility and platelet reactivity in individuals without a history of cardiovascular disease events. Psychosom Med. 2009;71:741–7.
28. Tsuboi H, Hamer M, Tanaka G, Takagi K, Kinae N, Steptoe A. Responses of ultra-weak chemiluminescence and secretory IgA in saliva to the induction of angry and depressive moods. Brain Behav Immun. 2008;22:209–14.
29. Karasek R, Baker D, Marxer F. Job decision latitude, job demands, and cardiovascular disease: a prospective study of Swedish men. Am J Public Health. 1981;71:694–705.
30. Collins SM, Karasek RA, Costas K. Job strain and autonomic indices of cardiovascular disease risk. Am J Ind Med. 2005;48:182–93.
31. Maina G, Bovenzi M, Palmas A, Larese Filon F. Associations between two job stress models and measures of salivary cortisol. Int Arch Occup Environ Health. 2009;82:1141–50.
32. Kivimäki M, Head J, Ferrie JE, Shipley MJ, Steptoe A, Vahtera J, Marmot MG. Hypertension is not the link between job strain and coronary heart disease in the Whitehall II study. Am J Hypertens. 2007;20:1146–53.

33. Steptoe A, Cropley M, Joekes K. Job strain, blood pressure, and responsivity to uncontrollable stress. J Hypertens. 1999;17:193–200.
34. Veiel HO. Buffer effects and threshold effects: an alternative interpretation of nonlinearities in the relationship between social support, stress, and depression. Am J Community Psychol. 1987;15:717–40.
35. Vagero D, Leon D. Effect of social class in childhood and adulthood on adult mortality. Lancet. 1994;343:1224–5.
36. Kittleson MM, Meoni LA, Chu NY, Ford DE, Klag J. Association of childhood socio-economic status with subsequent coronary heart disease in physicians. Arch Intern Med. 2006;166:2356–61.
37. Lynch JW, Kaplan GA, Cohen RD, et al. Childhood and adult socioeconomic status as predictors of mortality in Finland. Lancet. 1994;343:524–7.
38. Wannamethee SG, Whincup PH, Shaper G, et al. Influence of fathers' social class on cardio-vascular disease in middle-aged men. Lancet. 1996;348:1259–63.
39. Marmot M, Shipley M, Brunner E, Hemingway H. Relative contribution of early life and adult socioeconomic factors to adult morbidity in the Whitehall II study. J Epidemiol Community Health. 2001;55:301–7.
40. Forouhi N, Hall L, McKeigue P. A life course approaches to diabetes. In: Kuh D, Ben-Shlomo Y, editors. A life course approach to chronic disease epidemiology. Oxford: Oxford University Press; 2004. p. 165–88.
41. Latendresse G. The interaction between chronic stress and pregnancy: preterm birth from a biobehavioral perspective. J Midwifery Womens Health. 2009;54:8–17.
42. Sheikine Y, Hansson GK. Chemokines and atherosclerosis. Ann Med. 2004;36:98–118.
43. World Health Organization. The determinants of health. http://www.who.int/hia/evidence/doh/en/index.html. Accessed 4 July 2018.
44. Navarro V, Shi L. The political context of social inequalities and health. In: Navarro V, editor. The political economy of social inequalities: consequences for health and quality of life. Amityville, NY: Baywood; 2002. p. 403–18.
45. Poulton R, Caspi A, Milne BJ, et al. Association between children's experience of socioeconomic disadvantage and adult health: a life-course study. Lancet. 2002;360:1640–5.
46. Ben-Shlomo Y, Kuh D. A life course approach to chronic disease epidemiology: conceptual models, empirical challenges and interdisciplinary perspectives. Int J Epidemiol. 2002;31:285–93.

Open Access This chapter is licensed under the terms of the Creative Commons Attribution-NonCommercial-NoDerivatives 4.0 International License (http://creativecommons.org/licenses/by-nc-nd/4.0/), which permits any noncommercial use, sharing, distribution and reproduction in any medium or format, as long as you give appropriate credit to the original author(s) and the source, provide a link to the Creative Commons licence and indicate if you modified the licensed material. You do not have permission under this licence to share adapted material derived from this chapter or parts of it.

The images or other third party material in this chapter are included in the chapter's Creative Commons licence, unless indicated otherwise in a credit line to the material. If material is not included in the chapter's Creative Commons licence and your intended use is not permitted by statutory regulation or exceeds the permitted use, you will need to obtain permission directly from the copyright holder.

Chapter 6
Stroke

Naoki Kondo and Katsunori Kondo

1   Introduction

In Japan, the mortality from cerebrovascular disease reached a peak in the late 1960s, and then began to drop consistently. The current cerebrovascular disease mortality is two thirds of the peak rate (Fig. 6.1). However, cerebrovascular disease is the most common underlying disease in functionally dependent older adults and cannot be overlooked in public health. Moreover, given the recent call of amending the issue of health inequality in Japan and worldwide, success in terms of the reduction in the national average is not sufficient. This chapter examines future cerebrovascular disease measures by reviewing socioeconomic status (SES)-related inequalities in cerebrovascular disease based on previous academic knowledge.

N. Kondo (✉)
Graduate School of Medicine and School of Public Health, Kyoto University, Kyoto, Japan
e-mail: naoki-kondo@umin.ac.jp

K. Kondo
Professor of Social Epidemiology and Health Policy, Department of Social Preventive Medical Sciences, Center for Preventive Medical Sciences, Chiba University, Chiba, Japan

Head of Department of Gerontological Evaluation, Center for Gerontology and Social Science, National Center for Geriatrics and Gerontology, Obu City, Aichi, Japan

© The Author(s) 2020
K. Kondo (ed.), *Social Determinants of Health in Non-communicable Diseases*,
Springer Series on Epidemiology and Public Health,
https://doi.org/10.1007/978-981-15-1831-7_6

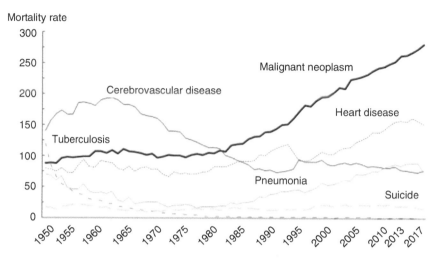

Fig. 6.1 Change of the mortality from cerebrovascular diseases and other leading causes (per 100,000 population). Cited from Trends of health of nation in 2009, pp. 54

2   SES-Related Inequalities in Cerebrovascular Disease and Risk Factors in Foreign Countries

SES is strongly associated with health condition, and cerebrovascular disease is no exception. Income, educational background, and occupational stratum are often used as measurements of SES. In several longitudinal studies performed mainly in Europe and the USA, it has been shown that SES can predict death by cerebrovascular disease by using any of these items [1]. For example, in a study performed in the USA, SES was separated into four categories by income, educational background, and occupational stratum to analyze mortality statistics by cause of death. The results showed that men with the lowest SES were 2.3 times more likely to die than men with the highest SES (data adjusted for age, survey year, sex, and race) [2]. According to a follow-up study in 50 million people per year in eight countries in Western Europe, similar to other primary disease, the cerebrovascular disease mortality was significantly higher (about 20–60%) in subjects with less education. Such impact was stronger with age [3]. There is also influential evidence in the Asian region. In a diachronic study performed in 580 thousand male public servants in Korea for mortality from both ischemic and hemorrhagic stroke, the worst group of the ranking that classified income into four groups was two times higher than the best group. In addition, SES-related inequalities were also observed in the fatality rate after onset [4].

Many studies have suggested that SES-related inequalities are found in the distribution of risk factors. A health and nutrition examination survey in the USA reported that cardiovascular disease risks such as smoking, lack of exercise, hypertension, and diabetes were most strongly accumulated in the lower-income class, regardless of race and sex [5]. However, for some risk factors the SES-related inequality has not been clear; for example, for the SES distribution of the serum cholesterol level, the results were heterogeneous [2].

3   SES-Based Inequality in Cerebrovascular Disease in Japan

Fukuda et al. [6] evaluated the SES at the local community level by five phases using the college-going rate and income per person at the local community level in Japan and ecologically estimated the ratio of the mortality from cerebral hemorrhage and from cerebral infarction. As a result, the mortality from cerebral hemorrhage in the local community with the lowest SES was 1.29 times (between 1973 and 1977) and 1.21 times (between 1993 and 1998) higher than the local community with the highest SES. Similarly, the mortality from cerebral infarction was 1.16 times and 1.19 times higher, respectively [6]. Fujino et al. [7, 8] analyzed 110,000 data from a JACC Study and examined the association between educational background and leading causes of death. In the group with 15 years or less of education history, risk of death caused by cerebrovascular diseases after having adjusted for age was 1.23 times (men) and 1.44 times (women) higher than the group with 18 years or more of education history. After having adjusted for smoking, drinking, working situation, and job type, this relative risk was slightly decreased (decreased to 1.21 and 1.38 for men and women, respectively) [7, 8].

4   SES-Related Inequalities of Cerebrovascular Disease Risk Factors in Japan

In an analysis of the individual data obtained from the Comprehensive Survey of Living Conditions 2001, the population with lower SES tended to show many risk behaviors [9]. The income was divided into quintiles and the percentage of smokers was estimated according to group. Regardless of age, occupation, and area of residence, the smoking odds in the lowest income group were significantly 1.29 times higher than the highest income group. Furthermore, most of the behaviors that become the main cardiovascular disease risks were associated with income level: no exercise habit (odds ratio, 1.42), undesirable dietary habits (1.28), holding psychological stress (1.15), no experience of medical examination (3.14). Notably, there was no significant association with drinking.

The association between smoking and SES was also observed in a survey performed with 1361 public employees in Hyogo Prefecture in 1998. However, the association of SES with drinking (consumption every day or not) and exercise habit (moderate to high or mild and below) was unclear. For the biomarkers, the group with higher educational background and higher occupation stratum tended to show significantly higher values for hemoglobin A1c, fasting blood glucose, triglyceride, and waist/hips ratio, and exceeded each diagnosis standard value for hypertension, hyperlipidemia, and diabetes [10]. In addition, the Aichi Gerontological Evaluation Study (AGES) (the early-stage project of the Japan Gerontological Evaluation Study: JAGES) performed with approximately 33,000 older people showed that the number of persons with the unfavored response for smoking and walking time was higher in the population with lower SES, by analysis of baseline data [11]. This study also suggested the presence of SES-related inequalities in medical access. According to the analysis by Murata et al. [12], the percentage of persons who responded that "I delayed the day of medical examination" was significantly higher in low-income persons. The common responses to explain this action were "cost," "distance," and "transportation" [12]. In addition, in a cohort of public employees in Toyama Prefecture, SES-related inequalities were related to psychosocial stress [13]. Thus, it was found that SES-related inequalities existed in cerebrovascular disease and its risk factors. However, for occupation stratum, associations between SES and risk factors were unclear in women (e.g., stress), while for some items, further examination is required (assay of SES and lifestyle risks and sex differences) [14].

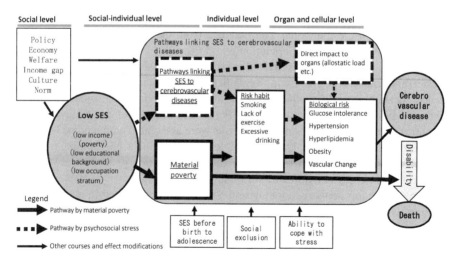

Fig. 6.2 Mechanism hypothesis that low SES increase risk of stroke

5 Pathways Linking SES and Cerebrovascular Disease

5.1 Material Poverty and Psychosocial Stress

There are two possible primary pathways linking SES and cerebrovascular diseases: material poverty and psychosocial stresses (Fig. 6.2). In the material poverty pathways, risk is increased by material deprivation in the population with lower SES: access to goods and services for health maintenance may be poor; appropriate health information may be difficult to obtain; long working hours leave little time for leisure activities. Poor neighborhood environment may also contribute to the effect. For example, people living in impoverished areas may have difficulty in exercising safely because of public security or poorly maintained sidewalks, while access to vendors of fresh fruit and vegetables may be limited and access to cheap fast food may be easy [15].

For psychosocial stress pathways, persistent stress caused by low SES might promote risk behavior such as smoking and excessive drinking. Stress could also increase physiological risks directly. In a Korean large-scale cohort, after adjusting for conventional risk factors of stroke (smoking, exercise, height, drinking, serum cholesterol level, blood glucose level, hypertension, high body mass index, and place of residence), there was no change in the conclusions that a higher number of patients with cerebrovascular disorders were found in the population with lower SES [4].

The MONICA study of the World Health Organization followed 50 million people in 32 countries. During 10 years or more of follow-up, there were few changes in the distribution of classic cerebrovascular disease risks including blood pressure and serum lipids. However, analysis of data from Russia and Denmark, where significant economic upheaval occurred at the time, suggested that psychosocial stress caused by the macroeconomic crisis might contribute to death from cerebrovascular diseases, rather than conventional behavioral risks [4]. This potential direct influence of stress is known as "allostatic load" [16]. Persistent stress could affect the circulatory organs, immunity, and glucose metabolism and directly increase the risks of cardiovascular diseases.

The extent of load on the body from stressful daily life depends on the capacity to cope with stress, which could be a congenital trait or acquired after birth. In the AGES data, the population with lower SES showed lower ability to cope with stress. It was pointed out that subjective feeling of health is lower in such cases [11].

SES shows a health effect in each life stage from the period before birth up to adulthood. Accumulation of the impact may be expressed as biological and psychosocial risks [17]. It is likely that there are critical or etiologic periods that may have great influence on cerebrovascular disease risks. Understanding these periods is important to develop strategies for prevention with life course perspectives [18].

6 Policy Recommendations

6.1 Monitoring SES Inequalities in Cerebrovascular Diseases

Many societal conditions can change rapidly through globalization, financial crises, and decentralization. This makes the complete removal of health inequalities difficult, so discussion is required to determine which health inequalities are unacceptable and how they should be removed. Therefore, monitoring the magnitude and characteristics of diseases their risks across subpopulations and prioritizing the issues and subpopulations are important [19].

As mentioned in other chapters, a population strategy to design the social and built environments should be a primary measure to address health inequality. There is evidence on the efficacy of such interventions [20]. For example, price adjustment by taxation to cigarette and high caloric fast foods may be effective in reducing smoking and total calories consumed, weight loss, and glucose tolerance in the overall population [21, 22]. Health-promoting measures involving local residents are effective in raising health consciousness in the overall community and in building suitable infrastructure like sidewalks and parks [23].

From the "Dynamic of population statistics" by the Ministry of Health, Labour and Welfare. (1): Cerebrovascular disease indicates the total of cerebral hemorrhage, cerebral infarction, and other cerebrovascular diseases. (2): For subarachnoid hemorrhage, the data of other cerebrovascular diseases are reused. (3): The mortality from cerebrovascular diseases classified by illness has been listed in the vital statistics since 1951. Author's note: The mortality from cerebrovascular disease has increased temporarily because of the issues for definition by application of ICD-10 in 1995.

References

1. Cox AM, McKevitt C, Rudd AG, Wolfe CDA. Socioeconomic status and stroke. Lancet Neurol. 2006;5(2):181–8.
2. Steenland K, Hu S, Walker J. All-cause and cause-specific mortality by socioeconomic status among employed persons in 27 US states, 1984-1997. Am J Public Health. 2004 Jun;94(6):1037–42.
3. Huisman M, Kunst AE, Bopp M, Borgan JK, Borrell C, Costa G, et al. Educational inequalities in cause-specific mortality in middle-aged and older men and women in eight western European populations. Lancet. 2005;365(9458):493–500.
4. Song YM, Ferrer RL, Cho SI, Sung J, Ebrahim S, Davey Smith G. Socioeconomic status and cardiovascular disease among men: the Korean national health service prospective cohort study. Am J Public Health. 2006;96(1):152–9.
5. Gillum RF, Mussolino ME. Education, poverty, and stroke incidence in whites and blacks: the NHANES I epidemiologic follow-up study. J Clin Epidemiol. 2003;56(2):188–95.
6. Fukuda Y, Nakamura K, Takano T. Cause-specific mortality differences across socioeconomic position of municipalities in Japan, 1973–1977 and 1993–1998: increased importance of injury and suicide in inequality for ages under 75. Int J Epidemiol. 2005;34(1):100.

7. Fujino Y, Tamakoshi A, Iso H, Inaba Y, Kubo T, Ide R, et al. A nationwide cohort study of educational background and major causes of death among the elderly population in Japan. Prev Med. 2005;40:444–51.

8. Fujino Y, Iso H, Tamakoshi A, Inaba Y, Koizumi A, Kubo T, et al. A prospective cohort study of employment status and mortality from circulatory disorders among Japanese workers. J Occup Health. 2005;47:510–7.

9. Fukuda Y, Nakamura K, Takano T. Accumulation of health risk behaviours is associated with lower socioeconomic status and women's urban residence: a multilevel analysis in Japan. BMC Public Health. 2005 May 27;5(1):53.

10. Nishi N, Makino K, Fukuda H, Tatara K. Effects of socioeconomic indicators on coronary risk factors, self-rated health and psychological Well-being among urban Japanese civil servants. Soc Sci Med. 2004;58(6):1159–70.

11. Kondo K. Evaluating health inequalities – a social epidemiological large-scale survey for care prevention [in Japanese: kensho kenkoukakusashakai]. Tokyo: Igakushoin; 2007.

12. Murata C, Yamada T, Chen C-C, Ojima T, Hirai H, Kondo K. Barriers to health care among the elderly in Japan. Int J Environ Res Public Health. 2010;7(4):1330–41.

13. Sekine M, Chandola T, Martikainen P, Marmot M, Kagamimori S. Socioeconomic inequalities in physical and mental functioning of Japanese civil servants: explanations from work and family characteristics. Soc Sci Med. 2006;63(2):430–45.

14. Fujino Y, Tamakoshi A, Ohno Y, Mizoue T, Tokui N, Yoshimura T. Prospective study of educational background and stomach cancer in Japan. Prev Med. 2002;35(2):121–7.

15. Cannuscio CC, Weiss EE, Asch DA. The contribution of urban foodways to health disparities. J Urban Health. 2010 May;87(3):381–93.

16. McEwen BS, Gianaros PJ. Central role of the brain in stress and adaptation: links to socioeconomic status, health, and disease. Ann N Y Acad Sci. 2010;1186(The Biology of Disadvantage: Socioeconomic Status and Health):190–222.

17. Gluckman PD, Hanson MA, Cooper C, Thornburg KL. Effect of in utero and early-life conditions on adult health and disease. N Engl J Med. 2008;359(1):61–73.

18. Berkman LF. Social epidemiology: social determinants of health in the United States: are we losing ground? Annu Rev Public Health. 2009;30(1):27–41.

19. WHO Commission on Social Determinants of Health. Closing the gap in a generation: health equity through action on the social determinants of health. Final report of the commission on social determinants of health. Geneva: World Health Organization; 2008.

20. Duffey KJ, Gordon-Larsen P, Shikany JM, Guilkey D, Jacobs DR Jr, Popkin BM. Food price and diet and health outcomes: 20 years of the CARDIA study. Arch Intern Med. 2010;170(5):420–6.

21. Chaloupka FJ, Cummings KM, Morley CP, Horan JK. Tax, price and cigarette smoking: evidence from the tobacco documents and implications for tobacco company marketing strategies. Tob Control. 2002;11(Suppl 1):I62–72.

22. Brownell KD, Farley T, Willett WC, Popkin BM, Chaloupka FJ, Thompson JW, et al. The public health and economic benefits of taxing sugar-sweetened beverages. N Engl J Med. 2009;361(16):1599–605.

23. Krieger J, Rabkin J, Sharify D, Song L. High point walking for health: creating built and social environments that support walking in a public housing community. Am J Public Health. 2009;99(S3):S593–9.

Open Access This chapter is licensed under the terms of the Creative Commons Attribution-NonCommercial-NoDerivatives 4.0 International License (http://creativecommons.org/licenses/by-nc-nd/4.0/), which permits any noncommercial use, sharing, distribution and reproduction in any medium or format, as long as you give appropriate credit to the original author(s) and the source, provide a link to the Creative Commons licence and indicate if you modified the licensed material. You do not have permission under this licence to share adapted material derived from this chapter or parts of it.

The images or other third party material in this chapter are included in the chapter's Creative Commons licence, unless indicated otherwise in a credit line to the material. If material is not included in the chapter's Creative Commons licence and your intended use is not permitted by statutory regulation or exceeds the permitted use, you will need to obtain permission directly from the copyright holder.

Chapter 7
Chronic Kidney Disease

Hideyo Tsutsui and Katsunori Kondo

1 Introduction

In 2018, chronic kidney disease (CKD) was estimated to affect approximately 850 million people worldwide. Up to 10.5 million patients worldwide with CKD need dialysis or a kidney transplant, although many patients cannot receive these lifesaving treatments because of high costs or lack of resources [1]. CKD has emerged as one of the highest-occurring, life-threatening, non-communicable diseases in both developing and developed countries.

As of December 31, 2017, there were 334,505 patients undergoing dialysis in Japan, an increase of 40,959 from January 2017. With the increasing number of new dialysis patients, the medical costs associated with this procedure now exceed 1 trillion yen annually [2]. Therefore, the Ministry of Health, Labour and Welfare (MHLW) is aiming to improve the care and outcomes for patients with kidney disease in Japan through the early detection of CKD and adequate standardized treatments. The MHLW set a goal of reducing the number of new dialysis patients to less than 35,000 by 2028 [3].

CKD is defined as kidney damage/injury for ≥3 months and/or a glomerular filtration rate (GFR) <60 mL/min per 1.73 m^2 for ≥3 months with or without kidney damage [4]. Socioeconomic status (SES) has been reported to be associated with the

H. Tsutsui (✉)
Department of Human Culture, Faculty of Modern Life, Teikyo Heisei University, Tokyo, Japan
e-mail: h.tsutsui@thu.ac.jp

K. Kondo
Professor of Social Epidemiology and Health Policy, Department of Social Preventive Medical Sciences, Center for Preventive Medical Sciences, Chiba University, Chiba, Japan

Head of Department of Gerontological Evaluation, Center for Gerontology and Social Science, National Center for Geriatrics and Gerontology, Obu City, Aichi, Japan

© The Author(s) 2020
K. Kondo (ed.), *Social Determinants of Health in Non-communicable Diseases*,
Springer Series on Epidemiology and Public Health,
https://doi.org/10.1007/978-981-15-1831-7_7

onset of CKD [5–11]. In addition, individuals with lower SES may suffer from unrecognized and untreated CKD as well as end-stage renal disease [5, 6].

Zeng et al. [5] and Vart et al. [6] performed meta-analyses to explore the association between SES and CKD. However, their meta-analyses did not include results in Japan. We explored the relationship between SES and CKD in other countries as well as in Japan and discuss factors related to the future direction of prevention measures for CKD.

2   Methods

2.1   Countries Other than Japan

Studies that measured the association between SES and CKD were systematically identified from PubMed. Studies published in English from the inception date of the database to June 2018 were retrieved. Keywords included "socioeconomic status," "income," "education level," "occupation," "chronic kidney disease," "chronic renal failure," and "dialysis." Abstracts without full articles were excluded. The search yielded 71 articles.

2.2   Japan

Suitable studies that measured the association between SES and CKD were systematically identified from PubMed. Studies published from the inception date of the database to June 2018 were retrieved. Keywords included "socioeconomic status," "income," "education level," "occupation," "chronic kidney disease," "chronic renal failure," "Japan," and "Japanese." Abstracts without full articles were excluded. The search yielded two articles. Moreover, Japanese studies that measured the association between SES and CKD were identified from the Japan Medical Abstracts Society. As a result of the search, there were no original articles; however, two abstracts were identified.

3   Results

3.1   Countries Other than Japan: Factors Associated with CKD

3.1.1   SES Status

Studies have compared different low SES areas and showed a higher incidence and worse prognosis of CKD among subjects living in the most deprived areas [5, 7–9]. A retrospective cohort study in Southampton and South-West Hampshire Health

Authority, United Kingdom (CKD incidence rate, 1701/100,000 persons per year) [7] examined the incidence of CKD in several low SES areas. Results showed that people living in the most deprived area had an approximately 40% higher incidence of CKD than those in other low SES areas. In another survey [8] in the United Kingdom, among five lower SES areas, the lowest rated area had the highest number of patients with CKD (19,599 patients per million population). In addition, living in the lowest SES quintile area (most deprived area) as compared with the highest SES area (least deprived area) was associated with a greater risk for a lower estimated glomerular filtration rate (eGFR). This study also analyzed the risk for progressive CKD among 1657 patients according to the SES of their area of residence. The risk for progressive CKD was 6.7 times higher among men and 9.8 times higher among women from the lowest SES area than for CKD patients from the highest SES area. Moreover, a cohort study from the United States that examined 12,856 participants [9] found that living in the lowest SES quartile was associated with more than twice the risk for progressive CKD compared with living in the highest quartile.

3.1.2   Income

A cohort study of 14,086 participants [10] in the United States reported that the hazard ratio (HR) for incident CKD was 1.10 [95% confidence interval (CI) 1.01–1.20] in a middle-income group ($12,000–24,999) and 1.30 (95% CI, 1.17–1.44) in a low-income group (<$12,000), with a high annual household income (≥$25,000) as reference. In a cohort study of 4735 participants in the United States [11], the HR for risk of progressive CKD among lower-income individuals (<$12,000) was 1.4 (95% CI, 1.0–1.9) compared with higher-income individuals (≥$35,000).

3.1.3   Education

A cohort study of 14,086 participants [10] reported that the HR for incident CKD was 1.09 (95% CI, 1.01–1.18) in the middle-education level group (high school/ equivalent) and 1.32 (95%CI, 1.20–1.45) in the low-education level group (<high school), using the high education level (>high school) as a reference. In a population-based case-control study of 1924 participants in Sweden, Fored et al. [12] demonstrated that the odds ratio (OR) for risk of CKD among subjects with 9 years or less of schooling was 1.3 (95% CI, 1.0–1.7) relative to those who went to university. In a study of 60,202 individuals in Brazil [13], it was reported that a higher occurrence of CKD was observed among individuals with a lower education (illiterate/elementary education incomplete) relative to those with higher education (higher education complete) (prevalence ratio 1.65; 95% CI, 1.10–2.46).

3.1.4 Occupation

Fored et al. [12] demonstrated that the OR of CKD among unskilled manual workers was 1.72 (95% CI, 1.2–2.5) relative to professionals. In addition, they showed that among patients in the unskilled manual workers group, 27% had a GFR in the lowest quartile, 24% in the second quartile, 27% in the third quartile, and 21% had a GFR in the highest quartile. A cross-sectional study in the United Kingdom showed that lower occupational grade (clerical and support staff) was associated with a greater OR for decreased eGFR (OR 1.31; 95% CI, 1.12–1.53) [14].

3.2 Factors Associated with CKD in Japan

3.2.1 SES Status

We could not find any original articles from Japan that reported the relationship between SES and CKD by living area.

3.2.2 Income

Takagi et al. [15] examined the relation between SES and mortality risk in 456 patients undergoing hemodialysis (HD). They found that patients undergoing HD from households with an annual income <two million yen had a mortality risk that was 2.19 times higher than patients from households with an annual income of ≥two million yen. In a study using data from the National Health and Nutrition Examination Survey in Japan, there were more people with CKD in low-income groups than in the higher-income group [16].

3.2.3 Education

Imanishi et al. [17] investigated the influences of education level on mortality and hospitalization among 7974 patients undergoing maintenance HD in Japan. They reported that patients with less than a high school education and patients who graduated high school with some college tended to have elevated mortality when compared with patients who graduated from university.

3.2.4 Occupation

We could not find any original articles from Japan that reported the relationship between occupational stratification and CKD.

4 Discussion

4.1 Relation of SES and Lifestyle with CKD

The incidence of CKD is closely related to unhealthy lifestyle behaviors, such as smoking, lack of exercise, and unhealthy eating styles [18–22]. According to Cockerham [23], lifestyle is fundamentally constrained by social hierarchy and an individual's living conditions. Health-related lifestyles related to SES for both individual and regional-level characteristics have been considered in some previous studies and different results have been reported [24, 25].

4.1.1 Smoking

Cigarette smoking is associated with an elevated risk for incident CKD/end-stage renal disease in the adult general population [18, 22]. Tobacco smoke is a major source of adult exposure to cadmium, and smoking contributes more to cadmium body burden than does the typical diet [26]. Cadmium is directly nephrotoxic and can induce renal tubular damage and a progressive reduction in eGFR [27]. Urine cadmium is an indicator of kidney and body burden, and the kidney is a critical target for cadmium toxicity, with renal tubular and glomerular damage manifested by proteinuria and progressive decreases in GFR, respectively [28]. There is also evidence that smoking is associated with many individual-level SES indicators, such as income, education, and occupation, and smoking is more frequent among socioeconomically disadvantaged people [29–31].

Smoking may be more common in people with a low SES for several reasons. First, smoking may serve as a coping mechanism that helps people deal with the different and stressful aspects of their daily lives. Lower family income was associated with higher severe uncertainty stress (OR 1.25; 95% CI, 1.06–1.49) [32]. Both men and women with low SES were shown to experience more stress than those with high SES [33]. Second, people with low SES may be less knowledgeable with regard to information and resources for healthy behavior. Furuya et al. [34] reported that health literacy scores of low-SES people were low. People with low SES have been shown to be less knowledgeable about the harmful effects of smoking [29].

Among studies in Japan, Yun et al. [30] indicated that the lowest household income group had a higher risk for smoking than the highest household income group in both men and women. A study of 32,981 older people in Japan observed smoking rates of 23.6% in men and 4.7% in women for those with less than 6 years of education and 18.9% in men and 1.9% in women for those with ≥13 years of education [31].

4.1.2 Exercise

A lack of habitual exercise is an independent risk factor for CKD [35]. Exercise has many different health-related parameters in CKD. Exercise training is effective in combating muscle atrophy associated with CKD through upregulation of protein synthesis, increasing muscle mitochondria content, and reducing muscle catabolism [36]. Physical activity also counteracts many of the metabolic disturbances that promote the progression of CKD [37]. It has been shown that exercise habits are also related to SES [24, 25, 33, 38]. Participants with a higher educational level are more likely to be physically active and involved in sports [38]. Several points may explain the lower exercise habits among people with lower SES. First, environmental barriers, such as neighborhood safety or inadequate street lighting, may directly and indirectly undermine exercise habits [39, 40]. Lack of parks and low-cost exercise facilities in lower SES areas may also contribute to these findings. Second, it is possible that the low-SES group spends more time watching television than the high-SES group. Andrade-Gómez et al. [41] indicated that television watching time was greater in those with a lower education. Increased time watching television, a passive and sedentary activity, may be associated with less recreational physical activity. Data on 32,981 elderly people in Japan also found that both men and women of low SES were more likely to walk <30 min/day. This finding was true for 47.3% of men with <6 years of education compared with 33.9% of men with ≥13 years of education [33].

4.1.3 Diet

The association between dietary macronutrients, especially protein intake, and the incidence and progression of kidney disease has been examined in multiple clinical trials [42]. Managing proper protein intake remains one of the most important modifiable lifestyle factors in the progression of kidney disease to CKD. More severe protein restriction (<0.3 g/kg per day) reduces the decline in GFR [43]. Furthermore, high salt intake has been related to the development of CKD [44]. In addition, high intake of fresh fruit, vegetables, fish, and unsaturated fats (mainly olive oil) is associated with a lower prevalence of CKD [45]. Several factors contributed to findings related to dietary habits and CKD. Poor eating habits are commonly found in people with low SES, partly because healthy diets are more expensive. Drewnowski et al. [46] demonstrated that higher consumption of fruit, vegetables, meats, and fish was associated with higher costs. In contrast, higher consumption of fats and oils, added sugars, and refined grains was associated with much lower costs. People of low SES may not be able to afford a healthy diet and thus tend to consume foods of lower nutritional value and lower quality. Second, people with less education may lack knowledge regarding healthy dietary patterns. Kuczmarski et al. [47] indicated that the relationship between health literacy and diet quality became stronger as the education level increased. Eating habits have also been reported to be related to SES in other studies [25, 46–49]. Daily consumption of fruits, vegetables, milk, meat, rice, fiber, fish, and dairy products was shown to be lower in people with low SES than those with high SES; those with a lower SES show a higher daily consumption of cakes, salty/fatty snacks, sweet drinks, fast foods, and potatoes [25, 48]. Moreover, Li et al. [49] reported that the highest prevalence of low fruit and vegetable consumption was observed among those aged ≥65 years and those who were illiterate or only had a primary school education.

4.2 Relation Between SES and Life Course in CKD

Previous studies have reported that adverse SES in adulthood is associated with adult CKD [50, 51]. The life-course perspective essentially reflects the study of long-term protective and risk factor effects of physical and social exposures from gestation through adult life, which may also reflect the incidence of CKD. That is, childhood SES may be related to the onset of CKD in adulthood.

Low birth weight (LBW) is strongly associated with childhood-onset CKD [52]. Brenner et al. [53] proposed that LBW may be associated with a congenital deficit in the number of nephrons, which would lead to a predisposition to reduced renal sodium excretion. Moreover, LBW can be attributed to intrauterine growth restriction (IUGR; birth weight less than the tenth percentile for gestational age) or premature birth. LBW associated with IUGR has a stronger association with adult CKD [54], and increased prevalence of microalbuminuria, proteinuria, and lower GFR are seen among adults who had LBW [55, 56]. Shoham et al. [51] reported that salient risk factors and markers that are associated with both SES and CKD early in life include diet and birth weight. Previous studies indicated that many infants of mothers with low SES had LBW [57–59]. Rammohan et al. [57] demonstrated that babies born to women with low family income were significantly more likely to have LBW than those born to women with medium family income (OR, 5.09; 95% CI 1.59–16.32) or high income (OR, 2.29; 95% CI, 0.82–6.38), while Yaya et al. [58] reported that compared to those who had higher education, the OR of experiencing LBW babies was 1.73 and 1.56 for those below the primary and secondary education levels, respectively.

Similarly, maternal diversity of nutritional intake before and during pregnancy is a critical factor influencing birth weight [59]. LBW was linked to poor diet, and poor diet is associated with low SES [57, 60]. Low education and income are considered a reason for LBW, which occurs frequently in low SES people. Lee et al. [60] indicated that women with high SES were more likely to consume healthier food and had better opportunities to maintain dietary profiles consistent with nutritional recommendations or dietary guidelines. Rammohan et al. [57] reported that a low diversity of foods was more common in the diets of women with less education/less income. Similarly, babies born to women with low family income were significantly more likely to have LBW than those born to women with medium family income (OR, 5.09; 95% CI; 1.59–16.32) or high income (OR, 2.29; 95% CI 0.82–6.38) [57]. It is possible that low maternal dietary diversity is caused by a lack of dietary knowledge. Kim et al. [61] reported that the consumption of fruit, vegetables, red meat, and milk was significantly higher in subjects with a higher education level. Another study supported the finding that people with a high education tend to have better dietary intake than people with a low education [62]. O'Brien et al. [63] reported that during pregnancy, a dietary education session was not effective among less educated women.

It is suggested that the low SES of parents leads to LBW in infants and increases the risk for developing adulthood CKD. In Japan, the proportion of LBW infants is increasing. According to the MHLW, the weight of LBW in infants has dropped 200 g in the past 40 years [64]. In the future, these children may have an increased risk of CKD.

5 Summary

We demonstrated that low SES is related to the onset and progression of CKD. Moreover, we found that low SES of parents is associated with an increased risk for developing CKD in children. There are approximately 13.3 million Japanese patients with CKD [3], and this number increases every year. The number of patients who ultimately need dialysis is also increasing and approximately 330,000 Japanese are undergoing HD [2]. There are few reports on the association between Japanese CKD patients and SES. However, it is reported that there are many patients of low SES that are undergoing HD and experiencing CKD. Because SES is strongly correlated with the onset and progression of CKD, it is likely that standard approaches to promoting improvements in individual lifestyle habits alone will not be effective. Therefore, the MHLW must consider the development of programs that target low SES citizens to educate them about CKD and address unhealthy lifestyle behaviors such as smoking, lack of exercise, and unhealthy eating styles.

References

1. Health Day News for Healthier Living. 850 million people worldwide have kidney disease. https://consumer.healthday.com/diseases-and-conditions-information-37/misc-kidney-problem-news-432/850-million-people-worldwide-have-kidney-disease-735411.html. Accessed 22 Feb 2019.
2. Nitta K, Masakane I, Hanafusa N, et al. 2017 Annual dialysis data report, JSDT renal data registry. J Jpn Soc Dial Ther. 2018;51:699–766; (In Japanese).
3. Kidney Disease Countermeasure Commission. Report of kidney disease countermeasure commission.. https://www.mhlw.go.jp/content/10901000/000332759.pdf. Accessed 25 Feb 2019; (In Japanese).
4. Levet AS, Eckardt KU, Tsukamoto Y, et al. Definition and classification of chronic kidney disease: a position statement from kidney disease: improving global outcomes (KDIGO). Kidney Int. 2005;67:2089–100.

5. Zeng X, Liu J, Tao S, Hong HG, Li Y, Fu P. Associations between socioeconomic status and chronic kidney disease: a meta-analysis. J Epidemiol Community Health. 2018;72:270–9.
6. Vart P, Gansevoort RT, Joosten MM, Bültmann U, Reijneveld SA. Socioeconomic disparities in chronic kidney disease: a systematic review and meta-analysis. Am J Prev Med. 2015;48:580–92.
7. Drey N, Roderick P, Mullee M, Rogerson M. A population-based study of the incidence and outcomes of diagnosed chronic kidney disease. Am J Kidney Dis. 2003;42:677–84.
8. Bello AK, Peters J, Rigby J, Rahman AA, Nahas ME. Socioeconomic status and chronic kidney disease at presentation to a renal service in the United Kingdom. Clin J Am Nephrol. 2008;3:1316–23.
9. Merkin SS, Coresh J, Diez Roux AV, Taylor HA, Powe NR. Area socioeconomic status and progressive CKD: the atherosclerosis risk in communities (ARIC) study. Am J Kidney Dis. 2005;46:203–13.
10. Vart P, Grams ME, Ballew SH, Woodward M, Coresh J, Matsushita K. Socioeconomic status and risk of kidney dysfunction: the atherosclerosis risk in communities study. Nephrol Dial Transplant. 2018. https://doi.org/10.1093/ndt/gfy142; 1–8.
11. Merkin SS, Diez Roux AV, Coresh J, Fried LF, Jackson SA, Powe NR. Individual and neighborhood socioeconomic status and progressive chronic kidney disease in an elderly population: the cardiovascular health study. Soc Sci Med. 2007;65:809–21.
12. Fored CM, Ejerblad E, Fryzek JP, et al. Socio-economic status and chronic renal failure: a population-based case-control study in Sweden. Nephrol Dial Transplant. 2003;18:82–8.
13. Malta DC, Bernal RT, de Souza MF, et al. Social inequalities in the prevalence of self-reported chronic non-communicable diseases in Brazil: national health survey 2013. Int J Equity Health. 2016;15:153.
14. Al-Qaoud TM, Nitsch D, Wells J, Witte DR, Brunner EJ. Socioeconomic status and reduced kidney function in the Whitehall II study: role of obesity and metabolic syndrome. Am J Kidney Dis. 2011;58:389–97.
15. Takaki J, Hashimoto H, Yano E, Ogino K. Relationship between survival and socioeconomic status in patients with chronic kidney disease. Jpn J Hyg. 2007;62:722; (In Japanese).
16. Amano H, Fukuda Y, Yamaoka K. Relationship between socioeconomic status and chronic kidney disease in Japan. Jpn J Hyg. 2017;72:S204; (In Japanese).
17. Imanishi Y, Fukuma S, Karaboyas A, et al. Associations of employment status and educational levels with mortality and hospitalization in the dialysis outcomes and practice patterns study in Japan. PLoS One. 2017;12:e0170731.
18. Ejerblad E, Fored CM, Lindblad P, et al. Association between smoking and chronic renal failure in a nationwide population-based case-control study. J Am Soc Nephrol. 2004;15:2178–85.
19. White SL, Polkinghorne KR, Cass A, Shaw JE, Atkins RC, Chadban SJ. Alcohol consumption and 5-year onset of chronic kidney disease: the AusDiab study. Nephrol Dial Transplant. 2009;24:2464–72.
20. Iseki K, Ikemiya Y, Kinjo K, Inoue T, Iseki C, Takishita S. Body mass index and the risk of development of end-stage renal disease in a screened cohort. Kidney Int. 2004;65:1870–6.
21. Michishita R, Matsuda T, Kawakami S, et al. The association between changes in lifestyle behaviors and the incidence of chronic kidney disease (CKD) in middle-aged and older men. J Epidemiol. 2017;27:389–97.
22. Xia J, Wang L, Ma Z, et al. Cigarette smoking and chronic kidney disease in the general population: a systematic review and meta-analysis of prospective cohort studies. Nephrol Dial Transplant. 2017;32:475–87.
23. Cockerham WC. Health lifestyles: bringing structure back. In: Cockerham WC, editor. The new Blackwell companion to medical sociology. Oxford: Blackwell; 2010. p. 159–83; ISBN 9781405188685.
24. Ottevaere C, Huybrechts I, Benser J, et al. Clustering patterns of physical activity, sedentary and dietary behavior among European adolescents: the HELENA study. BMC Public Health. 2011;11:328.

25. Kelishadi R, Qorbani M, Motlagh ME, Ardalan G, Heshmat R, Hovsepian S. Socioeconomic disparities in dietary and physical activity habits of Iranian children and adolescents: the CASPIAN-IV study. Arch Iran Med. 2016;19:530–7.
26. Galazyn-Sidorczuk M, Brzóska MM, Moniuszko-Jakoniuk J. Estimation of polish cigarettes contamination with cadmium and lead, and exposure to these metals via smoking. Environ Monit Assess. 2008;137:481–93.
27. Roels HA, Hoet P, Lison D. Usefulness of biomarkers of exposure to inorganic mercury, lead, or cadmium in controlling occupational and environmental risks of nephrotoxicity. Ren Fail. 1999;21:251–62.
28. Mortensen ME, Wong LY, Osterloh JD. Smoking status and urine cadmium above levels associated with subclinical renal effects in U.S. adults without chronic kidney disease. Int J Hyg Environ Health. 2011;214:305–10.
29. Stewart DW, Adams CE, Cano MA, et al. Associations between health literacy and established predictors of smoking cessation. Am J Public Health. 2013;103:e43–9.
30. Yun WJ, Rhee JA, Kim SA, et al. Household and area income levels are associated with smoking status in the Korean adult population. BMC Public Health. 2015;15:39.
31. Matsuda R. Lifestyle and history of falling. In: Kondo K, editor. Exploring "inequalities in health": a large-scale social epidemiological survey for care prevention in Japan. Tokyo: Igaku Shoin; 2007. p. p21–7.
32. Yang T, Yang XY, Yu L, Cottrell RR, Jiang S. Individual and regional association between socioeconomic status and uncertainty stress, and life stress: a representative nationwide study of China. Int J Equity Health. 2017;16:118.
33. Milas G, Klarić IM, Malnar A, Šupe-Domić D, Slavich GM. Socioeconomic status, social-cultural values, life stress, and health behaviors in a national sample of adolescents. Stress Health. 2019 Jan 4;35:217–24. https://doi.org/10.1002/smi.2854.
34. Furuya Y, Kondo N, Yamagata Z, Hashimoto H. Health literacy, socioeconomic status and self-rated health in Japan. Health Promot Int. 2015;30:505–13.
35. Michishita R, Matsuda T, Kawakami S, et al. The joint impact of habitual exercise and glycemic control on the incidence of chronic kidney disease (CKD) in middle-aged and older males. Environ Health Prev Med. 2017;22:76.
36. Watson EL, Kosmadakis GC, Smith AC, et al. Combined walking exercise and alkali therapy in patients with CKD4-5 regulates intramuscular free amino acid pools and ubiquitin E3 ligase expression. Eur J Appl Physiol. 2013;113:2111–24.
37. Robinson-Cohen C, Littman AJ, Duncan GE, et al. Physical activity and change in estimated GFR among persons with CKD. J Am Soc Nephrol. 2014;25:399–406.
38. Federico B, Falese L, Marandola D, Capelli G. Socioeconomic differences in sport and physical activity among Italian adults. J Sports Sci. 2013;31:451–8.
39. Grzywacz JG, Marks NF. Social inequalities and exercise during adulthood: toward an ecological perspective. J Health Soc Behav. 2001;42:202–20.
40. Murata C, Kondo K, Hirai H, Ichida Y, Ojima T. Association between depression and socioeconomic status among community-dwelling elderly in Japan: the Aichi Gerontological Evaluation Study (AGES). Health Place. 2008;14:406–14.
41. Andrade-Gómez E, García-Esquinas E, Ortolá R, Martínez-Gómez D, Rodríguez-Artalejo F. Watching TV has a distinct sociodemographic and lifestyle profile compared with other sedentary behaviors: a nationwide population-based study. PLoS One. 2017;12:e0188836.
42. Kasiske BL, Lakatua JD, Ma JZ, Louis TA. A meta-analysis of the effects of dietary protein restriction on the rate of decline in renal function. Am J Kidney Dis. 1998;31:954–61.
43. Klahr S, Levey AS, Beck GJ, et al. The effects of dietary protein restriction and blood-pressure control on the progression of chronic renal disease. Modification of diet in renal disease study group. N Engl J Med. 1994;330:877–84.
44. McMahon EJ, Bauer JD, Hawley CM, et al. A randomized trial of dietary sodium restriction in CKD. J Am Soc Nephrol. 2013;24:2096–103.

45. Hariharan D, Vellanki K, Kramer H. The western diet and chronic kidney disease. Curr Hypertens Rep. 2015;17:16.
46. Drewnowski A, Darmon N, Briend A. Replacing fats and sweets with vegetables and fruits--a question of cost. Am J Public Health. 2004;94:1555–9.
47. Kuczmarski MF, Adams EL, Cotugna N, et al. Health literacy and education predict nutrient quality of diet of socioeconomically diverse, urban adults. J Epidemiol Prev Med. 2016;2:13000115. https://doi.org/10.19104/jepm.
48. Allen L, Williams J, Townsend N, et al. Socioeconomic status and non communicable disease behavioural risk factors in low-income and lower-middle-income countries: a systematic review. Lancet Glob Health. 2017;5:e277–89.
49. Li YC, Jiang B, Zhang M, et al. Vegetable and fruit consumption among Chinese adults and associated factors: a nationally representative study of 170,847 adults. Biomed Environ Sci. 2017;30:863–74.
50. Brophy PD, Shoham DA, CKD Life Course Group, et al. Early-life course socioeconomic factors and chronic kidney disease. Adv Chronic Kidney Dis. 2015;22:16–23.
51. Shoham DA, Vupputuri S, Kshirsagar AV. Chronic kidney disease and life course socioeconomic status: a review. Adv Chronic Kidney Dis. 2005;12:56–63.
52. Hirano D, Ishikura K, Uemura O, et al. Association between low birth weight and childhood-onset chronic kidney disease in Japan: a combined analysis of a nationwide survey for paediatric chronic kidney disease and the National Vital Statistics Report. Nephrol Dial Transplant. 2016;31:1895–900.
53. Brenner BM, Garcia DL, Anderson S. Glomeruli and blood pressure. Less of one, more the other? Am J Hypertens. 1988;1:335–47.
54. Yiu V, Buka S, Zurakowski D, McCormick M, Brenner B, Jabs K. Relationship between birth-weight and blood pressure in childhood. Am J Kidney Dis. 1999;33:253–60.
55. Nelson RG, Morgenstern H, Bennett PH. Birth weight and renal disease in Pima Indians with type 2 diabetes mellitus. Am J Epidemiol. 1998;148:650–6.
56. Yudkin JS, Martyn CN, Phillips DI, Gale CR. Associations of micro-albuminuria with intra-uterine growth retardation. Nephron. 2001;89:309–14.
57. Rammohan A, Goli S, Singh D, Ganguly D, Singh U. Maternal dietary diversity and odds of low birth weight: empirical findings from India. Women Health. 2019;59(4):375–90.
58. Yaya S, Bishwajit G, Ekholuenetale M, Shah V. Inadequate utilization of prenatal care services, socioeconomic status, and educational attainment are associated with low birth weight in Zimbabwe. Front Public Health. 2017;5:35.
59. Abubakari A, Jahn A. Maternal dietary patterns and practices and birth weight in Northern Ghana. PLoS One. 2016;11:e0162285.
60. Lee SE, Talegawkar SA, Merialdi M, Caulfield LE. Dietary intakes of women during pregnancy in low- and middle-income countries. Public Health Nutr. 2013;16:1340–53.
61. Kim OY, Kwak SY, Kim B, Kim YS, Kim HY, Shin MJ. Selected food consumption mediates the association between education level and metabolic syndrome in Korean adults. Ann Nutr Metab. 2017;70:122–31.
62. Marques-Vidal P, Rousi E, Paccaud F, et al. Dietary intake according to gender and education: a twenty-year trend in a Swiss adult population. Nutrients. 2015;7:9558–72.
63. O'Brien EC, Alberdi G, Geraghty AA, McAuliffe FM. Lower education predicts poor response to dietary intervention in pregnancy, regardless of neighborhood affluence: secondary analysis from the ROLO randomized control trial. Public Health Nutr. 2017;20:2959–69.
64. Director-general or statistics and information, Ministry of Health, Labour and Welfare. Vital statistics in Japan. Trends up to 2016. https://www.mhlw.go.jp/english/database/db-hw/dl/81-1a2en.pdf. Accessed 25 Feb 2019; (In Japanese).

Open Access This chapter is licensed under the terms of the Creative Commons Attribution-NonCommercial-NoDerivatives 4.0 International License (http://creativecommons.org/licenses/by-nc-nd/4.0/), which permits any noncommercial use, sharing, distribution and reproduction in any medium or format, as long as you give appropriate credit to the original author(s) and the source, provide a link to the Creative Commons licence and indicate if you modified the licensed material. You do not have permission under this licence to share adapted material derived from this chapter or parts of it.

The images or other third party material in this chapter are included in the chapter's Creative Commons licence, unless indicated otherwise in a credit line to the material. If material is not included in the chapter's Creative Commons licence and your intended use is not permitted by statutory regulation or exceeds the permitted use, you will need to obtain permission directly from the copyright holder.

Chapter 8
Diabetes Mellitus

Hideyo Tsutsui, Go Tanaka, and Katsunori Kondo

1 Introduction

In 2017, diabetes mellitus (DM) was estimated to affect 452 million patients worldwide, a number that is predicted to grow to 693 million by 2045 [1]. DM has become one the most pressing and prevalent issues in the past few decades, hand- in- hand with the rising obesity crisis. It is now the seventh leading cause of death worldwide [2]. The number of deaths caused by DM increased from less than 1 million in 2000 to 1.6 million in 2016 [2]. DM is a major risk factor for the development of microvascular complications including nephropathy, retinopathy, and neuropathy as well as macrovascular complications including coronary artery disease, peripheral vascular disease, and carotid artery disease [3]. With the rapid and alarming growth of DM, both the prevalence and major complications associated with DM need to be addressed.

In Japan, the number of patients with DM reached ten million in 2017 [4]. Moreover, 16,492 patients had diabetic nephropathy (DMN), which is the most common cause of the need for dialysis [5]. Therefore, the Ministry of Health, Labour and Welfare (MHLW) created a program to prevent progression of DMN for

H. Tsutsui (✉)
Department of Human Culture, Faculty of Modern Life, Teikyo Heisei University, Tokyo, Japan
e-mail: h.tsutsui@thu.ac.jp

G. Tanaka
Human Development Department, Japan International Cooperation Agency, Tokyo, Japan

K. Kondo
Professor of Social Epidemiology and Health Policy, Department of Social Preventive Medical Sciences, Center for Preventive Medical Sciences, Chiba University, Chiba, Japan

Head of Department of Gerontological Evaluation, Center for Gerontology and Social Science, National Center for Geriatrics and Gerontology, Obu City, Aichi, Japan

© The Author(s) 2020
K. Kondo (ed.), *Social Determinants of Health in Non-communicable Diseases*,
Springer Series on Epidemiology and Public Health,
https://doi.org/10.1007/978-981-15-1831-7_8

those who have not been assessed or for those with high risk of severe DM who do not adhere to treatment regimens. This program aims to prevent the transition to kidney failure and the need for dialysis.

According to the International Diabetes Federation, diagnostic criteria for DM, include one or more of the following criteria: (1) fasting plasma glucose ≥7.0; or (2) 2-h plasma glucose ≥11.1 mmol/L (200 mg/dL) following a 75-g oral glucose load; or (3) a random glucose >11.1 mmol/L (200 mg/dL) or hemoglobin A1c (HbA1c) ≥48 mmol/mol (equivalent to 6.5%) [1]. The onset of DM and its relation to socio-economic status (SES) have been reported. Individuals with lower SES may suffer from unrecognized and untreated DM [6–10]. Furthermore, the association of DM with SES has been shown to be related to a higher number of socioeconomically disadvantaged individuals living in an area as well as the characteristics of the area itself.

Agardh et al. [6] performed a meta-analysis to explore the association between SES and DM. They reported that compared with high educational level, occupation, and income, low levels of these determinants were associated with an overall increased risk of type 2 DM (T2DM); [relative risk (RR), 1.41; 95% confidence interval (CI), 1.28–1.51], (RR, 1.31; 95% CI, 1.09–1.57), and (RR, 1.40; 95% CI, 1.04–1.88), respectively]. Wu et al. [7] demonstrated the relationship between low education and prevalence of DM in a meta-analysis and Suwannaphant et al. [8] showed this same relationship in a cross-sectional study. Nagata et al. [9] reported the association between occupation and prevalence of DM in a follow-up study in Japan, and Nagamine et al. [10] showed the relationship between low- income status and the prevalence of DM in a cross-sectional study. Moreover, Lamy et al. [11] and Green et al. [12] demonstrated that a high prevalence of DM was strongly correlated with indicators of low SES, poor environmental quality, and poor lifestyles in an ecological study.

In this chapter, we introduce findings on the relationship between SES and DM in Japan and other countries, and discuss the future direction of preventive measures.

2 Methods

2.1 Countries Other than Japan

Suitable studies that measured the association between SES and DM were systematically identified from PubMed. Studies published from the inception date of the database to June 2018 were retrieved. Studies were restricted to those published in English and within the past 5 years. Keywords included "socioeconomic status," "income," "education level," "occupation," "diabetes mellitus," "type 1 diabetes mellitus," and "type 2 diabetes mellitus." Abstracts without full articles were excluded. The search yielded 172 articles.

2.2 Japan

Suitable studies that measured the association between SES and DM were systematically identified from PubMed. Studies published from the inception date of the database to June 2018 were retrieved. Studies were restricted to those published in English and within the past 5 years. Keywords included "socioeconomic status," "income," "education level," "occupation," "diabetes mellitus," "type 1 diabetes mellitus," and "type 2 diabetes mellitus," "Japan," and "Japanese." Abstracts without full articles were excluded. The search yielded three articles. Moreover, Japanese studies that measured the association between SES and DM were identified from the Japan Medical Abstracts Society. As a result of the search, two original articles and two abstracts were retrieved.

3 Results

3.1 Countries Other than Japan

3.1.1 Living Area

A high incidence and poor control of DM were reported in areas with residents of low SES [11–15]. For instance, a study conducted in Winnipeg, Manitoba, Canada (DM prevalence rate of 47.3 cases/1000 population) [12] found a high DM prevalence clustered in the City of Winnipeg which has a high percentage of Aboriginal population, as well as people with low educational levels, low family income, a high percentage of single parent families, high levels of unemployment, high numbers of vacant and placarded houses, high levels of crime, and high rates of smoking. In a survey [13] in the United States, individuals with incident DM were shown to reside in neighborhoods of people with lower education levels, lower median household incomes, and greater proportions of people living below the poverty line. Lindner et al. [14] indicated that a low-SES area was associated with an increased risk for diabetic ketoacidosis at all ages. A cross-sectional study from 2012 to 2013 conducted using the Korean National Health Insurance Research Database [15] reported those living in rural areas were less likely to undergo HbA1c testing.

3.1.2 Individual Levels

Income

The Korea National Health and Nutrition Examination Survey (KNHANES) analyzed data from 2008 to 2014 in South Korea [16] and showed an increasing trend in the prevalence of DM in the low-income group. In assessing data from KNHANES

V, which was conducted from 2010 to 2012, Kim et al. [17] demonstrated that the odds ratio (OR) and 95% CI for the prevalence of DM among the lower income group was OR 2.87 (95% CI, 2.35–3.50) relative to higher income groups. Dinca-Panaitescu et al. [18] showed that the prevalence of T2DM in the lowest income group was 4.14 times higher than that in the highest income group. In addition, they reported that prevalence of DM decreased steadily as income went up [18].

Education

In a cross-sectional study, Suwannaphant et al. [8] demonstrated that the OR for the prevalence of DM among individuals with a lower education was 5.87 (95% CI, 4.70–7.33) relative to individuals with a higher education. A cross-sectional study of 664,969 adults [19] reported the rate of increase in prevalence of DM was higher for adults who had a high school education or less compared with those who had more than a high school education (for interaction, $P = 0.006$ for <high school and $P < 0.001$ for high school). In a population-based nationwide cross-sectional study of 19,303 individuals in Korea [20], educational status showed a significant association with DM; furthermore, the OR for DM increased with less education. The ORs were 1.41 (95% CI, 1.13–1.77) for elementary school or less, 1.33 (95% CI, 1.08–1.65) for middle school, and 1.30 (95% CI, 1.09–1.54) for high school.

Occupation

Reviriego et al. [21] performed a cross-sectional study and showed that the prevalence rates of impaired fasting glucose levels, type 1 DM, and T2DM by occupational categories in a nationwide sample of a Spanish working population were greater among blue-collar workers than among white-collar workers. Cleal et al. [22] showed that DM and low occupational status have a clear compound effect, showing that workers with DM with low-level occupations have a 1173% greater risk for early retirement than professionals without DM. Moreover, Shamshirgaran et al. [23] demonstrated that compared with people who were in paid employment, the age and sex-adjusted OR for prevalence of DM was higher in people who were retired (OR, 1.22; 95% CI, 1.16–1.29), or who were unemployed or involved in other types of work (OR, 1.17; 95% CI, 1.12–1.23).

3.2 Japan

3.2.1 Living Area

We could not find original articles from Japan reporting the relationship between SES and DM by living area.

3.2.2 Income

Nagamine et al. [10] showed that compared with people in the highest income category, prevalence ratios of women with DM for the lowest income category and the second-lowest category were 1.42 and 1.33 after adjusting for each SES factor. In a case-control study in 1993 [24], patients with DM had lower incomes than control participants, after adjusting for disability. Moreover, patients with low income were reported to have higher levels of complications of DM than those with higher income. For example, Funakoshi et al. [25] found that the ORs of having DMN were higher among patients with middle-income (OR, 3.61; 95% CI, 1.69–8.27) or low-income levels (OR, 2.53; 95% CI, 1.11–6.07), even after adjustment for covariates.

3.2.3 Education

Nishi et al. [26] found that Japanese men with a low level of education were more likely to have DM than those with a high level of education (OR, 2.55; 95% CI, 1.21–5.39). Moreover, patients who had only graduated from junior high school were shown to have more complications of DM than patients with a higher level of education. For example, Funakoshi et al. [25] found that the ORs of having diabetic retinopathy were greater among patients who had graduated from junior high school (OR, 1.91; 95% CI, 1.09–3.34) than for patients who had graduated from college. In addition, they reported that the ORs of having DMN were greater among patients who had graduated from junior high school (OR, 2.38; 95% CI, 1.06–5.31) than for patients who had graduated from college.

3.2.4 Occupation

Hayashino et al. [27] demonstrated that compared with white-collar workers, the age-adjusted OR for prevalent DM was 1.91 (95% CI, 1.37–2.64) in blue-collar workers. Another study [28] showed that among those aged 40–49 years, the incidence of DM in sales workers, which is considered a lower-level job, was significantly increased compared with clerical, with a multivariate-adjusted hazard ratio (HR) of 1.55 (95% CI, 1.02–2.35). In contrast, the incidence of DM in technical/professional workers and in managerial/administrative workers did not have a significant HR in any model.

4 Discussion

Common determinants of DM include excess body fat and high blood pressure and lifestyle factors such as inadequate diet, physical inactivity, and stress. Therefore, lifestyle interventions are appropriate strategies to help prevent DM. However, as mentioned in Chap. 7, unhealthy lifestyle habits are more common in low-SES groups [29, 30]. Moreover, in DM treatment, various self-care behaviors, such as diet, medication, and exercise, are required, and appropriate training is needed to help patients with DM to complete these self-management tasks. In addition, people of low SES have more difficulties with self-monitoring of blood glucose levels, because they cannot afford the test strips. The low-SES group may have worse self-care behavior than the high-SES group. Walker et al. [31] found that social determinants of health were significantly associated with diabetic knowledge, self-care, and outcomes. Uchmanowicz et al. [32] suggested that higher education was associated with higher cognitive function and better self-care.

4.1   Diet

Consumption of whole grains, coffee or tea, low-fat milk and dairy products, moderate alcohol consumption, fruit and vegetables, pulses, and nuts (in women only) are associated with a decreased risk for T2DM [33]. Conversely, consumption of foods high in fat and low in dietary fiber is associated with an increased risk for DM. High consumption of junk food, bread, and butter is associated with substantial increases in the risk for DM. Gittelsohn et al. [34] reported that high junk food consumption was associated with a 2.4 times greater risk for DM. As introduced in Chap. 7, the daily consumption of fruit, vegetables, milk, meat, rice, and dairy products was lower in those with a low SES than those with a high SES, whereas the daily consumption was higher for cakes, salty/fatty snacks, sweet drinks, fast foods, and potatoes [30]. In terms of the relationship between childhood SES and adult eating habits, Hardy et al. [35] indicated that compared with children from high-SES neighborhoods, children from low-SES neighborhoods were generally more than twice as likely to have a high junk food intake, not eat breakfast daily, and eat fast food once a week or more. Junk foods are high-calorie foods, with high sugar contents. Obesity, which is mostly caused by high-calorie food intake, often leads to insulin resistance [36]. An unfavorable impact on body composition caused by poor eating habits could be one mechanism linking early childhood growth with a later increased risk for T2DM. Yanagi et al. [37] found that those with low childhood SES in Japan were 1.36 times less likely to consume fruit and vegetables than those with a high childhood SES. Li et al. [38] found a 6% lower risk for T2DM per 1 serving/day increment of fruit intake and a 13% lower risk for T2DM per 0.2 servings/day increment of green leafy vegetable intake.

In addition, those who had been exposed to maternal malnutrition during pregnancy may have increased morbidity associated with metabolic diseases, including T2DM in adult life [39]. Similarly, Portrait et al. [40] showed significant associations between exposure to undernutrition during adolescence and the presence of DM at ages 60–76 years for women. These findings indicate that pregnancy and childhood diets are linked to the risk for developing DM in the future. The fetal origins of disease hypothesis suggests that the weight and nutritional status of a woman before and during pregnancy can affect the long-term health of her children through programming of the adrenal-pituitary-hypothalamic axis during gestation [41]. These effects also increase the risk for T2DM, obesity, and hypertension [41]. Obesity may increase the risk for hypertensive disorders among pregnant women [42]. Hypertension during pregnancy has been associated with increased insulin resistance during pregnancy [43]. Gestational hypertension has been shown to double the risk for development of T2DM in the mother within 17 years postpartum [43]. It has been reported that pregnant women and children with a low SES have poor eating habits. In a prospective cohort study in the United Kingdom [44], poorer nutrient intakes associated with deprivation were consistent with food choices: diets of the more deprived women were characterized by low intakes of fruit and vegetables and higher intakes of fried potatoes, crisps, snacks, and processed meat.

The reasons for poor eating habits in pregnant women with a low SES in childhood can be attributed to low income and less education, as discussed in Chap. 7. In Japan, recently pregnant women tend to lack energy intake, and gain insufficient weight during pregnancy [45]. Essentially, they are in a state of malnutrition. A preliminary prospective study [46] showed that a dietary pattern with a high intake of bread, confectioneries, and soft drinks, and a low intake of fish and vegetables during pregnancy might be associated with small birth weight and increased risk for having a small-for-gestational-age infant. Low birth weight is also associated with the onset of DM as well as chronic kidney disease [46].

4.2 Smoking

The World Health Organization recognizes smoking as a preventable risk factor for T2DM and endorses smoking avoidance/cessation as part of their lifestyle recommendations [47]. Cigarettes and other smoking products contain a mix of chemical additives with the potential to impact metabolic health. In particular, the effect of nicotine is great. Nicotine has been shown to directly alter glucose homeostasis [48]. Thus nicotine plays an important role in the incidence of T2DM. As mentioned in Chap. 7, people with low-SES status are more likely to smoke [49, 50]. In the Japan epidemiology collaboration on occupational health (J-ECOH) study, Akter et al. [51] indicated that DM risk increased with increasing numbers of cigarettes among current smokers. In addition, Fukuda et al. [52] reported that a low SES measured according to income and occupation in Japan was generally associated with higher likelihood of risky health behaviors, such as current smoking and excessive alcohol consumption. Furthermore, a Japanese study of a national integrated project for prospective observation of non-communicable disease and its trends in the aged in 2010 (NIPPON DATA 2010) [53] indicated that women with ≤9 years of education had a higher risk for passive smoking at home than women with ≥13 years of education (OR, 2.06; 95% CI, 1.31–3.25). The high proportion of smokers among people with a low-SES status is believed to be a result of inadequate stress-coping behaviors and a lack of knowledge about the harmful effects of smoking, as discussed in Chap. 7.

4.3   Exercise

Physical activity and exercise have a beneficial effect on a variety of factors relevant to DM. Exercise is recommended for both the prevention of DM and the treatment of people with DM [54]. However, many people of low- SES do not exercise [55, 56]. Lin et al. [55] found women with sub-high- school education had significantly lower average levels of physical activity than women with education of high school or above. In Japan, Murakami et al. [56] indicated that respondents with a higher education showed a higher prevalence of habitual exercise than those with a lower level of education in all stratified groups. Koohsari et al. [57] found that low-SES areas were disadvantaged in environmental attributes related to walking, such as lack of footpaths, high crime areas, and low street lighting. They suggested that improving environmental factors related to walking in lower-SES areas may enhance walking, and thus reduce the gap between low- and high-SES areas. Because a lower SES is associated with more work-related physical activity, and less travel-related, recreational, and total physical activity [58], providing an environment that makes access to exercise easier may lead to increased exercise habits among the low-SES group.

In addition, an experience of childhood poverty is associated with lack of exercise [59]. Low SES in childhood has a long-lasting adverse impact on numerous physical and mental health outcomes in adulthood [60]. Thus, low SES in childhood is linked to low SES in adulthood. Therefore, improving SES in childhood may promote better health behaviors in adulthood. Currently, childhood poverty is a major policy concern in Japan. The relative poverty rate of children in Japan was ranked 11th out of 41 developed countries [61], with a current relative poverty rate of children in Japan of 13.9% [62]. Therefore, providing health education for low-SES children may be important. DM often occurs in patients with low health literacy [63–65]. There are many patients with low health literacy in the low-SES group in Japan [65–67]. Therefore, strengthening health education for those with low-SES may help reduce the incidence of DM among patients with a low SES.

4.4   Stress

Excessive stress is a risk factor for the onset of DM. Exposure to long-term stress affects the entire neuroendocrine system, activating the hypothalamo-pituitary-adrenal axis and/or the central sympathetic nervous system, which results in an increase in cortisol levels [68]. Insulin resistance and increased hepatic glucose production induced by glucocorticoids result in increased plasma insulin levels [69].

Moreover, stress stimulates the release of various hormones, which can result in elevated blood glucose levels [70]. Thus, psychological distress can be a cause of insulin resistance [71].

People in low-SES groups have more psychological distress than people in high-SES groups [72, 73]. As mentioned earlier, the living environment can increase stress levels in people in low-SES groups. Baum et al. [72] suggested that lower SES is likely to be correlated with settings with higher population density, noise, crime, pollution, discrimination, poor access to resources, and with hazards or deprivations. In addition, they proposed that limited income, education, and/or lower social class may cause people to live in poorer, stressful settings or may perpetuate their living in such areas. Low household income and education level may also contribute to psychological stress. Markwick et al. [74] indicated that low household income results in less disposable income to purchase healthy foods, engage in leisure time activities that may be an important source of physical activity, and afford safe and adequate housing and healthcare. A low level of educational attainment puts people at higher risk for unemployment, limits their likelihood of obtaining a job that pays a living wage, and is associated with lower levels of health literacy. Furthermore, the heavy workload associated with the need to work to financially support their lives may limit time for healthy food preparation and cooking.

Moreover, people of low SES have been shown to have poor stress-coping abilities [75]. Low SES has been indirectly associated with poor mental health outcomes through the inability to adopt a suitable coping style [72]. Inadequate health behaviors such as smoking, poor diet, and lack of exercise are risk factors for developing DM. Psychological stress also decreases the motivation to take part in healthy lifestyle behaviors both before and after the onset of T2DM [76, 77]. Stress leads to unhealthy behaviors such as poor food intake [78]. Deasy et al. [79] reported that high psychological stress scores were correlated with poor diet (OR, 1.03) and increased consumption of convenience foods (OR, 1.04). Emami et al. [80] also reported that lower distress tolerance scores were related to higher levels of unhealthy eating. Cockerham et al. [81] indicated that psychological distress is associated with frequent drinking in men, and hypothesized that once drinking practices are established for an individual, they continue, as habitual drinking is perceived as suppressing distress. Furthermore, it has also been reported that distress is significantly associated with smoking in women who are distressed (OR, 1.064) [81]. Lipscombe et al. [82] indicated that smoking was associated with an increased probability of severe distress. The need for adequate stress-coping instructions for people of low SES is suggested.

5 Summary

We demonstrated that low SES is related to the onset of DM. In addition, we reported that there are many inappropriate health behaviors that increase the risk for developing DM in the low-SES group. In Japan, the MHLW, in as part of "Healthy Japan

21," is designed to implement "A basic direction for comprehensive implementation of national health promotion." [83] This initiative aims to improve lifestyle habits for people with DM and to reduce the number of patients with lifestyle-related diseases. The policy points out that it is important to classify target groups based on life stage, gender, and SES to improve lifestyle habits. Moreover, the policy points out the need to improve lifestyle factors, such as eating appropriate foods, taking part in moderate exercise, stopping smoking, etc., and to provide a social environment that is conductive to these activities. In addition, the policy aims to implement specific health checkups and health guidance for subjects with a low SES. However, many people who have medical examinations are in the high-SES group [50]. Therefore, to improve lifestyle-related diseases such as DM, it may be necessary to proceed with measures such as low-cost sale of low-calorie foods, maintenance of parks where exercise can be carried out, and cessation of smoking in all public places.

References

1. International Diabetes Federation. IDF diabetes atlas. 8th ed. 2017. www.diabetesatlas.org. Accessed 06 Mar 2019.
2. The World Health Organization. The top 10 causes of death. https://www.who.int/en/newsroom/fact-sheets/detail/the-top-10-causes-of-death. Accessed 06 Mar 2019.
3. Beckman JA, Creager MA, Libby P. Diabetes and atherosclerosis: epidemiology, pathophysiology, and management. JAMA. 2002;287:2570–81.
4. Ministry of Health, Labour and Welfare. Outline of the national health and nutrition survey 2017. https://www.mhlw.go.jp/content/10904750/000351576.pdf. Accessed 08 Mar 2019.
5. Nitta K, Masakane I, Hanafusa N, et al. 2017 Annual dialysis data report, JSDT renal data registry. J Jpn Soc Dial Ther. 2018;51:699–766; (In Japanese).
6. Agardh E, Allebeck P, Hallqvist J, Moradi T, Sidorchuk A. Type 2 diabetes incidence and socioeconomic position: a systematic review and meta-analysis. Int J Epidemiol. 2011;40:804e818.
7. Wu H, Meng X, Wild SH, Gasevic D, Jackson CA. Socioeconomic status and prevalence of type 2 diabetes in mainland China, Hong Kong and Taiwan: a systematic review. J Glob Health. 2017;7:011103.
8. Suwannaphant K, Laohasiriwong W, Puttanapong N, Saengsuwan J, Phajan T. Association between socioeconomic status and diabetes mellitus: the national socioeconomics survey, 2010 and 2012. J Clin Diagn Res. 2017;11:LC18–22.
9. Nagata T, Yoshida H, Takahashi H, Kawai M. Policemen and firefighters have increased risk for type-2 diabetes mellitus probably due to their large body mass index: a follow-up study in Japanese men. Am J Ind Med. 2006;49(1):30–5.
10. Nagamine Y, Kondo N, Yokobayashi K, et al. Socioeconomic disparity in the prevalence of objectively evaluated diabetes among older Japanese adults: JAGES cross-sectional data in 2010. J Epidemiol. 2019;29:295–301. https://doi.org/10.2188/jea.JE20170206.
11. Lamy S, Ducros D, Diméglio C, et al. Disentangling the influence of living place and socioeconomic position on health services use among diabetes patients: a population-based study. PLoS One. 2017;12:e0188295.
12. Green C, Hoppa RD, Young TK, Blanchard JF. Geographic analysis of diabetes prevalence in an urban area. Soc Sci Med. 2003;57:551–60.
13. Christine PJ, Young R, Adar SD, et al. Individual- and area-level SES in diabetes risk prediction: the multi-ethnic study of atherosclerosis. Am J Prev Med. 2017;53:201–9.

14. Lindner LME, Rathmann W, Rosenbauer J. Inequalities in glycaemic control, hypoglycaemia and diabetic ketoacidosis according to socio-economic status and area-level deprivation in type 1 diabetes mellitus: a systematic review. Diabet Med. 2018;35:12–32.
15. Yoo KH, Shin DW, Cho MH, et al. Regional variations in frequency of glycosylated hemoglobin (HbA1c) monitoring in Korea: a multilevel analysis of nationwide data. Diabetes Res Clin Pract. 2017;131:61–9.
16. Kim S, Lee B, Park M, Oh S, Chin HJ, Koo H. Prevalence of chronic disease and its controlled status according to income level. Medicine (Baltimore). 2016;95:e5286.
17. Kim YJ, Jeon JY, Han SJ, Kim HJ, Lee KW, Kim DJ. Effect of socio-economic status on the prevalence of diabetes. Yonsei Med J. 2015;56:641–7.
18. Dinca-Panaitescu S, Dinca-Panaitescu M, Bryant T, Daiski I, Pilkington B, Raphael D. Diabetes prevalence and income: results of the Canadian community health survey. Health Policy. 2011;99:116–23.
19. Geiss LS, Wang J, Cheng YJ, et al. Prevalence and incidence trends for diagnosed diabetes among adults aged 20 to 79 years, United States, 1980-2012. JAMA. 2014;312:1218–26.
20. Kim JH, Noh J, Choi JW, Park EC. Association of education and smoking status on risk of diabetes mellitus: A population-based nationwide cross-sectional study. Int J Environ Res Public Health. 2017;14; pii: E655.
21. Reviriego J, Vázquez LA, Goday A, Cabrera M, García-Margallo MT, Calvo E. Prevalence of impaired fasting glucose and type 1 and 2 diabetes mellitus in a large nationwide working population in Spain. Endocrinol Nutr. 2016;63:157–63.
22. Cleal B, Poulsen K, Hannerz H, Andersen LL. A prospective study of occupational status and disability retirement among employees with diabetes in Denmark. Eur J Pub Health. 2015;25:617–9.
23. Shamshirgaran SM, Jorm L, Bambrick H, Hennessy A. Independent roles of country of birth and socioeconomic status in the occurrence of type 2 diabetes. BMC Public Health. 2013;13:1223.
24. Matsushima M, Tajima N, Agata T, Yokoyama J, Ikeda Y, Isogai Y. Social and economic impact on youth-onset diabetes in Japan. Diabetes Care. 1993;16:824–7.
25. Funakoshi M, Azami Y, Matsumoto H, et al. Socioeconomic status and type 2 diabetes complications among young adult patients in Japan. PLoS One. 2017;12:e0176087.
26. Nishi N, Makino K, Fukuda H, Tatara K. Effects of socioeconomic indicators on coronary risk factors, self-rated health and psychological well-being among urban Japanese civil servants. Soc Sci Med. 2004;58:1159–70.
27. Hayashino Y, Yamazaki S, Nakayama T, Sokejima S, Fukuhara S. The association between socioeconomic status and prevalence of diabetes mellitus in rural Japan. Arch Environ Occup Health. 2010;65:224–9.
28. Nagaya T, Yoshida H, Takahashi H, Kawai M. Incidence of type-2 diabetes mellitus in a large population of Japanese male white-collar workers. Diabetes Res Clin Pract. 2006;74:169–74.
29. Ottevaere C, Huybrechts I, Benser J, et al. Clustering patterns of physical activity, sedentary and dietary behavior among European adolescents: the HELENA study. BMC Public Health. 2011;11:328.
30. Kelishadi R, Qorbani M, Motlagh ME, Ardalan G, Heshmat R, Hovsepian S. Socioeconomic disparities in dietary and physical activity habits of Iranian children and adolescents: the CASPIAN-IV study. Arch Iran Med. 2016;19:530–7.
31. Walker RJ, Gebregziabher M, Martin-Harris B, Egede LE. Independent effects of socioeconomic and psychological social determinants of health on self-care and outcomes in type 2 diabetes. Gen Hosp Psychiatry. 2014;36:662–8.
32. Uchmanowicz I, Jankowska-Polańska B, Mazur G, Sivarajan Froelicher E. Cognitive deficits and self-care behaviors in elderly adults with heart failure. Clin Interv Aging. 2017;12:1565–72.
33. Salas-Salvadó J, Martinez-González MÁ, Bulló M, Ros E. The role of diet in the prevention of type 2 diabetes. Nutr Metab Cardiovasc Dis. 2011;21(Suppl 2):B32–48.

34. Gittelsohn J, Wolever TM, Harris SB, Harris-Giraldo R, Hanley AJ, Zinman B. Specific patterns of food consumption and preparation are associated with diabetes and obesity in a native Canadian community. J Nutr. 1998;128:541–7.
35. Hardy LL, Baur LA, Wen LM, Garnett SP, Mihrshahi S. Descriptive epidemiology of changes in weight and weight-related behaviours of Australian children aged 5 years: two population-based cross-sectional studies in 2010 and 2015. BMJ Open. 2018;8:e019391.
36. Caceres M, Teran CG, Rodriguez S, Medina M. Prevalence of insulin resistance and its association with metabolic syndrome criteria among Bolivian children and adolescents with obesity. BMC Pediatr. 2008;8:31.
37. Yanagi N, Hata A, Kondo K, Fujiwara T. Association between childhood socioeconomic status and fruit and vegetable intake among older Japanese: the JAGES 2010 study. Prev Med. 2018;106:130–6.
38. Li M, Fan Y, Zhang X, Hou W, Tang Z. Fruit and vegetable intake and risk of type 2 diabetes mellitus: meta-analysis of prospective cohort studies. BMJ Open. 2014;4:e005497.
39. Yajnik CS. Early life origins of insulin resistance and type 2 diabetes in India and other Asian countries. J Nutr. 2004;134:205–10.
40. Portrait F, Teeuwiszen E, Deeg D. Early life undernutrition and chronic diseases at older ages: the effects of the Dutch famine on cardiovascular diseases and diabetes. Soc Sci Med. 2011;73:711–8.
41. de Boo HA, Harding JE. The developmental origins of adult disease (Barker) hypothesis. Aust N Z J Obstet Gynaecol. 2006;46:4–14.
42. Martin JA, Hamilton BE, Ventura SJ, et al. Births: final data for 2009. Natl Vital Stat Rep. 2011;60:1–70.
43. Feig DS, Shah BR, Lipscombe LL, et al. Preeclampsia as a risk factor for diabetes: a population-based cohort study. PLoS Med. 2013;10:e1001425.
44. Haggarty P, Campbell DM, Duthie S, et al. Diet and deprivation in pregnancy. Br J Nutr. 2009;102:1487–97.
45. Yachi Y, Sone H. Interim analysis of dietary intake and pregnancy course in Japanese pregnant women. Jpn J Nutr Dietetics. 2013;71:242–52.. (In Japanese)
46. Okubo H, Miyake Y, Sasaki S, et al. Maternal dietary patterns in pregnancy and fetal growth in Japan: the Osaka maternal and child health study. Br J Nutr. 2012;107:1526–33.
47. The World Health Organization. Global report on diabetes. https://apps.who.int/iris/bitstream/handle/10665/204871/9789241565257_eng.pdf;jsessionid=CB58B0A3768BDF8A4DC306F1C1A2C30D?sequence=1. Accessed 13 Mar 2019.
48. Epifano L, Di Vincenzo A, Fanelli C, et al. Effect of cigarette smoking and of a transdermal nicotine delivery system on glucoregulation in type 2 diabetes mellitus. Eur J Clin Pharmacol. 1992;43:257–63.
49. Yun WJ, Rhee JA, Kim SA, et al. Household and area income levels are associated with smoking status in the Korean adult population. BMC Public Health. 2015;15:39.
50. Matsuda R. Lifestyle and history of failing. In: Kondo K, editor. Exploring "inequalities in health": a large-scale social epidemiological survey for care prevention in Japan. Tokyo: Igaku Shoin; 2007. p. 21–7; (In Japanese).
51. Akter S, Okazaki H, Kuwahara K, et al. Smoking, smoking cessation, and the risk of type 2 diabetes among Japanese adults: Japan epidemiology collaboration on occupational health study. PLoS One. 2015;10:e0132166.
52. Fukuda Y, Nakamura K, Takano T. Accumulation of health risk behaviours is associated with lower socioeconomic status and women's urban residence: a multilevel analysis in Japan. BMC Public Health. 2005;5:53.
53. Nguyen M, Nishi N, Kadota A, et al. Passive smoking at home by socioeconomic factors in a Japanese population: NIPPON DATA 2010. J Epidemiol. 2018;28:S40–5.
54. Lumb A. Diabetes and exercise. Clin Med (Lond). 2014;14:673–6.
55. Lin CH, Chiang SL, Yates P, Tzeng WC, Lee MS, Chiang LC. Influence of socioeconomic status and perceived barriers on physical activity among Taiwanese middle-aged and older women. J Cardiovasc Nurs. 2017;32:321–30.

56. Murakami K, Hashimoto H, Lee JS, Kawakubo K, Mori K, Akabayashi A. Distinct impact of education and income on habitual exercise: a cross-sectional analysis in a rural city in Japan. Soc Sci Med. 2011;73:1683–8.
57. Koohsari MJ, Hanibuchi T, Nakaya T, et al. Associations of neighborhood environmental attributes with walking in Japan: moderating effects of area-level socioeconomic status. J Urban Health. 2017;94:847–54.
58. Matsushita M, Harada K, Arao T. Socioeconomic position and work, travel, and recreation-related physical activity in Japanese adults: a cross sectional study. BMC Public Health. 2015;15:916.
59. Umeda M, Oshio T, Fujii M. The impact of the experience of childhood poverty on adult health-risk behaviors in Japan: a mediation analysis. Int J Equity Health. 2015;14:145.
60. Loucks EB, Lynch JW, Pilote L, et al. Life-course socioeconomic position and incidence of coronary heart disease: the Framingham Offspring study. Am J Epidemiol. 2009;169:829–36.
61. United Nations Children's Fund (UNICEF), National Institute of Population & Social Security Research. Child well-being in rich countries: comparing Japan. https://www.unicef-irc.org/publications/pdf/rc11_comparing%20japan_fnl.pdf. Accessed 14 Mar 2019.
62. Cabinet Office. The situation of poverty of children and the implementation situation of poverty control of children.. https://www8.cao.go.jp/kodomonohinkon/taikou/pdf/h29_joukyo.pdf. Accessed 14 Mar 2019; (In Japanese).
63. Bailey SC, Brega AG, Crutchfield TM, et al. Update on health literacy and diabetes. Diabetes Educ. 2014;40:581–604.
64. Kim SH, Lee A. Health-literacy-sensitive diabetes self-management interventions: a systematic review and meta-analysis. Worldviews Evid-Based Nurs. 2016;13:324–33.
65. Lai AY, Ishikawa H, Kiuchi T, Mooppil N, Griva K. Communicative and critical health literacy, and self-management behaviors in end-stage renal disease patients with diabetes on hemodialysis. Patient Educ Couns. 2013;91:221–7.
66. Furuya Y, Kondo N, Yamagata Z, Hashimoto H. Health literacy, socioeconomic status and self-rated health in Japan. Health Promot Int. 2015;30:505–13.
67. Kaneko Y, Motohashi Y. Male gender and low education with poor mental health literacy: a population-based study. J Epidemiol. 2007;17:114–9.
68. Björntorp P. Heart and soul: stress and the metabolic syndrome. Scand Cardiovasc J. 2001;35:172–7.
69. Delaunay F, Khan A, Cintra A, et al. Pancreatic β cells are important targets for the diabetogenic effects of glucocorticoids. J Clin Invest. 1997;100:2094–8.
70. Surwit RS, Schneider MS, Feinglos MN. Stress and diabetes mellitus. Diabetes Care. 1992;15:1413–22.
71. Shomaker LB, Tanofsky-Kraff M, Young-Hyman D, et al. Psychological symptoms and insulin sensitivity in adolescents. Pediatr Diabetes. 2010;11:417–23.
72. Baum A, Garofalo JP, Yali AM. Socioeconomic status and chronic stress. Does stress account for SES effects on health? Ann N Y Acad Sci. 1999;896:131–44.
73. Zissi A, Stalidis G. Social class and mental distress in Greek urban communities during the period of economic recession. Int J Soc Psychiatry. 2017;63:459–67.
74. Markwick A, Ansari Z, Sullivan M, Parsons L, McNeil J. Inequalities in the social determinants of health of Aboriginal and Torres Strait Islander People: a cross-sectional population-based study in the Australian state of Victoria. Int J Equity Health. 2014;13:91.
75. Glasscock DJ, Andersen JH, Labriola M, Rasmussen K, Hansen CD. Can negative life events and coping style help explain socioeconomic differences in perceived stress among adolescents? A cross-sectional study based on the West Jutland cohort study. BMC Public Health. 2013;13:532.
76. Rod NH, Grønbaek M, Schnohr P, Prescott E, Kristensen TS. Perceived stress as a risk factor for changes in health behaviour and cardiac risk profile: a longitudinal study. J Intern Med. 2009;266:467–75.

77. Kato M, Noda M, Inoue M, Kadowaki T, Tsugane S, JPHC Study Group. Psychological factors, coffee and risk of diabetes mellitus among middle-aged Japanese: a population-based prospective study in the JPHC study cohort. Endocr J. 2009;56:459–68.
78. Lazzarino AI, Yiengprugsawan V, Seubsman SA, Steptoe A, Sleigh AC. The associations between unhealthy behaviours, mental stress, and low socio-economic status in an international comparison of representative samples from Thailand and England. Glob Health. 2014;10:10.
79. Deasy C, Coughlan B, Pironom J, Jourdan D, Mcnamara PM. Psychological distress and lifestyle of students: implications for health promotion. Health Promot Int. 2015;30:77–87.
80. Emami AS, Woodcock A, Swanson HE, Kapphahn T, Pulvers K. Distress tolerance is linked to unhealthy eating through pain catastrophizing. Appetite. 2016;107:454–9.
81. Cockerham WC, Hinote BP, Abbott P. Psychological distress, gender, and health lifestyles in Belarus, Kazakhstan, Russia, and Ukraine. Soc Sci Med. 2006;63:2381–94.
82. Lipscombe C, Smith KJ, Gariepy G, Schmitz N. Gender differences in the association between lifestyle behaviors and diabetes distress in a community sample of adults with type 2 diabetes. J Diabetes. 2016;8:269–78.
83. The Ministry of Health, Labour and Welfare. A basic direction for comprehensive implementation of national health promotion. https://www.mhlw.go.jp/file/06-Seisakujouhou-10900000-Kenkoukyoku/0000047330.pdf. Accessed 19 Mar 2019.

Open Access This chapter is licensed under the terms of the Creative Commons Attribution-NonCommercial-NoDerivatives 4.0 International License (http://creativecommons.org/licenses/by-nc-nd/4.0/), which permits any noncommercial use, sharing, distribution and reproduction in any medium or format, as long as you give appropriate credit to the original author(s) and the source, provide a link to the Creative Commons licence and indicate if you modified the licensed material. You do not have permission under this licence to share adapted material derived from this chapter or parts of it.

The images or other third party material in this chapter are included in the chapter's Creative Commons licence, unless indicated otherwise in a credit line to the material. If material is not included in the chapter's Creative Commons licence and your intended use is not permitted by statutory regulation or exceeds the permitted use, you will need to obtain permission directly from the copyright holder.

Chapter 9
Suicide

Go Tanaka and Katsunori Kondo

1 Introduction

Exogenous deaths occur more often than expected. According to demographic statistics, exogenous deaths such as suicide and accidental death make up around 5% of the total number of deaths in Japan [1]. These numbers also include accidental deaths such as falling, drowning, injuries from smoke and flame, asphyxiation, and poisoning, as well as murders. In other words, exogenous deaths cover almost all deaths other than those categorized as illness and natural causes. In 2006, suicide prevention was recognized as a crucial task in public health because of the succession of years in which the total number of suicides tallied over 30,000. This situation saw the establishment of the Basic Act on Suicide Prevention in 2006.

Several research studies have clarified that there are strong correlations between exogenous deaths and socioeconomic factors (SES). For example, the Japan Collaborative Cohort (JACC) Study for Evaluation of Cancer Risk found that people with a low academic level (aged 15 years or younger; junior high school level) are 1.8 times more likely to die by exogenous means than those with a high academic level (aged 19 years or over; college or university level) [2].

G. Tanaka (✉)
Human Development Department, Japan International Cooperation Agency, Tokyo, Japan
e-mail: go-tanaka@umin.net

K. Kondo
Professor of Social Epidemiology and Health Policy, Department of Social Preventive Medical Sciences, Center for Preventive Medical Sciences, Chiba University, Chiba, Japan

Head of Department of Gerontological Evaluation, Center for Gerontology and Social Science, National Center for Geriatrics and Gerontology, Obu City, Aichi, Japan

© The Author(s) 2020
K. Kondo (ed.), *Social Determinants of Health in Non-communicable Diseases*,
Springer Series on Epidemiology and Public Health,
https://doi.org/10.1007/978-981-15-1831-7_9

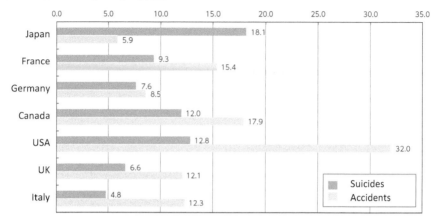

Fig. 9.1 International comparison of suicide and accidental death rate between G7 countries [population demographic statistics, Ministry of Health, Labour and Welfare (MHLW)]. Note: "Mortality rate" refers to the number of deceased persons per 100,000 persons in the population. (Reference source: World Health Organization documentation (December 2016))

Of the different exogenous deaths, this chapter focuses on suicide in particular, and introduces studies that have investigated its correlation with SES. Furthermore, the discussion also considers possible interventions against socio-environmental factors to prevent suicide.

2 Status Quo and Analysis

2.1 The Status Quo of Suicide in Japan

An international comparison by the World Health Organization (WHO) showed that the suicide rate in Japan has been the highest among the G7 countries (Fig. 9.1). Such trends can be used to explore negative correlations between each country's suicide rate and social indicators such as marriage rate, gross domestic product, and natural population growth rate. Thus, committing suicide can be triggered by factors such as being single (or loneliness), low-income, and living in a depopulated area [3]. Temporal changes in Japan show that the number of suicide victims increased drastically in 1998 by about 8000 (30% increase from the previous year) to give an abnormally high number of suicide deaths surpassing 30,000 for 12 years in a row (Fig. 9.2). However, since 2010, the number of suicides has decreased each year to around 21,000 in 2016 (35% decrease from 2003).

To help analyze the causes behind these trends, the National Police Agency (NPA) revised the suicide statistic registration slip in 2007, allowing up to three resources to corroborate that the death was suicide, and including attribution of the cause and motivation. The result showed that the most common reason for suicide

Number of suicide victims

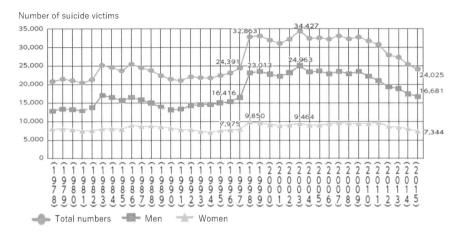

Fig. 9.2 Trend of suicide victims in Japan. Long-term trends in number of suicides (Reference source: "Demographic Statistics," Ministry of Health, Labour and Welfare)

Number of suicide victims

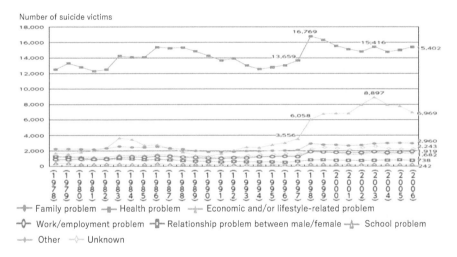

Fig. 9.3 Number of suicides by cause and incentive (Reference source: "Suicide Statistics" National Police Agency). Note: Due to the possibility of recording up to three reasons and/or motivations per suicide as confirmed by materials that account for such reasons, including suicide notes, etc.

was "health-related issues" with around 10,800 victims, followed by "financial and social problems" with around 3500 victims (Fig. 9.3) [4].

Around 70% of suicide victims in Japan are male. However, the lifelong prevalence rate of depression in Japan is around 5% for males and around 10% for females [5]. This implies that suicide ideation from mental illnesses cannot fully explain the causes of suicide. Thus, suicide may need to be analyzed by taking SES into account as one of the background factors.

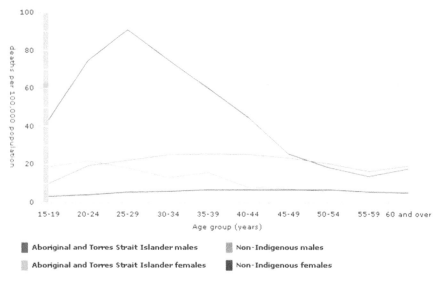

Fig. 9.4 Age-specific suicide rate by indigenous status and sex in Australia, 2001–2010. (Source: Department of Health)

2.2 Ecological Analysis Focusing on Regional, Ethnic, and Generational Factors

Fukuda et al. [6] compared samples by dividing into five groups, using SES (i.e., average income and academic history of residents) by municipalities in 1965. The municipalities with the lowest SES had more than 1.4 times higher suicide mortality rates than the municipalities with the highest SES. The trends in this data showed that the ratio had expanded to more than 1.6 times in 1990 [7]. In an Australian study conducted during the same period, regions were similarly divided into five groups. This study also indicated that the district with the lowest SES had a suicide mortality rate more than 1.4 times that of the district with the highest SES [8, 9].

Such disparities are not only seen among regions, but also among racial minorities that have historically been exposed to socioeconomic difficulties and received discrimination and abuse (Native Americans, Alaskan Natives, Maoris, Aborigines, and Korean residents in Japan). These groups have twice the suicide mortality rate than the average for where they are living (Fig. 9.4) [10, 11].

Although the suicide rate was low during World War II and during periods of high economic growth, studies have shown that suicide rate increased during the chaotic times immediately after the end of the War, from around 1955, around 1985, and when Japan experienced recession, as in 1998 (Fig. 9.5) [12, 13]. Sawada et al. [14] found a significant statistical correlation between unemployment rate and suicide mortality [15, 16]: correlation coefficient $R = 0.911$.

Furthermore, Émile Durkheim argued a birth cohort effect, in which a group born during the same generation exhibits a certain tendency in his *Study of Suicide*

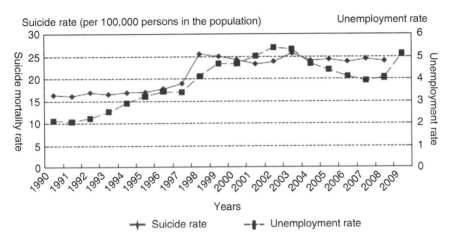

Fig. 9.5 Trends in suicide mortality rate and unemployment rate in Japan from 1990 to 2009

more than a century ago [17]. Experiencing major stress (i.e., poverty and militarist education during wartime) during one's susceptible infancy instills mental vulnerability. Thus, as years go by, these infants grow up and become unable to tolerate major socioeconomic changes (i.e., recession and associated unemployment), leading to taking their own lives. Recent epidemiology trends have also seen a gradual verification of the long-term (life course) impact; the biological and social factors during infancy can later influence the health state and illnesses during adulthood [18]. For example, a birth cohort of over 5300 subjects in Finland showed that approximately 80% of 27 men who attempted or committed suicide had suffered psychological problems by the age of 8 years [19]. In other words, low SES factors such as divorce, low income, depopulation, unprivileged ethnicity, recession, unemployment, and poor historical environment during infancy may exist in the backdrop of suicide [20].

2.3   Analysis Focusing on Individual Factors

According to the population demographic statistics published by the Ministry of Health, Labour and Welfare (MHLW) to investigate the background of suicide victims, 70% of victims are adult males, and, in particular, 63% are unemployed. However, from 1998 onward when the suicide increased drastically, it was revealed that the suicide rates of employed and self-employed individuals also increased as it did for unemployed individuals (Fig. 9.6). This fact may indicate that people take their own lives after becoming unemployed through corporate downsizing, but at the same time, people who have stayed in the workplace have considerable stress, which may be a consequence of excessive workload (after forced redundancies) or uncertainty about the future.

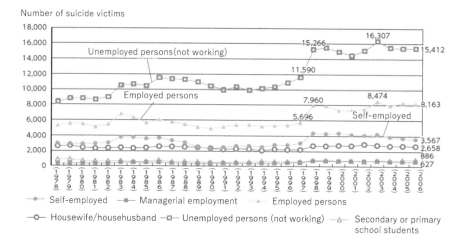

Fig. 9.6 Trend of suicide victims by occupation in Japan ("suicide statistics" National Police Agency (NPA))

Because studies that investigate individual etiologies in detail use an individual's private information, approval from the subject is required. However, it is impossible to earn the consent from victims of suicide. Furthermore, touching on the details of suicide may be considered taboo, and an individual analysis that goes back to the causes and motivation of suicide will be difficult. However, with the Basic Act on Suicide Prevention as an impetus, the Center for Suicide Prevention finally started to conduct psychological autopsy for clarifying actual conditions. They interviewed the family members and friends who knew the deceased well, based on the premise of providing care toward survivors [21].

Based on the data from over 300 suicide victims, there was an average of four reasons for people to take their own lives, confirming that the process that led up to suicide was by no means simple. The most common factors included family discord, exhaustion from taking care of senior citizens, multiple debts, bankruptcy, human relationships at work, unemployment, business slump, overwork, and depression.

3 Suggestion of Countermeasures

Partially because suicide has been considered as an individual issue, most administrative measures against suicide have only pertained to the health division such as depression countermeasures. However, suicide has been recognized as a significantly political issue involving the entire government and the focus was shifted from just the "cause" to the "cause of cause." Furthermore, it was confirmed that suicide needs to be prevented using multilateral initiatives, such as measures against bullying at schools and mental health awareness at workplaces.

Fig. 9.7 Suicide mortality in Finland for 1969–2014. (Source: Statistics Finland)

Finland is one of the countries that has achieved significant suicide prevention measures, and psychological autopsies have been conducted with almost all surviving families of the suicide victims. The national suicide prevention strategy has taken shape through support toward those who attempted suicide, collaboration with the police, and measures against drug and alcohol dependency. In addition, lifestyle support for youths and unemployment countermeasures were conducted even during the adverse time of an economic slump around 1990. As a result, Finland was successful in reducing the suicide mortality rate by 30% within a decade [13, 19]. Surprisingly the total participation-type countermeasures had been supported by the awareness of all citizens (Fig. 9.7). In South Korea, where the situation is very similar to Japan with its high suicide rate, a Comprehensive 5-Year Suicide Prevention Measure was formulated in which unemployed, divorcees, depression patients, and those who were close to suicide victims were perceived as a high-risk group. The policy aims for the society as a whole to take proactive responses, including enhancement of a consultation system and induction of early treatments.

In the previously mentioned Durkheim's *Study of Suicide*, egoistic suicide was also discussed [17]. He described this type of suicide as being caused by the excessive loneliness and frustration resulting from the weakening of ties between individuals and the group. Egoistic suicide was said to have increased by the spread of individualism that took place after the industrial revolution [16]. At the time in Europe, the suicide rate was higher in the city than in the country, and higher among unmarried individuals than those that were married. Analysis of these trends found that modernized society weakened the bond of groups (i.e., regional and occupational), causing the isolation of society members. Furthermore, Lane has also argued for the relation between the drastic increase in depression and the weakening of social ties caused by social pressure on saving time and the rise of a consumer

Table 9.1 Suicide prevention: A guideline for national strategies and their practice

1. Start from a measure that is feasible within the social and cultural circumstances and the financial situation of each country
2. Form an organization at a national level that fulfills the leading role in research, training, and practice of suicide prevention
3. Have people from various fields cooperate and coordinate to engage comprehensively from biological, psychological, and social perspectives
4. Accurately ascertain the state of suicide and the issues unique to each country that serve as background factors
5. Enhance the support system for high-risk groups
6. Strive to dispel prejudice related to psychological disorders and suicide
7. Enhance education systems for experts and supporters
8. Strive to educate general practitioners and strengthen their partnership with psychiatrists
9. Conduct suicide prevention education for youths
10. Provide psychological care for suicide survivors
11. Regulate the acquisition of a suicide method, such as firearms and poisons
12. Establish a cooperative system with the media to restrain copycat and cluster suicides caused by inappropriate broadcasting on suicide

Source: WHO, Preventing suicide; global imperative 2014 (SUPRE) [25]

culture [22, 23]. Motohashi et al. [5] claim that richness of social capital, which represents strong social bonds (i.e., social support, network, and sense of trust), is helpful in preventing suicide. In other words, having residents feel a sense of attachment to their region and having trust for one another, improves solidarity and brings about public safety [24].

Thus, an effort made by whole society in suicide prevention may be effective. The WHO also released *A Guideline for National Strategies and Their Practice*. This guideline advocates twelve comprehensive approaches (Table 9.1).

4 Summary

Suicide is an extremely individual issue. However, suicide is a social structural issue at the same time [4]. Based on past findings, countermeasure initiatives should not be limited to raising the awareness on mental health problems such as depression. Instead, for a more fundamental solution, it is necessary to focus on SES, which is indicative of the background factors behind suicide. Social security policies for income and livelihood should be positioned as a suicide prevention method along with policies of creating a livable regional society. Not only "health policy" but also "policy in health" is much anticipated.

References

1. Statistics and Information Policy Department, Ministry of Health, Labour and Welfare. Handbook of health and welfare statistics; 2018, pp. 1–30.
2. Fujino Y, et al. A nationwide cohort study of educational background and major causes of death among the elderly population in Japan (the JACC study group). Prev Med. 2005;40:444–51.
3. Watanabe N, et al. Regional differences of suicide. Mental Sci. 2004;118:34–9.
4. Health and Welfare for Persons with Disabilities Department, Ministry of Health, Labour and Welfare. White Paper on comprehensive measures to prevent suicide; 2019, pp. 1–5, 14.
5. Motohashi Y, et al. Suicide can be prevented. Supika; 2005.
6. Fukuda Y, et al. Cause-specific mortality differences across socioeconomic position of munici-palities in Japan, 1973-77 and 93-98: Increased importance of injury and suicide in inequality for ages under 75. Int J Epidemiol. 2005;34:100–9.
7. Fujita T. Rapid increase of suicide deaths in metropolitan areas. J Natl Inst Public Health. 2003;52(4):301.
8. Page A, et al. Divergent trends in suicide by socio-economic status in Australia. Soc Psychiatry Psychiatr Epidemiol. 2006;41(11):911–7.
9. Taylor R, et al. Mental health and socio-economic variations in Australian suicide. Soc Sci Med. 2005;61(7):1551–9.
10. Australian Government Department of Health and Ageing. National Aboriginal and Torres Strait Islander suicide prevention strategy; 2013, pp. 11–12.
11. Ishihara A, et al. Suicidology special. J Ment Health. 2003;49.
12. Cabinet Office. White Paper on suicide prevention; 2007.
13. Ministry of Health, Labour & Welfare. Population demographic statistics and labor force sur-vey No 598; 2010, pp. 59.
14. Sawada Y, et al. Correlation between recession, unemployment and suicide, No 598; 2010, pp. 59.
15. Inoue K, et al. The report in the correlation between the factor of unemployment and suicide in Japan. Am J Forensic Med Pathol. 2008;29(2):202–3.
16. Shah A. Possible relationship of elderly suicide rates with unemployment in society; a cross-national study. Psychol Rep. 2008;102(2):398–400.
17. Durkheim É. The study of suicide; 1897.
18. Kondo K. Life course approach; prescription for health inequality society. Public Health Nurse J. 2006;62(11):946–52.
19. Sourander A, et al. Childhood predictors of completed and severe suicide attempts; findings from the Finnish 1981 birth cohort study. Arch Gen Psychiatry. 2009;66(4):398–406.
20. Fujita T, et al. On the state of suicide seen from the population demographic statistics. 2nd national conference material for prefecture supervising managers on suicide countermeasure, 2009.
21. Fujino Y, et al. Prospective cohort study of stress, life satisfaction, self-rated health, insomnia, and suicide death in Japan. Suicide Life Threat Behav. 2005;35(2):227–37.
22. Center for Suicide Prevention. White Paper on the actual state of suicide; 2013, pp. 1–5.
23. Lane R. Friendship or commodities? The road not taken: friendship, consumerism, and happi-ness. Crit Rev. 1994;8(4):521–54.
24. Kawachi I. The health of nations: why inequality is harmful to your health. New York: The New Press; 2002.
25. WHO. Preventing suicide: global imperative (SUPRE); 2014, pp. 33–35.

Open Access This chapter is licensed under the terms of the Creative Commons Attribution-NonCommercial-NoDerivatives 4.0 International License (http://creativecommons.org/licenses/by-nc-nd/4.0/), which permits any noncommercial use, sharing, distribution and reproduction in any medium or format, as long as you give appropriate credit to the original author(s) and the source, provide a link to the Creative Commons licence and indicate if you modified the licensed material. You do not have permission under this licence to share adapted material derived from this chapter or parts of it.

The images or other third party material in this chapter are included in the chapter's Creative Commons licence, unless indicated otherwise in a credit line to the material. If material is not included in the chapter's Creative Commons licence and your intended use is not permitted by statutory regulation or exceeds the permitted use, you will need to obtain permission directly from the copyright holder.

Chapter 10
Depression

Chiyoe Murata and Katsunori Kondo

1 Introduction

An individual's health is influenced not only by genetic inheritance and/or personal lifestyle but also by social factors, including socioeconomic status (SES), which may reflect income, years of education, or social status. Most research in the field of depression is concentrated on the symptoms, and the biological and cognitive-behavioral explanations and treatments. A socioeconomic perspective offers different possibilities to approach this disorder and to apply prevention measures. To date, studies in Japan and abroad have repeatedly demonstrated that people with lower SES are more susceptible to various forms of illnesses. This chapter explores the extent to which such health inequalities are present in depression.

Symptoms of depression include depressed moods, loss of interest in usual activities, and loss of appetite. If depression is prolonged, it will start to interfere with daily life, and, in some cases, it may even result in suicidal ideations or an actual suicide [1]. When we refer to the mental disorder, we usually use the term "major

Chiyoe Murata revised and added new findings to the original manuscript written in Japanese.

C. Murata (✉)
School of Health and Nutrition, Tokaigakuen University, Nagoya, Japan

Department of Social Science, Center for Gerontology and Social Science, National Center for Geriatrics and Gerontology, Obu, Aichi, Japan
e-mail: murata-c@tokaigakuen-u.ac.jp

K. Kondo
Professor of Social Epidemiology and Health Policy, Department of Social Preventive Medical Sciences, Center for Preventive Medical Sciences, Chiba University, Chiba, Japan

Head of Department of Gerontological Evaluation, Center for Gerontology and Social Science, National Center for Geriatrics and Gerontology, Obu City, Aichi, Japan
e-mail: kkondo@chiba-u.jp

© The Author(s) 2020
K. Kondo (ed.), *Social Determinants of Health in Non-communicable Diseases*,
Springer Series on Epidemiology and Public Health,
https://doi.org/10.1007/978-981-15-1831-7_10

depression," although "depressive state/episode" is used when a person scores above the critical threshold on a screening test for depression and shows a variety of depressive symptoms. In this chapter, we use the term "depression" to refer to a broader definition that includes both a depressive state and the depressive disorder.

The prevalence of depression is highest among people suffering from other mental disorders. According to the Global Health Estimates published by the World Health Organization (WHO) in 2017 [1], more than 300 million people, or 4.4% of the world population, are suffering from depression. The report shows that the prevalence rate of depression increases with age. For example, almost 8% of women and 5.5% of men aged 60–64 years suffer from depression, compared with about 3% and 4.5%, respectively, for women and men aged 15–19 years. According to a study conducted from 2000 to 2001 [2] with 5363 senior citizens in four municipalities, 8.4–12.0% were found to be in a state of severe depression, scoring 10 points or higher on the 15-item Geriatric Depression Scale (GDS-15). In another study from 2003 [3] that used the same scale to assess senior citizens of 15 municipalities (excluding senior citizens who had been issued the Certification of Needed Long-Term Care), 8.1% were found to be in a state of severe depression. The average prevalence rate of depression in North America and Europe is estimated to be 9% [4], with a report [5] claiming that the lifetime prevalence in the USA was up to 16.2%. According to research conducted between July and September 2017 by the Japan Productivity Center [6], 24.4% of the companies that took part in the research stated that mental disorders, including depression, had been increasing in the past 3 years. According to the study, the peak of this trend was in 2006, when the majority of the companies (61.5%) had reported mental disorders among their workers. The number of workers suffering from mental disorders remains high, which has led to an increasing societal concern about depression. Depression is not only closely related to suicide [1], but is also a risk factor for developing heart disease [7] and is a predictive factor for the need for long-term care in the future [8]. Furthermore, the relationship between depression and the onset of dementia has also been pointed out [9]. The impact of depression on society is significant; depression was ranked fifth out of all illnesses in 2016 in terms of its burden on society according to the forecast of the WHO in the Global Burden of Disease, based on the Disability-Adjusted Life Year (DALY) measurement [10].

2   Depression and Socioeconomic Status

Although the causes involved in the etiology of depression could be physiological (e.g., medication or illnesses such as cerebrovascular disease) as well as psychosocial (e.g., stress) [11], the following sections mainly examine the psychosocial factors related to depression. To date, reasonably consistent data have been reported about depression being common among groups with lower SES [11]. A meta-analysis [4] (statistical analysis after integrating data from multiple papers) of 56 research papers from 1979 onward that examined the relation between SES (income, education, and occupation) and depression showed that people with the lowest SES were 1.25 times more likely to develop depression than those with higher SES. Moreover, it was found that the duration of suffering from depression was 1.25 times longer and depression was 1.81 times more common among people from the lowest SES. The Whitehall II study[11] with British public servants reported that depression was more common among people in lower-level job positions. A research paper [12] on 2472 Spanish workers reported that the workers with more unstable employment status had a lower level of mental health [scores of 3 or higher on the 12-item General Health Questionnaire (GHQ-12) that measures depression and anxiety]. It was found that while 5.6% of full-time male workers suffered from depression, the rate was 26.7% among those employed without a contract. Similarly, 12.5% of full-time female workers suffered from depression, but the rate was 32.5% for women without a full-time contract.

While there have been few studies in non-western countries that examine the relation between depression and SES, those studies have shown similar associations between depression and lower SES. According to a study based on the National Family Research of Japan survey in 1999 [13] that used a nationwide sample (6985 participants aged between 28 and 78 years), although no relation was found between depression and years of education, those from lower household income groups scored significantly higher on depression on the Center for Epidemiologic Studies Depression scale (CES-D). In a Japanese study conducted in 2003 [14] with 32,891 senior citizens, it was found that while 17.4% of males with less than 6 years of education were categorized as being in a depressive state (a score of 10 or higher on the GDS-15), this was the case for only 5.4% of those with 13 or more years of education; approximately a threefold difference. Furthermore, the rate of depression among males from the lowest income group was 15.8%, while that in the highest income group for males was 2.3%, which is a difference between the two groups of 6.9 times. Regional variations were also observed in the prevalence of depression in this study because higher rates of depression were identified in economically disadvantaged rural areas [3]. In their study from 2006, Kawakami et al. [15] used the occupational hierarchy of the International Standard Classification of Occupations (ISCO) [16] to show that the risk of being in a depressive state (a score of 16 points or higher on the CES-D) increased 1.05 times for males and 1.13 times for females for each step down in the occupational hierarchy levels. ISCO is an eight-level ranking of employment ranging from managerial positions at the top level to physical labor at the bottom level; the classification is based on the educational and skill levels required for each particular occupation.

3 Background of Inequalities

There are two hypotheses as to how inequalities in terms of SES are related to depression: social causation and social selection. The social causation hypothesis states that various stress factors related to lower SES, such as illness or unemployment, would lead to depression. The social selection hypothesis, in contrast, refers to the idea that those who are susceptible to suffering from depression to begin with (i.e., genetic vulnerability owing to family history related to depressive disorders) fall behind in society, which finally results in lower SES [17].

A British study [18] aimed to verify the social causation and social selection hypotheses by following 756 children of depressive patients for 17 years. The study showed that low parental education was related to increased risk of developing depression among the children. Furthermore, neither the parents' nor the children's depression was related to the children's future SES, such as income, educational level, and occupation. Thus, the results did not support the social selection hypothesis, which argues that suffering from depression will lead to a lower SES. A study [19] of 1803 American adolescents aged 18–23 years, found that adverse experiences such as long-term unemployment and divorce of their parents, unintended separation from parents, separation from one's own children (including stillbirth), life-threatening accidents and illnesses, betrayal from one's spouse, suicide or murder of one's acquaintance, various forms of abuse, and being exposed to a robbery were related to the development of clinical depression and anxiety disorder. These adverse experiences were found to be more prevalent among the lower socioeconomic groups. This association was even more prominent if the subject had suffered from post-traumatic stress disorder, drug addiction, and/or behavioral disorders in the past. Adverse experiences in childhood and being physically vulnerable at birth were also correlated with the development of mood disorders [11].

With regard to depression, the sense of control is also an important issue to consider. A state in which one's sense of control over a situation is deprived creates a feeling of helplessness, which increases the risk of developing depression [20]. It has been reported that when dogs are put in a situation in which they are being given electric shocks, with no means to escape from the shocks or to stop them, the dogs gradually become lethargic and do not attempt to escape even when they are given a chance to do so later. Subsequently, it was discovered that a depressed state could be artificially created in people as well, by depriving them of control [20]. The formation of such a sense of helplessness is perhaps one of the reasons that the rate of depression is higher among people with lower SES, because depression is strongly related to adverse experiences from one's birth onward. Such adverse experiences are frequently characterized by a lack of control over the events.

Although 33%–48% of the incidences of depression may be explained by genetic vulnerability, over half of the remaining depression cases are found to be caused by factors other than genetics [21]. This means that not only genetics but also the social environment, such as one's home, workplace, and region of residence, are important. The high prevalence of depression among workers from lower occupational levels may be related to the high job demands (i.e., quantity and quality of work) and the low level of control they are able to exert (e.g., the extent to which they can determine their work method based on their own judgement) [11, 12]. A study [6] conducted in Japan that examined workplace conditions found that poor communication between co-workers and a lack of opportunities for training or promotion were related to an increase in mental disorders among workers. Furthermore, a Danish longitudinal study [22] of 4133 workers found that a low level of control at the workplace, a lack of support from managers, and an unstable employment situation were significantly related to the onset of a depressive state within the following 5 years. Depressive symptoms were measured using the 36-item Short Form Health Survey (SF-36), a widely used quality-of-life scale. A similar correlation was also reported in the Whitehall II study [11]. The findings from the above-mentioned studies suggest that a lower SES increases an individual's susceptibility to falling into a state in which the sense of control has been taken away or denied, which, subsequently, could lead to the development of depression. Thus, this pattern could be considered a valid explanation of the inequalities in SES with regard to depression.

4   Possible Countermeasures

As discussed above, depressive states and depression are more frequent among people with low SES, and the development of depression is influenced not only by individual factors but by one's surrounding environment as well. There is no doubt that expansion of the knowledge on depression and early detection and treatment of depression are necessary [1]. According to the life course approach, which focuses on the impact of the environment during infancy on health during adulthood [11], an enhancement of health and welfare services is required to prevent depression in the socially vulnerable (i.e., the poor). Moreover, educational institutions, from pre-school to university education, should take caution not to induce disadvantages for students based on differences in income. Hence, the coordination of related organizations, such as welfare, educational, or medical organizations, and the cooperation of local societies are indispensable.

Measures to prevent depression at the workplace are also crucial. As mentioned above, lower levels of control facilitate the development of depression [20]. Thus, there may be some merit in providing opportunities for workers to become involved in decision making. Furthermore, given that lack of support and unstable employment are predictive factors of depression, support at the workplace (i.e., appropriate work management and hiring external experts) and improvements in working conditions, including compensation and holidays, are also important.

In considering the topic of depression, natural disaster victims cannot be overlooked, because adverse life experiences are strongly associated with this disorder [12]. Recent evidence [23] from Japan demonstrated that group exercise reduced depressive symptoms among survivors of the Great East Japan Earthquake. Although the authors did not specify the type of group activities used, they reported that peer social support or enjoyment were found to mitigate the worsening depression symptoms. This study result indicates that promoting participation in such activities for those at risk of depression is a worthwhile approach. Another study [24] demonstrated that lower socioeconomic gradients of depression are observed among the senior members of communities that are rich in social capital and foster social activities.

5 Summary

Research in western as well as non-western nations has reported that depression is common among people with lower SES, resulting in health inequalities, particularly among those with lower income, lower education, and low-paid occupations [11]. Individuals with fewer years of education and low income are more susceptible to suffering from depression, while an unprivileged environment during childhood increases the likelihood of developing depression during adulthood [4]. Measures against depression often tend to focus on an individual's genetic predisposition or are otherwise reduced to focus only on the individual. However, in addition to individual predisposition, adverse experiences also relate to depression. Furthermore, countermeasures for unstable employment and employment support for youths are essential. Given the impact that the social environment has on individual health, the discussion on countermeasures for depression should be widened to also focus on social environment factors.

References

1. World Health Organization. Depression and other common mental disorders: Global health estimates; 2017.
2. Wada T, Ishine M, Sakagami T, et al. Depression in Japanese community-dwelling elderly—prevalence and association with ADL and QOL. Arch Gerontol Geriatr. 2004;39(1):15–23.
3. Kondō K. Health inequalities in Japan: an empirical study of older people. Trans Pacific Press, Balwyn North; 2010.
4. Lorant V, Deliege D, Eaton W, Robert A, Philippot P, Ansseau M. Socioeconomic inequalities in depression: a meta-analysis. Am J Epidemiol. 2003;157(2):98–112.
5. Kessler RC, Berglund P, Demler O, et al. The epidemiology of major depressive disorder: results from the National Comorbidity Survey Replication (NCS-R). JAMA. 2003;289(23):3095–105.
6. Japan Productivity Center. The 8th corporate survey research result on "Initiatives on mental health" [In Japanese]. 2017. https://activity.jpc-net.jp/activity_detail.php. Accessed 14 June 2018.
7. Rugulies R. Depression as a predictor for coronary heart disease: a review and meta-analysis. Am J Prev Med. 2002;23(1):51–61.
8. Stuck AE, Walthert JM, Nikolaus T, Bula CJ, Hohmann C, Beck JC. Risk factors for functional status decline in community-living elderly people: a systematic literature review. Soc Sci Med. 1999;48(4):445–69.
9. Bennett S, Thomas AJ. Depression and dementia: cause, consequence or coincidence? Maturitas. 2014;79(2):184–90.
10. GBD 2016 Disease and Injury Incidence and Prevalence Collaborators. Global, regional, and national incidence, prevalence, and years lived with disability for 328 diseases and injuries for 195 countries, 1990-2016: a systematic analysis for the Global Burden of Disease Study 2016. Lancet. 2017;390(10100):1211–59.
11. Marmot MG. Status syndrome: how your social standing directly affects your health. London: Bloomsbury; 2005.
12. Commission on Social Determinants of Health. Final report. Closing the gap in a generation: health equity through action on the social determinants of health. Geneva: World Health Organization; 2008.

13. Inaba A, Thoits PA, Ueno K, Gove WR, Evenson RJ, Sloan M. Depression in the United States and Japan: gender, marital status, and SES patterns. Soc Sci Med. 2005;61(11):2280–92.
14. Murata C, Kondo K, Hirai H, Ichida Y, Ojima T. Association between depression and socio-economic status among community-dwelling elderly in Japan: the Aichi Gerontological Evaluation Study (AGES). Health Place. 2008;14(3):406–14.
15. Kawakami N, Takao S, Kobayashi Y, Tsutsumi A. Effects of web-based supervisor training on job stressors and psychological distress among workers: a workplace-based randomized controlled trial. J Occup Health. 2006;48(1):28–34.
16. Goldberg D, Williams P. A user's guide to the general health questionnaire. Windsor: NFER-NELSON; 1988.
17. Costello EJ, Compton SN, Keeler G, Angold A. Relationships between poverty and psychopathology: a natural experiment. JAMA. 2003;290(15):2023–9.
18. Ritsher JEB, Warner V, Johnson JG, Dohrenwend BP. Inter-generational longitudinal study of social class and depression: a test of social causation and social selection models. Br J Psychiatry. 2001;178(S40):84–90.
19. Turner RJ, Lloyd DA. Stress burden and the lifetime incidence of psychiatric disorder in young adults: racial and ethnic contrasts. Arch Gen Psychiatry. 2004;61(5):481–8.
20. Reivich K, Gillham JE, Chaplin TM, Seligman MEP. From helplessness to optimism: the role of resilience in treating and preventing depression in youth. In: Goldstein S, Brooks RB, editors. Handbook of resilience in children. Boston, MA: Springer; 2013. p. 201–14.
21. Hill MK, Sahhar M. Genetic counselling for psychiatric disorders. Med J Aust. 2006;185(9):507–10.
22. Rugulies R, Bultmann U, Aust B, Burr H. Psychosocial work environment and incidence of severe depressive symptoms: prospective findings from a 5-year follow-up of the Danish work environment cohort study. Am J Epidemiol. 2006;163(10):877–87.
23. Tsuji T, Sasaki Y, Matsuyama Y, et al. Reducing depressive symptoms after the great East Japan earthquake in older survivors through group exercise participation and regular walking: a prospective observational study. BMJ Open. 2017;7(3):e013706.
24. Haseda M, Kondo N, Ashida T, Tani Y, Takagi D, Kondo K. Community social capital, built environment, and income-based inequality in depressive symptoms among older people in Japan: an ecological study from the JAGES project. J Epidemiol. 2018;28(3):108–16.

Open Access This chapter is licensed under the terms of the Creative Commons Attribution-NonCommercial-NoDerivatives 4.0 International License (http://creativecommons.org/licenses/by-nc-nd/4.0/), which permits any noncommercial use, sharing, distribution and reproduction in any medium or format, as long as you give appropriate credit to the original author(s) and the source, provide a link to the Creative Commons licence and indicate if you modified the licensed material. You do not have permission under this licence to share adapted material derived from this chapter or parts of it.

The images or other third party material in this chapter are included in the chapter's Creative Commons licence, unless indicated otherwise in a credit line to the material. If material is not included in the chapter's Creative Commons licence and your intended use is not permitted by statutory regulation or exceeds the permitted use, you will need to obtain permission directly from the copyright holder.

Chapter 11
Dementia

Kokoro Shirai and Hiroyasu Iso

1 Worldwide Trend of Dementia

The number of people living with dementia worldwide is rising rapidly. Dementia is considered to be one of the greatest global challenges for health and social care in the twenty-first century. The condition is associated with physical, psychosocial, and economic burdens on individuals and society [1, 2], and is one of the principal causes of disability and dependency among older populations. It is a significant public health issue not only in Japan but all over the world, given the growing incidence and high prevalence rate, primarily due to global aging. It is reported that about 47.5 million people were living with dementia in 2015, and the number is projected to reach 65.7 million in 2030 and 115.4 million by 2050 worldwide [3]. Another estimate speculates that dementia patients will increase to 75.6 million by 2030 and reach 135.5 million by 2050 [4]. Furthermore, following the World Alzheimer Report 2018, the projection was revised upwardly and reached 50 million in 2018, 82 million in 2030, and 152 million in 2050 [5]. The total estimated global cost of dementia was US$818 billion in 2015, which is an increase of 35.4% over the estimates of previous years, and the global cost of dementia is expected to continue to increase [4]. About 85% of dementia costs are related to family and social care rather than medical costs. Dementia affects not only an individual but also the wider range of family, the community, and society in general; people

---

Kokoro Shirai is also the English translator for this chapter.

K. Shirai (✉) · H. Iso
Department of Public Health, Graduate School of Medicine, Osaka University, Osaka, Japan

© The Author(s) 2020   105
K. Kondo (ed.), *Social Determinants of Health in Non-communicable Diseases*,
Springer Series on Epidemiology and Public Health,
https://doi.org/10.1007/978-981-15-1831-7_11

affected by the disease lose potential opportunities to participate socially and economically and require health and social care.[1]

1.1   Dementia in Japan

Japan is one of the most rapidly graying societies in the world. Based on national statistics, the Ministry of Health, Labour and Welfare (MHLW) estimated the number of older people (those aged 65 years and over) living with dementia as 4.62 million in 2012 and another four million were estimated to have symptoms of mild cognitive impairment (MCI). However, the estimated prevalence rate varies depending on the data sources. A public long-term care insurance database estimates the prevalence of dementia patients among the over 65s as, 9.5% in 2010 and 12.8% in 2025. Those included in the estimated were people with a clinical diagnosis of Grade II-a or higher according to the national standardized long-term care insurance evaluation system. This number is 2.80 million in 2010 and predicted to be 3.45 million by 2015 and 4.70 million by 2025. The evaluation method of the long-term care insurance system uses information on physical, cognitive and social conditions including the availability of care resources for the patient. Details of the system are reported in a validation study examining identification of dementia diagnosis and evaluation in the public long-term care insurance system [6]. A synthesis for the findings from Japanese population-based studies suggested an increasing trend for dementia prevalence [7–13]. Among them, the Hisayama study only reported the long-term trends for age-standardized dementia prevalence of 6.8% in 1985, 4.6% in 1992, 5.3% in 1998, 8.4% in 2005 and 11.3% in 2012 in a rural community with a population size of around 8000 [7]. The trend for dementia in representative samples of Japanese, however, remains to be clarified.

Among global figures, it has been reported that age-specific new dementia incidences have declined in the past few decades in some high-income western countries, including the USA, France, Denmark, the Netherlands, Sweden, and the UK [14–20]. In 2013, the Framingham Heart Study [17] reported that age-specific incidence rates of dementia had decreased by almost 20% in the past three decades. These days, a limited number of countries have reported a sharp increment in the age-specific incidence rate among high-income countries. Japan, however, has not reported a decreasing trend of age-specific incident cases. Moreover, a review on 14 studies that investigated trends in dementia prevalence (nine studies) and incidences (five studies) from high-income countries suggested that except for the Japanese study, most of the studies indicated stable or declining trend of new incidences of dementia [15]. This may be due to different trends in dementia occurrence, or it may relate to

---

[1] In this chapter, we used the term 'dementia', which derives from the Latin words 'De' (= out of) and 'Meus' (= mind). In DSM-5 (Diagnostic and statistical manual of mental disorders, version 5) the term 'dementia' has been replaced by 'Major neurocognitive disorders'. However, in this chapter, we used 'dementia' based on its familiarity and its frequent use in the literature we reviewed.

different sources of data, diagnostic methods and changing criteria of dementia evaluation, which requires further examination.

At the same time, these findings of decreasing trend of age-specific incidence rate in some countries may suggest that dementia among the population can be preventable by targeting a number of modifiable risk factors. Some of the significant individual levels of behavioral and psychosocial changes and/or societal improvements in living conditions, including education, occupation, and healthcare conditions might be related to reduced risks of dementia incidence.

1.2   The Cost of Dementia

The transition phase during which a society from 'aging' (7% ≥ 65+) to 'aged society' (14% ≥ 65+) is considered to be a period in which preparation can be made for the infrastructure and social security systems to support an older population. Japan only took 24 years to become an aged society, while other European counties took a longer period; for example, 115 years in France or 45 years in the UK. However, other East Asian countries will take an even shorter time than Japan: 18 years in Korea and 20 years in Singapore to reach an aged society. Achieving preparedness for a dementia-friendly society is more difficult in those rapidly aging countries and the role of prevention is becoming increasingly important.

The World Alzheimer Report [21] pointed out that two-thirds of dementia patients currently live in low- or medium-income nations (Fig. 11.1), and these countries are expected to see a sharp increase in the number of such patients. In 2010, the total global societal costs of dementia were estimated to be US$ 604 billion, 818 billion in 2015, 1 trillion in 2018 and 2 trillion by 2030 [22]. This

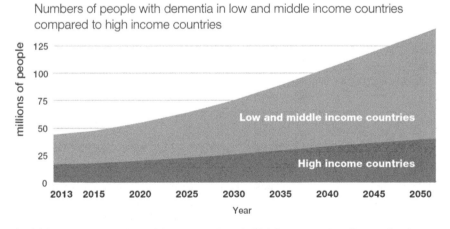

Fig. 11.1 Increasing numbers of dementia patients in high-income, and medium- to low-income countries. (**Source: World Alzheimer report**, 'The Global Impact of Dementia 2013–2050', *Alzheimer's Disease International*)

corresponds to 1.0% of worldwide gross domestic product (GDP) in 2010, or 0.6% if only direct costs are considered. The Japanese government reported the annual cost for medical and social care for dementia in 2014 to be 14.3 trillion Japanese yen which is 3% of Japanese GDP. Of these, the costs for healthcare, long-term care, and informal care are 1.91 trillion (se 4.91 billion), 6.44 trillion (se 63.2 billion), and 6.16 trillion (se 12.5 billion) Japanese yen, respectively. It is expected to increase to 24.3 trillion in 2060. The cost per person with dementia appeared to be 5.95 million (se 27 thousand) yen in 2015 [23]. If these estimates are accurate and 60% of dementia patients worldwide require care in developing countries, serious problems will emerge because the medical and social security systems in such countries are not yet able to support this number of advanced dementia patients.

It is important to understand the determinants of dementia from the perspectives of social determinants of health (SDH) to prevent the onset of disease and to minimize disparities in healthy aging among the older population in societies facing an era of worldwide aging.

2 Health Disparities in the Onset of Dementia Based on Socioeconomic Factors

Livingston et al. [3, 24] suggested that around 35% of dementia cases are preventable and attributable to a combination of modifiable lifestyle-related factors. These include early determination of education (at age 11 or 12 years), mid-life hypertension, obesity, hearing loss and later-life depression, diabetes, physical inactivity, smoking, and social isolation. On the other hand, unmodifiable factor, a well-known major genetic risk factor, including Apolipoprotein E (ApoE) ε4 allele [25, 26] is calculated to be related to a 7% of dementia cases based on a weighted population attributable fraction calculation [3, 27].

In 2018, the World Health Organization issued lifestyle guidelines to reduce the risk of dementia. It emphasized the basics of regular exercise, eating a balanced diet, stopping smoking, drinking in moderation, and staying socially and intellectually active. Furthermore, control of body weight, maintaining healthy blood pressure, cholesterol and blood sugar levels are suggested to be important factors related to dementia incidence.

Among the risk factors regarding social determinants of healthy aging, it is important to understand the socioeconomic background and its association with the incidence and prevalence of dementia, as it is strongly connected with lifestyles and elevated biomarkers. In this chapter, we review the relationship between onset of dementia and socioeconomic status (SES), which includes educational attainment, length of education, occupation, income, parents' educational history, and income level during childhood. Although some studies [28, 29] have found no association between SES and dementia onset, most have concluded that a disadvantaged SES is associated with increased risk of the onset of dementia including both Vascular dementia (VaD) and Alzheimer's dementia (AD) [30–36].

2.1 Education and Risk of Dementia

Researchers have long discussed the relationship between shorter education and higher risks of incidence and prevalence of dementia including its mechanism of occurrence. Meta-analysis of 13 cohort and 6 case-controlled studies concluded that a shorter period of education is associated with higher risks of developing dementia [37]. Those with a shorter education had a 1.59-fold greater relative risk of developing dementia than those with a longer education. This relative risk came from a 1.80-fold higher risk of Alzheimer's dementia (AD), and a 1.32-fold higher risk of non-Alzheimer's dementia. A pooled analysis of four European countries in the EURODEM Study (16,334 subjects) showed that a shorter education (8–11 years and less than 7 years) indicated a higher risk of developing dementia than those with 12 years or more education [38]. However, the results showed gender differences. For women, the findings suggested that compared with a longer education (12+ years), those with a middle-level (8–11 years) have a 2.5-fold greater risk, and those with a shorter education (up to 7 years) have a 3.8 times greater risk of developing all types of dementia. Considering the risk of developing AD in women, those with a middle-level education showed a 2.6-fold greater risk relative to longer education, while women with shorter education showed a 4.3-fold greater risk. However, no such association was observed in men [38]. Reports from the studies included in this research, such as the PAQUID project [39] and the Rotterdam Study [40], and the findings of previous studies in various countries, including Canada [41], Sweden [42, 43], USA [44, 45], and Italy [46], indicated that although the results on gender differences were inconsistent, most cohort studies showed that a shorter education indicated higher risk of dementia. A follow-up survey that targeted 3623 older people living in Massachusetts, USA, reported that for every 1-year increment in length of education, the risk of developing AD decreased by approximately 17% [44]. Recent studies also showed an association between duration of education and incidence of dementia after considering competing risks of death and onset of other diseases [47].

The association between length of education and the risk of dementia onset has also been reported in Japan. For example, both the Adult Health Study conducted by the Radiation Effects Research Foundation [13], and the Hisayama Study [48], have shown an association between shorter education and elevated risks of dementia incidence and prevalence. The results from the Hisayama study were introduced as a government report on the prevalence of dementia, and risk factors for dementia incidence in Japan. The Osaki-Tajiri Cohort Project [10] and the Japan Gerontological Evaluation Study (JAGES study) [49–51] showed that shorter education was associated with a higher risk of dementia. A number of other studies from Asian countries [52–54], have also reported on the relationship between length of education and incidence of dementia.

2.2 Occupation, Income, and Other SES with Risks of Dementia

Sociodemographic background other than the length of education, such as occupation, subjective and objective income level and, childhood SES also showed an association between risk of cognitive function and onset of dementia in various countries [34, 35, 38, 42–44, 53–55]. Qiu et al. [42] reported that manual labour, such as working on a factory production line, increased the risk of developing dementia. Occupation comprises several aspects which affect cognitive function, for instance, social status, economic status, psychosocial stress related to autonomy and reward-demand balance, work-life balance, work-family conflicts, complexity of the work, mentally challenging activity as cognitive stimulation, and exposure to certain environments including hazardous substances. The PAQUID study conducted in France reported that the risk of developing dementia was higher in female agricultural workers than in female specialists and/or managerial workers [56, 57]. Research by Evans et al. [44] showed that individual SES components including short education, limited income and low-status occupations were associated with increased risks of developing AD. After mutually controlling for those three components, only length of education was independently associated with incidence of AD. Likewise, research by Karp et al. [43] reported that if mutual influence was taken into account, length of education showed an independent relationship after adjusting for occupation and income, but neither occupation nor income showed an independent association. As a part of socioeconomic status, length of education showed an independent association with onset of dementia and the association cannot be fully explained by occupation nor income. Occupation showed association with risk of dementia based on the psychosocial factor of works, including complexity, challenges, control possibilities, and social demands at work [58–60]. Moreover, Karp et al. [43] stated that the relationship between length of education and the onset of AD could be explained by occupation after reaching adulthood, and suggested that other factors during early childhood, middle life, or early old age may have different effects on the onset of dementia throughout the life-course. In 2017, the Health and Retirement Study (HRS) compared various SES indicators including length of education, parental education level and individual income and their association with late-life memory performance and decline. That study showed a significant association between cognitive decline and individual income levels [61]. In terms of other aspect of SES, the English Longitudinal Study of Ageing (ELSA) reported that the index of multiple deprivation was associated with cognitive performance in older age independently of individual levels of education and SES [47, 62]. However, findings from the Seoul Dementia Management Project suggested that individual SES level contributed more to the development of cognitive impairment than district-level SES [63]. Discussion of area-level socioeconomic condition and individual SES and their association with cognitive decline and the onset of cognitive impairment remains ongoing [64].

2.3 Hypothesis on the Influence of Social Factors on Dementia Onset

There are several hypotheses regarding the relationship between SES and dementia. One of these is the cognitive reserve theory, and another, the brain battery theory [65–67]. The cognitive reserve theory was advocated by Katzman [68] and expanded by Stern [65] and is related to the influence of social determinants at a relatively early life stage. One of the arguments on the hypothesis is that education determines a person's ability to acquire accurate information and knowledge, which helps enhance cognitive function and keep it at a relatively high level, even when it declines in the later stage of life. High education, occupational work complexity, as well as a mentally and socially integrated lifestyle in late life could work as cognitive reserve factors and postpone the onset of clinical dementia and Alzheimer's Disease [67]. Furthermore, a higher level of education encourages individuals to adopt a healthier lifestyle which helps maintain cognitive function. This process happens through individual behavior and decision making, rather than securing a lifestyle associated with living circumstances with social status and elevated income level. This hypothesis supported the results shown by Karp et al. [43] who indicated that educational attainment was associated with the risk of dementia independently of social status or income. In his brain battery theory, Del Ser [57], argues that better education is associated with high income and high social status, since individuals with a higher education level will work in occupations that have little or no exposure to hazardous substances and enjoy better access to medical resources and healthier lifestyles. Ultimately, this will have both long-term and short-term health benefits.

Although discussions on the mechanisms have yet to reach a conclusion, a review of previous research appears to show that socioeconomic conditions influence the onset of dementia as an undisputable risk. We will next examine the possible pathways and countermeasures that target dementia. Similar to the other non-communicable diseases, it is important to understand the accumulating effects of individual behaviors and decision makings process influenced by the environment from the perspectives of the social determinants of health for effective prevention.

3 Disparities Related to Cognitive Health

The pathways to developing dementia and its countermeasures vary according to the types of dementia. Contributory factors to the development of dementia such as hypertension, obesity, type-2 diabetes, and hyperinsulinemia in middle and older age have been reported to have different effects on different types of dementia [69]; for example, Vascular dementia (VaD), Alzheimer's dementia (AD), Lewy Bodies (DLB) and others. However, sociodemographic factors have been reported to be risk factors for most types of dementia. Socioeconomic status and social disparities are argued to be related to the risk of dementia and unhealthy aging in the later stages of life. It is important to examine a broad range of primary, secondary and tertiary prevention measures to reduce the risk of dementia onset.

3.1 Material and Information Disparities

Researchers have discussed the pathways by which absolute and relative socioeconomic conditions affect individual health directly and indirectly: the materialist and the psychosocial pathways. The materialist pathway anticipates situations in which material deprivation relates to socioeconomic background. Conditions of deprivation can limit access to health resources such as healthy behaviors including diet and physical exercise, health screening and medical treatment [70]. A vulnerable group can also have difficulty in accessing accurate information and may suffer double or triple inequalities. Geographic and built environment can influence or design people's behavior and cognitive decisions. For example, 'walkability' [71] in the community may affect physical and cognitive health via difficulties in accessing shops that stock healthy food and in reaching a safe environment for physical activities and social interactions [72–74]. In order to support people in making healthier choices for physical and cognitive health, the following actions will be important; 1) Removing environmental barriers 2) Minimizing budget constraints 3) Improving information asymmetry 4) Leveraging social reinforcement 5) Designing individual behavioral plans 6) Constructing networks and build social capital. These approaches can be conducted on three levels: the individual, the community, and societal and policy levels.

It is anticipated that solutions to these structural or environmental disparities, will be generated through population-based approaches [75]. These may include imposing taxes on tobacco products and unhealthy foods [76], rather than approaching high-risk individuals and encouraging them to transform their behaviors by their own effort. For example, according to the results of a review of over 160 papers [77], raising the price of soft drinks by 10% causes consumption to fall by 8–10%. Further, a 20-year accumulation of data from the CARDIA Study showed that in the case of soft drinks and pizza, caloric intake decreased as price increases. When the price of these products was increased by $1, total caloric intake decreased by 124 kcal, body weight by 1.05 kg, and glucose tolerance, according to HOMA-IR scores, by 0.42 points [78, 79]. Altering environments to support unconscious healthier choices of irrational individuals is important. Instead of expecting an individual to make rational behavioral change, attempts are being made to use behavioral economic theories and environmental changes, it is hoped, to be more effective [80]. If Goffman's frame analysis theory were incorporated, re-capture of existing frameworks would become necessary [81]. Kahneman [82] has pointed out that individual actions and behaviors are determined by two systems: 'System 1', based on intuition, and 'System 2', based on rationalization. Provision of existing health information and offering health education are System 2 approach oriented that work on cognitive understanding and justify behaviors based on rational thought. To change unhealthy behaviors that people already know are bad behavior, but cannot stop doing, it is important to build methodologies that act on the sensory and awareness frames, as well as the cognitive understanding frames. As part of their advertising strategies, tobacco companies and fast-food industries spend huge amounts of money to work on the sensation of pleasure–displeasure, as well as operating at the unconscious level. On the other hand, in terms of public health measures, the key tactic is to work at the cognitive level, for example by providing accurate information, based on the results of epidemiological research on, say, the link between smoking and the high risk of developing lung cancer. With the latter method, however, differences in effects are seen; the technique is most effective among people with more education and in groups of people with a strong interest in health. Therefore, this technique has a risk to worsen health disparities. It is thus deemed imperative to recognize that there are disparities in people's access to socioeconomic resources, including information, and carry out health education and anti-poverty measures as a prelude to increasing basic opportunities, and to implement programs designed to narrow socioeconomic gaps.

Regarding social policies such as those related to education systems, Lynch and Kaplan [83] state that educational attainment is largely determined by the environment in which an individual is raised, and that it acts as an indicator when the individual moves from the socioeconomic background of their unbringing to new social and financial statuses which they themselves acquire. Considered from the perspective of life course epidemiology, a person's educational level, income, and occupation appear to influence different aspects of his or her life at different time points [27, 54, 61, 84, 85].

Many studies on occupation and income focus on a person's first job, as well as the longest held. However, it is necessary to study the different influences exerted by occupations and incomes during various life periods [61, 84, 85]. For example, the increased risk of developing AD attributable to high blood pressure and obesity was more strongly related to having these conditions during adolescence and midlife than in old age [86–88]. Enhancing educational opportunity is also likely to be significant in preventing dementia; although some researchers pointed out that emphasizing better education may counter-intuitively cause wider social gaps [89, 90]. Research suggests that a longer education reduces risks. However, improving public education during early childhood and supporting the rearing environment in infancy, rather than promoting higher education in adults, appears to guard more effectively against future dementia. Opportunities of higher education in adulthood can be effective for dementia prevention as it promotes social engagement and brain stimulation at a later stage of life. On the other hand, environment in infancy is a key factor in the development of person's physical, mental and cognitive health status in midlife and old age. For dementia prevention, treatment and care, early life and mid life support are important as well as old age interventions. There will inevitably be a considerable lag between the adoption of new policies including education and economic programs and the time when the affected persons reach old age. It will thus be necessary to monitor and evaluate the effects of these policies, taking the time axis into consideration.

3.2 Psychosocial Influences

According to psychosocial theory, there are routes from stress to illness: direct and indirect [91]. Even in countries where little or no absolute poverty exists, stress and psychological ill health caused by relative deprivation can be harmful to physical and cognitive health. A sense of social solidarity and consensus to invest in wealth redistribution may relate to avoid widening the disparities and the fixing of a person's ranking within a societal group. In a society where the haves and the have-nots are clearly delineated, a state of stress is likely to occur and persist as people compare themselves with those around them and find that they cannot obtain goods and services that should be within their reach. Psychological stress that comes from a sense of deficiency and dissatisfaction indirectly encourages unhealthy behaviors such as drinking and smoking, which worsen an individual's health status [92]. One study has also shown that stress increases the ingestion of sweets and high-salt, high-fat foods, although gender differences are seen [93]. A relationship between stress and obesity/diabetes, hypertension, cardiovascular disease and mortality is well reported [92, 94–98]. Researchers similarly point out that prolonged stress and accumulated allostatic load lead to the development of mental diseases such as depressive symptoms and suicide [99, 100]. Depressive states are also shown to increase the risk of dementia [101–103] and cardiovascular disease [104–106].

In addition to indirect influences mediated by unhealthy and risky behaviors, stress is known to exert a direct influence on the body. Stress cause the human body to accelerate or slow the action of the autonomic nervous system, endocrine system, and immune system [107, 108]. As a result, a variety of pathological responses can be observed, such as the elevation of blood pressure and blood sugar, a rise in blood aggregation capability, an increase in vascular load, a reduction in intestinal function, and a decline in immune function. The Whitehall II study shows that extended stressful states trigger inflammatory reactions, the progression of arteriosclerosis, and an increase in the risk of hypertension and coronary heart disease [98]. Countering stress is also thought to be a key factor for preventing the onset of dementia.

Folkman and Lazarus [109] used a two-stage stress source assessment and pointed out that identical events and challenges may or may not become a source of stress. It depends on an individual's coping strategy, empirical values and the quantity and quality of support resources available to them. Support resources include an individual's social network, social support and social capital in the community and workplace. Along with support resources that can be externalized, an individual's internal resources have also been noted. It has been reported that in addition to self-efficacy and self-esteem, an individual's ability to cope with stress through, resilience factors including optimistic personality traits, the ability to enjoy life, and positive emotions or so-called psychologically positive health resources, can alleviate the adverse effects of acute and prolonged stressors [108]. The accumulated effects of being loaded with stressors increase allostatic load [99]. These psychological traits and states are related to reducing the incidence of, and mortality from, cardiovascular disease [110–113] and dementia [114, 115]. Creating an environment that can readily foster rich social connection, positive emotions and enhance stress-coping skills may be an important measure for preventing dementia.

3.3 Social Participation and Social Activities

Social relations, social participation, and active engagement with society are one of the key components to maintaining the cognitive health of the older population. A meta-analysis examining social activity and dementia found that risk of incident dementia is elevated among people with lower participation in social activities (RR:1.41, 95%CI:1.31–1.75), and less frequent social contacts (RR:1.57, 95%CI: 1.32–1.85) [116]. Considering the ways that older people can participate socially and actively engage in life through social activities and creating forums in which they can play an active role may also be an important factor in reducing the risk of dementia. In the current literature on this topic based on the JAGES study which surveyed more than 100,000 older people in Japan, Saito T (2017) reported that diversity of social networks and support resources are related to a lower risk of dementia [117]. Nemoto M (2018) suggested that holding a responsible role in the occasion of social participation is related to a lower risk of dementia and loss of healthy life expectancy [118]. Takeda T (2010) has also reported on the relationship between older people's participation in hobbies and leisure activities and a reduced risk of developing dementia [119]. 'Silver human resources center' in Japan are public facilities that support older people's employment in order to support a sense of *'ikigai' (sense of life worth living, or purpose in life)*, rather than financial gain. Such employment service centers for older people have been introduced internationally and are being adopted in some countries, learning from Japan's experience in order to support successful aging [120]. It has also been recognized that loneliness and social isolation are key factors for increased risk of declining cognitive and physical health [121]. In 2018, the UK government added the role of 'Minister for Loneliness' to the remit of the Minister for Sport and Civil Society, to tackle the problem of isolation in the UK. Social services and programs targeting the older population in Japan have mostly focused on providing support for the older people by positioning them as recipients of support. However, in the super-aged society, the idea of older population as providers of services and schemes to support people in care needs by older population in the community is gaining ground. Old and young generations in the community can work as community designers as well as service providers together to support people with dementia in the community. The diversity and heterogeneity of the older population have been increasing. People aged 65 years and over are entitled to receive social security benefits and referred to as 'older people' in the Japanese system. However, the roles they are expected to play in the society and in the community have been dramatically increased, and understanding the potential contribution of the older population themselves to constructing a dementia-friendly environment is one of the keys to providing support and preventing dementia in the community. According to the concept of 'productive aging' proposed by Butler [122] in 1985, having a place for older people to carry out activities, and having a role for them to play in the society, encourages them to 'adapt themselves to their own aging', will contribute to realizing a better 'aging in the society'. It is reported that among older people, they do not only receive support but also provide it for others and that engaging with these two aspects of support in a well-balanced manner reduces an individual's risk of developing dementia [117, 118, 123, 124]. At present, services and programs for dementia prevention and treatments are implemented based on the "Comprehensive Strategy to Accelerate Dementia Countermeasures (New Orange Plan)" in Japan established by the Japanese Government in January 2015. And the establishment of the integrated community care system for a sustainable social security system is essential in japan. Kondo and Hirai [125] pointed out the importance of the broader population approach in the community.

As a measure for coping with older people who require long-term care, it is essential to reinforce both the formal and informal long-term care support systems. From the perspective of prevention, encouraging participation in social activities such as engaging in community salon which targets older people, encouraging them to participate, become community volunteers and working broadly to establish a society in which older people can play active roles may be generally adopted as measures to counter dementia in a super-aged society.

4 Social Determinants of Health and Dementia Prevention

This chapter attempted to provide an overview of research which examines the relationship between socioeconomic background and dementia. However, numerous researches and societal challenges remain undiscussed regarding the identification of social determinants of healthy aging.

In order to tackle the issue of dementia, collaboration among the health, medical, and welfare sectors are important when we consider relationship between prevention, treatment, and long-term care. Dementia countermeasures must be discussed not only in the medical and public health sector, but in the context of a broad range of social policies such as education, employment, economy, social participation, and the creation of 'ikigai' among the older population. Through our review of the literature and discussions in this chapter, the perspective of social determinants of health (SDH) was discussed as an important part of these multifaceted dementia countermeasures.

Challenges concerning SDH and dementia are likely to become the touchstones for realizing a sustainable society in today's Japan, in which we aim to ensure mature social growth and development. Life-course perspective that spans from infancy, middle age to old age is also important to understand dementia. The relationship between early years deprivation and later non-communicable diseases (NCDs) in developing countries has been attracting increased attention in recent years; for example, we are increasingly aware that children who suffer from poor nutrition during infancy have an increased risk of developing obesity and cardio-metabolic disease in middle to old age. Moreover, adverse childhood experiences were reported to be associated with an increased risk of dementia among older people [126, 127]. For dementia prevention, securing education and a healthy environment in childhood, and mentally and socially integrated lifestyle in late life could be both important as cognitive reserve factors. In other words, closing the disparities gaps that begin in infancy and focusing on lifestyle-related diseases are regarded as essential strategies for enhancing indexes of health in middle and old age, and for improving quality of life. We consider measures against dementia not as a medical challenge but rather as a complex challenge that society must meet from a SDH perspective. In addition, with a sharp increase in the number of dementia patients predicted in low- to medium-income nations in the coming years, Japan, as an advanced nation in terms of dementia prevention, treatment and care, will be expected to play an important role in the international community.

The perspective of SDH is essential for Japan, a super-aged society, to create a sustainable society and is increasingly needed worldwide.

5 Summary

Dementia is a significant public health issue in Japan and throughout the world. It is a major challenge for governments and policymakers given its growing incidence and high prevalence rate, primarily due to population aging worldwide. It is one of the principal causes of disability and dependency in the later stages of life, and is associated with physical, psychosocial, and economic burdens on individuals and society. However, several papers, especially from high-income countries, have reported declining trends in age-specific incidence rates of dementia cases [15–18], although the total number of dementia patient has sharply increased worldwide. Moreover, a Lancet commissioned paper suggested 35% of dementia cases are preventable. Modifiable risk factors for dementia include short education in early life, hearing loss, hypertension, obesity in midlife, smoking, depression, physical inactivity, social isolation, and diabetes in late life [3]. Specifically, education, smoking, physical activity, diabetes are reported as a modifiable risk factor related to the cognitive decline and dementia in several large cohort studies [128]. This chapter mainly reviewed the association between SES including the length of education and risks of dementia incidence and prevalence as one of the major social determinants of healthy aging. Further investigation is required to examine modifiable factors which may prevent dementia in Japan and the rest of the world. Also, the establishment of reliable evidence to understand dementia and to construct systems to support current and potential dementia patients and their families in society are required.

Acknowledgement The authors are grateful to Professor Ichiro Kawachi for his inspiring lectures and fruitful suggestions at T.H. Chan Harvard School of Public Health (HSPH) for this chapter. Original manuscript of this chapter was written during a research period in the HSPH as a research fellow.

References

1. Scholzel-Dorenbos CJ, Ettema TP, Bos J, et al. Evaluating the outcome of interventions on quality of life in dementia: selection of the appropriate scale. Int J Geriatr Psychiatry. 2007;22(6):511–9.
2. Tariq S, Barber PA. Dementia risk and prevention by targeting modifiable vascular risk factors. J Neurochem. 2018;144(5):565–81.
3. Livingston G, Sommerlad A, Orgeta V, et al. Dementia prevention, intervention, and care. Lancet. 2017;390(10113):2673–734.
4. Prince M, Ali GC, Guerchet M, et al. Recent global trends in the prevalence and incidence of dementia, and survival with dementia. Alzheimers Res Ther. 2016;8(1):23.
5. Alzheimer's Disease International. World Alzheimer Report 2018: the state of the art of dementia research: new frontiers. London: Alzheimer's Disease International; 2018.
6. Noda H, Yamagishi K, Ikeda A, et al. Identification of dementia using standard clinical assessments by primary care physicians in Japan. Geriatr Gerontol Int. 2018;18(5):738–44.
7. Ohara T, Hata J, Yoshida D, et al. Trends in dementia prevalence, incidence, and survival rate in a Japanese community. Neurology. 2017;88(20):1925–32.
8. Dodge HH, Buracchio TJ, Fisher GG, et al. Trends in the prevalence of dementia in Japan. Int J Alzheimers Dis. 2012;2012:956354.
9. Meguro K, Ishii H, Yamaguchi S, et al. Prevalence of dementia and dementing diseases in Japan: the Tajiri project. Arch Neurol. 2002;59(7):1109–14.
10. Meguro K, Ishii H, Kasuya M, et al. Incidence of dementia and associated risk factors in Japan: the Osaki-Tajiri Project. J Neurol Sci. 2007;260(1–2):175–82.
11. Kasai M, Nakamura K, Meguro K. Alzheimer's disease in Japan and other countries: review of epidemiological studies in the last 10 years (in Japanese). Brain Nerve. 2010;62(7):667–78.
12. Okamura H, Ishii S, Ishii T, Eboshida A. Prevalence of dementia in Japan: a systematic review. Dement Geriatr Cogn Disord. 2013;36(1–2):111–8.
13. Yamada M, Sasaki H, Mimori Y, et al. Prevalence and risks of dementia in the Japanese population: RERF's adult health study Hiroshima subjects. Radiation Effects Research Foundation. J Am Geriatr Soc. 1999;47(2):189–95.
14. Ahmadi-Abhari S, Guzman-Castillo M, Bandosz P, et al. Temporal trend in dementia incidence since 2002 and projections for prevalence in England and Wales to 2040: modelling study. BMJ. 2017;358:j2856.
15. Wu YT, Beiser AS, Breteler MMB, et al. The changing prevalence and incidence of dementia over time current evidence. Nat Rev Neurol. 2017;13(6):327–39.
16. Matthews FE, Stephan BC, Robinson L, et al. A two decade dementia incidence comparison from the Cognitive Function and Ageing Studies I and II. Nat Commun. 2016;7:11398.
17. Satizabal CL, Beiser AS, Chouraki V, et al. Incidence of dementia over three decades in the Framingham Heart Study. N Engl J Med. 2016;374(6):523–32.
18. Stephan BCM, Birdi R, Tang EYH, et al. Secular trends in dementia prevalence and incidence worldwide: a systematic review. J Alzheimers Dis. 2018;66(2):653–80.
19. Schrijvers EM, Verhaaren BF, Koudstaal PJ, et al. Is dementia incidence declining?: trends in dementia incidence since 1990 in the Rotterdam Study. Neurology. 2012;78(19):1456–63.
20. Qiu C, von SE, Backman L, Winblad B, Fratiglioni L. Twenty-year changes in dementia occurrence suggest decreasing incidence in central Stockholm, Sweden. Neurology. 2013;80(20):1888–94.
21. Alzheimer's Disease International. World Alzheimer Report 2010. The global economic impact of dementia. London: Alzheimer's Disease International; 2010.
22. Hurd MD, Martorell P, Delavande A, et al. Monetary costs of dementia in the United States. N Engl J Med. 2013;368(14):1326–34.
23. Sado M, Ninomiya A, Shikimoto R, et al. The estimated cost of dementia in Japan, the most aged society in the world. PLoS One. 2018;13:e0206508.

24. Livingston G, Frankish H. A global perspective on dementia care: a Lancet Commission. Lancet. 2015;386(9997):933–4.

25. Corder EH, Saunders AM, Strittmatter WJ, et al. Gene dose of apolipoprotein E type 4 allele and the risk of Alzheimer's disease in late onset families. Science. 1993;261:921–3.

26. Reiman EM, Caselli RJ, Yun LS, et al. Preclinical evidence of Alzheimer's disease in persons homozygous for the epsilon 4 allele for apolipoprotein E. N Engl J Med. 1996;334:752–8.

27. Ritchie K, Carriere I, Ritchie CW, et al. Designing prevention programmes to reduce incidence of dementia: prospective cohort study of modifiable risk factors. BMJ. 2010;341:c3885.

28. Cobb JL, Wolf PA, Au R, et al. The effect of education on the incidence of dementia and Alzheimer's disease in the Framingham Study. Neurology. 1995;45(9):1707–12.

29. Yip AG, Brayne C, Matthews FE, Study MCFaA. Risk factors for incident dementia in England and Wales: the Medical Research Council Cognitive Function and Ageing Study. A population based nested case-control study. Age Ageing. 2006;35(2):154–60.

30. Gatz M, Mortimer JA, Fratiglioni L, Johansson B, Berg S, Andel R, Crowe M, Fiske A, Reynolds CA, Pedersen NL. Accounting for the relationship between low education and dementia: a twin study. Physiol Behav. 2007;92:232–7.

31. Gilleard CJ. Education and Alzheimer's disease: a review of recent international epidemiological studies. Aging Ment Health. 1997;1(1):33–46.

32. Sharp ES, Gatz M. Relationship between education and dementia: an updated systematic review. Alzheimer Dis Assoc Disord. 2011;25(4):289–304.

33. Valenzuela MJ, Sachdev P. Brain reserve and dementia: a systematic review. Psychol Med. 2006;36(4):441–54.

34. Russ TC, Stamatakis E, Hamer M, et al. Socioeconomic status as a risk factor for dementia death: individual participant meta-analysis of 86 508 men and women from the UK. Br J Psychiatry. 2013;203(1):10–7.

35. Sattler C, Toro P, Schonknecht P, Schroder J. Cognitive activity, education and socioeconomic status as preventive factors for mild cognitive impairment and Alzheimer's disease. Psychiatry Res. 2012;196(1):90–5.

36. Harrison SL, Sajjad A, Bramer WM, et al. Exploring strategies to operationalize cognitive reserve: a systematic review of reviews. J Clin Exp Neuropsychol. 2015;37(3):253–64.

37. Caamano-Isorna F, Corral M, Montes-Martinez A, Takkouche B. Education and dementia: a meta-analytic study. Neuroepidemiology. 2006;26(4):226–32.

38. Letenneur L, Launer LJ, Andersen K, et al. Education and the risk for Alzheimer's disease: sex makes a difference. EURODEM pooled analyses. EURODEM Incidence Research Group. Am J Epidemiol. 2000;151(11):1064–71.

39. Letenneur L, Gilleron V, Commenges D, et al. Are sex and educational level independent predictors of dementia and Alzheimer's disease? Incidence data from the PAQUID project. J Neurol Neurosurg Psychiatry. 1999;66(2):177–83.

40. Ott A, van Rossum CT, van Harskamp F, et al. Education and the incidence of dementia in a large population-based study: the Rotterdam Study. Neurology. 1999;52(3):663–6.

41. Lindsay J, Laurin D, Verreault R, et al. Risk factors for Alzheimer's disease: a prospective analysis from the Canadian Study of Health and Aging. Am J Epidemiol. 2002;156(5):445–53.

42. Qiu C, Karp A, von Strauss E, et al. Lifetime principal occupation and risk of Alzheimer's disease in the Kungsholmen project. Am J Ind Med. 2003;43(2):204–11.

43. Karp A, Kareholt I, Qiu C, et al. Relation of education and occupation-based socioeconomic status to incident Alzheimer's disease. Am J Epidemiol. 2004;159(2):175–83.

44. Evans DA, Hebert LE, Beckett LA, et al. Education and other measures of socioeconomic status and risk of incident Alzheimer disease in a defined population of older persons. Arch Neurol. 1997;54(11):1399–405.

45. Reuser M, Willekens FJ, Bonneux L. Higher education delays and shortens cognitive impairment: a multistate life table analysis of the US Health and Retirement Study. Eur J Epidemiol. 2011;26(5):395–403.

46. De Ronchi D, Fratiglioni L, Rucci P, et al. The effect of education on dementia occurrence in an Italian population with middle to high socioeconomic status. Neurology. 1998;50(5):1231–8.

47. Cadar D, Lassale C, Davies H, et al. Individual and area-based socioeconomic factors associated with dementia incidence in England: evidence from a 12-year follow-up in the English longitudinal study of ageing. JAMA Psychiatry. 2018;75(7):723–32.

48. Yoshitake T, Kiyohara Y, Kato I, et al. Incidence and risk factors of vascular dementia and Alzheimer's disease in a defined elderly Japanese population: the Hisayama Study. Neurology. 1995;45(6):1161–8.

49. Takeda T, Kondo K, Hirai H. Psychosocial risk factors in certifying the need for long-term care accompanied by dementia in the elderly living in the community: AGES Project, a 3-year cohort study. J Jpn Publ Health. 2010;57:1054–65.

50. Shirai K, Hirai H, Kondo K, et al. Socioeconomic status and its association with incidence of dementia among older Japanese men and women: JAGES study. Intel Epidemiol Assoc World Congr Epidemiol. 2017;46(1):60.

51. Takasugi T, Tsuji T, Kondo K, et al. Socio-economic status and dementia onset among older Japanese: a 6-year prospective cohort study from the Japan Gerontological Evaluation Study. Int J Geriatr Psychiatry. 2019;34(11):1642–50.

52. Chen RL, Ma Y, Wilson K, et al. A multicentre community-based study of dementia cases and subcases in older people in China—the GMSAGECAT prevalence and socio-economic correlates. Int J Geriatr Psychiatry. 2012;27(7):692–702.

53. Zhang ZX, Zahner GE, Román GC, et al. Socio-demographic variation of dementia subtypes in China: methodology and results of a prevalence study in Beijing, Chengdu, Shanghai, and Xian. Neuroepidemiology. 2006;27(4):177–87.

54. Chiao C, Botticello A, Fuh JL. Life-course socio-economic disadvantage and late-life cognitive functioning in Taiwan: results from a national cohort study. Int Health. 2014;6(4):322–30.

55. Bonaiuto S, Rocca WA, Lippi A, et al. Education and occupation as risk factors for dementia: a population-based case-control study. Neuroepidemiology. 1995;14(3):101–9.

56. Helmer C, Letenneur L, Rouch I, et al. Occupation during life and risk of dementia in French elderly community residents. J Neurol Neurosurg Psychiatry. 2001;71(3):303–9.

57. Del Ser T, Hachinski V, Merskey H, Munoz DG. An autopsy-verified study of the effect of education on degenerative dementia. Brain. 1999;122(Pt 12):2309–19.

58. Seidler A, Nienhaus A, Bernhardt T, et al. Psychosocial work factors and dementia. Occup Environ Med. 2004;61(12):962–71.

59. Kroger E, Andel R, Lindsay J, et al. Is complexity of work associated with risk of dementia? Am J Epidemiol. 2008;167(7):820–30.

60. Andel R, Crowe M, Hahn EA, et al. Work-related stress may increase the risk of vascular dementia. J Am Geriatr Soc. 2012;60(1):60–7.

61. Marden JR, Tchetgen Tchetgen EJ, et al. Contribution of socioeconomic status at 3 life-course periods to late-life memory function and decline: early and late predictors of dementia risk. Am J Epidemiol. 2017;186(7):805–14.

62. Lang IA, Llewellyn DJ, Langa KM, et al. Neighborhood deprivation, individual socioeconomic status, and cognitive function in older people: analyses from the English Longitudinal Study of Ageing. J Am Geriatr Soc. 2008;56(2):191–8.

63. Kim GH, Lee HA, Park H, et al. Effect of individual and district-level socioeconomic disparities on cognitive decline in community-dwelling elderly in Seoul. J Korean Med Sci. 2017;32(9):1508–15.

64. Meyer OL, Mungas D, King J, et al. Neighborhood socioeconomic status and cognitive trajectories in a diverse longitudinal cohort. Clin Gerontol. 2018;41(1):82–93.

65. Stern Y. What is cognitive reserve? Theory and research application of the reserve concept. J Int Neuropsychol Soc. 2002;8(3):448–60.

66. Schmand B, Smit JH, Geerlings MI, Lindeboom J. The effects of intelligence and education on the development of dementia. A test of the brain reserve hypothesis. Psychol Med. 1997;27(6):1337–44.

67. Fratiglioni L, Wang H-X. Brain reserve hypothesis in dementia. J Alzheimers Dis. 2007;12(1):11–22.
68. Katzman R. Education and the prevalence of dementia and Alzheimer's disease. Neurology. 1993;43(1):13–20.
69. Dufouil C, Richard F, Fievet N, et al. APOE genotype, cholesterol level, lipid-lowering treatment, and dementia: the Three-City Study. Neurology. 2005;64(9):1531–8.
70. Murata C, Yamada T, Chen C-C, et al. Barriers to health care among the elderly in Japan. Int J Environ Res Public Health. 2010;7(4):1330–41.
71. Frank LD, Sallis JF, Saelens BE, et al. The development of a walkability index: application to the Neighborhood Quality of Life Study. Br J Sports Med. 2010;44(13):924–33.
72. Morland K, Wing S, Diez Roux A, et al. Neighborhood characteristics associated with the location of food stores and food service places. Am J Prev Med. 2002;22(1):23–9.
73. Kikuchi H, Nakaya T, Hanibuchi T, et al. Objectively measured neighborhood walkability and change in physical activity in older Japanese adults: a five-year cohort study. Int J Environ Res Public Health. 2018;15(9):E1814.
74. Hanibuchi T, Kondo K, Nakaya T, et al. Does walkable mean sociable? Neighborhood determinants of social capital among older adults in Japan. Health Place. 2012;18(2):229–39.
75. Rose G. Sick individuals and sick populations. Int J Epidemiol. 2001;30(3):427–32.
76. Brownell KD, Farley T, Willett WC, et al. The public health and economic benefits of taxing sugar-sweetened beverages. N Engl J Med. 2009;361(16):1599–605.
77. Andreyeva T, Long MW, Brownell KD. The impact of food prices on consumption: a systematic review of research on the price elasticity of demand for food. Am J Public Health. 2010;100(2):216–22.
78. Duffey KJ, Gordon-Larsen P, Shikany JM, et al. Food price and diet and health outcomes: 20 years of the CARDIA Study. Arch Intern Med. 2010;170(5):420–6.
79. Meyer KA, Guilkey DK, Ng SW, et al. Sociodemographic differences in fast food price sensitivity. JAMA Intern Med. 2014;174(3):434–42.
80. Glanz K, Rimer BK, Viswanath K. Health behavior and health education: theory, research, and practice. 4th ed. San Francisco, CA: Jossey-Bass; 2008.
81. Johnston H. A methodology for flame analysis: from discourse to cognitive schemata. In: Johnston H, Klandermans B, editors. Social movements and culture. 4th ed. London: Routledge; 1995.
82. Kahneman D. Maps of bounded rationality: psychology for behavioral economics. Am Econ Rev. 2003;93(5):1449–75.
83. Lynch J, Kaplan G. Socioeconomic position. In: Berkman LF, Kawachi I, editors. Social epidemiology. Oxford: Oxford University Press; 2000. p. 13–35.
84. Marengoni A, Fratiglioni L, Bandinelli S, Ferrucci L. Socioeconomic status during lifetime and cognitive impairment no-dementia in late life:the populationbased aging in the Chianti area (InCHIANTI) Study. J Alzheimers Dis. 2011;24(3):559–68.
85. Sha TT, Yan Y, Cheng WW. Associations of childhood socioeconomic status with mid-life and late-life cognition in Chinese middle-aged and older population based on a 5-year period cohort study. Int J Geriatr Psychiatry. 2018;33(10):1335–45.
86. Bendlin BB, Carlsson CM, Gleason CE, et al. Midlife predictors of Alzheimer's disease. Maturitas. 2010;65:131–7.
87. Qiu C, Winblad B, Fratiglioni L. The age-dependent relation of blood pressure to cognitive function and dementia. Lancet Neurol. 2005;4:487–99.
88. Whitmer RA, Gunderson EP, Quesenberry CP Jr, et al. Body mass index in midlife and risk of Alzheimer disease and vascular dementia. Curr Alzheimer Res. 2007;4:103–9.
89. Kawachi I, Adler NE, Dow WH. Money, schooling, and health: mechanisms and causal evidence. Ann N Y Acad Sci. 2010;1186:56–68.
90. Vera MR. France's educational attainment inflation and disparate society. Tokyo: Akashi Shoten; 2007. Hayashi, M. (translated).

 91. Rozanski A, Kubzansky LD. Psychologic functioning and physical health: a paradigm of flexibility. Psychosom Med. 2005;67:S47–53.
 92. Torres SJ, Nowson CA. Relationship between stress, eating behavior, and obesity. Nutrition. 2007;23:887–94.
 93. Mikolajczyk RT, El Ansari W, Maxwell AE. Food consumption frequency and perceived stress and depressive symptoms among students in three European countries. Nutr J. 2009;8:31.
 94. McEwen BS. Protective and damaging effects of stress mediators. N Engl J Med. 1998;338:171–9.
 95. Kivimäki M, Steptoe A. Effects of stress on the development and progression of cardiovascular disease. Nat Rev Cardiol. 2017;15:215–29.
 96. Arnold SV, Smolderen KG, Buchanan DM, et al. Perceived stress in myocardial infarction: long-term mortality and health status outcomes. J Am Coll Cardiol. 2012;60:1756–63.
 97. Hackett RA, Steptoe A. Type 2 diabetes mellitus and psychological stress—a modifiable risk factor. Nat Rev Endocrinol. 2017;13:547–60.
 98. Stansfeld SA, Fuhrer R, Shipley MJ, Marmot MG. Psychological distress as a risk factor for coronary heart disease in the Whitehall II Study. Int J Epidemiol. 2002;31(1):248–55.
 99. Logan JG, Barksdale DJ. Allostasis and allostatic load: expanding the discourse on stress and cardiovascular disease. J Clin Nurs. 2008;17:201–8.
100. Edelstein BA, Heisel MJ, McKee DR, et al. Development and psychometric evaluation of the reasons for living-older adults scale: a suicide risk assessment inventory. Gerontologist. 2009;49:736–45.
101. Byers AL, Yaffe K. Depression and risk of developing dementia. Nat Rev Neurol. 2011;7:323–31.
102. Underwood EA, Davidson HP, Azam AB, et al. Sex differences in depression as a risk factor for Alzheimer's disease: a systematic review. Innov Aging. 2019;3(2):igz015.
103. Diniz BS, Butters MA, Albert SM, et al. Late-life depression and risk of vascular dementia and Alzheimer's disease: systematic review and meta-analysis of community-based cohort studies. Br J Psychiatry. 2013;202(5):329–35.
104. Van der Kooy K, van Hout H, Marwijk H, et al. Depression and the risk for cardiovascular diseases: systematic review and meta analysis. Int J Geriatr Psychiatry. 2007;22(7):613–26.
105. Fan AZ, Strine TW, Jiles R, Mokdad AH. Depression and anxiety associated with cardiovascular disease among persons aged 45 years and older in 38 states of the United States, 2006. Prev Med. 2008;46(5):445–50.
106. Gan Y, Gong Y, Tong X, et al. Depression and the risk of coronary heart disease: a meta-analysis of prospective cohort studies. BMC Psychiatry. 2014;14:371.
107. Cohen S, Kessler RC, Gordon LU. Measuring stress: guide for health and social scientists. Oxford: Oxford University Press; 1995.
108. Steptoe A, Wardle J, Marmot M. Positive affect and health-related neuroendocrine, cardiovascular, and inflammatory processes. Proc Natl Acad Sci U S A. 2005;102:6508–12.
109. Folkman S, Lazarus RS. Coping as a mediator of emotion. J Pers Soc Psychol. 1988;54(3):466–75.
110. Kubzansky LD, Sparrow D, Vokonas P, Kawachi I. Is the glass half empty or half full? A prospective study of optimism and coronary heart disease in the Normative Aging Study. Psychosom Med. 2001;63:910–6.
111. Giltay EJ, Kamphuis MH, Kalmijn S, et al. Dispositional optimism and the risk of cardiovascular death: the Zutphen Elderly Study. Arch Intern Med. 2006;166:431–6.
112. Shirai K, Iso H, Ohira T, et al. Perceived level of life enjoyment and risks of cardiovascular disease incidence and mortality: the Japan public health center-based study. Circulation. 2009;120:956–63.
113. Chida Y, Steptoe A. Positive psychological well-being and mortality: a quantitative review of prospective observational studies. Psychosom Med. 2008;70:741–56.
114. Sutin A, Stephan Y, Terracciano A. Psychological well-being and risk of dementia. Int J Geriatr Psychiatry. 2018;33(5):743–7.

115. Gawronski KAB, Kim ES, et al. Dispositional optimism and incidence of cognitive impairment in older adults. Psychosom Med. 2016;78(7):819–28.
116. Kuiper JS, Zuidersma M, Oude Voshaar RC, et al. Social relationships and risk of dementia: a systematic review and meta-analysis of longitudinal cohort studies. Ageing Res Rev. 2015;22:39–57.
117. Saito T, Murata C, Saito M, et al. Influence of social relationship domains and their combinations on incident dementia: a prospective cohort study. J Epidemiol Community Health. 2018;72(1):7–12.
118. Nemoto Y, Saito T, Kanamori S, et al. An additive effect of leading role in the organization between social participation and dementia onset among Japanese older adults: the AGES cohort study. BMC Geriatr. 2017;17(1):297.
119. Takeda T, Kondo K, Hirai H. Relations between the onset of dementia and the content of hobbies of elderly local residents based on a cohort study, AGES Project. In: The 68th Meeting of the Japanese Society of Public Health, Nara City. Tokyo: JPHA; 2009.
120. Rowe JW, Kahn RL. Successful aging. Gerontologist. 1997;37:433–40.
121. Evans I, Martyr A, Collins R, et al. Social isolation and cognitive function in later life: a systematic review and meta-analysis. J Alzheimers Dis. 2019;70(S1):S119–44.
122. Butler RN. The study of productive aging. J Gerontol B Psychol Sci Soc Sci. 2002;57:S323.
123. Murata C, Saito T, Saito M, et al. The association between social support and incident dementia: a 10-year follow-up study in Japan. Int J Environ Res Public Health. 2019;16(2):239.
124. Shirai K, Iso H, Aida J, et al. Reciprocal social support and onset of dementia—relationship with a loss of healthy life expectancy; AGES Project. Nihon Koshu Eisei Zasshi. 2009;56(10):510.
125. Kondo K, Hirai H. To what extent is high-risk strategy of preventing long-term care effective?—a study based on a cohort research. In: The 18th Annual Scientific Meeting of the Japan Epidemiological Association, January 25–26, 2008, National Center for Sciences, Tokyo. Tokyo: JPHA; 2008.
126. Tani Y, Fujiwara T, Kondo K. Association between adverse childhood experiences and dementia in older Japanese adults. JAMA Netw Open. 2020;3(2):e1920740.
127. Ritchie K, Jaussent I, Stewart R, et al. Adverse childhood environment and late-life cognitive functioning. Int J Geriatr Psychiatry. 2011;26(5):503–10.
128. Lipnicki DM, Makkar SR, Crawford JD, et al. Determinants of cognitive performance and decline in 20 diverse ethno-regional groups: a COSMIC collaboration cohort study. PLoS Med. 2019;16(7):e1002853.

Open Access   This chapter is licensed under the terms of the Creative Commons Attribution-NonCommercial-NoDerivatives 4.0 International License (http://creativecommons.org/licenses/by-nc-nd/4.0/), which permits any noncommercial use, sharing, distribution and reproduction in any medium or format, as long as you give appropriate credit to the original author(s) and the source, provide a link to the Creative Commons licence and indicate if you modified the licensed material. You do not have permission under this licence to share adapted material derived from this chapter or parts of it.

The images or other third party material in this chapter are included in the chapter's Creative Commons licence, unless indicated otherwise in a credit line to the material. If material is not included in the chapter's Creative Commons licence and your intended use is not permitted by statutory regulation or exceeds the permitted use, you will need to obtain permission directly from the copyright holder.

Chapter 12
Falls and Related Bone Fractures

Takahiro Hayashi and Joji Onishi

1 Introduction

According to the 2016 Vital Statistics of Japan, 8030 people die from falling each year, 88% of whom are 65 years and older [1]. The primary cause of functional disability is a bone fracture in 12% of the cases [2], and falls and related bone fractures are a critical public health issue among the elderly population. In this chapter, we first look at the frequency of falls and related bone fractures and the regional differences in their distribution. This is followed by a review of the literature regarding the association between falls and related bone fractures and socioeconomic status (SES), and a discussion of the reasons for the association and possible approaches to preventing falls.

2 Frequency of and Regional Differences in Falls and Related Bone Fractures

Approximately 10–20% of community-dwelling older adults living in Japan fall at least once per year [3–7]. Bone fracture occurs in approximately 10% of falls [8], and it is estimated that slightly fewer than 10% of those are hip fractures [9]. The annual

Takahiro Hayashi is also the English translator for this chapter.

T. Hayashi (✉)
Department of Rehabilitation and Care, Seijoh University, Tokai, Japan
e-mail: hayashi-taka@seijoh-u.ac.jp

J. Onishi
Department of Community Healthcare & Geriatrics, Nagoya University Graduate School of Medicine, Nagoya, Japan

© The Author(s) 2020
K. Kondo (ed.), *Social Determinants of Health in Non-communicable Diseases*,
Springer Series on Epidemiology and Public Health,
https://doi.org/10.1007/978-981-15-1831-7_12

125

rate of falls is 5% among persons aged 65–69 years, and increases with age to 22% among those aged 85 years and older [5]. The relationship between bone fracture and aging is striking, with hip fracture occurring in 7.3 per 10,000 people in their 60s, and occurring more frequently in 271.7 per 10,000 people in their 90s [10].

In terms of geographical occurrence, it may be reasonable to expect that bone fractures would be more frequent in cold regions where road surfaces freeze in the winter. However, contrary to this expectation, an ongoing nationwide survey conducted by Orimo et al. [10, 11] since 1987 has continually shown that the incidence of hip fracture is less frequent in cold regions (Fig. 12.1). In a regional correlation study conducted by Yaegashi et al. [12], a relationship with vitamin K is cited as a reason for this regional difference, and although Kaneki et al. [13] have reported that the large amount of *natto* (fermented soybean) consumed in eastern Japan may correlate to the incidence of bone fracture, the reason for this regional difference is still under debate.

3   Association Between Falls and Related Bone Fractures and SES

In a regional correlation study using a deprivation index calculated from the average income, unemployment rate, and other factors for each region, and in a study using individual income, it has been reported that the incidence of falls and related bone fractures is high among socioeconomically impoverished regions and individuals.

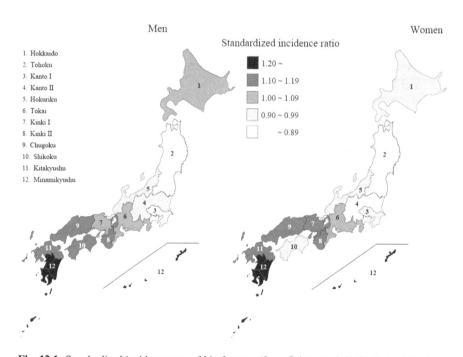

Fig. 12.1 Standardized incidence rate of hip fracture (from Orimo et al. [11]). Note: Calculated from the European standard incidence rate

Below, we introduce the relationships of falls (and related bone fractures) with (1) the regional deprivation index, (2) individual income, (3) education index, and (4) other indices.

$$\text{Standardized incidence ratio} = \frac{B}{\Sigma(I \times P)}$$

where B is the estimated number of patients by regional block, I is the estimated national incidence rate by gender/age, and P is the estimated regional block population by gender/age.

3.1   Regional Deprivation Index and Falls and Related Bone Fractures

First, considering falls, in a cross-sectional study conducted by Lawlor et al. [14] among 4050 older women aged 60–79 years in Britain, no significant difference in the incidence of falls was seen depending on the level of regional impoverishment or social class. In a study on the relationship between the probability of hospitalization because of injury (including injuries from causes other than falls) and regional impoverishment (at five levels) conducted in Wales by Lyons et al. [15] among 90,935 subjects, hospitalization because of injury tended to be more frequent in more impoverished regions overall, but there was variability in the association depending on the age and cause. Although the rate of hospitalization because of falls among people aged 75 years and older was the lowest in the wealthiest region and the highest in the poorest region, there was a nonlinear association between impoverishment and hospitalization [15].

No significant correlation was found between bone fracture and income in a study conducted in the United States by Gornick et al. [16] in 1996 ($n = 26,253,266$). However, in an analysis of 5167 discharged Caucasian patients aged 50 years and older performed by Bacon and Hadden [17], a negative linear correlation was observed between the regional average income and the rate of hospitalization caused by hip fracture. In a study of 43,806 older people aged 75 years and older in England conducted by West et al. [18], the hospitalization rate caused by all bone fractures was 1.10 times higher (95% confidence interval, 1.01–1.19) in the poorest region than in the wealthiest region, and there was no significant difference considering hip fracture alone. Furthermore, recent reports included a cross-sectional study conducted by Bhimjiyani et al. [19] among 747,369 patients with hip fractures aged 50 years and older in Britain as subjects. While the authors did not find a correlation between regional impoverishment and the incidence rate of falls between the central and southern regions of Britain, they reported a high incidence rate of falls in the poorest parts of the northern region. Regarding the mortality rate associated with hip fractures, an analysis performed by Hsu et al. [20] of 193,158 patients with hip fractures aged 65 years and older as subjects reported that the mortality rate was low 1 year after the onset in regions with the highest household income compared to regions with the lowest household income.

3.2 Individual Income and Falls and Related Bone Fractures

Wallace et al. [21] conducted a study on falls by surveying 42,044 older adults aged 65 years and older in California. They found that the annual incidence of falls in 2003 increased with decreasing income, with the incidence rate of the poorest group (18%) being twice as high as that of the wealthiest group (9%).

In a cross-sectional study conducted by Chang and Do [22] among 14,881 community-dwelling older people aged 65 years and older as subjects, the incidence rate of falls was lower among women with household incomes of $20,000 and above ($20,000–39,999, $40,000–59,999, and ≥$60,000), in comparison to women with household income <$20,000.

However, no significant association was observed in cross-sectional studies with fewer subjects compared with those studies. A study conducted in Brazil by Siqueira et al. [23], involving a random sample of 6616 older adults aged 60 years and above, revealed that while the incidence rate of falls tended to decrease with increasing income, no significant difference was found among the income groups.

Moreover, no significant correlation between falling and income was observed in the abovementioned study conducted by Lawlor et al. [14], a study of 1709 randomly selected older people aged 65 years and older conducted in the USA by Boyd and Stevens [24], or in a telephone survey of 2619 older people aged 65 years and older conducted in Australia by Gill et al. [25] Among these studies, Gill et al. [25] showed that the rate of falls was high in groups that did not answer questions about income (odds ratio, 1.34; 95% confidence interval, 1.04–1.73), but this is with the caveat that in this situation, the study was on the subject of income, which is difficult to respond to, or study results were being interpreted.

A longitudinal study conducted by Hanlon et al. [26] among 2996 people in the USA revealed no significant association between income and falls.

A prospective cohort study of a random sample of 16,578 people aged 20–74 years in the Netherlands conducted by van Lenthe et al. [27] indicated that the lower the income, the higher was the incidence rate of hip fractures, and that the adjusted hazard ratio was 2.28 times higher in the lowest income group than in the highest income group (95% confidence interval, 1.40–3.73). Similar results were also found in a study conducted by Brennan et al. [28] A case-control study conducted by Hansen et al. [29] with inpatients and outpatients as subjects (case group: 351,379 people, control group: 351,379 people) indicated that there was a low risk of hip fractures, humeral fractures, and wrist fractures in the highest income group when compared with the average income group. Farahmand et al. [30] conducted a case-control study on bone fracture among postmenopausal women in Sweden (case group: 1327, control group: 3262), and found that the rate of hip fracture was significantly lower in individuals with high income (adjusted odds ratio, 0.74; 95% confidence interval, 0.60–0.90). A study conducted by Kristensen et al. [31] with 25,324 patients with hip fractures aged 65 years and older as subjects in Denmark, a study conducted by Quah et al. [32] with 6300 patients aged 65 years and older in Britain, and a study conducted by Leslie et al. [33] among 104,293 community-dwelling residents aged 50 years and older in Canada all reported that the mortality rate associated with hip fractures was high in the low income group.

The association between regional impoverishment or income and bone fractures is relatively clear, as shown in Table 12.1, but a significant difference has only been seen in large-scale studies on falls with 10,000 or more subjects, suggesting that a large sample size is required to detect an association between impoverishment or income and falls. In addition, a regional correlation study conducted by Jones et al. [41], which analyzed the injury database of Wales, provided important suggestions for interpreting the variability in findings. They compared the bone fracture injury rate of impoverished regions and wealthy regions by age group and found that although the bone fracture injury rate was noticeably high in impoverished regions in the younger strata, the difference was small in the older strata. The difference in bone fracture rate between impoverished regions and wealthy regions was greatest in the 35–44 years age group, at 1.64 times (95% confidence interval, 1.57–1.72), but in the ≥85 years age group, it was 0.94 times (95% confidence interval, 0.87–1.01) without a significant difference. Although extrinsic factors are strong and socioeconomic factors have a large influence on bone fracture in middle-aged patients, it is estimated that intrinsic factors are strong in later old age and the influence of socioeconomic factors is small.

3.3   Level of Education and Falls and Related Bone Fractures

Some studies have shown that the rate of falls is high among people with a higher level of education, while other studies show the converse; thus, there is still no consensus. Among cross-sectional studies, Boyd and Stevens [24] reported no difference in the incidence rate of falls regardless of whether subjects were high school graduates ($n = 1709$). However, Cevizci et al. [43] reported a difference in the fall rate between subjects who were high school graduates and those who were not ($n = 1001$). Gill et al. [25] reported that the fall rate was lower among 2619 subjects who were university graduates or had achieved higher education (adjusted odds ratio, 0.63; 95% confidence interval, 0.43–0.94). In a review of recent reports, Vieira et al. [36] reported that in a random sample of 1451 people aged ≥60 years in Brazil, the adjusted odds ratio for the incidence of falls was higher among people with 4–7 years of education (adjusted odds ratio, 1.40; 95% confidence interval, 1.09–1.80) and uneducated people (adjusted odds ratio, 1.47; 95% confidence interval, 1.09–1.80) in comparison to people with ≥12 years of education. In addition, a study of a random sample of 1182 people aged ≥60 years in Saudi Arabia by Almegble et al. [37] revealed a higher adjusted odds ratio for the incidence of falls among middle school graduates and uneducated people in comparison to university graduates.

Regarding longitudinal studies, in a 2-year cohort study conducted by Reyes-Ortiz et al. [44] among 3050 older adults of Mexican descent in the United States, there was no significant difference in the rate of falls according to the level of educa-

Table 12.1 Relationship between income and regional impoverishment and falls and related bone fractures

Outcome	Authors	Year of publication	Country	Study type	Subjects	Age (years)	No. of subjects	Primary result regarding income or deprivation index
Falls	Hayashi et al. [34]	2014	Japan	Cross-sectional study	Community-dwelling older persons	>65	90,610	The incidence rate of falls was high in the low-income group compared to the high-income group
	Wallace et al. [21]	2007	USA	Regional correlation study	Regional representative sample	>65	42,044	The lower the income, the higher the incidence rate of falls
	Matsuda et al. [35]	2005	Japan	Cross-sectional study	Community-dwelling older persons	>65	29,131	More frequent history of falling in lower income strata ($P < 0.001$)
	Chang et al. [22]	2015	Canada	Cross-sectional study	Community-dwelling older persons	>65	14,881	The incidence rate for falls was low among the wealthiest and second wealthiest groups in comparison to the lowest income group (only for women)
	Lyons et al. [15]	2003	Britain	Regional correlation study	Data of hospitalized patients	≥75	13,277	In the wealthiest region, the standardized hospitalization rate due to injury was significantly lower, at 0.900, but in the next-wealthiest region, it was the highest, at 1.088

	Year	Country	Study type	Sample	Age	Sample size	Findings
Siqueira et al. [23]	2011	Brazil	Cross-sectional study	Regional representative sample	>60	6616	The higher the income of the group, the lower was the tendency of the incidence rate for falls
Lawlor et al. [14]	2003	Britain	Cross-sectional study	Regional representative sample	60–79	4050	No significant association was observed between regional impoverishment and the incidence rate of falls
Boyd and Stevens [24]	2009	USA	Cross-sectional study	Regional representative sample	>65	1709	No significant association was observed between income and the incidence rate of falls
Hanlon et al. [26]	2002	USA	Prospective cohort study	Community-dwelling older persons	>65	2996	No significant association was observed between income and the incidence rate of falls
Gill et al. [25]	2005	Australia	Cross-sectional study	Community-dwelling older persons	>65	2619	No significant association was observed between income and the incidence rate of falls
Vieira et al. [36]	2018	Brazil	Cross-sectional study	Regional representative sample	>60	1451	The lower the income of the group, the higher was the incidence rate of falls
Almegbel et al. [37]	2018	Saudi Arabia	Cross-sectional study	Regional representative sample	>60	1182	The incidence rate of falls was high among people who rented houses compared to those who owned houses
Yasumura et al. [3]	1994	Japan	Cross-sectional study	Community-dwelling older persons	>65	807	No significant association was observed between income and the incidence rate of falls
Brito et al. [38]	2014	Brazil	Cross-sectional study	Community-dwelling older persons	>60	316	No significant association was observed between income and the incidence rate of falls

(continued)

Table 12.1 (continued)

Outcome	Authors	Year of publication	Country	Study type	Subjects	Age (years)	No. of subjects	Primary result regarding income or deprivation index
Bone fractures	Gornick et al. [16]	1996	USA	Regional correlation study	Medicare beneficiaries	>65	26,253,266	No significant association was observed between income and the hip fracture treatment rate
	Lin et al. [39]	2018	Taiwan	Retrospective cohort study	Regional representative sample	All ages	1,000,000	No significant association was observed between income and the hip fracture incidence rate
	Bhimjiyani et al. [19]	2018	Britain	Continuous cross-sectional study	Hip fracture patients	>50	747,369	The incidence rate of bone fractures was high in the poorest regions (only in north England)
	Hansen et al. [29]	2018	Danish	Case-control study	Inpatients and outpatients	>50	Case group 351,379; control group 351,379	The bone fracture incidence rate was low in the wealthiest income group compared to the average income group
	Hsu et al. [20]	2018	Taiwan	Retrospective cohort study	Patients hospitalized due to hip fracture	>65	193,158	The mortality rate was low 1 year after onset in regions with the highest average household income compared to regions with the lowest average household income
	Brennan et al. [28]	2015	Canada	Retrospective cohort study	Undescribed	>50	Undescribed	The bone fracture incidence rate was high in the poorest income group compared to the wealthiest income group
	Leslie et al. [33]	2013	Canada	Case-control study	Community-dwelling older persons	>50	First Nation peoples = 63,081 Non-First Nation peoples = 41,211	The risk of mortality associated with bone fractures was high in the low-income group compared to the high-income group

Oliveira et al. [40]	2014	Portugal	Regional correlation study	Discharged hip fracture patients	>50	96,905	The bone fracture rate was low for women in wealthy regions compared to women in poor regions
Jones et al. [41]	2004	Britain	Regional correlation study	Bone fracture patients	All ages	60,106	In younger strata, the bone fracture rate was particularly high in impoverished regions, and the difference decreased with increasing age
Brennan et al. [42]	2014	Canada	Retrospective cohort study	Community-dwelling older persons	>50 (females)	51,327	The incidence rate of osteoporosis and falls were high for the poorest income group compared to the wealthiest income group
West et al. [18]	2004	Britain	Regional correlation study	Patients hospitalized due to fall or bone fracture	>75	43,806	In low-income regions, the hospitalization rate due to bone fracture was 1.1 times higher
Kristensen et al. [31]	2016	Danish	Prospective cohort study	Patients hospitalized due to hip fracture	>65	25,354	The mortality rate within 30 days after injury was low in the high-income group compared to the low-income group

(continued)

Table 12.1 (continued)

Outcome	Authors	Year of publication	Country	Study type	Subjects	Age (years)	No. of subjects	Primary result regarding income or deprivation index
	van Lenthe et al. [27]	2011	Netherlands	Prospective cohort study	Regional representative sample	20–74	16,578	The incidence rates of falls were high in the low- and middle-income groups compared to the high-income group
	Quah et al. [32]	2011	Britain	Prospective cohort study	Patients hospitalized due to hip fracture	>65	6300	The poorest group had a high bone fracture incidence rate and mortality rate compared to the wealthiest group
	Bacon et al. [17]	2000	USA	Regional correlation study	Discharged hip fracture patients	>50	5167	Negative correlation between the hip fracture incidence rate and income
	Farahmand et al. [30]	2000	Sweden	Case-control study	Postmenopausal female hip fracture patients	50–81 (females)	Case group 1327; control group 3262	The hip fracture incidence rate was significantly lower with higher income (odds ratio 0.74)

"Community-dwelling elderly persons" excludes institutional residents; "Regional representative sample" indicates a study in which a sample was extracted from a resident database.

tion. However, in a study conducted by Hanlon et al. [26] ($n = 2996$), the group with ≥13 years of education showed a 1.49 higher adjusted odds ratio for the incidence rate of falls compared with the group with ≤8 years of education (95% confidence interval, 1.05–2.12). Ryu et al. [45] ($n = 12,286$) also reported a 1.29 times higher adjusted odds ratio for people with high school or less compared with university graduates or those that had achieved higher education (95% confidence interval, 1.00–1.66).

In a study conducted by Woo et al. [46] in Hong Kong that followed 3890 people for 2 years, the incidence rate for falls was 1.77 times higher (95% confidence interval, 1.09–2.88) among female university graduates than among women with an elementary school education, but no significance was observed in multiple logistic regression analysis. Similarly, in a study conducted in Hong Kong by Chu et al. [47] that followed 1517 people for 1 year, there was no significant difference in the fall rate depending on the level of education. In a longitudinal study of 335 Koreans aged ≥60 years, there was also no significant association between falls and the level of education [48]. In a longitudinal aging study conducted in Amsterdam, among 1365 community-dwelling older persons who had fallen, those who had repeatedly fallen two or more times in 6 months had significantly higher levels of education than those who had not ($p = 0.020$) [49]. Among persons with ≥11 years of education, the recurrence rate of falls was significantly higher (univariate analysis odds ratio, 1.36; 95% confidence interval, 1.04–1.77), and Cox proportional hazards analysis with respect to the total number of bone fractures in 6 years demonstrated that whether a person had ≥11 years of education was not a significant variable [50]. Regarding the mortality rate after falls, a prospective cohort study with 566,478 community-dwelling older people aged 50–75 years in Sweden as subjects reported an adjusted hazard ratio of 1.4 for mortality among men with less than 10–12 years of education (95% confidence interval, 1.1–1.8), and 1.8 (95% confidence interval, 1.4–2.3) among men with less than 0–9 years of education compared to men with ≥12 years of education. Thus, the mortality rate was higher after falls among the group of men with poor education [51].

The above review indicates that for cross-sectional studies, there has been a recent increase in reports of a low incidence rate of falls among subjects with increasing level of education. However, longitudinal studies have not reached a consensus to date.

3.4   Other Indices

Regarding community correlation studies, a study conducted by Gribbin et al. [52] that followed 61,248 persons aged ≥60 years in Britain reported an increase in the fall rate with decreasing SES of the community, as calculated from census data for occupation and private automobile ownership ($p < 0.0001$). In a study conducted by

Turner et al. [53] among 5250 hospitalized older Australians, the subjects were divided into five strata of SES by region graded according to income, unemployment rate, and education level, and the association with hospitalization rate caused by hip fracture was assessed. Compared with the region with the lowest SES, the regions with the second and third lowest SES had significantly lower standardized hospitalization rates, at 0.837 (95% confidence interval, 0.717–0.972) and 0.855 (95% confidence interval, 0.743–0.989), respectively. In a report from the USA by Wallace et al. [21], there were differences in the fall rate depending on race, with a rate of 12% among both Caucasians and African-Americans; a high rate of 19% and 17% among Native Americans and the indigenous people of Alaska, respectively; and a low rate of 8% among Asians and Pacific Islanders.

In the Swedish case-control study conducted by Farahmand et al. [30] (case group 1327, control group 3262), the rate of hip fracture injury was significantly lower among employed persons (adjusted odds ratio, 0.74; 95% confidence interval, 0.56–0.96) and homeowners (adjusted odds ratio, 0.85; 95% confidence interval, 0.72–0.99). In the cross-sectional study conducted in Australia by Gill et al. [25] ($n = 2619$), the fall rate was significantly higher among persons living alone (adjusted odds ratio, 1.45; 95% confidence interval, 1.22–1.73).

In a longitudinal study conducted by Chu et al. [47] in Hong Kong ($n = 1517$), there was no significant difference in the fall rate depending on whether a person was employed. However, in a cross-sectional study conducted by Ho et al. [54] in Hong Kong among 1947 subjects aged ≥70 years, the fall rate was significantly lower among those who used to be blue-collar workers than among those who used to be white-collar workers (odds ratio, 0.8; 95% confidence interval, 0.6–0.9).

In summary, although it has been reported that the fall rate is high among people living alone, people who do not own homes, unemployed people, and people living in a region of low SES, some authors have also reported a higher fall rate for white-collar workers than for blue-collar workers, indicating a lack of consensus.

3.5   Findings in Japan

Although few studies on falls and fractures in Japan have investigated the correlation with SES, a number of interesting studies have been conducted. A study of 807 people in Japan conducted by Yasumura et al. [3] showed that there was no significant correlation between falling and SES (income/education). However, studies using large-scale data reported a correlation between income, education, and falling incidence. In the Aichi Gerontological Evaluation Study, which surveyed 29,131 community-dwelling older people, when divided into groups of equivalent income of <2 million yen, 2–4 million yen, and >4 million yen, Matsuda et al. [35] reported a higher rate of falls among both men and women (all $p < 0.001$) with decreasing income. When the subjects were divided into those with <6 years, 6–9 years,

10–12 years, and ≥13 years of education, the adjusted fall rate was significantly higher among women with fewer years of education ($p < 0.001$). A study conducted by Hayashi et al. [34] with 90,610 older adults aged ≥65 years in 31 cities, towns, and villages in Japan as subjects divided the subjects according to three levels of income (<1.5 million yen, 1.5–2.5 million yen, and ≥2.5 million yen). The authors reported that while the adjusted odds ratio was high for fall incidence among subjects with an income of <1.5 million yen, this significant correlation disappeared after the addition of variables of regional environment (neighborhood built environment and population density) and adjustment. Similarly, an ecological study conducted by Hayashi et al. [55] discussed the incidence rate of falls and its related factors between regions among 16,102 subjects from nine cities and towns and 64 elementary school districts. This study identified the regions with fewer falls (elementary school district with the fewest falls: 7.4%, elementary school district with the most falls: 31.1%), and indicated a higher incidence rate of falls among low-income earners ($r_s = -0.54$, $p < 0.01$) and poorly educated people ($r_s = -0.41$, $p < 0.01$) in the regions. Furthermore, this study indicated a higher participation rate in regional sports groups (indicative of a form of social participation) with a lower incidence rate of falls in the regions after adjusting for SES. The study indicated a correlation between the regional incidence rate of falls and social participation [55]. In terms of the regional disparity in the incidence rate of falls, a study conducted by Yamada et al. [56], which had 8943 people from seven cities and towns as subjects, reported a significant disparity in the incidence rate of falls among cities, towns, and villages (range, 8.0–10.1%), even after adjustment for individual-level and environmental factors correlated to falls.

4   Reasons for the Influence of SES on Falls and Related Bone Fractures

As described above, although some findings lack consistency, in studies that used a large sample size and standard variables, it was observed that the strata of lower SES tend to have a higher incidence of falls and bone fractures. If this is true, we may be able to explain the path of influence.

Factors that affect the occurrence of falls include intrinsic factors such as reduced sensation, muscular strength, and balance, as well as extrinsic factors such as the living environment and the effects of medication. As shown in the guidelines of the American Geriatrics Society [57] and a systematic review performed by Moreland et al. [58], in addition to low muscular strength and visual impairment, depression, cerebrovascular disorder, dementia, and use of multiple medications are strong risk factors for falls, but several of these are known to be associated with SES (Table 12.2).

Low muscular strength, particularly of the legs, is strongly associated with falls [59]. Muscular strength correlates with the amount of physical activity, but

Table 12.2 Risk factors of falls

	Number of studies indicating significant difference/total number of studies[a]	Mean relative risk[b] (or mean odds ratio)	95% confidence interval
Low muscular strength	10/11	4.4	1.5–10.3
History of a fall	12/13	3.0	1.7–7.0
Walking disability	10/12	2.9	1.3–5.6
Balance disability	8/11	2.9	1.6–5.4
Use of walking assistance device	8/8	2.6	1.2–4.6
Visual impairment	6/12	2.5	1.6–3.5
Arthritis	3/7	2.4	1.9–2.9
ADL disability	8/9	2.3	1.5–3.1
Depression	3/6	2.2	1.7–2.5
Cognitive impairment	4/11	1.8	1.0–2.3
Age >80 years	5/8	1.7	1.1–2.5

Data from American Geriatrics Society British Geriatrics Society and American Academy of Orthopaedic Surgeons Panel on Falls Prevention [57]
ADL activity of daily living
[a]Number of studies in which a significant relative risk or odds ratio was indicated in the univariate analysis
[b]Relative risk was calculated from a prospective survey; odds ratio was calculated from a retrospective survey

in a Canadian study on income and amount of physical activity, habitually active people accounted for 12.6% of the low-income strata and 17.9% of the high-income strata, whereas inactive people made up a greater proportion of the low-income strata at 67.4% compared with the high-income strata at 56.1% [60]. In an analysis of the Aichi Gerontological Evaluation Study data, Murata et al. [61] reported that low-income subjects often had a visual impairment and were affected by disease, and people who walked for less than 30 min/day and did not participate in sports were often in the low-income strata. del Rio Barquero et al. [62] compared bone density between central Barcelona and the suburban regions of low SES, and made the interesting observation that bone density was better maintained in the city center than in the suburbs among both men and women.

A Brazilian study observed that visual impairment often occurs when income and education level are low [63–65], but the frequency of cataract surgery is also lower when the education level is low [66].

Chou and Chi [65], Chiriboga et al. [67], Perrino et al. [68], Murata et al. [69] in the Aichi Gerontological Evaluation Study, and Yoshii et al. [70] reported that depression is closely associated with SES and that lack of social support, low level of education, and low SES indicated by low income are risk factors for depression. In a review performed by Darowski et al. [71], antidepressants were a risk factor that increased the rate of falls and related bone fractures. It is also known that sleep-inducing drugs, which can lead to falls, are often taken by people of low SES [72]. Moreover, low SES as indicated by lower income is associated with a poor living environment and barriers to healthcare services, which might, in turn, affect health status and increase the risk of falls [73].

We believe that SES affects these risk factors of falls and related bone fractures in a multifaceted and complex manner.

5 Measures Against Falls and Related Bone Fractures that Consider Their Association with SES

Measures against falls and related bone fractures are one of the six key topics of preventive care, and classes on fall prevention are given in various places. However, studies that prove the effect of bone fracture prevention are extremely limited [74], and a significant effect has not been adequately demonstrated by meta-analysis [40, 75, 76]. Falling and related bone fracture prevention projects must always be accompanied by an evaluation of their results. In light of the information provided thus far, we discuss measures that should be taken, in consideration of the association of falls and related bone fractures with SES.

The first measure is an approach that enables high-risk persons to participate in fall-prevention programs. It has been shown that the number of people who do not participate in health checkups to screen for subjects for preventive care programs and the number of people who do not respond to mail surveys are high in low-income groups [77, 78], and that few high-risk people of low SES participate in preventive care programs. In a study conducted by Vind et al. [79], it was shown that the incidence of falls was greater among nonparticipants of a fall-prevention program than among participants. First off, an approach that provides information on the need for prevention to high-risk persons of low SES and urges them to participate in fall-prevention programs is required.

Second, the development of an integral fall and related bone fracture prevention program should be considered. Fall and bone fracture prevention in the past often consisted of a simple intervention program such as muscle-strengthening training, but it is important to provide a multifaceted intervention program that is also relevant to SES, such as maintaining activity, addressing visual impairment, assisting with depression, appropriate use of medications, and maintaining a living environment. This was demonstrated by Chang et al. [80], who, through meta-analysis, found that an integrated program rather than simple exercise reduced the risk of falls (adjusted odds ratio, 0.82; 95% confidence interval, 0.72–0.99). The more socioeconomically disadvantaged people are, the more risk factors they have, and an integrated program may be more effective for persons in the lower socioeconomic strata.

Third, the importance of social participation to promote personal connections and social support should be emphasized. This is particularly important because many socioeconomically disadvantaged people do not leave the house often and interact little with others, thus receiving little social support [81, 82]. Therefore, it is possible that physical activity decreases and the fall risk increases. The aforementioned study conducted by Hayashi et al. [55] indicated a regional difference in the incidence rate of falls and its correlation with SES. However, it was also reported that the lower the regional incidence rate of falls, the higher the participation rate was for regional sports groups, indicative of a form of social participation. In addition, another report of a cross-sectional study indicated a significantly low fall incidence among people who participated once or more a week in sports groups in comparison to those who did not participate. This suggested the possibility that falls could be prevented if individuals exercised [83]. Participation in sports groups was also reported to be effective in not only preventing falls, but also preventing depression and certification of the need for long-term care [84]. Therefore, it is possible that an approach that promotes social participation, such as participation in regional sports groups, can prevent falls through a population strategy with the entire regional population as subjects. The effectiveness of this approach is also anticipated among people of low SES. To proceed with such an approach, support will be required from not only community-dwelling residents participating in such groups, but also local government bodies and experts.

Finally, there is a need for large-scale longitudinal studies. As seen in the above discussion, low SES seems to exert an adverse effect on falls and related bone fractures, but nearly all of those studies were conducted outside Japan, and the validity of their findings must be verified in Japan. Unfortunately, however, there is still little research that longitudinally examines the association between health and SES in Japan. The main point examined in most of the foreign studies discussed in this chapter was not falls and related bone fractures, and the analyses were performed using data from large-scale studies of community-dwelling residents or patients. A system for evaluating the effect of preventive care and health promotion programs over time, including falls and related bone fractures, must be promptly created in Japan.

6 Summary

Poverty increases the incidence of bone fractures, and this association is especially strong in middle age. Because falls and related bone fractures are a primary reason for older adults requiring care and sometimes lead to life-and-death situations, measures must be taken. There is still little medical basis for the effect of prevention measures for falls and related bone fractures, and assessment studies must be conducted in parallel with prevention activities. In light of the association with SES, there is an urgent need for implementation and management of a large-scale longitudinal study that can appropriately evaluate the effectiveness of prevention activities and can be used as feedback while effective integrated prevention programs are developed and community assistance systems are put in place.

References

1. Ministry of Health, Labour and Welfare. 2016 Vital statistics of Japan. Available at https://www.mhlw.go.jp/toukei/saikin/hw/jinkou/kakutei16/dl/11_h7.pdf.
2. Ministry of Health, Labour and Welfare. 2016 National livelihood survey. Available at https://www.mhlw.go.jp/toukei/saikin/hw/k-tyosa/k-tyosa16/dl/05.pdf.
3. Yasumura S, Haga H, Nagai H, et al. Rate of falls and the correlates among elderly people living in an urban community in Japan. Age Ageing. 1994;23:323–7.
4. Yasumura S, Haga H, Niino N. Circumstances of injurious falls leading to medical care among elderly people living in a rural community. Arch Gerontol Geriatr. 1996;23:95–109.
5. Aoyagi K, Ross PD, Davis JW, et al. Falls among community-dwelling elderly in Japan. J Bone Miner Res. 1998;13:1468–74.
6. Niino N, Tsuzuku S, Ando F, et al. Frequencies and circumstances of falls in the National Institute for Longevity Sciences, Longitudinal Study of Aging (NILS-LSA). J Epidemiol. 2000;10:S90–4.
7. Kitayuguchi J, Kamada M, Okada S, et al. Association between musculoskeletal pain and trips or falls in rural Japanese community-dwelling older adults: a cross-sectional study. Geriatr Gerontol Int. 2015;15:54–64.
8. Cabinet Office, Government of Japan. 2005 Survey of housing and activities of the elderly. Available at https://www8.cao.go.jp/kourei/ishiki/h17_sougou/pdf/gaiyou.pdf.
9. Yasumura S. Frequency of falls and related bone fractures in the elderly. J Jpn Med Assoc. 1999;122:1945–9. (In Japanese)
10. Orimo H, Sakata K. Results of fourth nationwide hip fracture frequency survey: hip fracture incidence in Japan: estimates of new patients in 2002 and 15-year trends. Jpn Med J. 2004;4180:25–30. (In Japanese)
11. Orimo H, Yaegashi Y, Onoda T, et al. Hip fracture incidence in Japan: estimates of new patients in 2007 and 20-year trends. Arch Osteopor. 2009;4:71–7.
12. Yaegashi Y, Onoda T, Tanno K, et al. Association of hip fracture incidence and intake of calcium, magnesium, vitamin D, and vitamin K. Eur J Epidemiol. 2008;23:219–25.
13. Kaneki M, Hodges SJ, Hosoi T, et al. Japanese fermented soybean food as the major determinant of the large geographic difference in circulating levels of vitamin K2: possible implications for hip-fracture risk. Nutrition. 2001;17:315–21.
14. Lawlor DA, Patel R, Ebrahim S. Association between falls in elderly women and chronic diseases and drug use: cross sectional study. BMJ. 2003;327:712–7.
15. Lyons RA, Jones SJ, Deacon T, et al. Socioeconomic variation in injury in children and older people: a population based study. Inj Prev. 2003;9:33–7.
16. Gornick ME, Eggers PW, Reilly TW, et al. Effects of race and income on mortality and use of services among Medicare beneficiaries. N Engl J Med. 1996;335:791–9.
17. Bacon WE, Hadden WC. Occurrence of hip fractures and socioeconomic position. J Aging Health. 2000;12:193–203.
18. West J, Hippisley-Cox J, Coupland CA, et al. Do rates of hospital admission for falls and hip fracture in elderly people vary by socio-economic status? Public Health. 2004;118:576–81.
19. Bhimjiyani A, Neuburger J, Jones T, et al. Inequalities in hip fracture incidence are greatest in the North of England: regional analysis of the effects of social deprivation on hip fracture incidence across England. Public Health. 2018;162:25–31.

20. Hsu IL, Chang CM, Yang DC, et al. Socioeconomic inequality in one-year mortality of elderly people with hip fracture in Taiwan. Int J Environ Res Public Health. 2018;15
21. Wallace SP, Molina LC, Jhawar M. Falls, disability and food insecurity present challenges to healthy aging. Policy Brief UCLA Cent Health Policy Res. 2007:1–12.
22. Chang VC, Do MT. Risk factors for falls among seniors: implications of gender. Am J Epidemiol. 2015;181:521–31.
23. Siqueira FV, Facchini LA, Silveira DS, et al. Prevalence of falls in elderly in Brazil: a country-wide analysis. Cad Saude Publica. 2011;27:1819–26.
24. Boyd R, Stevens JA. Falls and fear of falling: burden, beliefs and behaviours. Age Ageing. 2009;38:423–8.
25. Gill T, Taylor AW, Pengelly A. A population-based survey of factors relating to the prevalence of falls in older people. Gerontology. 2005;51:340–5.
26. Hanlon JT, Landerman LR, Fillenbaum GG, et al. Falls in African American and white community-dwelling elderly residents. J Gerontol A Biol Sci Med Sci. 2002;57:M473–8.
27. van Lenthe FJ, Avendano M, van Beeck EF, et al. Childhood and adulthood socioeconomic position and the hospital-based incidence of hip fractures after 13 years of follow-up: the role of health behaviours. J Epidemiol Community Health. 2011;65:980–5.
28. Brennan SL, Yan L, Lix LM, et al. Sex- and age-specific associations between income and incident major osteoporotic fractures in Canadian men and women: a population-based analysis. Osteoporos Int. 2015;26:59–65.
29. Hansen L, Judge A, Javaid MK, et al. Social inequality and fractures-secular trends in the Danish population: a case-control study. Osteoporos Int. 2018;29:2243–50.
30. Farahmand BY, Persson PG, Michaelsson K, et al. Socioeconomic status, marital status and hip fracture risk: a population-based case-control study. Osteoporos Int. 2000;11:803–8.
31. Kristensen PK, Thillemann TM, Pedersen AB, et al. Socioeconomic inequality in clinical outcome among hip fracture patients: a nationwide cohort study. Osteoporos Int. 2017;28:1233–43.
32. Quah C, Boulton C, Moran C. The influence of socioeconomic status on the incidence, outcome and mortality of fractures of the hip. J Bone Joint Surg. 2011;93:801–5.
33. Leslie WD, Brennan SL, Prior HJ, et al. The contributions of First Nations ethnicity, income, and delays in surgery on mortality post-fracture: a population-based analysis. Osteoporos Int. 2013;24:1247–56.
34. Hayashi T, Kondo K, Suzuki K, et al. Factors associated with falls in community-dwelling older people with focus on participation in sport organizations: the Japan gerontological evaluation study project. Biomed Res Int. 2014;2014:537614.
35. Matsuda R, Hirai H, Kondo K, et al. Large-scale epidemiological survey on preventive care in Japanese elderly (3) health behavior and falling history – correlation with socioeconomic status. Koshu-Eisei. 2005;69:231–5. (In Japanese)
36. Vieira LS, Gomes AP, Bierhals IO, et al. Falls among older adults in the South of Brazil: prevalence and determinants. Rev Saude Publica. 2018;52:22.
37. Almegbel FY, Alotaibi IM, Alhusain FA, et al. Period prevalence, risk factors and consequent injuries of falling among the Saudi elderly living in Riyadh, Saudi Arabia: a cross-sectional study. BMJ Open. 2018;8:e019063.
38. Brito TA, Coqueiro Rda S, Fernandes MH, et al. Determinants of falls in community-dwelling elderly: hierarchical analysis. Public Health Nurs. 2014;31:290–7.
39. Lin KB, Yang NP, Lee YH, et al. The incidence and factors of hip fractures and subsequent morbidity in Taiwan: an 11-year population-based cohort study. PLoS One. 2018;13:e0192388.
40. Oliver D, Connelly JB, Victor CR, et al. Strategies to prevent falls and fractures in hospitals and care homes and effect of cognitive impairment: systematic review and meta-analyses. BMJ. 2007;334:82.
41. Jones S, Johansen A, Brennan J, et al. The effect of socioeconomic deprivation on fracture incidence in the United Kingdom. Osteoporos Int. 2004;15:520–4.
42. Brennan SL, Leslie WD, Lix LM, et al. FRAX provides robust fracture prediction regardless of socioeconomic status. Osteoporos Int. 2014;25:61–9.

43. Cevizci S, Uluocak S, Aslan C, et al. Prevalence of falls and associated risk factors among aged population: community based cross-sectional study from Turkey. Cent Eur J Public Health. 2015;23:233–9.
44. Reyes-Ortiz CA, Al Snih S, Loera J, et al. Risk factors for falling in older Mexican Americans. Ethn Dis. 2004;14:417–22.
45. Ryu E, Juhn YJ, Wheeler PH, et al. Individual housing-based socioeconomic status predicts risk of accidental falls among adults. Ann Epidemiol. 2017;27:415–20.e2.
46. Woo J, Leung J, Wong S, et al. Development of a simple scoring tool in the primary care setting for prediction of recurrent falls in men and women aged 65 years and over living in the community. J Clin Nurs. 2009;18:1038–48.
47. Chu LW, Chi I, Chiu AY. Incidence and predictors of falls in the Chinese elderly. Ann Acad Med Singapore. 2005;34:60–72.
48. Shin KR, Kang Y, Hwang EH, et al. The prevalence, characteristics and correlates of falls in Korean community-dwelling older adults. Int Nurs Rev. 2009;56:387–92.
49. Stel VS, Pluijm SM, Deeg DJ, et al. A classification tree for predicting recurrent falling in community-dwelling older persons. J Am Geriatr Soc. 2003;51:1356–64.
50. Pluijm SM, Smit JH, Tromp EA, et al. A risk profile for identifying community-dwelling elderly with a high risk of recurrent falling: results of a 3-year prospective study. Osteoporos Int. 2006;17:417–25.
51. Ahmad Kiadaliri A, Turkiewicz A, Englund M. Educational inequalities in falls mortality among older adults: population-based multiple cause of death data from Sweden. J Epidemiol Community Health. 2018;72:68–70.
52. Gribbin J, Hubbard R, Smith C, et al. Incidence and mortality of falls amongst older people in primary care in the United Kingdom. QJM. 2009;102:477–83.
53. Turner RM, Hayen A, Dunsmuir WT, et al. Spatial temporal modeling of hospitalizations for fall-related hip fractures in older people. Osteoporos Int. 2009;20:1479–85.
54. Ho SC, Woo J, Chan SS, et al. Risk factors for falls in the Chinese elderly population. J Gerontol A Biol Sci Med Sci. 1996;51:M195–8.
55. Hayashi T, Kondo K, Yamada M, et al. Does a region with few people who fall – considerations of regional gaps and related factor: JAGES project. J Health Welf Stat. 2014;61:1–7. (In Japanese)
56. Yamada M, Matsumoto D, Hayashi T, et al. Does a city with few people who fall: AGES project. J Health Welf Stat. 2012;59:1–7. (In Japanese)
57. American Geriatrics Society British Geriatrics Society and American Academy of Orthopaedic Surgeons Panel on Falls Prevention. Guideline for the prevention of falls in older persons. J Am Geriatr Soc. 2001;49:664–72.
58. Moreland J, Richardson J, Chan D, et al. Evidence-based guidelines for the secondary prevention of falls in older adults. Gerontology. 2003;49:93–116.
59. Moreland JD, Richardson JA, Goldsmith CH, et al. Muscle weakness and falls in older adults: a systematic review and meta-analysis. J Am Geriatr Soc. 2004;52:1121–9.
60. Tang M, Chen Y, Krewski D. Gender-related differences in the association between socioeconomic status and self-reported diabetes. Int J Epidemiol. 2003;32:381–5.
61. Murata C, Yamada T, Chen CC, et al. Barriers to health care among the elderly in Japan. Int J Environ Res Public Health. 2010;7:1330–41.
62. del Rio Barquero L, Romera Baures M, Pavia Segura J, et al. Bone mineral density in two different socio-economic population groups. Bone Miner. 1992;18:159–68.
63. Jack CI, Smith T, Neoh C, et al. Prevalence of low vision in elderly patients admitted to an acute geriatric unit in Liverpool: elderly people who fall are more likely to have low vision. Gerontology. 1995;41:280–5.
64. Chong EW, Lamoureux EL, Jenkins MA, et al. Sociodemographic, lifestyle, and medical risk factors for visual impairment in an urban Asian population: the Singapore Malay eye study. Arch Ophthalmol. 2009;127:1640–7.

65. Chou KL, Chi I. Financial strain and depressive symptoms in Hong Kong elderly Chinese: the moderating or mediating effect of sense of control. Aging Ment Health. 2001;5:23–30.
66. Salomao SR, Soares FS, Berezovsky A, et al. Prevalence and outcomes of cataract surgery in Brazil: the Sao Paulo eye study. Am J Ophthalmol. 2009;148:199–206.e2.
67. Chiriboga DA, Black SA, Aranda M, et al. Stress and depressive symptoms among Mexican American elders. J Gerontol B Psychol Sci Soc Sci. 2002;57:P559–68.
68. Perrino T, Brown SC, Mason CA, et al. Depressive symptoms among Urban Hispanic older adults in Miami: prevalence and sociodemographic correlates. Clin Gerontol. 2009;32:26–43.
69. Murata C, Kondo K, Hirai H, et al. Association between depression and socio-economic status among community-dwelling elderly in Japan: the Aichi Gerontological Evaluation Study (AGES). Health Place. 2008;14:406–14.
70. Yoshii K, Kondo K, Hirai H, et al. Large-scale epidemiological survey on preventive care in Japanese elderly (2) socioeconomic differences and regional differences in physical and mental health of the elderly. Koshu-Eisei. 2005;69:145–8. (In Japanese)
71. Darowski A, Chambers SA, Chambers DJ. Antidepressants and falls in the elderly. Drugs Aging. 2009;26:381–94.
72. Blennow G, Romelsjo A, Leifman H, et al. Sedatives and hypnotics in Stockholm: social factors and kinds of use. Am J Public Health. 1994;84:242–6.
73. World Health Organization. WHO global report on falls prevention in older age. Geneva: World Health Organization; 2007.
74. Japan Public Health Association. Report on comprehensive survey project of preventive care. Tokyo: Japan Public Health Association; 2010. (In Japanese)
75. Gillespie LD, Gillespie WJ, Robertson MC, et al. Interventions for preventing falls in elderly people. Cochrane Database Syst Rev. 2003;(4):Cd000340.
76. Gates S, Fisher JD, Cooke MW, et al. Multifactorial assessment and targeted intervention for preventing falls and injuries among older people in community and emergency care settings: systematic review and meta-analysis. BMJ. 2008;336:130–3.
77. Hiramatsu M, Kondo K, Hirai H. Background factors related to preventive care subjects not getting checkups. J Health Welf Stat. 2009;56:1–8. (In Japanese)
78. Suemori K. Trends in non-response. In: Kondo K, editor. Review "Health Gap Society" large-scale epidemiological survey on preventive care in Japanese elderly. Tokyo: Igaku Shoin; 2007. p. 124. (In Japanese)
79. Vind AB, Andersen HE, Pedersen KD, et al. Baseline and follow-up characteristics of participants and nonparticipants in a randomized clinical trial of multifactorial fall prevention in Denmark. J Am Geriatr Soc. 2009;57:1844–9.
80. Chang JT, Morton SC, Rubenstein LZ, et al. Interventions for the prevention of falls in older adults: systematic review and meta-analysis of randomised clinical trials. BMJ. 2004;328:680.
81. Hirai H, Kondo K, Ichida Y, et al. Large-scale epidemiological survey on preventive care in Japanese elderly (6) "Homeboundness" among the elderly. Koshu-Eisei. 2005;69:485–9. (In Japanese)
82. Saito Y, Kondo K, Yoshii K, et al. Large-scale epidemiological survey on preventive care in Japanese elderly (8) health and social support of the elderly: accepted support and provided support. Koshu-Eisei. 2005;69:661–5. (In Japanese)
83. Hayashi T, Kondo K, Kanamori S, et al. Differences in falls between older adult participants in group exercise and those who exercise alone: a cross-sectional study using Japan Gerontological Evaluation Study (JAGES) data. Int J Environ Res Public Health. 2018;15:1413.
84. Kanamori S, Kai Y, Kondo K, et al. Participation in sports organizations and the prevention of functional disability in older Japanese: the AGES Cohort Study. PLoS One. 2012;7:e51061.

Open Access   This chapter is licensed under the terms of the Creative Commons Attribution-NonCommercial-NoDerivatives 4.0 International License (http://creativecommons.org/licenses/by-nc-nd/4.0/), which permits any noncommercial use, sharing, distribution and reproduction in any medium or format, as long as you give appropriate credit to the original author(s) and the source, provide a link to the Creative Commons licence and indicate if you modified the licensed material. You do not have permission under this licence to share adapted material derived from this chapter or parts of it.

The images or other third party material in this chapter are included in the chapter's Creative Commons licence, unless indicated otherwise in a credit line to the material. If material is not included in the chapter's Creative Commons licence and your intended use is not permitted by statutory regulation or exceeds the permitted use, you will need to obtain permission directly from the copyright holder.

Chapter 13
Malnutrition in Older People

Miyo Nakade and Katsunori Kondo

1 Introduction

Malnutrition is an important health issue in people of all ages. For children, it is a risk for hindering normal growth and development, and in pregnancy it affects both mother and child, leading to low birth weight. In old age, malnutrition is a risk leading to the need for care, or endangers life through a person becoming bedridden or affected with pneumonia (Fig. 13.1) [1]. To maintain a proper state of nutrition, required nutrients must be eaten, and obtaining food is the first step. Food intake and malnutrition are affected by income and household economy. In the results of studies in infants and children not only in developing countries in Africa and Asia but also in developed countries in Europe and America, it has been reported that there is more malnutrition in children of parents in lower-income strata than higher-income strata [1]. For example, in a 2010 survey in Iran, a clear relationship was observed between socioeconomic status (SES) and stunting as a result of malnutrition, with a stunting frequency of 17.4% in children under 5 years in the poorest socioeconomic quintile compared to 6.4% in the richest [2].

Miyo Nakade is also the English translator for this chapter.

M. Nakade (✉)
Department of Nutrition, School of Health and Nutrition, Tokai Gakuen University, Nagoya, Japan
e-mail: nakade-m@tokaigakuen-u.ac.jp

K. Kondo
Professor of Social Epidemiology and Health Policy, Department of Social Preventive Medical Sciences, Center for Preventive Medical Sciences, Chiba University, Chiba, Japan

Head of Department of Gerontological Evaluation, Center for Gerontology and Social Science, National Center for Geriatrics and Gerontology, Obu City, Aichi, Japan

© The Author(s) 2020
K. Kondo (ed.), *Social Determinants of Health in Non-communicable Diseases*,
Springer Series on Epidemiology and Public Health,
https://doi.org/10.1007/978-981-15-1831-7_13

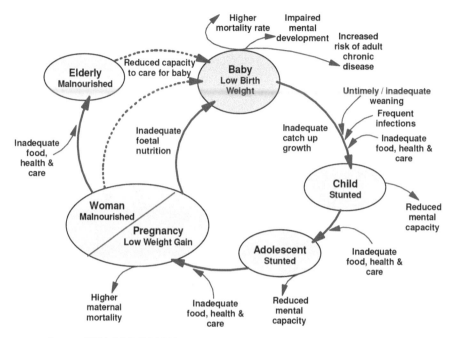

Source: UNACC/SCN 2000. In: UN Millenium Project 2005.

Fig. 13.1 Nutrition throughout the life cycle. (Source: Modification of UNACC/SCN2000. In: UN Millennium Project 2005)

In this chapter, we provide an overview of the problem of malnutrition inside and outside Japan, and then, narrowing our focus to community-dwelling older persons, we introduce findings that demonstrate the association between malnutrition and social determining factors of health, primarily SES components such as income and years of education. Finally, we discuss the future direction of measures to combat malnutrition.

2 The Problem of Malnutrition Inside and Outside Japan

Looking at the global situation, it was indicated in a World Health Organization report on integrating poverty and gender into health programs [1] that underweight young women remained underweight even as they aged and that growth of their children after birth was poor. In South Asia, a relationship between short stature in childhood and incidence of chronic disease in adulthood was reported. A 2017 report [3] by the Food and Agricultural Organization of the United Nations on food security and nutrition found that the number of malnourished people in the world was estimated to be 815 million in 2016, following a global rise in malnutrition from 2014. Africa has the highest prevalence of malnutrition in the world, with an average of 20% compared with the global average of 11%. Asia has the highest absolute number of undernourished people in the world, owing to population size [3].

For children, the global rate of stunting decreased from 29.5% in 2005 to 22.9% in 2016. However, there are still 155 million children under 5 years across the globe who suffer from stunting. In 2016, 52 million children under 5 years were affected by wasting, with around 27.6 million of that number living in southern Asia [4].

To summarize the worldwide state of nutrition, malnutrition is a health problem that is widespread in children in households of low social class in both developing countries and in developed countries. As described above, it is known that malnutrition is seen more widely in low-income strata, but that does not mean that material deprivation (poverty) alone brings about poor health such as malnutrition [5]. An association between years of education and nutritional state has also been reported [1], and this is thought to be caused by the kind of diet provided to children depending on parental knowledge about nutrition and health, differences in hygiene, and differences in health services that are utilized. In a study on stunting and trends toward being underweight or overweight in Indonesian children aged 2.0–4.9 years, it was found that a mother's lack of formal education was closely associated with stunting and being underweight [6].

In Japan, for younger people, being underweight especially amongst women is a public health problem. According to the results of the 2016 National Health and Nutrition Survey in Japan [7], the proportion of people considered underweight [body mass index (BMI) < 18.5 kg/m^2] stands at 4.4% for men, and 11.6% for women, with a significant increase in the percentage of underweight women over the past decade. The number of young women in their twenties considered underweight is 20.7%. For this reason, "Health Japan 21" [8] (a national health initiative) has specified a target value to reduce the number of underweight women in their twenties. It is considered that among underweight young Japanese women, a desire to be thin or excessive concern with body image are the main causes of being underweight [9], which is a different modality from the worldwide situation of being underweight described above (malnutrition because of low SES).

In middle-aged and older persons, there are people who are obese because of metabolic syndrome and require correction of high nutrition, while there are also people who are malnourished or at risk of malnutrition. According to a survey conducted in 2016, the percentage of obese people over 20 years of age (BMI ≥ 25 kg/m^2) was 31.3% for men and 20.6% for women. These figures have remained relatively unchanged over the past decade. However, the percentage of older people aged over 65 years at risk of malnutrition (BMI ≤ 20 kg/m^2) is 12.8% for men and 22.0% for women, of which the percentage for women has increased over the past decade [7]. To combat this problem among older people, "nutrition improvement" has been positioned as a key issue in preventative care measures, with a "nutrition improvement program" implemented to address issues associated with malnutrition and to target people at risk of malnutrition.

As summarized above, malnutrition has been very widely studied, from developing countries to developed countries and from childhood to old age. Next, we review the literature while narrowing our focus to community-dwelling older people as primary subjects.

3   Malnutrition in Older People (Determination of Nutritional State)

The most critical nutritional problem in older people is improvement of protein-energy malnutrition (PEM). PEM is a cause of disease in older people and is closely associated with an increased nursing care requirement level. The state of PEM and its causes must be understood, and improvement and prevention measures taken as early as possible.

In preventive care nutrition improvement programs in Japan, a person's state of nutrition is assessed according to nutrition risk level, using indices such as the rate of weight loss, BMI, serum albumin level, food intake quantity, nutrition supply method, the presence of bedsores, and others. In older people, those with a serum albumin level of 3.5 g/dL or less in a basic health exam, or those who have lost 2–3 kg of weight in 6 months and are extremely thin with a BMI less than 18.5 kg/m^2 on a basic checklist (checking performance of 25 vital functions), are determined to be at risk of malnutrition. Because there are people who maintain a healthy state even with a BMI less than 18.5 kg/m^2, if such people have also lost weight they are judged as being at risk of malnutrition [10].

In an international comparison of malnutrition in older people, Kuzuya [11] cited the definition of malnutrition as a reason that there are almost no reports comparing rates of malnutrition in older people. BMI is used throughout the world, but it is only an indicator of physique and not necessarily an indicator of malnutrition. Furthermore, BMI is greatly influenced by differences in physical function and cognitive function in older people (regardless of whether reduction of these functions is included in the object of research) and class differences such as wealth or poverty. As a tool for assessing nutritional state, the mini nutritional assessment (MNA) has been used in various European countries as well as in Asian countries as a comprehensive method for nutrition assessment of older people [12, 13]. MNA is made up of 18 items in four categories: (1) physical measurements, (2) general state (ambulatory capacity, number of medicines taken, etc.), (3) dietary situation, and (4) self-assessment of nutritional state and state of health. First, 6 of the 18 items (total of 14 points) are evaluated as a screening step, and a score of 12 points or higher is considered normal. For subjects scoring 11 points or lower, the remaining 12 items are evaluated, and the nutritional state is determined based on the total score, where 30 points is a perfect score (24 points or more, good nutritional state; 17–23.5 points, at risk of malnutrition; less than 17 points, poor nutrition) [14, 15].

A variety of factors are associated with malnutrition in older people, including physical, psychological, environmental, and social factors such as chronic disease, missing teeth that directly affect food intake, poorly fitting dentures, reduced level of activity, taking medicine, psychological states such as depression, difficulty in buying food (no stores nearby, difficulty in shopping on foot), and lack of cooking skills and knowledge [10].

4   Association of SES and Older People's Malnutrition and Food Intake Situation

4.1   SES and Nutritional State Assessment Using MNA

For studies in countries other than Japan that used MNA for nutritional assessment of community-dwelling older people, differences that were attributed to individual SES were seen in numerous reports [16–21].

For example, in Japan, when 130 healthy, community-dwelling older people attending a senior university were screened for malnutrition using MNA, 12.6% of participants were at risk of malnutrition, and many were in the poor economic status strata [16]. It has also been reported that many at risk of malnutrition (weight loss of at least 3 kg in 6 months) are in the strata of limited education and low income, and that more live in agricultural regions than in metropolitan areas [17]. In regard to extensive tooth loss as a cause of malnutrition, Aida et al. [18] reported that the odds ratio of people 65 years and older having 19 or fewer remaining teeth was 1.4 times higher in people with 9 or fewer years of education than those with 13 or more years, even after adjustment for age, gender, income, health behavior, smoking habit, and so forth.

In an MNA-SF (Mini Nutritional Assessment short form) survey of 698 community-dwelling older people in Italy, an association was found between low education levels, low economic status, and malnutrition [19], while a different survey reported a relationship between malnutrition and factors such as low income, distance from supermarkets, and lack of transport [20].

The prevalence rate is also higher when the degree of development of a country is lower. In a report from Bangladesh on 457 people aged 60 years and older who were not receiving nursing care services, an association was demonstrated between high degree of education or high level of household consumption and high MNA score (good nutritional state) even after adjustment for age and state of health [21]. In that survey, the prevalence rate of malnutrition was a high 62%, and it was shown that people with depression or low cognitive function had a poor nutritional state, as well as uneducated people and women with no income or irregular financial assistance [22].

In a survey of 1200 older people in Lebanon, it was found that while 8% of men were at risk of malnutrition, the percentage for women was much higher at 29.1%, with lower rates of literacy and income as well as high frequency of depression in women rather than men [23].

4.2 Association Between Individual SES and Quality of Food Consumed

A large-scale cohort survey conducted in Europe found that men in particular of lower income status and socioeconomic class consumed fewer different fruits or vegetables [24]. A similar survey in England found that older men with low SES had a poor-quality diet. Married men had higher diet quality than men living alone, with diet quality in older men also adversely influenced by factors such as SES (including manual social class of parents) in childhood [25].

In a review of epidemiological data, Darmon and Drewnowski [26] found that persons of higher SES tended to consume whole grains, fish, low-fat dairy products, and fresh fruit and vegetables, while consumption of refined grains and added fats is associated with persons of lower SES. However, it has been shown that while some European countries have comparatively lower SES than America, consumption of fruit and vegetables is not adversely affected. A relationship has also been identified between children's food consumption and their parents' level of education, where a lower level of schooling resulted in less fruit and vegetables, and more sugary beverages being consumed by the children of such parents [26].

In Japan, large-scale studies have shown that in recent years an individual's SES has an influence on general health, meals, and dietary environment. The National Health and Nutrition Survey of Japan showed a direct correlation between household income and fat intake, while there was an inverse correlation with carbohydrate intake. Women with low education levels and household income were likely to be overweight or obese, but for men, there was no direct correlation between lower education level and rate of obesity [27, 28].

In a Japan Gerontological Evaluation Study (JAGES) of 100,000 participants, men with 19 teeth or less were found to be 1.5 times more at risk of being underweight, while women under the same conditions that did not consume fruit and vegetables on a daily basis had a 1.2 times higher risk of being underweight [29]. It was found that risk of death with a BMI of 18.5 kg/m^2 or under increased, while obese males of low SES were also at a higher risk of dying [30]. In a 3-year study conducted by Tani et al. [31], older people with lower SES in childhood were 1.27 times more likely to develop depression as adults than those with a higher childhood SES. Moreover, men who ate meals alone had a higher risk of developing depression, higher risk of death, and even men who lived with family had a higher risk of death if eating alone [32, 33]. From these reports, it is seen that the SES of an individual is related in no small measure to quality and quantity of food consumed, and affects an individual's state of health not only through malnutrition, but through obesity, improper nutrition intake, and so forth.

4.3 Association Between Community SES and Individual Food Intake

Several reports have stated that not only is an individual's SES associated with his or her food intake, but also the socioeconomic environment of the community in which the individual lives [34–36]. For example, in a study of women living in 3204 communities in 26 states of India, a multilevel analysis by dividing the communities into wealthy, moderate, and poor communities found that community wealth was associated with BMI after adjusting for individual factors [34]. Furthermore, when adjusted for individual SES including household wealth (work, education, etc.), BMI was 0.29 kg/m² higher in the wealthiest communities than in the poorest communities [34]. From the results of a survey of Cambodian women, Hong and Hong [36] demonstrated that the nutritional state of women was lower in low-SES communities and that differences were large depending on the community, even after adjustment for individual household economy level by multilevel analysis. In a different survey from 2010 of 4000 older people in Japan, after adjustment for individual factors were made, a relationship was reported between community income levels and the number of remaining teeth [37].

In a report on a large-scale survey in people aged 65 years and older based on the 2000 USA census [38], the death rate due to malnutrition was extracted by tracking the data of 190,000 households in 3141 counties over 4 years. The death rate was significantly higher in the lower education level strata, and even when adjusted for that, it was shown that social, physical, and social isolation factors are involved in regional patterns of death based on malnutrition in older people. As an example of the traditional diet of a community being related to SES, in a study in residents of the eastern Mediterranean islands of Greece (eight islands) aged 65–100 years [39], an association was seen between consumption of a Mediterranean diet (using a Mediterranean diet score) and education or financial status. The results indicated that people of the highest SES level more often consumed a traditional diet (i.e., fish, vegetables, wine, etc.) than people of other levels.

In a seven-country comparative study of SES and variances in fruit and vegetable consumption, an association was found between neighborhood-level SES and fruit consumption in Canada, New Zealand, and Scotland. In Australia, Canada, New Zealand, and Portugal, those residing in higher SES neighborhoods had an increased chance of greater vegetable intake [40].

Regarding community influences on diet, access or proximity to certain food stores such as supermarkets has been used as a normalizing factor of obesity and eating behavior [41]. For example, Zenk et al. [42] reported that women who shopped at supermarkets or specialty stores consumed fruit and vegetables more than people who shopped at grocery stores that were not specialty stores. There are also reports demonstrating the association between fast food and obesity [43, 44]. In the results of a study in 65 Los Angeles communities with a large low-income population, it was reported that BMI was high in communities with a large number of restaurants and fast food places, even after adjustment for individual factors and community SES [43].

In Japan, communities in which it is difficult to find inexpensive, good-quality perishable food in city centers and changes in community shops threaten to affect the health of residents living there. This situation has been called the food desert problem [45–47]. As smaller food stores disappear from communities, older people become disadvantaged, consuming less variety of foods and at higher risk of not consuming enough meat, fish, fruit, and vegetables. These factors were particularly pronounced in older men with low levels of neighborhood contact [48]. It is clear that community-dwelling SES, geographical factors, and lack of social contact with neighbors is linked to malnutrition.

5   Future Direction of Measures Against Malnutrition

Considering the association between malnutrition and social determining factors of health described above, we draw attention to four points regarding the future direction of measures against malnutrition.

First is the importance of a population-wide strategy. Although Japan has a "nutrition improvement" program in place as part of the country's preventive care policy, the small number of program participants or people qualifying as at risk for malnutrition and the contents of the program have been pointed out as issues. The reasons cited include: many participants are healthy people with no nutritional problems; it is difficult to attract malnourished people who want to participate in a nutrition improvement program; information about nutrition is difficult for subjects to understand; and the albumin level of people who were anticipated to be malnourished was not low. Older people are inevitably at risk of malnutrition sooner or later. It is therefore important to take the view that malnutrition in older people is not just a problem for the people who participate in nutrition programs, but is a topic of preventive care in all community-dwelling older people, and a population-wide strategy must be established.

Second is the importance of perspective on the disparity among socioeconomic classes. As has been seen, however, there are disparities in food intake depending on individual SES, which influences malnutrition and the health of older people. People with a high level of education generally have a high level of knowledge about nutrition, consume healthy foods, as well as a variety of foods. Some reports have also shown that low-income groups demonstrate low serum albumin levels compared with middle-income groups. These results suggest that intake of meat and fish may be low [49]. Malnutrition countermeasures need to take differences in social classes into consideration, and food environments are required to provide older people with safe and appropriate dining options. For this to happen, the enhancement of food delivery services and communal dining facilities would be a welcome step [50].

Third is the importance of focusing on community environmental factors. The association between health and socioeconomic factors at a community level, rather than just differences in individual socioeconomic factors, has started to be reported. If there are no nearby stores where one can buy fresh fruit and vegetables, the nutritional state of people without access to transportation becomes affected. To establish a population-wide strategy and to counteract health disparities among social classes, measures against malnutrition must be examined in the future by compiling research that focuses on community environmental factors rather than just individual factors.

Although not touched upon here because of space constraints, the fourth point is the importance of research and countermeasures from a life course approach. As an example, in a Brazilian study, the quality of a child's diet was associated with having no father in the household or having two parents with a low education level, and, in particular, it was four times worse in children whose parents did not finish elementary school than in children of parents who did [51]. A child's SES is determined by the parents' SES, and an undesirable foundation of eating habits is created by a parent's SES being low, with the risk of it leading to poor health. This must be addressed while looking at all generations through the life course. Long-term comprehensive measures are required, such as improving the education level, knowledge about nutrition, and income security of mothers bearing the next generation.

6   Summary

"Nutrition improvement" is an important undertaking not only because it improves the state of malnutrition, but also because it leads to the maintenance of biological rhythm. The everyday act of eating is the foundation of individual self-actualization, through improvement of vital functions, restoration of communication, and social participation. It should be guaranteed regardless of SES or the community in which a person lives. On the other hand, nutritional state is influenced by social determining factors of health. To improve the nutritional state of all people, we must treat it as a population-wide problem rather than an individual one, and we must devise countermeasures with a life course approach while focusing on both disparities among socioeconomic classes and community environmental factors.

References

1. World Health Organization. Integrating poverty and gender into health programmes: a sourcebook for health professionals: module on nutrition. Geneva: WHO; 2010. Available at https://apps.who.int/iris/handle/10665/207658. Accessed Oct 2018.
2. Almasian Kia A, Rezapour A, Khosravi A, Afzali Abarghouei V. Socioeconomic inequality in malnutrition in under-5 children in Iran: evidence from the multiple indicator demographic and health survey, 2010. J Prev Med Public Health. 2017;50(3):201–9.

3. Food and Agricultural Organization of the United Nations (FAO). The state of food security and nutrition in the world. Rome: FAO; 2017. Available at http://www.fao.org/3/a-I7695e.pdf. Accessed Oct 2018.
4. UNICEF/WHO/The World Bank Group. Joint child malnutrition estimates - levels and trends. Geneva: WHO; 2017. Available at https://www.who.int/nutgrowthdb/jme_brochoure2017. pdf?ua=1. Accessed Oct 2018.
5. Kondo K. New public health paradigm: introduction to social epidemiology 2 - socioeconomic status and health. J Public Health Pract. 2004;68(2):132–6. (In Japanese).
6. Rachmi CN, Agho KE, Li M, Baur LA. Stunting, underweight and overweight in children aged 2.0-4.9 years in Indonesia: prevalence trends and associated risk factors. PLoS One. 2016;11(5):e0154756.
7. Office for Life-Style Related Diseases Control, General Affairs Division, Health Service Bureau, Ministry of Health, Labour and Welfare. Outline of results from 2016 National Health and Nutrition Survey in Japan. Tokyo: Ministry of Health, Labour and Welfare; 2017. Available at http://www.mhlw.go.jp/stf/houdou/0000177189.html. Accessed Oct 2018.
8. Japan Health Promotion and Fitness Foundation. Health Japan 21. Tokyo: JHPFF; 2013. Available at https://www.mhlw.go.jp/file/05-Shingikai-10601000-Daijinkanboukousei-kagakuka-Kouseikagakuka/0000166300.pdf. Accessed Oct 2018. (In Japanese).
9. Yasutomo H, Yamanaka M, Tachibana E, et al. Study of body image and nutritional intake status among female students, vol. 7. Aichi: School of Nutritional Sciences, Nagoya University of Arts and Sciences; 2015. p. 15–23. (In Japanese).
10. "Nursing Care Prevention Manual" Distribution Research Group (Sugiyama M, Chairperson). Nutrition Improvement Manual (revised edition). 2009. Available at https://www.mhlw.go.jp/topics/2009/05/dl/tp0501-1e_0001.pdf. Accessed Oct 2018. (In Japanese).
11. Kuzuya M. Malnutrition in the elderly: international comparison of status and countermeasures. Ger Med. 2010;48(7):895–9. (In Japanese).
12. Malek Mahdavi A, Mahdavi R, Lotfipour M, et al. Evaluation of the Iranian mini nutritional assessment short-form in community-dwelling elderly. Health Promot Perspect. 2015;5(2):98–103.
13. Ferrari Bravo M, Gallo F, Marchello C, et al. Assessment of malnutrition in community-dwelling elderly people: cooperation among general practitioners and public health. Iran J Public Health. 2018;47(5):633–40.
14. Nestle Nutrition Institute. Mini Nutritional Assessment (MNA®). Available at https://www.mna-elderly.com/forms/MNA_english.pdf. Accessed Oct 2018.
15. Vellas B, Guigoz Y, Garry PJ, et al. The Mini Nutritional Assessment (MNA) and nomic differences in fruit and System • 8: 582--its use in grading the nutritional state of elderly patients. Nutrition. 1999;15(2):116–22.
16. Iizaka S, Tadaka E, Sanada H, et al. Comprehensive assessment of nutritional status and associated factors in the healthy, community-dwelling elderly. Geriatr Gerontol Int. 2008;8(1):24–31.
17. Kondo K, editor. Review "Health Disparity Society": large-scale socio-epidemiological survey on preventive care in Japanese elderly. Tokyo: Igaku Shoin; 2007. (In Japanese).
18. Aida J, Hanibuchi T, Nakade M, et al. The different effects of vertical social capital and horizontal social capital on dental status: a multilevel analysis. Soc Sci Med. 2009;69(4):512–8.
19. Timpini A, Facchi E, Cossi S, et al. Self-reported socio-economic status, social, physical and leisure activities and risk for malnutrition in late life: a cross-sectional population-based study. J Nutr Health Aging. 2011;15(3):233–8.
20. Donini LM, Scardella P, Piombo L, et al. Malnutrition in elderly: social and economic determinants. J Nutr Health Aging. 2013;17(1):9–15.
21. Kabir ZN, Ferdous T, Cederholm T, et al. Mini Nutritional Assessment of rural elderly people in Bangladesh: the impact of demographic, socio-economic and health factors. Public Health Nutr. 2006;9(8):968–74.

22. Ferdous T, Kabir ZN, Wahlin A, et al. The multidimensional background of malnutrition among rural older individuals in Bangladesh - a challenge for the Millennium Development Goal. Public Health Nutr. 2009;12(12):2270–8.
23. Boulos C, Salameh P, Barberger-Gateau P. The AMEL study, a cross sectional population-based survey on aging and malnutrition in 1200 elderly Lebanese living in rural settings: protocol and sample characteristics. BMC Public Health. 2013;13:573.
24. Conklin AI, Forouhi NG, Suhrcke M, et al. Variety more than quantity of fruit and vegetable intake varies by socioeconomic status and financial hardship. Findings from older adults in the EPIC cohort. Appetite. 2014;83:248–55.
25. Atkins JL, Ramsay SE, Whincup PH, et al. Diet quality in older age: the influence of childhood and adult socio-economic circumstances. Br J Nutr. 2015;113(9):1441–52.
26. Darmon N, Drewnowski A. Does social class predict diet quality? Am J Clin Nutr. 2008;87(5):1107–17.
27. Nakamura T, Nakamura Y, Saitoh S, et al. Relationship between socioeconomic status and the prevalence of underweight, overweight or obesity in a general Japanese population: NIPPON DATA 2010. J Epidemiol. 2018;28(Suppl 3):S10–6.
28. Sakurai M, Nakagawa H, Kadota A, et al. Macronutrient intake and socioeconomic status: NIPPON DATA 2010. J Epidemiol. 2018;28(3):S17–22.
29. Nakamura M, Ojima T, Nakade M, et al. Poor oral health and diet in relation to weight loss, stable underweight, and obesity in community-dwelling older adults: a cross-sectional study from the JAGES 2010 project. J Epidemiol. 2016;26(6):322–9.
30. Nakade M, Takagi D, Suzuki K, et al. Influence of socioeconomic status on the association between body mass index and cause-specific mortality among older Japanese adults: the AGES Cohort Study. Prev Med. 2015;77:112–8.
31. Tani Y, Fujiwara T, Kondo N, et al. Childhood socioeconomic status and onset of depression among Japanese older adults: the JAGES prospective cohort study. Am J Geriatr Psychiatry. 2016;24(9):717–26.
32. Tani Y, Sasaki Y, Haseda M, Kondo K, et al. Eating alone and depression in older men and women by cohabitation status: the JAGES longitudinal survey. Age Ageing. 2015;44(6):1019–26.
33. Tani Y, Kondo N, Noma H, et al. Eating alone yet living with others is associated with mortality in older men: the JAGES cohort survey. J Gerontol B Psychol Sci Soc Sci. 2018;73(7):1330–4.
34. Ackerson LK, Kawachi I, Barbeau EM, et al. Geography of underweight and overweight among women in India: a multilevel analysis of 3204 neighborhoods in 26 states. Econ Hum Biol. 2008;6(2):264–80.
35. Subramanian SV, Kawachi I, Smith GD. Income inequality and the double burden of under - and overnutrition in India. J Epidemiol Community Health. 2007;61(9):802–9.
36. Hong R, Hong R. Economic inequality and undernutrition in women: multilevel analysis of individual, household, and community levels in Cambodia. Food Nutr Bull. 2007;28(1):59–66.
37. Tashiro A, Aida J, Shobugawa Y, et al. Association between income in quality and dental status in Japanese older adults: analysis of data from JAGES2013. Jpn Soc Public Health. 2017;64(4):190–6. (In Japanese).
38. Lee MR, Berthelot ER. Community covariates of malnutrition based mortality among older adults. Ann Epidemiol. 2010;20:371–9.
39. Katsarou A, Tyrovolas S, Psaltopoulou T, et al. Socio-economic status, place of residence and dietary habits among the elderly: the Mediterranean islands study. Public Health Nutr. 2010;13(10):1614–21.
40. Ball K, Lamb KE, Costa C, et al. Neighbourhood socioeconomic disadvantage and fruit and vegetable consumption: a seven countries comparison. Int J Behav Nutr Phys Act. 2015;12:68.
41. Frank BH. Epidemiology of obesity: Chapter 17 Social determining factors of obesity. Nagoya: The University of Nagoya Press; 2010.
42. Zenk SN, Schulz AJ, Hollis-Neely T, et al. Fruit and vegetable intake in African Americans income and store characteristics. Am J Prev Med. 2005;29(1):1–9.

43. Inagami S, Cohen DA, Brown AF, et al. Body mass index, neighborhood fast food and restaurant concentration, and car ownership. J Urban Health. 2009;86(5):683–95.
44. Fraser LK, Edwards KL, Cade J, et al. The geography of fast food outlets: a review. Int J Environ Res Public Health. 2010;7(5):2290–308.
45. Iwama N, Takana K, Sasaki M, et al. The dietary life of the elderly in local cities and food desert issues: a case study of Mito City, Ibaraki Prefecture. Hum Geograph Soc Jpn. 2009;61(2):139–56. (In Japanese).
46. Iwama N, Tanaka K, Komori N, et al. Mapping residential areas of elderly people at high risk of undernutrition: analysis of mobile sales wagons from the viewpoint of food desert issues. J Geogr. 2016;125(4):583–606. (In Japanese).
47. Asakawa T, Iwama N, Tanaka K, et al. Food deserts issues in a local city: empirical study in a local city that is composed of urban and rural area. Ann Jpn Assoc Urban Soc. 2016;34:1–13. (In Japanese).
48. Nakamura H, Nakamura M, Okada E, et al. Association of food access and neighbor relationships with diet and underweight among community-dwelling older Japanese. J Epidemiol. 2017;27(11):546–51.
49. Ota A, Kondo N, Murayama N, et al. Serum albumin levels and economic status in Japanese older adults. PLoS One. 2016;11(6):e0155022.
50. Takemi Y, Koiwai K. Strategy for prevention of undernutrition in the elderly: meal delivery service and eating together in the community for health care and promotion. J Natl Inst Public Health. 2017;66(6):603–11. (In Japanese).
51. Molina MCB, Lopéz PM, Faria CP, et al. Socioeconomic predictors of child diet quality. Rev Saude Publica. 2010;44(5):785–32.

Open Access This chapter is licensed under the terms of the Creative Commons Attribution-NonCommercial-NoDerivatives 4.0 International License (http://creativecommons.org/licenses/by-nc-nd/4.0/), which permits any noncommercial use, sharing, distribution and reproduction in any medium or format, as long as you give appropriate credit to the original author(s) and the source, provide a link to the Creative Commons licence and indicate if you modified the licensed material. You do not have permission under this licence to share adapted material derived from this chapter or parts of it.

The images or other third party material in this chapter are included in the chapter's Creative Commons licence, unless indicated otherwise in a credit line to the material. If material is not included in the chapter's Creative Commons licence and your intended use is not permitted by statutory regulation or exceeds the permitted use, you will need to obtain permission directly from the copyright holder.

Chapter 14
Oral Health

Jun Aida and Katsunori Kondo

1 Introduction

Dental diseases, particularly dental caries (cavities) and periodontal disease, are a significant burden to society, even though they are not fatal, and represent some of the most prevalent diseases in the world [1, 2]. In Japan, the national medical cost of dental diseases in 2015 amounted to 2,829,400 million yen, which was third behind the cost of cardiovascular diseases including hypertension (5,981,800 million yen) and neoplasms such as cancer (4,125,700 million yen). In particular, the cost of dental diseases for individuals younger than 65 years of age is highest compared with other diseases. In addition, recent studies have shown that oral health may affect general health. Accordingly, public health policies, such as the Health Promotion Campaign for the Twenty-First Century (Health Japan 21) and the "8020 Campaign" to retain 20 natural teeth by 80 years of age, have been promoted in Japan.

A difference in health status, such as variation of height among the population, maybe natural. However, it becomes a problem when such differences are considered

Jun Aida is also the English translator for this chapter.

J. Aida (✉)
Department of Oral Health Promotion Graduate School of Medical and Dental Sciences, Tokyo Medical and Dental University, Tokyo, Japan
e-mail: j-aida@umin.ac.jp

K. Kondo
Professor of Social Epidemiology and Health Policy, Department of Social Preventive Medical Sciences, Center for Preventive Medical Sciences, Chiba University, Chiba, Japan

Head of Department of Gerontological Evaluation, Center for Gerontology and Social Science, National Center for Geriatrics and Gerontology, Obu City, Aichi, Japan

© The Author(s) 2020
K. Kondo (ed.), *Social Determinants of Health in Non-communicable Diseases*, Springer Series on Epidemiology and Public Health,
https://doi.org/10.1007/978-981-15-1831-7_14

to be avoidable health inequalities because they are caused by systemic differences in the social determinants of health, which are also found in dental diseases.

2 Health Inequalities in Dental Disease in Japan

Many reports have described health inequalities in dental diseases and medical conditions around the world [3–7]. This section introduces the health inequalities in dental diseases in Japan according to generation, disease, and condition.

Several studies have reported caries inequalities in preschool children [8–11]. The disease map of the caries prevalence for each municipality indicates that the prevalence rate was higher mainly in the areas of Hokkaido, Tohoku, Shikoku, and Kyushu (Fig. 14.1) [8]. In multivariate analysis of municipalities in these areas, the

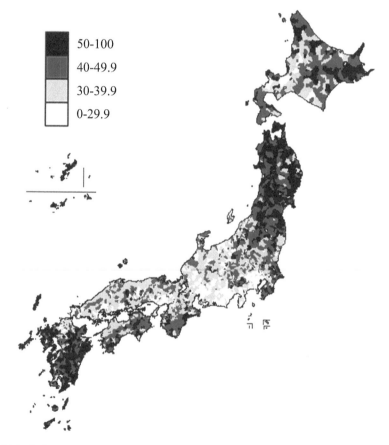

Fig 14.1 Caries prevalence (%) for 3-year-old-children in Japan (2000, Empirical Bayes Approach). (Quoted and modified from Aida et al. [8])

percentage of university graduates most significantly contributed to this geographical difference, and the rate of higher education was inversely associated with the prevalence of caries. On the other hand, the association with dentistry-related indicators was weak. A study examining the life course trajectory of caries inequalities revealed inequalities in children aged 1.5–2.5 years, which widened following the growth of these children until 5.5 years of age at the end of the follow-up [10]. Caries inequalities in school-age children have also been reported [12, 13]. An ecological study reported that higher income level was associated with lower caries experience [12].

Inequalities in dental diseases among adults have also been reported. In a cross-sectional study involving 15,803 Japanese adults by Morita et al. [14], nonprofessionals were at significantly higher risk for periodontal disease than professionals, even after the data were adjusted for age, diabetes history, and smoking history. When professionals were scored as 1, the relative risk for other occupational groups were: drivers, 2.0 times; workers in service industries, 1.5 times; salespersons, 1.4 times; managers, 1.4 times. A cohort study also confirmed inequalities in periodontal disease related to occupation [15]. Such occupational "social gradients" can be also found in other oral health indicators. Similarly, in a study investigating caries experience in 16,261 adults, the condition of oral cavities was better in professionals, managers, and businesspersons than in workers in service industries and drivers [16].

The number of remaining teeth in older adults can be considered the result of experience with dental diseases and access to dental care throughout life. Aida et al. [17] reported that educational background—an index of socioeconomic status at a younger age—was significantly associated with dental status (remaining teeth) in older people even after adjustment for covariates. Interestingly, other studies have shown that not only individual income, but also community income levels, were associated with inequalities in having no teeth (edentulousness) [18].

3   New Viewpoint on Health Inequalities

The phrase "health inequality" evokes the image "the most deprived people have the poorest health condition." However, health inequalities are not only a problem for the deprived, but also for the nondeprived. Nevertheless, health inequality has emerged as a "social gradient," with a stepwise difference in health according to socioeconomic status. Here, recent viewpoints regarding health inequalities are introduced.

When considering the causes of differences in health among individuals, there are two viewpoints: compositional effects based on differences in members (because there is a group consisting mostly of individuals in poor health, and another consisting mostly of those in good health, health inequalities among groups are observed); and contextual effects based on differences in social circumstances (because some groups live under social circumstances that cause poor health and others that are not affected by such environments, health inequalities arise). Social epidemiological studies using multilevel analyses have enabled us to distinguish compositional effects and contextual effects. For example, a study involving older Japanese adults determined individual and community-level income inequalities in edentulousness [18]. There was an individual-level social gradient: participants with lower incomes had a higher risk for edentulousness. Multilevel analysis also determined the association between community-level income (adjusted for individual-level income) and other covariates: regardless of individual-level income, income levels in communities were also associated with the possibility of edentulousness. This study suggested that dental status is partially determined by where individuals live because it is affected by the community social environment. As such, not only individual income, but also community income levels cause health inequalities.

Multilevel studies have suggested that an individual's health is determined not only by individual characteristics but also community-level environments. Individuals living in poorer areas possibly become poorer in health even if they are economically affluent. For example, an individual living in a poor area, where there are few dentists, may find it difficult to receive dental care. Other community-level environmental factors, such as social capital [19], income inequality [20], accessibility to grocery stores [21], and fluoride concentration in municipal water [22], have been reported to be associated with dental health. Therefore, health inequalities are an issue—not only for individuals—but society as a whole.

4   Causes of Oral Health Inequalities

Four theoretical models have been proposed to explain how social determinants influence inequalities in dental disease [23]. First, the "materialist explanation" posits that the availability of foods and medical services varies according to socioeconomic conditions, especially income. Second, the "cultural/behavioral explanation" is a model in which health behavior and culture, such as smoking, alcohol use, dietary habits, and tooth brushing, vary according to social strata, which leads to health inequalities. Third, in the "psychosocial perspective," individuals in a lower social stratum experience various stresses: in the "direct model," physiological mechanisms caused by stress increase the incidence of disease; and in the "indirect model," increased smoking, alcohol use, and intake of sweet foods caused by stress increase the incidence of disease. Fourth, the "life course perspective" is a model in which factors related to the previous three explanations accumulate throughout life and affect health and disease in later life. The "accumulation model" describes health influences that gradually accumulate throughout life, while the "critical period model" targets the importance of a particular time point; for example, when one's lifestyle changes completely by leaving home in adolescence to begin a new phase of life living alone. Both models are supported by empirical research investigating dental diseases. In a cohort study from New Zealand by Poulton et al. [24], 980 individuals were followed for 26 years to examine the association between socioeconomic conditions and general and oral health index at two key time points in childhood and adulthood. Participants who experienced poor socioeconomic conditions during childhood exhibited poorer general and oral health at 26 years of age. In comparing subjects in various socioeconomic conditions at the two time points, those with a higher socioeconomic position in childhood and a lower socioeconomic position in adulthood exhibited better dental health than those who were of lower socioeconomic status in childhood and higher socioeconomic status in adulthood. In other words, a lifestyle acquired in childhood may be difficult to change and may become greatly influential in subsequent years.

5 How to Tackle Oral Health Inequalities

5.1 Social Determinants and Population Strategy

Even if evidence-based methods are used, health inequalities cannot be eliminated unless social determinants are considered. Interventions primarily depend on the efforts of individuals which fail to improve health inequalities. Such interventions are usually more beneficial for healthy individuals who experience good social conditions and are at lower risk of disease, while those at higher risk of disease may find it difficult to benefit from these interventions. This issue is well known as the "inverse care law" or "inverse prevention law" [25, 26]. For example, an intervention through dental health education in 5-year-old children in the United Kingdom improved the oral health of those with higher socioeconomic status; however, oral health did not improve among those with lower socioeconomic status [27].

From this perspective, a population strategy that affects the entire population in a community or group is required [28, 29]. Fluoride application is a well-known preventive measure for dental caries throughout the world [30]. If it is applied only in dental clinics, the benefit reaches only those who can afford to visit a clinic. However, if fluoride is used in community/municipal water fluoridation, the fluoride concentration in tap water is adjusted to the same level as green tea (approximately 1 mg/L). All residents of areas where fluoridation has been established can receive benefits regardless of social condition, and health inequalities in dental caries are, therefore, reduced [31, 32]. The World Health Organization published a book summarizing public health programs that reduce health inequalities, including a chapter on oral health [33, 34]. Several measures, such as water fluoridation, smoking regulations, and removal of taxes for oral health products, were introduced. School-based health interventions can also be a population strategy for students. In the Philippines, the "Fit for School" program offers general and oral health interventions, including soap for hand washing and fluoride toothpaste for brushing, to students of public elementary schools [35].

5.2   Reducing Dental Caries Inequalities in Japan

Although water fluoridation is not established in Japan, school-based fluoride mouth-rinsing programs have been conducted as a population strategy since 1970 [36]. It is a gargling method that is conducted once per week at school using mouth rinse solution containing almost the same concentration of fluoride as fluoride toothpaste (Fluoride concentration = 900 mg/L). To reduce the risk for excessive intake of fluoride in preschool children, a mouth-rinse liquid with a lower concentration of fluoride (approximately 250 mg/L) is used five times per week. This school-based program enables all students to receive the benefits of fluoride regardless of socioeconomic status or attitude of caregivers.

School-based fluoride mouth-rinse programs reduce both caries and caries inequalities [12]. In Niigata Prefecture, fluoride mouth rinsing was launched in elementary schools for the first time in Japan in 1970, and its rate of dissemination has gradually increased [36]. Recently, 12-year-old children in Niigata Prefecture had the lowest rate of dental caries in 47 prefectures in Japan, although caries levels in Niigata among 3-year-old children before starting the mouth-rinse program ranked in the middle. In Japan, most toothpastes contain fluoride; however, the use of fluoride toothpaste is believed to be affected by socioeconomic status and the knowledge of children's caregivers. In contrast, school-based fluoride programs can overcome these types of barriers and reach all students. As a result, inequalities in caries have been reduced [12].

5.3   Overcoming Opposition and Building a Healthy Society

Generally, there is much opposition to public health interventions such as tobacco regulations [37], vaccination programs [38], and the use of fluoride for public health [39]. Gray [40] pointed out that if the magnitude of a health problem is large (many are affected), the strength of opposition to public health intervention is larger. Because public health interventions to reduce health inequalities require changes in social determinants that work as a population strategy, large numbers of individuals become concerned about the intervention(s) and opposition tends to become larger.

To overcome opposition, it is the responsibility of scientists not only to provide empirical evidence, but also to communicate with society [39, 41]. In the Ottawa Charter on health promotion, "Enable," "Mediate," and "Advocate" were described as the core activities [42–44]. Scientists need to advocate evidence to mediate conflict among groups to enable public health interventions. In the United States, following these efforts, the number of individuals with access to water fluoridation increased from 5.1 million in 1951 to 211.4 million in 2014 [39].

In Japan, school-based fluoride mouth-rinse programs have gradually increased since 1970. In addition to positions on fluoride, collaboration between the health and education sectors is also one of the barriers to implementing the program. To promote the dissemination of this method, the Ministry of Health, Labour and Welfare in Japan issued the "Fluoride mouth rinsing guidelines" in 2003. As a result of continuous efforts, a total of 7479 schools and 777,596 children participated in the program in 2010 [36]. Fluoride mouth rinsing in schools is performed after informed consent is received from caregivers. In elementary schools in Date City, Hokkaido, the rate of participation in mouth rinsing gradually increased from 87% in 1990 to 97% in 2005 [45]. The majority of guardians recognized the significance of the program, thanks to appropriate explanations based on scientific evidence.

6   Summary

Dental diseases are prevalent, and inequalities exist from children to older adults. To reduce oral health inequalities, population strategies aimed at changing social determinants are required. Decision making regarding changes in social determinants is the responsibility of residents and politicians. Therefore, scientists and healthcare professionals must provide and advocate scientific evidence supporting these interventions to reduce inequalities in oral health.

References

1. Marcenes W, Kassebaum NJ, Bernabe E, Flaxman A, Naghavi M, Lopez A, et al. Global burden of oral conditions in 1990-2010: a systematic analysis. J Dent Res. 2013;92:592–7.
2. Disease GBD, Injury I, Prevalence C. Global, regional, and national incidence, prevalence, and years lived with disability for 310 diseases and injuries, 1990-2015: a systematic analysis for the global burden of disease study 2015. Lancet. 2016;388:1545–602.
3. Schwendicke F, Dorfer CE, Schlattmann P, Page LF, Thomson WM, Paris S. Socioeconomic inequality and caries: a systematic review and meta-analysis. J Dent Res. 2015;94:10–8.
4. Boillot A, El Halabi B, Batty GD, Range H, Czernichow S, Bouchard P. Education as a predictor of chronic periodontitis: a systematic review with meta-analysis population-based studies. PLoS One. 2011;6:e21508.
5. Schuch HS, Peres KG, Singh A, Peres MA, Do LG. Socioeconomic position during life and periodontitis in adulthood: a systematic review. Community Dent Oral Epidemiol. 2017;45:201–8.
6. Seerig LM, Nascimento GG, Peres MA, Horta BL, Demarco FF. Tooth loss in adults and income: systematic review and meta-analysis. J Dent. 2015;43:1051–9.
7. Barbato PR, Peres KG. Contextual socioeconomic determinants of tooth loss in adults and elderly: a systematic review. Rev Bras Epidemiol. 2015;18:357–71.
8. Aida J, Ando Y, Aoyama H, Tango T, Morita M. An ecological study on the association of public dental health activities and sociodemographic characteristics with caries prevalence in Japanese 3-year-old children. Caries Res. 2006;40:466–72.
9. Kato H, Tanaka K, Shimizu K, Nagata C, Furukawa S, Arakawa M, et al. Parental occupations, educational levels, and income and prevalence of dental caries in 3-year-old Japanese children. Environ Health Prev Med. 2017;22:80.

10. Aida J, Matsuyama Y, Tabuchi T, Komazaki Y, Tsuboya T, Kato T, et al. Trajectory of social inequalities in the treatment of dental caries among preschool children in Japan. Community Dent Oral Epidemiol. 2017;45:407–12.

11. Aida J, Matsuyama Y, Koyama S, Sato Y, Ueno M, Tsuboya T, et al. Oral health and social determinants – oral health inequality and social determinants of oral health. In: Fukai K, editor. The current evidence of dental care and oral health for achieving healthy longevity in an aging society. Tokyo: Japan Dental Association; 2015. p. 216–34.

12. Matsuyama Y, Aida J, Taura K, Kimoto K, Ando Y, Aoyama H, et al. School-based fluoride mouth-rinse program dissemination associated with decreasing dental caries inequalities between Japanese prefectures: an ecological study. J Epidemiol. 2016;26:563–71.

13. Aida J, Ando Y, Yanagisawa T. Oral health inequalities through life-stages among Japanese: a study linking the survey of dental diseases and comprehensive survey of living conditions. J Dent Health. 2016;66:458–64. (In Japanese).

14. Morita I, Nakagaki H, Yoshii S, Tsuboi S, Hayashizaki J, Igo J, et al. Gradients in periodontal status in Japanese employed males. J Clin Periodontol. 2007;34:952–6.

15. Irie K, Yamazaki T, Yoshii S, Takeyama H, Shimazaki Y. Is there an occupational status gradient in the development of periodontal disease in Japanese workers? A 5-year prospective cohort study. J Epidemiol. 2017;27:69–74.

16. Morita I, Nakagaki H, Yoshii S, Tsuboi S, Hayashizaki J, Mizuno K, et al. Is there a gradient by job classification in dental status in Japanese men? Eur J Oral Sci. 2007;115:275–9.

17. Aida J, Hanibuchi T, Nakade M, Hirai H, Osaka K, Kondo K. The different effects of vertical social capital and horizontal social capital on dental status: a multilevel analysis. Soc Sci Med. 2009;69:512–8.

18. Ito K, Aida J, Yamamoto T, Otsuka R, Nakade M, Suzuki K, et al. Individual- and community-level social gradients of edentulousness. BMC Oral Health. 2015;15:34.

19. Koyama S, Aida J, Saito M, Kondo N, Sato Y, Matsuyama Y, et al. Community social capital and tooth loss in Japanese older people: a longitudinal cohort study. BMJ Open. 2016;6:e010768.

20. Aida J, Kondo K, Kondo N, Watt RG, Sheiham A, Tsakos G. Income inequality, social capital and self-rated health and dental status in older Japanese. Soc Sci Med. 2011;73:1561–8.

21. Aida J, Ando Y, Oosaka M, Niimi K, Morita M. Contributions of social context to inequality in dental caries: a multilevel analysis of Japanese 3-year-old children. Community Dent Oral Epidemiol. 2008;36:149–56.

22. Do LG, Ha DH, Spencer AJ. Factors attributable for the prevalence of dental caries in Queensland children. Community Dent Oral Epidemiol. 2015;43:397–405.

23. Sisson KL. Theoretical explanations for social inequalities in oral health. Community Dent Oral Epidemiol. 2007;35:81–8.

24. Poulton R, Caspi A, Milne BJ, Thomson WM, Taylor A, Sears MR, et al. Association between children's experience of socioeconomic disadvantage and adult health: a life-course study. Lancet. 2002;360:1640–5.

25. Adams J, White M. Are the stages of change socioeconomically distributed? A scoping review. Am J Health Promot. 2007;21:237–47.

26. Hart JT. The inverse care law. Lancet. 1971;1:405–12.

27. Schou L, Wight C. Does dental health education affect inequalities in dental health? Community Dent Health. 1994;11:97–100.

28. Watt RG. From victim blaming to upstream action: tackling the social determinants of oral health inequalities. Community Dent Oral Epidemiol. 2007;35:1–11.

29. Aida J. Challenges in reducing oral health inequalities in Asia–Pacific. Nature India special issue 2017; Oral Health Inequalities & Health Systems in Asia-Pacific: S7–S8.

30. FDI World Dental Federation. Promoting oral health through fluoride: adopted by the FDI General Assembly: August 2017, Madrid, Spain. Int Dent J. 2018;68:16–7.

31. Riley JC, Lennon MA, Ellwood RP. The effect of water fluoridation and social inequalities on dental caries in 5-year-old children. Int J Epidemiol. 1999;28:300–5.

32. Kim HN, Kim JH, Kim SY, Kim JB. Associations of community water fluoridation with caries prevalence and oral health inequality in children. Int J Environ Res Public Health. 2017;14:E631.
33. Blas E, Kurup AS. Equity, social determinants and public health programmes. Geneva: WHO; 2010.
34. Petersen PE, Kwan S. Equity, social determinants and public health programmes - the case of oral health. Community Dent Oral Epidemiol. 2011;39:481.
35. Monse B, Benzian H, Naliponguit E, Belizario V, Schratz A, van Palenstein Helderman W. The fit for school health outcome study - a longitudinal survey to assess health impacts of an integrated school health programme in the philippines. BMC Public Health. 2013;13:256.
36. Komiyama K, Kimoto K, Taura K, Sakai O. National survey on school-based fluoride mouth-rinsing programme in Japan: regional spread conditions from preschool to junior high school in 2010. Int Dent J. 2014;64:127–37.
37. Ferriman A. Vilified for tackling tobacco. BMJ. 2000;320:1482.
38. Tanaka Y, Ueda Y, Yoshino K, Kimura T. History repeats itself in Japan: failure to learn from rubella epidemic leads to failure to provide the hpv vaccine. Hum Vaccin Immunother. 2017;13:1859–60.
39. Allukian M Jr, Carter-Pokras OD, Gooch BF, Horowitz AM, Iida H, Jacob M, et al. Science, politics, and communication: the case of community water fluoridation in the US. Ann Epidemiol. 2018;28:401–10.
40. Gray M. Evidence-based healthcare and public health: how to practice and teach evidence-based decision making. 3rd ed. Edinburgh; New York, NY: Churchill Livingstone; 2008. p. 303–32.
41. Weed DL, Mink PJ. Roles and responsibilities of epidemiologists. Ann Epidemiol. 2002;12:67–72.
42. WHO. Ottawa charter on health promotion. Geneva: World Health Organization; 1986.
43. Saan H, Wise M. Enable, mediate, advocate. Health Promot Int. 2011;26(Suppl 2):ii187–93.
44. Kokeny M. Ottawa revisited: 'enable, mediate and advocate'. Health Promot Int. 2011;26(Suppl 2):ii180–2.
45. Hatakeyama Y, Katada S, Shinohara T, Honda O, Tange T. Effect of continuous implementation of fluoride mouth rinse program in elementary school in date city. J Hokkaido Dent Assoc. 2007:157–9. (In Japanese).

Open Access This chapter is licensed under the terms of the Creative Commons Attribution-NonCommercial-NoDerivatives 4.0 International License (http://creativecommons.org/licenses/by-nc-nd/4.0/), which permits any noncommercial use, sharing, distribution and reproduction in any medium or format, as long as you give appropriate credit to the original author(s) and the source, provide a link to the Creative Commons licence and indicate if you modified the licensed material. You do not have permission under this licence to share adapted material derived from this chapter or parts of it.

The images or other third party material in this chapter are included in the chapter's Creative Commons licence, unless indicated otherwise in a credit line to the material. If material is not included in the chapter's Creative Commons licence and your intended use is not permitted by statutory regulation or exceeds the permitted use, you will need to obtain permission directly from the copyright holder.

Chapter 15
Healthy Aging: IADL and Functional Disability

Masashige Saito

1 Introduction

Extension of healthy life expectancy is an important topic in Japanese healthy aging policy, which has already achieved extended life expectancy. In 2013, there was about a 9-year gap between life expectancy and healthy life expectancy among men, and a 13-year gap of them among women. Although the definition of healthy life expectancy is diverse, one definition is measured by a period that has not seen the onset of functional disability in public long-term care certification, or that has independence in instrumental activities of daily living (IADL; a higher-living functional capacity of older adults). About 18% of older adults were certified for long-term care/support needs, and the number was about 5.9 million people (as of 2014).

Many studies indicate that the ability to conduct IADL, the onset of functional disability, and death are intimately related to not only lifestyles and health behaviors, but also to socioeconomic situations. While several systematic reviews focusing on the daily functions of older adults exist [1–3], overseas findings are not necessarily applicable to Japan because of genetic, environmental, and cultural factors. There is thus a need to review findings on older adults in Japan. Longitudinal studies are needed when doing so because there is a bidirectional relationship between health and other variables (for example, the unhealthier one is, the harder it is to acquire income; the poorer one is, the easier it is to become unhealthy). As opposed to cross-sectional studies, which are based on synchronic data, longitudinal studies trace individuals. Furthermore, considering that there are few cases in which

Masashige Saito is also the English translator for this chapter.

M. Saito (✉)
Department of Social Welfare, Faculty of Social Welfare, Nihon Fukushi University, Mihama, Japan
e-mail: masa-s@n-fukushi.ac.jp

© The Author(s) 2020
K. Kondo (ed.), *Social Determinants of Health in Non-communicable Diseases*,
Springer Series on Epidemiology and Public Health,
https://doi.org/10.1007/978-981-15-1831-7_15

individuals incur functional disabilities or die when tracked for only a few years, it is preferable to conduct large-scale baseline surveys to acquire more robust data.

The number of studies based on large-scale epidemiological surveys in Japan has increased in recent years. The Japan Epidemiological Association website introduces 16 studies, each of which track over 10,000 people for longer than 5 years (as of April 2018). A search for articles based on longitudinal studies discussing the health and life functions of older adults in Japan[1] revealed 53 studies in Japanese and 212 in English. These were narrowed down to those covering 10,000 or more people, review papers and articles that discussed specific diseases and medical treatments were excluded, and hand-searching was added to give a set of 48 articles. This set was reduced to 34 articles after excluding those covering depressive symptoms, falls, and dementia outcomes, which are discussed in another chapter. This chapter provides an overview of the findings of these articles with large-scale longitudinal research on Japanese older adults that discussed factors relating to their IADL, functional disability levels, and mortality.

2 Overview of Large-Scale Longitudinal Studies

The outcomes covered by the articles were as follows: death (20 articles), functional disability (16 articles), and IADL (2 articles). The primary explanatory variables were classified as follows: mental health and psychological well-being [4, 5], health behaviors (e.g., smoking and obesity) [6–11], oral function/dental status [12–14], socioeconomic status (SES) [15–23], social participation [24–29], social network and social support [30–36], and others [37] (Table 15.1).

The Japan Gerontological Evaluation Study, from which approximately 80% of the articles are derived, is a research project that aims to create a scientific foundation for preventative policies that seek to create a healthy aging and long-living society (principal investigator: Katsunori Kondo, Professor, Chiba University). Since 2003, the self-administered postal survey has worked with municipalities to survey (through a questionnaire) tens of thousands of older individuals without certified functional disabilities. The response rate was 60–70% (there were approximately 13,000 responses in 2003, 40,000 in 2006, and over 100,000 from 2010 onward, see Fig. 15.1). The survey also included prospective cohort data that enabled understanding of the subsequent outcomes (e.g., death and functional disability level) based on information regarding public long-term care insurance records. At the same time, the survey is also notable for simultaneously collecting

---

[1] For Japanese language journals, The National Diet Library Online Search and Request Service was used to search for the terms "高齢者AND コホート研究" (kōreisha AND kōhōto kenkyū; "elderly AND cohort study") and "高齢者AND 縦断研究 AND 健康" (kōreisha AND jūdan kenkyū AND kenkō; "elderly AND longitudinal study AND health"). For English language journals, PubMed was used to search for "older Japanese AND cohort study" and "Japanese AND cohort study AND older."

Table 15.1 Main results of associated factors with functional disability or mortality

Articles	Data	Explanatory variables	Outcome	Main results
Mental health and psychological well-being				
Nishi et al. [4][a]	2003–2007 cohort (n = 14,668)	Self-rated health (SRH)	Mortality	Fair/poor self-rated health was a stronger predictor of mortality in both sexes (HR = 1.67, 95% CI: 1.35–2.07).
Wada et al. [5][a]	2003–2007 cohort (n = 14,286)	GDS (short version)	Mortality and functional disability	Compared to older adults with nondepressive symptoms, depressive people were 1.26 times higher for functional disability, and 1.33 times higher for mortality than nondepressive.
Health behavior				
Iso et al. [6]	1989–1999 cohort (n = 94,683) including <65 years	Smoking cessation	Mortality	The multivariate relative risks for current smokers compared with never smokers were 1.41 (95% CI: 1.19–1.67) in older men, 1.69 (95% CI: 1.32–2.15) in older women for mortality from total cardiovascular disease.
Sakata et al. [7]	1963 to 1992–2008 cohort (n = 67,973) including <65 years	Smoking	Mortality	Current smokers compared with never smokers were 1.47 (95% CI: 1.41–1.52) among those born before 1920, 1.84 (95% CI: 1.74–1.96) among those born during 1920–1945 for all-cause mortality.
Tamakoshi et al. [8]	1988–2003 cohort (n = 26,747)	BMI	Mortality	The underweight group was associated with a statistically higher risk of all-cause mortality; 1.78-fold (95% CI: 1.45–2.20) and 2.55-fold (95% CI: 2.13–3.05) increase in mortality risk among severest thin men and women (BMI: <16.0), respectively.
Nakade et al. [9][a]	2003–2007 cohort (n = 14,931)	BMI	Mortality	Among low income group, hazard ratios for mortality by all causes was 1.96 (95% CI: 1.02–3.73) for overweight.
Yamazaki et al. [10]	1999–2009 cohort (n = 13,280)	BMI	Mortality	Compared with normal-weight participants, overweight/obese participants tended to have lower hazard ratios; the multivariate hazard ratios were 0.86 (95% CI: 0.62–1.19) for obesity, 0.83 (95% CI: 0.73–0.94) for overweight, and 1.60 (95% CI: 1.40–1.82) for underweight.

(continued)

Table 15.1 (continued)

Articles	Data	Explanatory variables	Outcome	Main results
Tomata et al. [11]	2006–2011 cohort ($n = 14,260$)	Dietary pattern	Functional disability	Japanese pattern as one of three dietary patterns was associated with a lower risk of incident functional disability (HR = 0.77; 95% CI: 0.68–0.88). An animal food pattern and a high dairy pattern tended to have a higher risk of incident functional disability.
Oral function/dental status				
Hayasaka et al. [12]	2006–2010 cohort ($n = 21,730$)	Dental care	Mortality	Participants who practiced all three types of oral care (brushed teeth two or more times per day, had dental visits at least once a year, or used dentures) was 0.54 (95% CI: 0.45–0.64) times lower for mortality than participants who practiced none of the three.
Sato et al. [13][a]	2010–2013 panel ($n = 62,333$)	Tooth loss	IADL	IPW models estimated the increment in TMIG-IC score ($\beta = 0.170$, 95% CI: 0.114–0.227) if edentulous participants gained 20 or more natural teeth.
Matsuyama et al. [14][a]	2010–2013 cohort ($n = 85,161$)	Tooth loss	Functional disability	Among the participants aged ≥ 85 years old, those with ≥ 20 teeth had a longer life expectancy (men: +57 days; women: +15 days) and healthy life expectancy (men: +92 days; women: +70 days).
Socio-economic status				
Kondo N. et al. [15][a]	2003–2007 cohort ($n = 7673$)	Relative income	Functional disability	The hazard ratio of incident physical/cognitive disability per one standard deviation increase in relative deprivation ranged from 1.13 (95% CI: 0.99–1.29) to 1.15 (95% CI: 1.01–1.31) in men.
Hirai et al. [16][a]	2003–2006 cohort ($n = 22,829$)	Household income	Mortality and functional disability	Using governmental administrative data, comparing the lowest to the highest income level were 3.50 for men and 2.48 for women for mortality and 3.71 for men and 2.27 for women for loss of healthy life.

(continued)

Table 15.1 (continued)

Articles	Data	Explanatory variables	Outcome	Main results
Kondo K. et al. [17][a]	2003–2007 cohort (n = 14,652)	Income and education	Mortality and functional disability	In men, significant health inequalities were observed between the highest income group and lowest one (HR: 1.55–1.75), and between the highest educational attainment group and lowest one (HR = 1.45–1.97).
Kondo N. et al. [18][a]	2003–2007 cohort (n = 16,023)	Relative income	Mortality	1 SD unit increase in income deprivation relative to others was associated with increased death hazard in men (HR = 1.20, 95% CI: 1.06–1.36) and in women (HR = 1.17, 95% CI: 0.97–1.41).
Saito M. et al. [19][a]	2003–2007 cohort (n = 13,310)	Poverty, social isolation, etc.	Mortality	Those with simultaneously relative poverty and social isolation and/or social inactivity were 1.29 times more likely to die prematurely than those who were not socially excluded.
Kondo N. et al. [20][a]	2003–2007 cohort (n = 21,031)	Relative income	Cause-specific mortality	The HR for death from cardiovascular diseases per SD increase in relative deprivation was 1.50 (95% CI: 1.09–2.08) in men, whereas HRs for mortality by cancer and other diseases were close to the null value.
Tani et al. [21][a]	2010–2013 cohort (n = 15,449)	Childhood SES	Mortality	Compared with men growing up in more advantaged childhood socioeconomic circumstances, the age-adjusted HR for men from low childhood SES backgrounds was 0.75 (95% CI: 0.56–1.00). This association was stronger among men aged 75 years or older.
Murayama et al. [22][a]	2010–2013 panel (n = 11,601)	Childhood SES	IADL	Childhood SES was independently associated with functional decline in the older cohort. In the 75–79 years group, lower childhood SES was associated with functional decline.

(continued)

Table 15.1 (continued)

Articles	Data	Explanatory variables	Outcome	Main results
Inoue et al. [23][a]	2003–2013 cohort (*n* = 12,290)	Month of birth	Mortality	Men born in December were more likely to die earlier (14%) while those born in January had lower mortality (10%). Time period when a birth is officially registered might be reflected in socioeconomic factors in early life.
Social participation				
Hirai et al. [24][a]	2003–2006 cohort (*n* = 12,031)	Social participation, SES, etc.	Functional disability	In both sexes, frequency of going out, frequency of contact with friends, social participation were significantly related to onset of certification of long-term care insurance.
Ueshima et al. [25]	1999–2006 cohort (*n* = 10,385)	Physical activities	Mortality	Physical activity was associated with a reduced risk of all-cause and CVD mortality. The HRs among participants with 5 or more days of nonexercise physical activity per week and those with pre-existing disease were 0.38 (95% CI: 0.22–0.55) and 0.35 (95% CI: 0.24–0.52), respectively.
Kanamori et al. [26][a]	2003–2007 cohort (*n* = 11,581)	Sports activity	Functional disability	Compared to the active participant group, the exercise alone group had HR of 1.29 (95% CI: 1.02–1.64) for incident functional disability. No significant difference was seen with the passive participant group.
Kanamori et al. [27][a]	2003–2007 cohort (*n* = 12,951)	Social participation	Functional disability	Compared to nonparticipants, the HR was 0.83 (95% CI: 0.73–0.95) for participation in one, 0.72 (95% CI: 0.61–0.85) for in two, and 0.57 (95% CI: 0.46–0.70) for in three or more different types of organizations.
Ishikawa et al. [28][a]	2003–2008 cohort (*n* = 14,286)	Social participation	Mortality	Relative to regular members, the IPTW-HR for all-cause mortality was 0.88 (95% CI: 0.79–0.99) for participants occupying leadership positions (e.g. president, manager, or having administrative roles).

(continued)

Table 15.1 (continued)

Articles	Data	Explanatory variables	Outcome	Main results
Ashida et al. [29][a]	2003–2007 cohort (*n* = 12,991)	Social participation	Functional disability	Participants in sports (HR = 0.66, 95% CI: 0.51–0.85) or hobby group (HR = 0.69, 95% CI: 0.55–0.87), or who had a group facilitator role (HR = 0.82, 95% CI: 0.66–1.02) were less likely to be disabled.
Social network and social support				
Aida et al. [30][a]	2003–2008 cohort (*n* = 14,668)	Social network	Mortality	Lower friendship network was significantly associated with higher all-cause mortality among men (HR = 1.30, 95% CI: 1.10–1.53) and women (HR = 1.81, 95% CI: 1.02–3.23).
Aida et al. [31][a]	2003–2007 cohort (*n* = 14,589)	Community-level social capital	Functional disability	Women living in communities with higher mistrust had 1.68 (95% CI: 1.14–2.49) times higher OR of onset of disability, even after adjusting for covariates.
Saito M. et al. [32][a]	2003–2007 cohort (*n* = 13,310)	Social isolation and satisfaction	Functional disability	The isolated older people were 1.34 (95% CI: 1.18–1.53) times more likely to develop functional disability. In men, satisfied isolation was associated with 1.27 (95% CI: 1.02–1.58) times higher risk of functional disability.
Saito M. et al. [33][a]	2003–2013 cohort (*n* = 12,085)	Social network	Mortality and functional disability	The hazard ratios for functional disability and premature death increase in those with contact frequency of "less than once a month" were 1.37 (95% CI: 1.16–1.61) and 1.34 (95% CI: 1.16–1.55), respectively.
Tani et al. [34][a]	2010–2013 cohort (*n* = 71,781)	Eating alone	Mortality	The HR were 1.48 (95% CI: 1.26–1.74) for men who ate alone yet lived with others. Among women, HR was 1.18 (95% CI: 0.97–1.43) who ate alone yet lived with others and 1.10 (95% CI: 0.93–1.29) who ate and lived alone.

(continued)

Table 15.1 (continued)

Articles	Data	Explanatory variables	Outcome	Main results
Saito T. et al. [35][a]	2003–2013 cohort (n = 13,460)	Household	Functional disability	Men living only with nonspousal cohabitants and those living alone were more likely to develop disability. Social support exchange explained 24.4% and 15.8% of the excess risk of disability onset in those men.
Murata et al. [36][a]	2003–2013 cohort (n = 14,088)	Social support	Functional disability	Social ties with co-residing family members, and those with friends or neighbors, independently protected functional health (HR = 0.81, 0.85) among men. Among women, ties with friend or neighbors had a stronger effect.
Others				
Tsuji et al. [37][a]	2011–2015 cohort (n = 72,127)	Functional disability risk scale	Functional disability	A risk assessment scale of 0–55 developed from the Kihon Checklist's 10 items (included in the Needs Survey's essential items) is useful for predicting the incidence of Needed Support/ Long-Term Care certification.

[a]From JAGES (AGES) longitudinal survey

panel data that individually compares cross-sectional data at certain intervals. Since 2010, the survey has expanded to cover more areas and has changed in name from AGES to JAGES (see website for details: https://www.jages.net/). In the 14 years from 2004 to 2017, the JAGES project has published 364 articles and books (267 in Japanese, 97 in English), including 55 papers based on longitudinal studies (including sub-projects).

3   Mental Health, Health Behavior, and Oral Functions

While subjective health indicators have been criticized as unreliable, large-scale Japanese longitudinal studies have found them to be important indicators for predicting future objective health. For example, regardless of age, chronic conditions, or disabilities at the baseline survey, both older men and women who stated that their health was poor had an approximately 1.7 higher risk of unmature death compared to those who answered that their health was good [4]. Furthermore, individuals with depression were found to have a 1.26 higher risk of functional disability and a 1.33 times higher mortality risk [5].

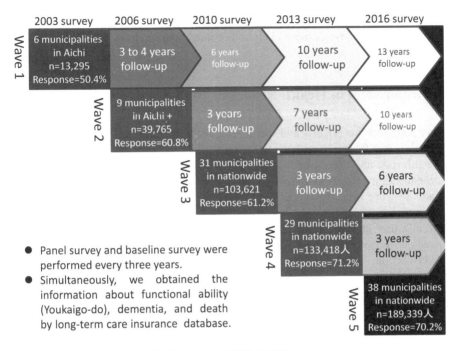

Fig. 15.1 Overview of longitudinal survey in JAGES (AGES)

Regarding health behaviors, older male smokers were found to have 1.41 times the risk of death due to cardiovascular disease compared to nonsmokers. For women, the risk was 1.69 times higher [6]. In addition, smokers in the pre-1920 birth cohort had 1.47 times the risk of death [7]. Regarding body mass index (BMI), some large-scale cohort studies have consistently shown that Japanese older adults have approximately 1.6–2.6 times the risk of subsequent death if obese or underweight [8, 10]. Regarding food, Japanese dietary habits may reduce subsequent functional disability risk (HR = 0.77; 95% CI: 0.68–0.88) [11].

Oral health indicators such as bite strength and number of teeth are closely related to subsequent healthy aging. For example, it has been reported that people without teeth were more likely to experience a significant IADL decline compared to people with 20 or more remaining teeth; this influence was nearly equal to having a history of stroke [13]. The risk of death for older adults who brushed their teeth two or more times per day, visited the dentist at least once per year, or used dentures was reported as being 0.54 times those who performed none of these activities [12]. Furthermore, men aged 85 years or older with 20 or more remaining teeth had an estimated lifespan of 92 days longer that those who did not, while women with the same characteristics lived an average of 70 days longer [14].

Although it analyzed fewer than 10,000 subjects, another study reported that those with 19 or fewer remaining teeth had 1.21 times the risk of functional disability onset [38] and 1.83 times the risk of death because of cardiovascular or respiratory disease [39]. In addition, young-old persons aged 65–74 with fewer than 20 remaining teeth were 1.78 times more likely to become housebound [40].

4 Differences in Health Risks Due to SES

It is a solid fact that poverty and social exclusion are one of the social determinants of health [41]. Research on Japanese older adults has found that low SES could be a health risk, and these trends are remarkable among men [41]. Older men with less education or income were found to have 1.6–2.0 times the risk of unmature death [17]. The same trend was also found in objective income data from levy cost in public long-term care insurance [16]. It has been reported that income that is low in either absolute terms or when compared to others creates psychosocial stress and becomes a risk for functional disability [15], overall death [18], and cardiovascular disease death [20]. Furthermore, research indicates that economic poverty in both old age and childhood increases the overall risk of death during old age [21] in addition to causing declines in IADL [22]. In other words, the influence of SES on health extends throughout the course of people's lives, suggesting the effectiveness of countermeasures that begin at a young age. It is also clear that the destruction of one's house or job loss resulting from natural disaster (e.g., the Great East Japan Earthquake) is connected to worsening IADL [42].

5 Differences in Health Risks Due to Social Participation and Social Networks

Social participation is an important element of successful aging. According to activity theory in social gerontology, older individuals who actively participate in society maintain a sense of happiness due to steady social relationships and increased opportunities to receive positive feedback from others. One would therefore expect that social participation protects older adult health; this has in fact been confirmed by some large-scale cohort studies. People who hold positions and participate in social organizations (e.g., residents' associations) have significantly lower subsequent risks of functional disability [29] and death [28], and there is a lower risk of death and functional disability among older individuals who participate in sports or physical activities [25–27]. In addition, an intervention study in Taketoyo Town, Aichi Prefecture, indicated that those who participated in community salon activities had more positive health self-assessments 2 years later than those who did not [43]. Their risk of functional disability was 51% lower [44], while their risk of functional disability involving dementia was approximately 30% lower [45].

Large-scale longitudinal studies have also found that having a poor social network (i.e., social isolation) is also a health risk. It has been reported that isolated older individuals had 1.3–1.8 times the risk of functional disability [32]. Reports have also indicated that contact with others less than once per week was a functional onset disability risk and that less than once per month was a mortality risk [33]. In addition, eating alone while living with someone else increased the risk of death for both men and women [34]. It has also been found that those who belonged to an infrequently meeting sports club had lower functional disability risks than those who frequently played sports alone [23]. This suggests that connecting with others is an important element for health. Studies focusing on social support (i.e., the functional side of social networks) have found that men and women without social support had 1.25 and 1.08 times the risk of functional disability, respectively [36]. While individuals in single-person households were more likely to have functional disabilities, social support could possibly reduce these risks by 25% [35].

Although individual-level social participation and social relationships are important, community-level social participation (social capital) is also associated with health among older adults. There have been efforts to develop a health-related community-level social capital instrument (comprised of three factors: civic participation, social cohesion, and reciprocity) [46]. For example, it has been found that even after adjusting for individual attributes, older women living in communities in which there is a 1% higher prevalence of the view that people cannot generally be trusted were 1.68 times more likely to receive functional disability certification [31]. Such studies suggest the importance of developing age-friendly community/cities in addition to individual interventions in healthcare and social welfare.

6 Summary

The proper handling of population aging is a global health problem that must be addressed for sustainable development. While a diverse set of issues must be addressed, one of the most important is healthy aging. In 2017, the World Health Organization released "10 Priorities for a Decade of Action on Healthy Ageing" [47], which presents a collection of high-quality data regarding healthy aging as a priority and points out the need for analytical reviews of current data sources to identify where gaps exist in measuring healthy aging over the life course.

As demonstrated in this review, large-scale studies of the older adults in Japan have found that, in addition to lifestyle, health behaviors, and medical history, the following items were also related to the healthy aging: mental health and psychological well-being, oral function/dental status, the up-stream factors of social participation, social networks/social support, educational attainment, income, income disparities, SES throughout one's life course, loss of living environment, and community-level social capital including civic participation, social cohesion, and reciprocity.

"Healthy Japan 21 (The Second Term)" [48], which established the basic policy for health promotion in Japan, discusses improving the quality of social environments as a way to increase healthy aging and decrease health disparities. The results of this review also suggest that along with approaches that focus on high-risk individuals, it is important to implement social policies that increase social capital, reduce socioeconomic disparities, construct environments that promote social participation and physical activity, and offer education to individuals from a young age (thus enabling anyone to develop their abilities without relying on household economic resources). However, with the exception of some, the articles considered in this review are observation studies, and there is a need to elucidate the mechanisms behind the discussed factors in addition to conducting intervention studies.

Acknowledgements This study was supported by Health Labour Sciences Research Grant (H29-chikyukibo-ippan-001) and grants (29-42) from the National Center for Gerontology and Geriatrics.

References

1. Stuck AE, Walthert JM, Nikolaus T, et al. Risk factors for functional status decline in community-level elderly people; a systematic literature review. Soc Sci Med. 1999;48(4):445–69.
2. Rodrigues MA, Facchini LA, Thumé E, et al. Gender and incidence of functional disability in the elderly: a systematic review. Cad Saude Publica. 2009;25(Suppl 3):S464–76.
3. Soares WJS, Lopes AD, Nogueira E, et al. Physical activity level and risk of falling in community-dwelling older adults: systematic review and meta-analysis. J Aging Phys Act. 2018;15:1–28.
4. Nishi A, Kawachi I, Shirai K, et al. Sex/gender and socioeconomic differences in the predictive ability of self-rated health for mortality. PLoS One. 2012;7(1):e30179.
5. Wada Y, Murata C, Hirai H, et al. AGES project data wo mochiita GDS5 no yosokuteki datousei ni kansuru kentou. J Health Welf Stat. 2014;61(11):7–12. (In Japanese).
6. Iso H, Date C, Yamamoto A, et al. Smoking cessation and mortality from cardiovascular disease among Japanese men and women: the JACC Study. Am J Epidemiol. 2005;161(2):170–9.
7. Sakata R, McGale P, Grant EJ. Impact of smoking on mortality and life expectancy in Japanese smokers: a prospective cohort study. BMJ. 2012;345:e7093.
8. Tamakoshi A, Yatsuya H, Lin Y, et al. BMI and all-cause mortality among Japanese older adults: findings from the Japan collaborative cohort study. Obesity. 2010;18(2):362–9.
9. Nakade M, Takagi D, Suzuki K, et al. Influence of socioeconomic status on the association between body mass index and cause-specific mortality among older Japanese adults: the AGES cohort study. Prev Med. 2015;77:112–8.
10. Yamazaki K, et al. Is there an obesity paradox in the Japanese elderly population? A community-based cohort study of 13 280 men and women. Geriatr Gerontol Int. 2017;17(9):1257–64.
11. Tomata Y, Watanabe T, Sugawara Y, et al. Dietary patterns and incident functional disability in elderly Japanese: the Ohsaki Cohort 2006 Study. J Gerontol A Biol Sci Med Sci. 2014;69(7):843–51.
12. Hayasaka K, Tomata Y, Aida J, et al. Tooth loss and mortality in elderly Japanese adults: effect of oral care. J Am Geriatr Soc. 2013;61(5):815–20.
13. Sato Y, Aida J, Kondo K, et al. Tooth loss and decline in functional capacity: a prospective cohort study from the Japan Gerontological Evaluation Study. J Am Geriatr Soc. 2016;64(11):2336–42.

14. Matsuyama Y, Aida J, Watt RG, et al. Dental status and compression of life expectancy with disability. J Dent Res. 2017;96(9):1006–13.
15. Kondo N, Kawachi I, Hirai H, et al. Relative deprivation and incident functional disability among older Japanese women and men: prospective cohort study. J Epidemiol Community Health. 2009;63(6):461–7.
16. Hirai H, Kondo K, Kawachi I. Social determinants of active aging: differences in mortality and the loss of healthy life between different Income levels among older Japanese in the AGES Cohort Study. Curr Gerontol Geriatr Res. 2012;2012:701583.
17. Kondo K, Ashida T, Hirai H, et al. The relationship between socio-economic status and the loss of health aging, and relevant gender differences in the Japanese older population; AGES project longitudinal study. Iryo Shakai. 2012;22(1):19–30. (In Japanese with English Abstract).
18. Kondo N, Kondo K, Yokomichi Y, et al. Relative deprivation in income and mortality in Japanese older adults; AGES cohort study. Iryo Syakai. 2012;22(1):91–101. (In Japanese with English Abstract).
19. Saito M, Kondo N, Kondo K, et al. Gender differences on the impacts of social exclusion on mortality among older Japanese: AGES cohort study. Soc Sci Med. 2012;75:940–5.
20. Kondo N, Saito M, Hikichi H, et al. Relative deprivation in income and mortality by leading causes among older Japanese men and women: AGES cohort study. J Epidemiol Community Health. 2015;69(7):680–5.
21. Tani Y, Kondo N, Nagamine Y, et al. Childhood socioeconomic disadvantage is associated with lower mortality in older Japanese men: the JAGES cohort study. Int J Epidemiol. 2016;45(4):1226–35.
22. Murayama H, Fujiwara T, Tani Y, et al. Long-term impact of childhood disadvantage on late-life functional decline among older Japanese: results from the JAGES prospective cohort study. J Gerontol A Biol Sci Med Sci. 2018;73(7):973–9. https://doi.org/10.1093/gerona/glx171.
23. Inoue Y, Stickley A, Yazawa A, et al. Month of birth is associated with mortality among older people in Japan; Findings from the JAGES cohort. Chronobiol Int. 2016;33(4):441–7.
24. Hirai H, Kondo K, Ojima T, et al. Examination of risk factors for onset of certification of long-term care insurance in community-dwelling older people: AGES project 3-year follow-up study. Jpn J Public Health. 2009;56(8):501–12. (In Japanese with English Abstract).
25. Ueshima K, Ishikawa-Takata K, Yorifuji T, et al. Physical activity and mortality risk in the Japanese elderly: a cohort study. Am J Prev Med. 2010;38(4):410–8.
26. Kanamori S, Kai Y, Kondo K, et al. Participation in sports organizations and the prevention of functional disability in older Japanese: the AGES cohort study. PLoS One. 2012;7(11):e51061.
27. Kanamori S, Kai Y, Aida J, et al. Social participation and the prevention of functional disability in older Japanese: the JAGES cohort study. PLoS One. 2014;9(6):e99638.
28. Ishikawa Y, Kondo N, Kondo K, et al. Social participation and mortality: does social position in civic groups matter? BMC Public Health. 2016;16(1):394.
29. Ashida T, Kondo N, Kondo K. Social participation and the onset of functional disability by socioeconomic status and activity type; the JAGES cohort study. Prev Med. 2016;89:121–8.
30. Aida J, Kondo K, Hirai H, et al. Assessing the association between all-cause mortality and multiple aspects of individual social capital among the older Japanese. BMC Public Health. 2011;11:499.
31. Aida J, Kondo K, Kawachi I, et al. Does social capital affect the incidence of functional disability in older Japanese? A prospective population-based cohort study. J Epidemiol Community Health. 2013;67:42–7.
32. Saito M, Kondo K, Ojima T, et al. Different association between the loss of healthy life expectancy and social isolation by life satisfaction among older people: a four-year follow-up study of AGES project. Jpn J Gerontol. 2013;35(3):331–41. (In Japanese with English Abstract).
33. Saito M, Kondo K, Ojima T, et al. Criteria for social isolation based on associations with health indicators among older people. A 10-year follow-up of the Aichi Gerontological Evaluation Study. Jpn J Public Health. 2015;62(3):95–105. (In Japanese with English Abstract).

34. Tani Y, Kondo N, Noma H, et al. Eating alone yet living with others is associated with mortality in older men: the JAGES cohort survey. J Gerontol B Psychol Sci Soc Sci. 2018;73(7):973–9. https://doi.org/10.1093/geronb/gbw211.
35. Saito T, Murata C, Aida J, et al. Cohort study on living arrangements of older men and women and risk for basic activities of daily living disability: findings from the AGES project. BMC Geriatr. 2017;17(1):183.
36. Murata C, Saito T, Tsuji T, et al. A 10-year follow-up study of social ties and functional health among the old: the AGES project. Int J Environ Res Public Health. 2017;14:717.
37. Tsuji T, Takagi D, Kondo N. Development of risk assessment scales for needed support/long-term care certification: a longitudinal study using the Kihon Checklist and medical assessment data. Jpn J Public Health. 2017;64(5):246–57. (In Japanese with English Abstract).
38. Aida J, Kondo K, Hirai H, et al. Association between dental status and incident disability in an older Japanese population. J Am Geriatr Soc. 2012;60(2):338–43.
39. Aida J, Kondo K, Yamamoto T, et al. Oral health and cancer, cardiovascular, and respiratory mortality of Japanese. J Dent Res. 2011;90(9):1129–35.
40. Koyama S, Aida J, Kondo K, et al. Does poor dental health predict becoming homebound among older Japanese? BMC Oral Health. 2016;16(1):51.
41. Wilkinson R, Marmot M. Social determinants of health: the solid facts. 2nd ed. København: WHO Regional Office for Europe; 2003.
42. Tsuboya T, Aida J, Hikichi H, et al. Predictors of decline in IADL functioning among older survivors following the Great East Japan Earthquake: a prospective study. Soc Sci Med. 2017;176:34–41.
43. Ichida Y, Hirai H, Kondo K, et al. Does social participation improve self-rated health in the older population? A quasi-experimental intervention study. Soc Sci Med. 2013;94:83–90.
44. Hikichi H, Kondo N, Kondo K, et al. Effect of community intervention program promoting social interactions on functional disability prevention for older adults; propensity score matching and instrumental variable analyses, JAGES Taketoyo study. J Epidemiol Community Health. 2015;69(9):905–10.
45. Hikichi H, Kondo K, Takeda T, et al. Social interaction and cognitive decline; results of a 7-year community intervention. Alzheimers Dement. 2017;3:23–32.
46. Saito M, Kondo N, Aida J, et al. Development of an instrument for community-level health related social capital among Japanese older people: the JAGES project. J Epidemiol. 2017;27(5):221–7.
47. WHO. 10 Priorities for a decade of action on healthy ageing. Geneva: WHO; 2017. Available at http://www.who.int/ageing/WHO-ALC-10-priorities.pdf.
48. Ministry of Health, Labour and Welfare. Kenkou Nihon 21 (dai 2 ji) no suisin ni kansuru sankoushiryo. Tokyo: Ministry of Health, Labour and Welfare; 2012. Available at http://www.mhlw.go.jp/bunya/kenkou/kenkounippon21.html. (In Japanese).

Open Access This chapter is licensed under the terms of the Creative Commons Attribution-NonCommercial-NoDerivatives 4.0 International License (http://creativecommons.org/licenses/by-nc-nd/4.0/), which permits any noncommercial use, sharing, distribution and reproduction in any medium or format, as long as you give appropriate credit to the original author(s) and the source, provide a link to the Creative Commons licence and indicate if you modified the licensed material. You do not have permission under this licence to share adapted material derived from this chapter or parts of it.

The images or other third party material in this chapter are included in the chapter's Creative Commons licence, unless indicated otherwise in a credit line to the material. If material is not included in the chapter's Creative Commons licence and your intended use is not permitted by statutory regulation or exceeds the permitted use, you will need to obtain permission directly from the copyright holder.

Chapter 16
Life Course Epidemiology

Toshiyuki Ojima and Katsunori Kondo

1 Definition of Life Course Epidemiology

Life course epidemiology is defined as "the study of long-term effects on later health or disease risk of physical or social exposures during gestation, childhood, adolescence, young adulthood, and later adult life" [1, 2]. This term has been used widely since the first edition of the book by Kuh and Ben-Shlomo was published in 1997. A similar term is "life course approach," which was used by psychologists, sociologists, demographers, anthropologists, and biologists for many years before being adopted in the field of epidemiology [1]. In Japan, Kondo [3] has discussed the use of the life course approach for some time.

One famous historical study is the fetal origins hypothesis, which was published by Barker et al. in 1986 [4]. From an ecological study of 220 regions in England, they found that the standardized mortality ratio for ischemic heart disease and bronchitis in adults between 1968 and 1978 was high in regions with high infant mortality between 1921 and 1925. These findings led them to speculate that undernutrition during gestation or infancy could cause the development of disease in adulthood. Even earlier in 1951, the World Health Organization published a report [5] by

Toshiyuki Ojima is also the English translator for this chapter.

T. Ojima (✉)
Department of Community Health and Preventive Medicine, Faculty of Medicine, Hamamatsu University School of Medicine, Hamamatsu, Japan
e-mail: ojima@hama-med.ac.jp

K. Kondo
Professor of Social Epidemiology and Health Policy, Department of Social Preventive Medical Sciences, Center for Preventive Medical Sciences, Chiba University, Chiba, Japan

Head of Department of Gerontological Evaluation, Center for Gerontology and Social Science, National Center for Geriatrics and Gerontology, Obu City, Aichi, Japan

© The Author(s) 2020
K. Kondo (ed.), *Social Determinants of Health in Non-communicable Diseases*,
Springer Series on Epidemiology and Public Health,
https://doi.org/10.1007/978-981-15-1831-7_16

Bowlby regarding the poor development of children after separation from their mother and placed in the care of an institution such as an orphanage (deprivation of maternal care). Although the term "life course" has only been used in recent years, the concept has existed for some time and relevant research has been conducted.

2 Significance and Recent Development

Life course epidemiology has recently gained increased attention, probably as a result of several factors. One is that the links between lifestyle habits during adulthood and subsequent lifestyle diseases have become well understood, so that understanding the factors preceding adulthood has become important for future research. Although it is still possible for people to change their lifestyle habits during adulthood, albeit with great effort, they cannot change the factors that impacted them during childhood or in utero, which are important social determinants of health. Life course epidemiology provides researchers with the capability to understand such factors. On that account, interventions in earlier life stages may be more cost effective than interventions in adult life to prevent noncommunicable diseases. Furthermore, life course epidemiology is gaining attention because it can bring researchers closer to understanding the causal associations and mechanisms of development of diseases. In other words, longitudinal studies from childhood would be useful to determine which factors are actual causes, confounding factors, or intermediate stages among various factors. Moreover, life course epidemiology can also be used to study biological factors jointly with socioeconomic factors.

Common study designs in life course epidemiology have included ecological studies and retrospective cohort studies. The results from prospective cohort studies that have tracked participants from birth are now starting to be published. Although we do not discuss the issue of study design in detail, we point out the analytical problems such as repeat observations, hierarchical data, latent exposures, and multiple interactive or small effects [1], as well as this emerging field with respect to factors such as developments in epidemiological research methodologies. Advances in computing capabilities that have made it easier to conduct complex statistical analyses, such as multilevel analysis (also called hierarchical linear modeling or latent growth modeling), have also driven the growth of life course epidemiology.

3 Basic Theories

Two types of conceptual model, as shown in Table 16.1, the critical period model and the accumulation of risk model, address why early life factors including in utero and childhood factors increase the risk for diseases during adulthood [6]. The critical period model postulates that certain periods in life have an important meaning. The simplest example of this model is that children whose mothers took thalidomide

Table 16.1 Life course conceptual models	Critical period model
	• Does/does not become a risk factor in adulthood
	• Becomes a modifying factor in adulthood
	Accumulation of risk
	• Caused by independent, noncorrelated factors
	• Caused by correlated factors
	−"Risk clustering"
	−"Chains of risk" caused by additive effects or a trigger effect

during a certain period of gestation developed phocomelia; no such danger exists if the mother takes thalidomide at any other time. In this example, phocomelia develops because exposure occurs during the period of in utero growth, when the structure of the limbs develops. Recent studies have shown that the same phenomenon occurs with function, and it is now believed that the in utero environment has a profound effect on shaping the functions related to metabolism and hormones. However, unlike the effects on structure, the effects on function can be changed even during adulthood. At a more detailed level, even if genes themselves are determined at conception, gene expression (epigenetics) later in life can also affect function [7]. A similar concept is "biological programming." It should be noted that the term "sensitive period," which is a similar concept to the critical period, is often used without clear differentiation. Strictly speaking, the "critical period" denotes that the effects of exposure appear only when the exposure occurs during that period and do not occur during any other period. The term "sensitive period" is used if the effects are more likely to appear during that period but can still occur during other periods. A slightly more complex mechanism within the critical period model is the influence of effect modifiers (interactions). For example, it is now known that low birth weight increases the risk of ischemic heart disease during adulthood in individuals who develop obesity in childhood or adulthood, but not in those who do not develop obesity. In addition, a better understanding of the interactions between social and biological factors is anticipated.

Another conceptual model is the accumulation of risk model. This model postulates that various factors gradually accumulate throughout life and cause diseases to develop in adulthood. This accumulation can arise from various independent factors that do not correlate with each other. For example, the factors of being involved in a car accident, incurring a job loss, and experiencing the death of a spouse may accumulate incidentally, leading to the onset of a disease. In another pattern called "risk clustering," various factors correlate with one another. For example, low birth weight, childhood undernutrition, secondhand smoke, and a low education level can overlap. Such factors likely arise from a common cause of low socioeconomic status (SES) during childhood. Another concept is "chains of risk," in which, for example, job loss could bring about financial difficulties, causing marital discord or domestic violence, subsequently leading to divorce. It is important to understand the chain of risk because intervening in the chain at some point can prevent the situation from deteriorating.

In the broader picture of life course epidemiology, it is important to consider intergenerational effects. The environments of the grandparental generation, the parental generation, and the generation of children and their siblings intertwine at the country level, the community level, and the household level. When a person is living far from their grandparents, they share only a country-level environment. On the other hand, community-level and household-level environments directly affect parents and their children, as well as children and their siblings. If time is added as a variable, various effects such as cohort effects from childhood and period effects common to three generations can intertwine. Although it is complex, life course epidemiology is an important and interesting field of research.

4   Research Results

Studies in life course epidemiology have revealed various findings, which are briefly summarized in the literature [8, 9]. In particular, factors such as low birth weight and low SES during childhood increase the risk of coronary artery disease, cerebral hemorrhage, and chronic obstructive pulmonary disease. Conversely, the risk of breast cancer increases when birth weight and SES during childhood are high. Reviews also summarize various risk factors for type 2 diabetes such as the increased risks associated with abnormally high or low birth weight.

Infectious diseases are another important topic in life course epidemiology [10]. For example, it is well known that hepatitis C infection increases the risk of hepatoma later in life and that varicella zoster infection during childhood can cause herpes zoster during adulthood.

Several studies have also been conducted in Japan. In a cohort study of adults, Tamakoshi et al. [11] examined maternity health records and found that low birth weight increased a person's susceptibility to hypertension in adulthood. Sekine et al. [12] followed a birth cohort in Toyama Prefecture until the subject's first year of high school and analyzed relationships with lifestyles in their health check-up data at the age of 3 years as baseline data. They revealed that having a large number of undesirable lifestyle habits such as skipping breakfast, physical inactivity, and long hours of watching television is associated with an increased risk of developing obesity in later life [12]. Suzuki et al. [13] followed a group of children from before birth to 10 years of age as Project Koshu and found that boys whose mothers smoked during pregnancy had a higher body mass index, but the same association was not observed in girls.

The Japan Gerontological Evaluation Study (JAGES) have published several papers that revealed relationships between childhood events or SES and health status in older years. Matsuyama et al. [14] reported that adverse childhood experiences

(ACEs) were significantly associated with fewer remaining teeth after adjusting for covariates (odds ratio = 1.14). Amemiya et al. [15] revealed that ACEs showed significantly greater higher-level functional limitation (prevalence ratio = 1.46, adjusting for age, sex, and childhood disadvantage). Moreover, Tani et al. [16] showed that low childhood SES was positively associated with depression onset (risk ratio = 1.44). Yanagi et al. [17] reported that older people with low childhood SES were 1.36 times more likely to have poor fruit and vegetable intake (FVI) than those with high childhood SES. They suggested that a school lunch program could help improve FVI because the relationship was not observed among people aged 65–69 years who were fully exposed to such a program [17].

In Japan, a couple of national projects on life course epidemiology are ongoing. The Ministry of Health, Labour and Welfare has been conducting the Longitudinal Survey of Newborns in the Twenty-First Century since 2001 and since 2010 [18]. The Ministry of the Environment has conducted the Japan Environment and Children's Study since 2011, involving 100,000 mother–child pairs living throughout Japan [19].

5   Future Outlook

The research results from life course epidemiology have started to be used for development of health policy. Through its Recommendations for the Control of Lifestyle-Related Diseases from Before Birth through Childhood, which summarize research findings from Japan and abroad, the Science Council of Japan advocates the importance of awareness and education on the health problems that can arise in adolescent and young women who are underweight, among other issues [20].

Although targeting lifestyle habits during adulthood plays a specific role in preventing adult diseases, it is difficult to substantially reduce the incidence of such diseases with that approach alone; it is important to target childhood influences, intergenerational influences, physiological factors, and socioeconomic factors. Progress in life course epidemiology research should help to build a more detailed understanding of such factors and make it possible to target them effectively.

References

1. Kuh D, Ben-Shlomo Y, Lynch J, Hallqvist J, Power C. Life course epidemiology. J Epidemiol Community Health. 2003;57(10):778–83.
2. Kuh D, Ben-Shlomo Y, editors. A life course approach to chronic disease epidemiology. 2nd ed. Oxford: Oxford University Press; 2004.
3. Kondo K. Life course approach: people with long legs die of cancer? Public Health Nurse J [Hokenshi Janaru]. 2006;62(11):946–52. (In Japanese).
4. Barker DJ, Osmond C. Infant mortality, childhood nutrition, and ischaemic heart disease in England and Wales. Lancet. 1986;1(8489):1077–81.

5. Bowlby J. Maternal care and mental health. Geneva: World Health Organization; 1951.
6. Ben-Shlomo Y, Kuh D. A life course approach to chronic disease epidemiology: conceptual models, empirical challenges and interdisciplinary perspectives. Int J Epidemiol. 2002;31(2):285–93.
7. Fujiwara T. Parent/child health and school health: the parental environment during gestation and early childhood alters children's genes. Jpn J Public Health [Nihon Koshu Eisei Zasshi]. 2008;55(5):344–9. (In Japanese).
8. Lynch J, Smith GD. A life course approach to chronic disease epidemiology. Annu Rev Public Health. 2005;26:1–35.
9. Fujiwara T. Life-course approach for the prevention of adult diseases from fetal and early periods of life. J Natl Inst Public Health [Hoken Iryo Kagaku]. 2007;56(2):90–8. (In Japanese).
10. Hall AJ, Yee LJ, Thomas SL. Life course epidemiology and infectious diseases. Int J Epidemiol. 2002;31(2):300–1.
11. Tamakoshi K, Yatsuya H, Wada K, Matsushita K, Otsuka R, Yang PO, Sugiura K, Hotta Y, Mitsuhashi H, Kondo T, Toyoshima H. Birth weight and adult hypertension. Circ J. 2006;70:262–7.
12. Sekine M, Yamagami T, Kagamimori S. Lifestyle and childhood obesity: results from the Toyama Birth Cohort Study. Pediatr Cardiol Cardiac Surg [Nihon Shoni Jyunkanki Gakkai Zasshi] 2008;24(5): 589–597. (In Japanese).
13. Suzuki K, Kondo N, Sato M, Tanaka T, Ando D, Yamagata Z. Gender differences in the association between maternal smoking during pregnancy and childhood growth trajectories: multilevel analysis. Int J Obes (Lond). 2011;35(1):53–9.
14. Matsuyama Y, Fujiwara T, Aida J, Watt RG, Kondo N, Yamamoto T, Kondo K, Osaka K. Experience of childhood abuse and later number of remaining teeth in older Japanese: a life-course study from Japan Gerontological Evaluation Study project. Community Dent Oral Epidemiol. 2016;44(6):531–9.
15. Amemiya A, Fujiwara T, Murayama H, Tani Y, Kondo K. Adverse childhood experiences and higher-level functional limitations among older Japanese people: results from the JAGES study. J Gerontol A Biol Sci Med Sci. 2018;73(2):261–6.
16. Tani Y, Fujiwara T, Kondo N, Noma H, Sasaki Y, Kondo K. Childhood socioeconomic status and onset of depression among Japanese older adults: the JAGES prospective cohort study. Am J Geriatr Psychiatry. 2016;24(9):717–26.
17. Yanagi N, Hata A, Kondo K, Fujiwara T. Association between childhood socioeconomic status and fruit and vegetable intake among older Japanese: the JAGES 2010 study. Prev Med. 2018;106:130–6.
18. Ministry of Health, Labour and Welfare. Longitudinal survey of newborns in the 21st Century. Available at https://www.mhlw.go.jp/english/database/db-hw/vs03.html
19. Ministry of the Environment. Japan Environment and Children's Study (JECS). Available at http://www.env.go.jp/chemi/ceh/en/
20. Science Council of Japan Committee on Clinical Medicine and Committee on Health/Human Life Science Subcommittee on Lifestyle-related Disease Control. Science Council of Japan, 2008. Available at http://www.scj.go.jp/ja/info/kohyo/pdf/kohyo-20-t62-4.pdf

Open Access This chapter is licensed under the terms of the Creative Commons Attribution-NonCommercial-NoDerivatives 4.0 International License (http://creativecommons.org/licenses/by-nc-nd/4.0/), which permits any noncommercial use, sharing, distribution and reproduction in any medium or format, as long as you give appropriate credit to the original author(s) and the source, provide a link to the Creative Commons licence and indicate if you modified the licensed material. You do not have permission under this licence to share adapted material derived from this chapter or parts of it.

The images or other third party material in this chapter are included in the chapter's Creative Commons licence, unless indicated otherwise in a credit line to the material. If material is not included in the chapter's Creative Commons licence and your intended use is not permitted by statutory regulation or exceeds the permitted use, you will need to obtain permission directly from the copyright holder.

Chapter 17
Social Capital and Health

Jun Aida and Katsunori Kondo

1 Introduction

Social capital (SC), "resources that are accessed by individuals as a result of their membership of a network or a group," [1] has been considered a determinant of health [2]. People obtain various resources from social relationships, and these may affect their lives. Such phenomena are sometimes serious, and the consequences may reach beyond health. In January 2018, Tracey Crouch was appointed as the first Minister for Loneliness in the UK in move that is indicative of the worldwide concern about loneliness—the lack of social relationships—not only in terms of its effects on health, but also for the effects on the lives of individuals and on society. This chapter introduces SC with a focus on its effects on health.

Jun Aida is also the English translator for this chapter.

J. Aida (✉)
Department of Oral Health Promotion Graduate School of Medical and Dental Sciences,
Tokyo Medical and Dental University, Tokyo, Japan
e-mail: j-aida@umin.ac.jp

K. Kondo
Professor of Social Epidemiology and Health Policy, Department of Social Preventive
Medical Sciences, Center for Preventive Medical Sciences, Chiba University, Chiba, Japan

Head of Department of Gerontological Evaluation, Center for Gerontology and
Social Science, National Center for Geriatrics and Gerontology, Obu City, Aichi, Japan

© The Author(s) 2020   191
K. Kondo (ed.), *Social Determinants of Health in Non-communicable Diseases*,
Springer Series on Epidemiology and Public Health,
https://doi.org/10.1007/978-981-15-1831-7_17

2   The Roseto Effect

In the 1950s, a strange phenomenon was discovered in the small town of Roseto, Pennsylvania, in the USA. Many of the residents of Roseto were Italian emigrants, who lived in a close-knit community. Although their lifestyles were not superior to their neighbors, it was observed that the residents of Roseto showed lower mortality from myocardial infarction than neighboring areas [3].

SC was considered to be the cause of the lower mortality in Roseto [4]. SC is a concept that has been used in various academic fields. Putnam [5] defined SC as "features of social organization, such as trust, norms and networks that can improve the efficiency of society by facilitating coordinated actions." Until now, epidemiology researches have reported that people who live in communities with deep trust, helping each other and enjoying social participation, have better health conditions.

3   Social Capital

There are various definitions and measurements of SC, because it has been discussed and considered in the fields of sociology, economics, and political science [6, 7]. Recently, the definition mentioned above, "resources that are accessed by individuals as a result of their membership of a network or a group," [1] seemed suitable for social epidemiology.

In addition to this definition, there are many classifications and subordinate concepts in SC [8, 9], including classification by cognitive SC and structural SC. Cognitive SC includes cognitive components of SC such as social trust and social support, while structural SC includes concepts related to network structure such as social networks and social participation. Classification as horizontal SC and vertical SC focuses on the structure of networks: SC obtained from horizontal and vertical networks can be distinguished. Classification as bonding SC, bridging SC, and linking SC focuses on the characteristics of networks: bonding SC is obtained from close and intense social ties; bridging SC is obtained from weak and diverse social ties; and linking SC is obtained from different power levels and positions. Following the background and hypothesis of a social epidemiological study as needed, these classifications and subordinate concepts should be selected as appropriate.

Figure 17.1 shows the theoretical explanation of the pathways between community-level SC and health. Living in a community with rich SC produces various resources. Social influence and informal social control affect health behaviors. Collective efficacy and social security contribute to establishment of health care policies. SC also buffers psychological stress. These mechanisms from community-level SC are considered to promote the health of residents [1].

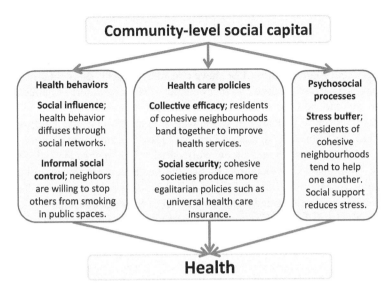

Fig. 17.1 Theoretical explanation of the pathways between community-level social capital and health

4 Individual and Community Social Capital and Multilevel Analysis

In social epidemiology, the distinction of individual-level SC and community (neighborhood)-level SC is an important issue. Studies often use components of SC such as social participation, social trust, and social networks as the variables of individual-level SC. Aggregated values of individual-level SC or community variables such as voting rate are often used as the variables of community-level SC.

Social epidemiology studies using multilevel analysis have revealed that SC in the community affects the health of residents regardless of individual-level SC. Such types of multilevel studies are interesting because they indicate that the health of an individual is not only determined by the individual's characteristics but also by the social environments in which they live. Such community-level SC also contributes to health inequalities between areas or groups. This community-level effect is called the "contextual effect". By contrast, the "compositional effect" causes some health inequality owing to differences among individuals in areas or groups. The concept of the contextual effect was new when SC studies began in the health field. Therefore, studies of SC have emphasized community-level SC.

However, studies of individual-level SC also seem to be important, especially when determining the mechanism of SC in health. Recent studies of social epidemiology seem to focus more on individual-level variables related to SC.

5 Social Capital and Health: Benefits and Downsides

Since the late 1990s, associations between SC and various health outcomes have been examined. Many studies of SC have considered effects on mental health, but other studies have also focused on other outcomes. SC is considered to affect mental well-being and to reduce the risk of mental health problems [10–12], mortality [13], and chronic noncommunicable diseases such as diabetes [14, 15], cardiovascular disease [13, 15], cancer [13], and oral diseases [16]. Recently, intervention studies relating to SC have suggested beneficial effects of SC on the health of older people [17, 18]. Although the associations of SC and health are not always robust, and high-quality research is required, SC generally seems to be beneficial for health.

Studies have also suggested a buffering effect of SC on socioeconomic inequalities in health [19, 20], and SC is considered a beneficial resource for health in developing countries [21]. In spite of these positive effects, we should also consider the potential downsides of SC in terms of health [22]. A systematic review reported behavioral contagion cross-level interactions as the primary negative effect of SC on health. As a behavioral contagion, SC may contribute to the diffusion of harmful health behaviors and negative health. A study that examined cross-level interactions reported that people with low trust experienced more harmful health effects in high-trust communities. Such downsides should be considered when SC is used for health promotion.

6 Social Capital Studies in Japan

There are relatively large reports of SC and health in Japan, even though SC studies have mainly been conducted in Western countries [23]. Although fewer longitudinal studies of community-level SC were reported, several longitudinal studies have been conducted in Japan; the outcomes considered were functional disability [24], cognitive decline [25], and oral health [26]. Many studies focused on the components of individual-level SC such as social support, social participation, social networks, and social trust. There were also studies of the development of measurements of community-level SC [27]. As a result of these studies, the Japanese government includes the concept of SC in the health field, especially in the prevention of functional disabilities among the older population. Therefore, levels of SC in communities are sometimes measured for health policy planning. In this section, two recent important topics are introduced: SC intervention and SC in the disaster context.

6.1   Intervention Study of Social Capital and Health

Possibilities for interventions that improve SC and promote health have been reported [17, 18]. In Japan, local governments and researchers in the Japan Gerontological Evaluation Study (JAGES) conduct a community-based intervention program that aims to improve SC and health. The Taketoyo town government has established community salons, where older people participate in several activities; the salon is managed by older volunteers. This community-based intervention program provides the opportunity for improved social participation and interaction among older people and reduces the problem of being homebound, which increases the risk of frailty. Its effects on health were evaluated by researchers, showing reduction in the risks of poor self-rated health [28], onset of functional disability [29], and cognitive decline [30]. This kind of community intervention program has been introduced to other municipalities in Japan, and further reports on its effects in other municipalities are anticipated.

6.2   Social Capital and Health in a Post-disaster Context

The health effects of natural disasters are enormous around the world, making it an important public health issue [31]. Disasters change various social determinants of health including SC. SC is considered to play an important role in mitigating the health effects of disasters [32–34]; for example, as in the Great East Japan Earthquake and Tsunami in 2011 during which 15,894 people lost their lives, and 2546 people remain missing. The Tohoku area was the main affected area, and one of the areas, Iwanuma City, was the site of a JAGES cohort health survey before and after the disaster. Studies in Iwanuma contribute important insights to SC and health in a post-disaster context.

SC prior to the disaster contributed to preventing incidents of post-traumatic stress disorder following the disaster [35]. Because the tsunami destroyed housing, residents were obliged to move to other residences. The detrition of SC owing to the disaster increased the risk of cognitive decline [25], and obligatory relocation changed the SC of disaster survivors [36]. As an important implication of this study, group relocation to temporary housing with neighbors by the government aimed at maintaining social networks of neighbors, and was reported to protect SC. Other studies showed that physical exercise and participation in sports activity groups reduced the risk of depression after a disaster [37]. Therefore, intervention to provide opportunities for sports activity group participation may reduce risk of depression among disaster survivors.

7 Summary

SC is considered a social determinant of health. SC in a community affects the health of residents regardless of individual characteristics. Recent studies have suggested the possibility that intervention to improve SC reduces health risks. SC is also important in the post-disaster health of survivors. Studies are required to determine the effect of SC on health as a health promotion resource of communities.

References

1. Kawachi I, Berkman LF. Social capital, social cohesion, and health. In: Berkman LF, Kawachi I, Glymour MM, editors. Social epidemiology. 2nd ed. Oxford: Oxford University Press; 2014. p. 290–319.
2. Solar O, Irwin A. A conceptual framework for action on the social determinants of health. Discussion paper for the commission on social determinants of health. Geneva: WHO; 2007.
3. Egolf B, Lasker J, Wolf S, Potvin L. The Roseto effect: a 50-year comparison of mortality rates. Am J Public Health. 1992;82:1089–92.
4. Putnam R. Bowling alone: the collapse and revival of American community. New York, NY: Simon and Schuster; 2000.
5. Putnam RD. Making democracy work: civic traditions in modern Italy. Princeton, NJ: Princeton University Press; 1993. p. 167.
6. Kawachi I, Subramanian SV, Kim D. Social capital and health. New York, NY: Springer; 2008.
7. Francis P. Social capital at the World Bank: strategic and operational implications of the concept; 2002.
8. Harpham T. The measurement of community social capital through surveys. In: Kawachi I, Subramanian SV, Kim D, editors. Social capital and health. New York, NY: Springer; 2008. p. 51–62.
9. Islam MK, Merlo J, Kawachi I, Lindstrom M, Gerdtham UG. Social capital and health: does egalitarianism matter? A literature review. Int J Equity Health. 2006;5:3.
10. Ehsan AM, De Silva MJ. Social capital and common mental disorder: a systematic review. J Epidemiol Community Health. 2015;69:1021–8.
11. McPherson KE, Kerr S, McGee E, Morgan A, Cheater FM, McLean J, et al. The association between social capital and mental health and behavioural problems in children and adolescents: an integrative systematic review. BMC Psychol. 2014;2:7.
12. Nyqvist F, Forsman AK, Giuntoli G, Cattan M. Social capital as a resource for mental well-being in older people: a systematic review. Aging Ment Health. 2013;17:394–410.
13. Choi M, Mesa-Frias M, Nuesch E, Hargreaves J, Prieto-Merino D, Bowling A, et al. Social capital, mortality, cardiovascular events and cancer: a systematic review of prospective studies. Int J Epidemiol. 2014;43:1895–920.
14. Flor CR, Baldoni NR, Aquino JA, Baldoni AO, Fabbro ALD, Figueiredo RC, et al. What is the association between social capital and diabetes mellitus? A systematic review. Diab Metab Synd. 2018;12:601.
15. Hu F, Hu B, Chen R, Ma Y, Niu L, Qin X, et al. A systematic review of social capital and chronic non-communicable diseases. Biosci Trends. 2014;8:290–6.
16. Batra M, Tangade P, Rajwar YC, Dany SS, Rajput P. Social capital and oral health. J Clin Diagn Res. 2014;8:Ze10–1.
17. Coll-Planas L, Nyqvist F, Puig T, Urrutia G, Sola I, Monteserin R. Social capital interventions targeting older people and their impact on health: a systematic review. J Epidemiol Community Health. 2017;71:663–72.

18. Flores EC, Fuhr DC, Bayer AM, Lescano AG, Thorogood N, Simms V. Mental health impact of social capital interventions: a systematic review. Soc Psychiatry Psychiatr Epidemiol. 2018;53:107–19.
19. Uphoff EP, Pickett KE, Cabieses B, Small N, Wright J. A systematic review of the relationships between social capital and socioeconomic inequalities in health: a contribution to understanding the psychosocial pathway of health inequalities. Int J Equity Health. 2013;12:54.
20. Vyncke V, De Clercq B, Stevens V, Costongs C, Barbareschi G, Jonsson SH, et al. Does neighbourhood social capital aid in levelling the social gradient in the health and well being of children and adolescents? A literature review. BMC Public Health. 2013;13:65.
21. Story WT. Social capital and health in the least developed countries: a critical review of the literature and implications for a future research agenda. Glob Public Health. 2013;8:983–99.
22. Villalonga-Olives E, Kawachi I. The dark side of social capital: a systematic review of the negative health effects of social capital. Soc Sci Med. 2017;194:105–27.
23. Murayama H, Fujiwara Y, Kawachi I. Social capital and health: a review of prospective multilevel studies. J Epidemiol. 2012;22:179–87.
24. Aida J, Kondo K, Kawachi I, Subramanian SV, Ichida Y, Hirai H, et al. Does social capital affect the incidence of functional disability in older Japanese? A prospective population-based cohort study. J Epidemiol Community Health. 2013;67:42–7.
25. Hikichi H, Tsuboya T, Aida J, Matsuyama Y, Kondo K, Subramanian SV, et al. Social capital and cognitive decline in the aftermath of a natural disaster: a natural experiment from the 2011 great east japan earthquake and tsunami. Lancet Planet Health. 2017;1:e105–e13.
26. Koyama S, Aida J, Saito M, Kondo N, Sato Y, Matsuyama Y, et al. Community social capital and tooth loss in Japanese older people: a longitudinal cohort study. BMJ Open. 2016;6:e010768.
27. Saito M, Kondo N, Aida J, Kawachi I, Koyama S, Ojima T, et al. Development of an instrument for community-level health related social capital among Japanese older people: the JAGES Project. J Epidemiol. 2017;27:221–7.
28. Ichida Y, Hirai H, Kondo K, Kawachi I, Takeda T, Endo H. Does social participation improve self-rated health in the older population? A quasi-experimental intervention study. Soc Sci Med. 2013;94:83–90.
29. Hikichi H, Kondo N, Kondo K, Aida J, Takeda T, Kawachi I. Effect of a community intervention programme promoting social interactions on functional disability prevention for older adults: propensity score matching and instrumental variable analyses, JAGES Taketoyo study. J Epidemiol Community Health. 2015;69:905–10.
30. Hikichi H, Kondo K, Takeda T, Kawachi I. Social interaction and cognitive decline: results of a 7-year community intervention. Alzheimers Dement (N Y). 2017;3:23–32.
31. Guha-Sapir D, Hoyois P, Below R. Annual disaster statistical review 2013 the numbers and trends. Brussels: Center for Research on the Epidemiology of Disasters; 2014.
32. Aida J, Kawachi I, Subramanian SV, Katsunori K. Disaster, social capital, and health. In: Kawachi I, Takao S, Subramanian SV, editors. Global perspectives on social capital and health. New York, NY: Springer; 2013. p. 167–87.
33. Noel P, Cork C, White RG. Social capital and mental health in post-disaster/conflict contexts: a systematic review. Disaster Med Public Health Prep. 2018;12:791–802.
34. Aldrich DP. Building resilience: social capital in post-disaster recovery, vol. xii. Chicago, IL: The University of Chicago Press; 2012. 232 pages.
35. Hikichi H, Aida J, Tsuboya T, Kondo K, Kawachi I. Can community social cohesion prevent posttraumatic stress disorder in the aftermath of a disaster? A natural experiment from the 2011 Tohoku earthquake and tsunami. Am J Epidemiol. 2016;183:902–10.
36. Hikichi H, Sawada Y, Tsuboya T, Aida J, Kondo K, Koyama S, et al. Residential relocation and change in social capital: a natural experiment from the 2011 great east japan earthquake and tsunami. Sci Adv. 2017;3:e1700426.
37. Tsuji T, Sasaki Y, Matsuyama Y, Sato Y, Aida J, Kondo K, et al. Reducing depressive symptoms after the great east japan earthquake in older survivors through group exercise participation and regular walking: a prospective observational study. BMJ Open. 2017;7:e013706.

Open Access This chapter is licensed under the terms of the Creative Commons Attribution-NonCommercial-NoDerivatives 4.0 International License (http://creativecommons.org/licenses/by-nc-nd/4.0/), which permits any noncommercial use, sharing, distribution and reproduction in any medium or format, as long as you give appropriate credit to the original author(s) and the source, provide a link to the Creative Commons licence and indicate if you modified the licensed material. You do not have permission under this licence to share adapted material derived from this chapter or parts of it.

The images or other third party material in this chapter are included in the chapter's Creative Commons licence, unless indicated otherwise in a credit line to the material. If material is not included in the chapter's Creative Commons licence and your intended use is not permitted by statutory regulation or exceeds the permitted use, you will need to obtain permission directly from the copyright holder.

Chapter 18
Access to Healthcare and Health Disparities

Chiyoe Murata and Katsunori Kondo

1 Introduction

The notion of healthcare access is often considered in discussions of the state of healthcare systems. Arguments concerning the problem of healthcare access usually focus on two main aspects. One refers to access problems caused by physical constraints including availability of healthcare facilities or staff, distance to healthcare facilities, and the existence of means of transportation. The other aspect refers to access problems caused by financial constraints such as the costs of receiving treatment [1]. In addition to these two aspects, psychological barriers such as health illiteracy or distrust of medical systems are also prominent [2]. For there to be equity of access to healthcare, every person in need of healthcare services must make use of them. A major indicator for measuring access to healthcare is "delayed care," which refers to refraining from visiting a doctor despite the need to do so [2]. This chapter presents Japanese and international research investigating whether healthcare access disparities are caused by socioeconomic status (SES). We also suggest possible measures to eliminate healthcare access inequality based on SES.

Chiyoe Murata revised and added new findings to the original manuscript written in Japanese.

C. Murata (✉)
School of Health and Nutrition, Tokaigakuen University, Nagoya, Japan

Department of Social Science, Center for Gerontology and Social Science, National Center for Geriatrics and Gerontology, Obu, Aichi, Japan
e-mail: murata-c@tokaigakuen-u.ac.jp

K. Kondo
Professor of Social Epidemiology and Health Policy, Department of Social Preventive Medical Sciences, Center for Preventive Medical Sciences, Chiba University, Chiba, Japan

Head of Department of Gerontological Evaluation, Center for Gerontology and Social Science, National Center for Geriatrics and Gerontology, Obu City, Aichi, Japan
e-mail: kkondo@chiba-u.jp

© The Author(s) 2020
K. Kondo (ed.), *Social Determinants of Health in Non-communicable Diseases*,
Springer Series on Epidemiology and Public Health,
https://doi.org/10.1007/978-981-15-1831-7_18

2   Access to Healthcare and SES

Evidence shows that the lower the income of the country, the lower the rate of basic maternal and child health service use [3]. Studies of representative samples of the US population demonstrate high death rates of admitted patients with acute myocardial infarctions in sparsely populated rural areas, especially among people with low income [4, 5]. The reasons cited were medical staff shortages, lack of nearby healthcare facilities [4], and financial (cost) barriers [5].

Disparities between the type of medical service received based on the patient's SES also exist in countries with universal healthcare systems. Comparative research between the USA and Canada shows that in both countries, the proportion of people not receiving essential treatment or primary care is greater among low-income and poorly educated groups [6]. However, the research also showed that Canada, which has a universal healthcare system, has less income-related healthcare inequality than the USA, which does not have universal healthcare.

Income or education-based health inequality is also found in the quality of healthcare received. A systematic review [7] of 26 papers covering 12 individual studies and 3 comparative studies, along with a study covering 21 countries with universal healthcare systems from the Organization for Economic Co-operation and Development (OECD), found that primary care service usage equity is assured to a degree, but specialized medical service usage in hospitals is lower among low-income groups.

Japan has maintained a universal healthcare system, built on the German model, for more than 30 years. The insurance component covers most of the population and is financed by premiums paid by insured persons, employers, and government compensation. Japan's National Health Insurance System reimburses by percentage and patients pay co-insurance. The system currently pays 70% of medical charges and patients (with the exception of children and elders) pay the remaining 30%. Healthcare access was previously believed to be broadly guaranteed under Japan's universal national insurance system. However, in recent years, income-based disparities have been noted. The Health Policy Institute's 2008 "Public Survey on Healthcare in Japan" [8] found that low-income groups delay seeking medical care more than twice the rate of high-income groups. The survey also found that within the past 12 months, 39% of sick people in low-income groups did not seek healthcare because of costs versus 18% of those in high-income groups. The proportion of reported low-income people not having a medication prescribed because of costs was 16% versus 2% for high-income people [8]. Another Japanese study (Japanese General Social Survey 2008) using data from a nationally representative sample (2160 people aged 20–89 years), also reported a higher delay rate in seeking medical care within low-income groups [9]. Furthermore, a 2006 study ($N = 15,302$) of older people from the Aichi Gerontological Evaluation Study project [10] found similar associations between delayed care, low income, and limited education.

The Agency for Healthcare Research and Quality (AHRQ), which is part of the US Department of Health and Human Services, reported that lower SES leads to lower rates of preventative actions, such as the reception of health screenings or vaccinations [4]. Similarly, the proportion of low-income people that underwent cancer-screening procedures, such as fecal occult blood tests, fiber-optic colonoscopies, or sigmoidoscopies, was smaller than the proportion of high-income people [11]. In Japan, the rate of older people without health screenings was linked to low SES [10].

In addition to unhealthy habits such as smoking, unbalanced diet, or sedentary life, an individual's SES, including income, education level, and profession, is related to his or her health. It is reported that people with mental health problems, such as those who are clinically depressed, are more prone to unhealthy behaviors [12]. A US study using data from the Medical Expenditure Panel Survey found a relationship between psychological distress and low reception rates for a variety of health examinations [13]. A study of Japanese elders also found a link between clinical depression and low reception rates for health examinations [1].

3 Background of Inequalities Based on SES

3.1 Financial Barriers to Access to Healthcare

Disparities in seeking medical consultation are related to a country's health insurance system. Commonly cited reasons for delayed healthcare include health insurance type and treatment (co-insurance) costs [4]. A recent 2-month study in the USA compared the medical consultation frequency of uninsured and insured people [14]. The odds ratio of an uninsured person receiving treatment for unintentional injuries was 0.47, which is less than half that of an insured person. Similarly, the odds ratio of an uninsured person receiving treatment for chronic illness was 0.45. Furthermore, uninsured persons were more unlikely to receive recommended follow-up care and remained in poor health 7 months after being injured [14].

Delays in seeking medical consultations do not just occur among uninsured people, but also among those with insurance. In the USA, coverage varies by insurance type, hence the existence of an underinsured or partially covered group. In a study of 2498 patients with acute myocardial infarctions, researchers compared the group not seeking medical consultations because of costs (18.1%) with all of the other groups [15]. Among those not seeking medical consultation because of cost, 68.9% had some type of insurance. After 1 year, patients with cost barriers were 1.3 times more likely to be re-hospitalized for heart disease than those without cost barriers. Therefore, individuals with inadequate health insurance may delay seeking healthcare, which can lead to worsened health and more re-hospitalizations.

An increase in patient cost share is also linked to delays in seeking medical care. According to impact reports on the European healthcare system reform and OECD countries [16, 17], when out-of-pocket expenses increase, treatments decline. According to the National Institute of Population and Social Security Research July

2007 survey [18] on social security in Japan, 17% of households did not visit a healthcare provider when someone was ill. The most common reason was economic, such as "the co-insurance being high" (38.4%). Babazono et al. [19] reported that among Japanese enrolled in health insurance plans, increases in direct treatment costs caused delayed care among low-income people. The study also found that fewer diabetes patients without comorbidities received outpatient treatment because of the rise of co-insurance rates from 20% to 30%. This suggests that delayed care frequently occurs among patients with diseases that develop without initial symptoms.

A comparative study of universal healthcare systems in France, Germany, and Spain reported that as patient cost share increased, outpatient consultations decreased, particularly among people with low income or social status [20]. Similar findings were reported in studies from South Korea [21] and Taiwan [22]. In 2003, a Japanese survey on healthcare usage among elders aged 65 years and over was conducted [1]. At that time, co-insurance for people under 70 years of age was 30% versus 10% for people 70 years of age and older. The survey showed that people under 70 years of age were more likely to refrain from seeking medical consultation because of cost barriers (35.8% of people 65–69 years of age vs. 20.1% of those 70 years of age and older) [1].

3.2 Physical Barriers to Access to Healthcare

Physicality is another barrier to healthcare access. In the aforementioned study of Japanese elders [1], physical access became more problematic with age. Reasons for not receiving needed medical treatment included "no medical facilities nearby" (9.0% for people aged 65–69 years and 15.4% for those aged 70 years and older) and "no means of transportation" (4.7% for people aged 65–69 years and 13.2% for those aged 70 years and older). In the USA, it has been reported that distance from healthcare facilities causes barriers to medical care, particularly among older people [4]. In the UK [23] and Nigeria [24], it was found that residents tend to be healthier as physical access to public health services improves.

3.3 Psychological Barriers to Access to Healthcare

Psychological factors [2] also comprise reasons that low-income groups are less likely to visit medical doctors. A Japanese study showed that people without a happy outlook on the future rated lower rates of receiving health checks than others [25]. In addition, people of low SES, regardless of their health condition, tended to be anxious about not receiving medical care, thus delaying necessary treatment [9]. Furthermore, people of low SES tended to have low trust in healthcare systems [26]. A report from Sweden found that people with minimal trust in healthcare systems were unlikely to seek medical consultations [27]. In 2004, the East Asian Social Survey compared China, Japan, South Korea, and Taiwan [9]. Results indicated that 50.8% of people that responded "I do not like to see a doctor" were South Korean while 25% were Japanese. In Japan and the USA, communication quality is related to healthcare access [28]. When asked "Did your doctor explain things in a way that is easy to understand?" or "Did your doctor listen to what you have to say?," those who answered "no" were dissatisfied with their medical care. Such communication problems are more linked to medical care satisfaction than waiting time or medical facility distance [28].

Health illiteracy is another psychological barrier to healthcare. A 2009 meta-analysis [29] of multiple qualitative studies suggested that health illiteracy (i.e., the inability to analyze and understand issues related to health) was linked to poor communication quality between patients and medical staff. The AHRQ recently reported that low SES begets higher diabetes hospitalization and comorbid condition rates [4]. In Japan, lower education was associated with lower exposure to health-related information [30]. Lack of information may undermine communication between healthcare providers and people with low SES, which leads to delayed or unmet healthcare needs.

4   Measures against Healthcare Access Disparities

As patient cost share increases, not only unnecessary medical procedures but also those that are necessary become less accessible to low-income groups. Although their healthcare needs may increase as their income decreases, low-income groups are often excluded from necessary healthcare. Accessible health insurance systems for low-income earners are vital for elimination of health disparity. Under the slogan "Health for All," the World Health Organization [3] has called upon governments to "ensure public sector leadership in healthcare systems financing, focusing on tax-/insurance-based funding, ensuring universal coverage of healthcare regardless of ability to pay, and minimizing out-of-pocket health spending." These inequalities must be resolved via healthcare system revisions.

Out-of-pocket expenses and the dilemma of uninsured people are healthcare access issues that warrant discussion. In the USA, the establishment of the State Children's Health Insurance Program for low-income children has reduced healthcare access inequalities [31]. In 2009, a revised version of Japan's National Health Insurance Act went into effect. It issues short-term insurance cards to uninsured young children who have become uninsured following parental payment delinquency.

Healthcare system revisions alone do not address healthcare access problems sufficiently. Mistrust of medicine and miscommunication problems are also related to health inequality [2]. UK initiatives are instructive examples of policies that can be implemented in local areas [32]. In August 2010, a program called "Healthy Homes" emerged in Liverpool (https://liverpool.gov.uk/healthyhomes). Using the slogan "Healthier homes, Healthier lives," the program designated 40 poverty-affected areas (with high immigrant populations) where "Healthy Homes advocates" visited homes to conduct on-site inspections. If a house posed any health risks, the owner was ordered to make improvements. When visiting, advocates informed residents of healthcare services. The program helped bring early treatment to immigrants who, because of language barriers or low health awareness, may not have sought treatment until their conditions became serious.

Economic factors also contribute to mothers not receiving antenatal care. Infant mortality rates in London's poorest areas rate 1.3 times higher than the national average. In 2008, local midwives called upon universities and hospitals to act, which led to the formation of a response team. In turn, the team called upon young local mothers to act, which led to the inauguration of the volunteer group called Bump Buddies (http://www.shoreditchtrust.org.uk/health-and-wellbeing/bump-buddies/). Young group members that may be of the same ethnicity or have a similar appearance (i.e., same skin color) reach out to local pregnant women. By connecting them with medical services, the Bump Buddies have helped increase antenatal care reception rates by 50% [32]. This is an excellent example of volunteer activities bringing medical care to underserved people.

5   Summary

Socioeconomically based healthcare access inequality must be addressed via healthcare system revisions. In addition, financial, physical, and psychological barriers to healthcare also need to be addressed. Health illiteracy or mistrust in medicine are often seen among people with low SES, and several underlying factors need to be emphasized, such as lack of necessary information provision or poor communication with healthcare providers. Such issues should be addressed when discussing possible countermeasures to healthcare inequalities. To provide disadvantaged groups with the necessary healthcare, community outreach activities (e.g., Bump Buddies) and the resource redistribution mentioned above are important. In Japan, partnerships between social welfare councils, local governments, local residents, and private businesses traditionally conduct a variety of activities to promote local volunteer efforts to support children, mothers, and older people. In other nations, peer support interventions that use the strength of local communities, such as those conducted in the UK [32], will continue to grow in importance.

References

1. Murata C, Yamada T, Chen CC, Ojima T, Hirai H, Kondo K. Barriers to health care among the elderly in Japan. Int J Environ Res Public Health. 2010;7(4):1330–41.

2. Cabinet Office, Government of Japan Policy evaluation report no. 20. Tokyo: Cabinet Office, Government of Japan. 2006. Available at https://www5.cao.go.jp/keizai3/seisakukoka.html. Accessed 14 Mar 2019. (In Japanese).
3. Commission on Social Determinants of Health. Final report. Closing the gap in a generation: health equity through action on the social determinants of health. Geneva: World Health Organization; 2008.
4. Agency for Healthcare Research and Quality. 2016 national healthcare quality & disparities reports. Agency for Healthcare Research and Quality Rockville, MD 2017. . Available at http://www.ahrq.gov/research/findings/nhqrdr/index.html. Accessed Jun 2018.
5. Shi L, Stevens GD. Vulnerability and unmet health care needs: the influence of multiple risk factors. J Gen Intern Med. 2005;20(2):148–54.
6. Lasser KE, Himmelstein DU, Woolhandler S. Access to care, health status, and health disparities in the United States and Canada: results of a cross-national population-based survey. Am J Public Health. 2006;96(7):1300–7.
7. Hanratty B, Zhang T, Whitehead M. How close have universal health systems come to achieving equity in use of curative services? A systematic review. Int J Health Serv. 2007;37(1):89–109.
8. Health Policy Institute. Nihon no Iryō ni Kan Suru 2007-nen Yoron Chōsa [public survey on healthcare in Japan 2007]. Health Policy Institute, Tokyo 2007Available at https://hgpi.org/research/45.html. Accessed Mar 2019. (In Japanese).
9. Iwai N, Hanibuchi T, editors. Health and society in East Asia: a comparison among Japan, South Korea, China and Taiwan based on east Asian social survey 2010. Kyoto: Nakanishiya; 2014.
10. Murata C, Kondo K, Hirai H, Ichida Y, Ojima T. Association between depression and socioeconomic status among community-dwelling elderly in Japan: the Aichi Gerontological evaluation study (AGES). Health Place. 2008;14(3):406–14.
11. U.S. Department of Health and Human Services, Centers for Disease Control and Prevention. CDC health disparities and inequalities report – United States. Atlanta, GA: CDC; 2011.
12. Lett HS, Blumenthal JA, Babyak MA, et al. Depression as a risk factor for coronary artery disease: evidence, mechanisms, and treatment. Psychosom Med. 2004;66(3):305–15.
13. Thorpe JM, Kalinowski CT, Patterson ME, Sleath BL. Psychological distress as a barrier to preventive care in community-dwelling elderly in the United States. Med Care. 2006;44(2):187–91.
14. Hadley J. Insurance coverage, medical care use, and short-term health changes following an unintentional injury or the onset of a chronic condition. JAMA. 2007;297(10):1073–84.
15. Rahimi AR, Spertus JA, Reid KJ, Bernheim SM, Krumholz HM. Financial barriers to health care and outcomes after acute myocardial infarction. JAMA. 2007;297(10):1063–72.
16. Mossialos E, Dixon A, Figueras J, Kutzin J, editors. Funding health care: options for Europe. Buckingham: Open University Press; 2002.
17. Organization for Economic Co-operation and Development. Towards high-performing health systems: policy studies. Paris: OECD; 2004.
18. National Institute of Population and Social Security Research. The 2nd national survey on social security and people's life (2012). National Institute of Population and Social Security Research Tokyo 2013. Available at http://www.ipss.go.jp/ss-seikatsu/e/2012/seikatsu2012_e.asp. Accessed Jul 2018.
19. Babazono A, Miyazaki M, Imatoh T, et al. Effects of the increase in co-payments from 20 to 30 percent on the compliance rate of patients with hypertension or diabetes mellitus in the employed health insurance system. Int J Technol Assess. 2005;21(2):228–33.
20. Lostao L, Regidor E, Geyer S, Aiach P. Patient cost sharing and social inequalities in access to health care in three western European countries. Soc Sci Med. 2007;65(2):367–76.
21. Kim J, Ko S, Yang B. The effects of patient cost sharing on ambulatory utilization in South Korea. Health Policy. 2005;72(3):293–300.
22. Huang JH, Tung CM. The effects of outpatient co-payment policy on healthcare usage by the elderly in Taiwan. Arch Gerontol Geriatr. 2006;43(1):101–16.

23. Barnett S, Roderick P, Martin D, Diamond I. A multilevel analysis of the effects of rurality and social deprivation on premature limiting long term illness. J Epidemiol Commun Health. 2001;55(1):44–51.
24. Onwujekwe O. Inequities in healthcare seeking in the treatment of communicable endemic diseases in Southeast Nigeria. Soc Sci Med. 2005;61(2):455–63.
25. Asida T, Kondo K, Hirai H. The association between happy outlook on the future, depression, health check-up, and socioeconomic status among the old: the AGES project. J Health Welf Stat. 2012;59(12):12–21. (In Japanese).
26. Doescher MP, Saver BG, Franks P, Fiscella K. Racial and ethnic disparities in perceptions of physician style and trust. Arch Fam Med. 2000;9(10):1156–63.
27. Mohseni M, Lindstrom M. Social capital, trust in the health-care system and self-rated health: the role of access to health care in a population-based study. Soc Sci Med. 2007;64(7):1373–83.
28. Saha S, Arbelaez JJ, Cooper LA. Patient-physician relationships and racial disparities in the quality of health care. Am J Public Health. 2003;93(10):1713–9.
29. Edwards M, Davies M, Edwards A. What are the external influences on information exchange and shared decision-making in healthcare consultations: a meta-synthesis of the literature. Patient Educ Couns. 2009;75(1):37–52.
30. Ishikawa Y, Nishiuchi H, Hayashi H, Viswanath K. Socioeconomic status and health communication inequalities in Japan: a nationwide cross-sectional survey. PLoS One. 2012;7(7):e40664.
31. Shone LP, Dick AW, Klein JD, Zwanziger J, Szilagyi PG. Reduction in racial and ethnic disparities after enrollment in the state Children's health insurance program. Pediatrics. 2005;115(6):e697–705.
32. Iwanaga N, Kondo K. Kenkō no Shakaiteki Kettei Yōin e no Kainyū Igirisu NHS no Genba ni Miru Kenkō Kakusa Taisaku. Byōin. 2001;70(1):19–23. (In Japanese).

Open Access This chapter is licensed under the terms of the Creative Commons Attribution-NonCommercial-NoDerivatives 4.0 International License (http://creativecommons.org/licenses/by-nc-nd/4.0/), which permits any noncommercial use, sharing, distribution and reproduction in any medium or format, as long as you give appropriate credit to the original author(s) and the source, provide a link to the Creative Commons licence and indicate if you modified the licensed material. You do not have permission under this licence to share adapted material derived from this chapter or parts of it.

The images or other third party material in this chapter are included in the chapter's Creative Commons licence, unless indicated otherwise in a credit line to the material. If material is not included in the chapter's Creative Commons licence and your intended use is not permitted by statutory regulation or exceeds the permitted use, you will need to obtain permission directly from the copyright holder.

Chapter 19
Measures of Health Disparities and Health Impact Assessment

Yoshihisa Fujino and Katsunori Kondo

1 Introduction

Health disparities have only recently come to the forefront in Japan, despite the topic being of interest in foreign countries since the 1980s. With increasing awareness comes corresponding interest in measures to address health disparities. One potential solution is the implementation of a health impact assessment (HIA).

An HIA is a series of methodologies aimed at predicting the potential impact of a newly proposed policy on health. The strategy optimizes policies for promoting health benefits while minimizing conditions that will have negative effects. Today, HIAs are widely used as a tool to prepare national or local policies related to employment, housing, traffic, education, and urban development, particularly in Europe [1]. They can be categorized into three types, focusing on environmental impact, social effects, and health inequity.

In Asia, HIAs are also becoming increasingly popular. Implementation of HIAs in Japan is similar to that for environmental impact assessments, which are required before large-scale development. However, differences in HIA types can cause

Yoshihisa Fujino is also the English translator for this chapter.

Y. Fujino (✉)
Department of Environmental Epidemiology, Institute of Industrial Ecological Sciences, University of Occupational and Environmental Health Japan, Kitakyushu, Japan
e-mail: zenq@med.uoeh-u.ac.jp

K. Kondo
Professor of Social Epidemiology and Health Policy, Department of Social Preventive Medical Sciences, Center for Preventive Medical Sciences, Chiba University, Chiba, Japan

Head of Department of Gerontological Evaluation, Center for Gerontology and Social Science, National Center for Geriatrics and Gerontology, Obu City, Aichi, Japan

© The Author(s) 2020
K. Kondo (ed.), *Social Determinants of Health in Non-communicable Diseases*,
Springer Series on Epidemiology and Public Health,
https://doi.org/10.1007/978-981-15-1831-7_19

problems, because standardized protocols for one type may not apply in all cases. Here, we focus on HIAs targeting health disparities.

2 Health Disparities and Health Inequity

There is no general consensus regarding Japanese terms such as health disparities, disparities of health, health inequity, and unfairness. Thus, it is necessary to clarify the context in which each term is used.

Health disparities refers to differential between-group distribution of good health and factors related to health. For example, older people and young people differ in disease prevalence, while geographical regions differ in mortality rates. The source of health disparities may be from variation in biological (genetics) or demographic (sex and age) factors between groups.

Because intervention to correct biological factors may be impossible or unethical, health disparities caused by such reasons cannot be completely avoided. However, in many cases, variation in physical environment or socioeconomic status can also generate between-group health differences. While such environmental variation results from factors that cannot be easily corrected through personal effort, intervention targeting the environment is more acceptable. In addition, health disparities derived from the socioeconomic situation are considered unethical. Such instances can thus be associated with health inequity.

Health inequity refers to health disparities caused by social disadvantage, resulting in more moral and ethical judgement [4]. The World Health Organization (WHO) advocates "health for all," a concept that maintains all people have equal right to health.

In Japan, the term "health disparities" now directly implies health inequity and all of the associated ethical issues. Nevertheless, the distinction between health disparities and inequity should be preserved whenever possible.

3 Domestic and Overseas Health Disparities

Four comprehensive reviews regarding health disparities worldwide have been conducted, with the first being the Black Report [2], followed by the Acheson Report [3]. Then, in 2008, the WHO-established Commission on Social Determinants of Health (CSDH) presented "Closing the gap in a generation: health equity through action on the social determinants of health" [4]. Two years later, the Marmot Review was published [5]. Based on these reviews, several countries (e.g., the Netherlands and Sweden) have presented comprehensive plans of national strategies to correct health disparities [6, 7].

In Japan, health disparity is closely associated with educational background, income, and employment [8–15].

4 Applying HIAs to Correct Health Disparities

Health equity involves equalizing access to opportunities that improve health [16]. A report by the CSDH emphasized the need to treat these issues under the framework of social justice.

Most of the reports have suggested HIAs as a means of correcting health disparities [3–6, 17]. A common understanding of these strategies is that interventions with potential to reduce health inequities are mainly in areas other than healthcare. Therefore, most issues related to the effects of socioeconomic status on health can only be resolved through implementing cross-sectional policies. These include regulations for income and housing, taxes on recreational drugs (cigarettes or alcohol), as well as improved labor regulation. In summary, health disparities cannot be mitigated unless HIAs cover relevant fields in addition to healthcare [3, 18].

The Acheson Report [3] lists HIAs at the top of its recommendations for decreasing health inequity. All health-associated policies use HIAs to assess potential impacts on health inequalities and then to reduce those inequalities as much as possible. Similarly, the CSDH report [7] indicated that an HIA should be implemented for all policies, and recommended a system for doing so at the national level.

5 What Is an HIA and Health Equity Impact Assessment (HEqIA)?

The current definitions for HIA come from the WHO and the International Association for Impact Assessment (IAIA). The WHO Gothenburg Paper [19] defines an HIA as "a combination of procedures, methods, and tools by which a policy, a program, or a project may be judged as to its potential effects on health of a population and the distribution of effects within the population." Notably, this early-stage definition [20] did not include any mention of health disparities. However, the Gothenburg Paper confirmed that assessing health disparities was an indispensable function of an HIA, so such language was explicitly included in revised definitions.

Both the CSDH report [4] and the Marmot Review [5] used the term "Health Equity Impact Assessment" (HEqIA). Based on assessment from the International HIA Conference, HEqIA was essentially the same as an HIA, because the latter automatically includes a disparities assessment. Taken together, these reports indicate ongoing refinement of appropriate methods and evaluation of HIA performance focusing on health disparities.

6   Social Environment Model for Health

In general, HIAs are based on the social environment model, which states that social structure and socioeconomic factors directly and indirectly influence the health of an individual or population [16]. These social health determinants have been recently validated in the field of public health and are now recognized widely. Social health determinants are associated with many fields. The Ottawa Charter for Health Promotion, for example, cited the following variables as preconditions of health: peace, housing, education, food, income, environmental stability, sustainable resources, social justice, and fairness. Assessment of policies using an HIA would thus account for the complex variation in social environments.

7   "Health in All Policies" and Governance

The Healthy Public Policy in the Ottawa Charter suggests that we can optimize the impact of "non-health policies" to improve societal health, by requiring the inclusion of health-promotion measures at every policy opportunity. In other words, policies other than those related to healthcare should be considered under the jurisdiction of HIAs, as mentioned earlier. However, in many cases, we do not have sufficient infrastructure to determine the relation with health when planning for non-health policies.

To address this absent infrastructure, the Ottawa Charter has refined the concept of non-health-policy inclusion, generating the "Health in All Policies" initiative. This aims to facilitate the preparation of policies in all fields, including education, real estate, development, and employment, to better consider their relative impact on health. Specifically, health-conscious governance should form well-regulated policies based on scientific knowledge and the social environment model of health [17]. HIAs are valuable tools for realizing the "Health in All Policies" initiative.

8   How Does an HIA Evaluate Disparities?

First, differential impact of policies or projects on social strata (various populations with distinct attributes) must be assessed. This necessity is based on an awareness that the health effects of a policy vary according to a given population's characteristics. In particular, socially disadvantaged populations are especially vulnerable to adverse effects. The following points are typically considered when determining whether a policy is unequal [21, 22]:

- Socially disadvantaged populations are more likely to be affected.
- Does a newly proposed policy promote health disparity?
- Will a new policy increase disparity in a certain population?
- What is the distribution of and exposure to specific health determinants and risk factors or changes in accessibility to services?

9 Prospective Effects of Including Health Disparities in an HIA

9.1 Influence on the Decision-Making Process

In an HIA, merits and demerits of proposed policies are assessed from standpoints of health disparities and fairness. The goal of an HIA is to obtain the best evidence possible, collecting and analyzing data regarding the potential influence of proposed policies on health disparities. Thus, various protocols can be used, including both quantitative and qualitative evaluations, such as a participatory approach.

9.2 Promoting a Better Understanding of Associations Between Policies and Health

By demonstrating the association between policies and health disparities, an HIA allows leaders to determine how their proposals affect public health. Findings on social health determinants using HIAs allow for beneficial revisions to governmental strategies that can address health disparities effectively.

9.3 Participatory Approaches and Empowerment

A participatory approach is often used in HIAs. Both the findings and the process of an HIA have important uses. One particular advantage of a participatory approach is that populations potentially at risk of negative health effects can undergo detailed health-disparity assessments through their involvement in an HIA. Furthermore, such an approach allows subjects to voice their opinion on health. The immediate disclosure of this information increases population self-effectiveness. In short, a participatory approach promotes health through increasing the opportunity for individuals to participate in decision making regarding their lives.

10 Future Directions

Numerous fields in Japan can benefit from HIAs. In particular, we recommend the implementation of "Health in All Policies," with the goal of eliminating health disparities in the future. To do so successfully, we first must understand the social environment model in all departments responsible for policy making. Next, we should prepare a system that can effectively implement HIAs and collect the resultant data. We should also aim to have interdisciplinary cooperation and discussion regarding direct and indirect health effects. Finally, specialists responsible for HIAs must be trained and developed.

References

1. Kemm J, Parry J, Palmer S. Health impact assessment: concepts, theory, techniques and applications. Oxford: Oxford University Press; 2004.
2. Great Britain. Working Group on Inequalities in Health. In: Black D, Townsend P, Davidson N, editors. Inequalities in health: the Black report. Harmondsworth: Penguin; 1982.
3. Acheson D, Great Britain. Department of Health. Independent inquiry into inequalities in health: report. London: Stationery Office; 1998.
4. WHO Commission on Social Determinants of Health., World Health Organization. Closing the gap in a generation: health equity through action on the social determinants of health: final report of the commission on social determinants of health. Geneva: World Health Organization; 2008.
5. Marmot MG. Fair society, healthy lives: the Marmot review; strategic review of health inequalities in England post-2010. London: The Marmot Review; 2010.
6. Mackenbach JP, Stronks K. A strategy for tackling health inequalities in the Netherlands. BMJ. 2002;325(7371):1029–32.
7. Oestlin P, Diderichsen F, World Health Organization. Regional Office for Europe & European Centre for Health Policy. Equity-oriented national strategy for public health in Sweden. Copenhagen: WHO Regional Office for Europe; 2011.
8. Fujino Y, Japan Collaborative Cohort Study for Evaluation of C. Occupational factors and mortality in the Japan collaborative cohort study for evaluation of Cancer (JACC). Asian Pac J Cancer Prev. 2007;8(Suppl):97–104.
9. Honjo K, Iso H, Inoue M, Tsugane S, Japan Public Health Center-based Prospective Study G. Education, social roles, and the risk of cardiovascular disease among middle-aged Japanese women: the JPHC study cohort I. Stroke. 2008;39(10):2886–90.
10. Ito S, Takachi R, Inoue M, Kurahashi N, Iwasaki M, Sasazuki S, Iso H, Tsubono Y, Tsugane S, Group JS. Education in relation to incidence of and mortality from cancer and cardiovascular disease in Japan. Eur J Pub Health. 2008;18(5):466–72.
11. Murata C, Kondo K, Hirai H, Ichida Y, Ojima T. Association between depression and socioeconomic status among community-dwelling elderly in Japan: the Aichi Gerontological evaluation study (AGES). Health Place. 2008;14(3):406–14.
12. Honjo K, Iso H, Ikeda A, Inoue M, Tsugane S, Group JS. Education level and physical functional limitations among Japanese community residents-gender difference in prognosis from stroke. BMC Public Health. 2009;9:131.
13. Ichida Y, Kondo K, Hirai H, Hanibuchi T, Yoshikawa G, Murata C. Social capital, income inequality and self-rated health in Chita peninsula, Japan: a multilevel analysis of older people in 25 communities. Soc Sci Med. 2009;69(4):489–99.
14. Kondo N, Sembajwe G, Kawachi I, van Dam RM, Subramanian SV, Yamagata Z. Income inequality, mortality, and self rated health: meta-analysis of multilevel studies. BMJ. 2009;339:b4471.
15. Kondo K, Kawachi I. Health inequalities in Japan: an empirical study of older people. Balwyn North, VIC: Trans Pacific Press; 2010.
16. Whitehead M, World Health Organization. Regional Office for Europe. The concepts and principles of equity and health. Copenhagen: World Health Organization, Regional Office for Europe; 1990.
17. Ståhl T, Wismar M, Ollila E, Lahtinen E, Leppo K. Health in all policies: prospects and potentials. Helsinki: Ministry of Social Affairs and health and European Observatory on Health systems and policies; 2006.
18. Rose G. The strategy of preventive medicine. Oxford: Oxford University Press; 1992.
19. WHO European Centre for Health Policy. Health impact assessment: main concepts and suggested approach. Gothenburg consensus paper. Brussels: European Centre for Health Policy, WHO Regional Office for Europe; 1999.

20. Barnes R, Scott-Samuel A. Health impact assessment and inequalities. Rev Panam Salud Publica. 2002;11(5–6):449–53.
21. Parry J, Scully E. Health impact assessment and the consideration of health inequalities. J Public Health Med. 2003;25(3):243–5.
22. Taylor L, Gowman N, Quigley R, NHS Health Development Agency. Addressing inequalities through health impact assessment. London: Health Development Agency; 2003.

Open Access This chapter is licensed under the terms of the Creative Commons Attribution-NonCommercial-NoDerivatives 4.0 International License (http://creativecommons.org/licenses/by-nc-nd/4.0/), which permits any noncommercial use, sharing, distribution and reproduction in any medium or format, as long as you give appropriate credit to the original author(s) and the source, provide a link to the Creative Commons licence and indicate if you modified the licensed material. You do not have permission under this licence to share adapted material derived from this chapter or parts of it.

The images or other third party material in this chapter are included in the chapter's Creative Commons licence, unless indicated otherwise in a credit line to the material. If material is not included in the chapter's Creative Commons licence and your intended use is not permitted by statutory regulation or exceeds the permitted use, you will need to obtain permission directly from the copyright holder.

Chapter 20
What Measures Can Be Taken to Reduce Health Disparity?

Katsunori Kondo

1 Introduction

This book has considered numerous non-communicable diseases and health problems and has described the importance of the "social determinants of health" (SDH), based on the findings of research from Japan and other countries. Even in Japan, which was a country regarded as "a nation with little inequality by achieving universal health and pension coverage half a century ago," we could find health disparities.

Up until the early 1980s, Japan was trending toward reducing income inequality as measured by the Gini coefficient (a measure of inequality in the distribution of income). However, inequality began to grow thereafter, and Japan is now one of the countries among the members of the OECD that have high Gini coefficients (i.e., higher levels of inequality). Compared to an average among the 30 OECD member countries in the mid-2000s of 10.6%, Japan's poverty rate (the proportion with less than 50% of the median income) is 14.9%, the fourth highest after Mexico, Turkey, and the United States [1]. The unemployment rate among youth approaches 10%, and, even among those who are employed, the proportion in unstable, irregular employment, including as temporary workers, has climbed to a level of one out of every three young persons. As has been presented in the preceding chapters, there is an extensive body of research corroborating the fact that ill health is prevalent

Katsunori Kondo is also the English translator for this chapter.

K. Kondo (✉)
Professor of Social Epidemiology and Health Policy, Department of Social Preventive Medical Sciences, Center for Preventive Medical Sciences, Chiba University, Chiba, Japan

Head of Department of Gerontological Evaluation, Center for Gerontology and Social Science, National Center for Geriatrics and Gerontology, Obu City, Aichi, Japan
e-mail: kkondo@chiba-u.jp

© The Author(s) 2020
K. Kondo (ed.), *Social Determinants of Health in Non-communicable Diseases*,
Springer Series on Epidemiology and Public Health,
https://doi.org/10.1007/978-981-15-1831-7_20

among the poor, the unemployed, and those in irregular employment. Therefore, it is likely that this issue is also relevant in Japan, despite the relatively few studies, and that health disparities do exist. Indeed, the past decade has seen the release of findings from studies of Japanese older people [2] and children [3] at the micro level, and it is becoming evident that Japan does have health disparities.

The WHO (World Health Organization) has put emphasis on problems of health inequalities, treating the issue in a 2009 resolution adopted by the World Health Assembly and urging its member states to engage with the issue. In Japan, the publicized basic goal of the National Movement of Health Promotion—Health Japan 21 (The Second Term)—to be implemented during the *10*-year period from 2013 is "Extension of healthy life expectancy and reduction of health disparities" (see Appendices).

It is necessary to refer to the recommendations and other materials provided by the WHO and to begin implementing measures. Therefore, this final chapter discusses the reasoning of the WHO and others in stressing the social determinants of health, the background to this development, and its meaning. This chapter presents these matters with a focus on the actions of the WHO to consider the sorts of measures that ought to be implemented to reduce health disparities.

2 Why Is Attention Paid to the Social Determinants of Health?

The focus on the "social determinants of health" within the field of public health seems like a dramatic epochal shift to rival those of primary healthcare and health promotion; this shift should be examined each decade. The authors would like to confirm how the trends of the day have shifted, the background to them, and the direction of the latest trends, and they would like to use this information as the foundation for formulating new policies.

The following three background conditions or factors can be pointed out: (1) the limitations of medicine and medical technology; (2) the difficulty of modifying lifestyles; and (3) health disparities.

2.1 Limitations of Medicine and Medical Technology

Since the founding of the WHO, numerous essential technologies have appeared that eliminate the causes of disease at the root level, including vaccines and antibiotics against infectious diseases, as well as nutrient supplements against undernutrition and nutrient deficiencies. Because of these technologies, infant mortality and other health indicators have improved dramatically. Medical treatments and technologies, which were developed one after another, contributed greatly to eliminating many health problems.

However, problems *that cannot be* solved by technology *have* remained. Even when the technology exists, there can be problems of access, such as when the costs are high or the places providing treatment are not located nearby. These problems can affect, for instance, people excluded from society or those of low social standing, such as the poor or *those on* low incomes, as well as the unemployed or irregularly employed. Some people cannot pay for insurance and become uninsured; others have insurance but give up treatment by themselves because they cannot afford the *co-payments* when using services; yet others are unaware of the existence of free or inexpensive systems for health examinations; still others do not avail themselves of services because of the demands of daily life; and some, finally, can only receive care of low quality [4].

If people cannot access technologies and cannot make use of them, then these will be ineffective regardless of how advanced they are. What such people need to resolve their health issues is not further advances in medical technology but rather the removal of socioeconomic factors that act as barriers to access and usage. This is why the WHO and UN pursue universal health coverage.

2.2 The Difficulty of Modifying Lifestyles

The importance of noncommunicable diseases and healthy aging has increased even in developing countries as control over infectious diseases has been achieved to some degree. Representative of these are lifestyle diseases caused by the accumulated effects of unhealthy living habits. It was expected that living habits could be improved by inform citizens that lifestyle could cause disease and functional decline along with aging; thus, resources were poured into health education. However, no matter how much information is communicated, it will be ineffective if it does not change behavior and if lifestyles remain the same. Because of this, techniques have been developed based on the insights of behavioral science with the aim to bring about behavioral modifications. The effects of these programs have been validated in randomized controlled trials that provide high-quality evidence. However, these trials studied a comparatively small number of cases in the short term and under ideal laboratory conditions. Therefore, the observed effects would not necessarily be obtained under ordinary implemental conditions. Long-term effects that impact ordinary life were not sufficiently demonstrated in systematic reviews [5], and neither were effects sufficiently demonstrated in systematic reviews of intervention research on groups composed of a larger number of cases [6, 7]. Symbolic of this is obesity, which has only increased, rather than decreased, in spite of a redoubling of measures against it in Europe, North America, and even in Japan—measures implemented because obesity leads to innumerable diseases.

The people needed to improve their lifestyles are likely to be difficult to be influenced through a behavioral modification approach focused on communicating information and based on health education. As it is discussed in the preceding chapters, the social determinants of health are behind the difficulty of modifying lifestyles.

2.3   Health Disparities

It is now clear that undeniable health disparities, or gaps in health status between the groups created by differences in community or socioeconomic status, are observable not just among nations but also within single countries. It has become clear that there are considerable disparities even in the fundamental human right to "life," and, moreover, clear that this gap appeared to be on an expansionary trend. At that point, the WHO, which had adopted the slogan "Health for All," dealt with these disparities as issues of social justice concerning health equity in a resolution adopted at the World Health Assembly [8], and the organization urged its member states to act. Within the resolution, the WHO placed emphasis on the social determinants of health, and it also called for action in non-health sectors.

Looking at these three background factors, it is apparent that the social determinants of health have arisen as unavoidable, central issues that are the root causes of the health problems that have persisted despite efforts to combat them over the past few decades. Initiatives to deal with the social determinants of health will presumably only produce results "in a generation" [9] rather than immediately, but it is expected that they will gradually permeate throughout various fields. Greater resources were put into health education not after all the evidence had come in as to what specifically should be done or as to how effective it would be. Similarly, interest in the social determinants of health, the development of intervention policies, and the investigation of their effects will presumably be advanced little by little as attempts based on necessity build upon one another.

3   Three Concepts Should Be Pursued

There are at least three concepts for dealing with the social determinants of health that should be paid much attention.

3.1   The Approach Aimed at the Root Causes Upstream

The first concept is the notion of looking not only at the causes of problems but also at the "causes of the causes." This is an approach in which, using a river as a metaphor, to overcome health problems—which are occurring downstream—the root causes farther upstream must be dealt with. In a life course approach, measures to deal with even those health problems presenting in adulthood are formulated while tracing the causes of the problems back through adolescence, childhood, birth, and then further back to the parents' generation, based on the insights of life course epidemiology. Such an approach could thus be said to be an expression of this first concept. Therefore, the WHO included in its recommendations the elimination of social inequalities themselves, as these are the root causes of health inequalities.

3.2   Environmental Interventions

There are two methods for modification of behaviors: (1) a method in which appeals are made to the individuals who are the principals engaging in behaviors, and (2) interventions are made in the environment to make it easy to engage in behaviors favorable to health, and, as a result, the behavior of the people living there changes in a favorable way. It is "primordial prevention." [10]

Preventive medicine also has two strategies available to it: (1) high-risk strategies aimed at individuals who possess risk factors, and (2) population strategies aimed at entire population groups. It is necessary to combine these methods and strategies. For instance, smoking cessation guidance aimed at smokers is an example of an individual intervention employing a high-risk strategy, while such techniques as smoking bans in workplaces and public spaces and increased tobacco taxes are environmental interventions employing population strategies.

As the difficulty of modifying people's lifestyles has become apparent, it has become clear that it is important to combine high-risk and population strategies rather than relying on the former alone. Among population strategies, in addition to the publicizing of information about health that had already been long practiced, emphasis has also come to be placed on creating environments conducive to good health. Moreover, there are not only natural and physical environments but also a socioeconomic environment, and it is now known that this exerts a great effect on people. To give an example, within an apparently physical environment (read: "cause") of a local community containing residential areas with parks and sidewalks built nearby and a developed public transportation system that means not having to rely on cars—which would tend to increase the amount of walking—the "cause of the cause" that would not permit people to buy or rent houses in the desirable environment of that community might be problems of economic power.

As a factor behind health disparities, people of low social status tend to be placed in poor environmental conditions. As this has become clear, the importance of population strategies and that of environmental interventions have been recognized. The Health Japan 21 (The Second Term) program called for "improvement of the quality of the social environment."

3.3   Consideration of Health in All Policies

The slogan of the Adelaide Statement [11] is "Health in All Policies" (HiAP). When looking for the causes of causes upstream and attempting to approach them from a life course perspective, issues can no longer be dealt with entirely within a health or medical framework.

Such things as measures to deal with child poverty, as well as education policy, are indispensable. That being so, the framers of the statement did not insist that health and medical experts are powerless to deal with health inequalities. Instead, the WHO declared that they should involve and collaborate with non-health sectors. This includes, for instance, making appeals to departments in charge of transportation policy or to city planners to reconsider policy, or to devise future plans from the perspective of increasing the amount of walking done by the people living in an area.

4   WHO Policy Documents

The final report of the Commission on Social Determinants of Health [8] set out three recommendations, and these were reflected in a 2009 resolution adopted at the World Health Assembly [9]. In 2010, the WHO highlighted the necessity of initiatives that go beyond the framework of health and medicine in its Adelaide Statement [11]. Meanwhile, it also produced documents [12] on what should be attempted within public health programs.

4.1   The Three Recommendations of the Commission on Social Determinants of Health

The first recommendation is to improve the conditions of daily life—the circumstances in which people are born, grow, live, work, and age. The second recommendation is to tackle the inequitable distribution of power, money, and resources—the structural drivers of those conditions of daily life—globally, nationally, and locally. The third recommendation is to measure and understand the problem and assess the impact of action—measure the problem, evaluate action, expand the knowledge base, develop a workforce that is trained in the social determinants of health, and raise public awareness about the social determinants of health. Health (Equity) Impact Assessments—H(E)IA (see Chap. 18)—should be conducted to predict and assess the effects of policies on health (equity).

4.2   Adelaide Statement

Many of the policies that have an effect on the social determinants of health are proposed and implemented in non-health sectors. Therefore, it is necessary to have a perspective that considers HiAP. Some examples of initiatives involving partnerships with non-health sectors include those relating to: the economy and employment; public order and justice; education and early life; agriculture and food; social infrastructure, national lands, and land use planning; transportation; the environment and sustainability; housing and community services; and national lands and culture.

4.3   Public Health Programs

These documents concern how to approach the social determinants of health in 12 public health programs, including those dealing with alcohol and tobacco, cardiovascular disease and diabetes, and mental health [12].

Figure 20.1 [12] presents an analytical framework common to all of these programs. This framework divides factors into four levels that ultimately give rise to differential health at the individual level. Directly, differences in the healthcare that individuals receive are observed, but, prior to that, there are differences in the vulnerability of different population groups, which might, for instance, cause different risks of becoming ill when exposed to the same factor to the same degree. There are also differences in exposure to harmful social and physical environments. Even further upstream from those, there are the social factors consisting of the types of socioeconomic contexts and positions. These overlap to give rise to health disparities. Table 20.1 [12] gives examples of social determinants of health at each of these five levels. With these, one may be able to analyze individual public health issues, find the important social determinants of health at each of the five levels, and intervene there. Then it will be necessary to ask which sort of initiatives will have what magnitude of effect—and on which people. It will be necessary to evaluate the effects and to proceed while constantly improving the initiatives.

5   Latent Possibilities in the Approach Toward the Social Determinants of Health

In November 2011, the WHO established the World Conference on Social Determinants of Health as a high-level meeting attended by officials at the ministerial level; the conference was held in Brazil. Approaches toward the social determinants of health characterized by such things as "an approach toward the root causes upstream," "Health in All Policies," and "environmental intervention" are more

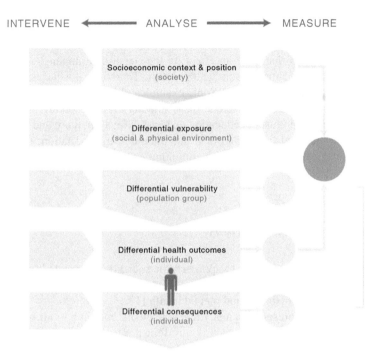

INTERVENE ◄────────── ANALYSE ──────────► MEASURE

Socioeconomic context & position
(society)

Differential exposure
(social & physical environment)

Differential vulnerability
(population group)

Differential health outcomes
(individual)

Differential consequences
(individual)

Fig. 20.1 Priority public health conditions analytical framework. (Blas E, Kurup AS: Equity, social determinants and public health programmes. World Health Organization (WHO), https://apps.who.int/iris/bitstream/handle/10665/44289/9789241563970_eng.pdf?sequence=1&isAllowed=y, 2010)

difficult to achieve than initiatives focused on medicine, medical technology, or lifestyle. However, the latent impact of these approaches that will be expeceted when they have developed is great. If these were to lead to continued increases in smoking cessation and physical activity, improvements of diets, reductions of psychosocial stress, or other favorable developments, then—as has been seen within the present book—one could expect effects limiting not just individual diseases but instead nearly all lifestyle diseases and stress-related conditions, as well as diseases overall.

This is similar to how improved environmental sanitation led to decreases in infectious diseases overall and thus death rates continued to decline long before technologies for treating specific diseases, such as anti-tubercular drugs, appeared. It is also similar to how, if measures to treat metabolic syndrome pay off, then high blood pressure, diabetes, and dyslipidemia will also tend to improve. Those initiatives are not exactly simple, but they will still hold great importance if undertaken.

Within Japan, developments following the WHO recommendations have begun, starting within academia. The Japanese Society of Public Health has established a working group on social inequalities and health under its monitoring and reporting committee, and it has released three reports and recommendations aimed at children,

Table 20.1 Social determinants occurring on the pathways

Level of the priority public health conditions framework	Major social determinants at play
Socioeconomic context and position *Society*	Globalization and urbanization Social status and inequality Gender Minority situation and social exclusion Rapid demograptic change, including aging population
Differential exposure *Social and physical environment*	Social norms Community settings and infrastructures Unhealthy and harmful consumables Non-regulated markets and outlets Advertisement and television exposure
Differential vulnerability *Population group*	Poverty and unemployment Hard-to-reach populations Health care-seeking and low access to health care Low education and knowledge Tobacco use and substance abuse Family and community dysfunction Food insecurity and malnutrition
Differential health care outcomes Individual	Poor-quality and discriminatory treatment and care services Limited patient interaction and adherence
Differential consequences *Individual*	Social, educational, employment and financial consequences Social exclusion and stigma Exclusion from insurance

Blas E, Kurup AS: Equity, social determinants and public health programmes. World Health Organization (WHO), https://apps.who.int/iris/bitstream/handle/10665/44289/9789241563970_eng.pdf?sequence=1&isAllowed=y, 2010

the generation in the labor force, and older people (see Appendices). The Science Council of Japan has also compiled recommendations concerning health and social inequalities through a joint public health science subcommittee of their basic medicine committee and their health and life sciences committee (see Appendices).

In dealing with health disparities, a focus on the social determinants of health and a perspective of HiAP are indispensable. These will presumably begin with actions in the health and medical sector. It will start with health and medical professionals increasing their understanding of health disparities and the importance of the social determinants of health, and they will then urge those around them to act.

Health Japan 21 (The Second Term), published in 2012, set a reduction of disparity of healthy longevity (a period without limitations in everyday life) among prefectures as its goal. Healthy longevity by prefecture for 2010 was 71.74–68.95 years for men and 75.32–72.37 years for women, with a difference of 2.79 and 2.95 years for men and women, respectively (see Fig. 20.2). There were concerns on whether health disparities, which has its root cause in social disparities, could be reduced or

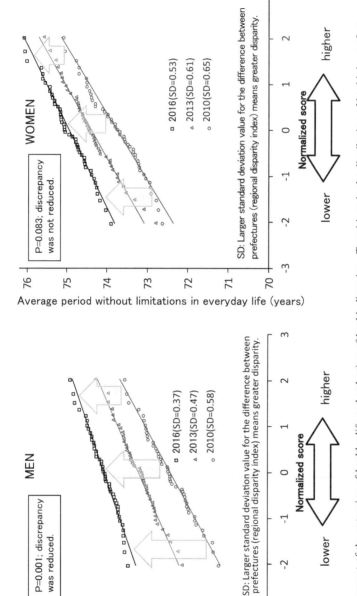

Fig. 20.2 Achievement of the extension of healthy life and reduction of health disparity—Transitions in the distribution of health by prefectures (average period without limitations in everyday life) between 2010 and 2016. Notes: The values are different from the official values for health life by prefectures since the figure uses values where the impact of chance fluctuation due to standard deviation is corrected. 2016 does not include Kumamoto Prefecture because of the earthquake. (Source: 11th Health Japan 21 (Second term) Technical Committee (March 9, 2018) Document 1-1)

not. However, mid-term evaluation of Health Japan 21 (The Second Term) published 5 years later showed that disparities in healthy longevity by prefectures (standard deviation: SD) reduced from 0.58 to 0.37 for men and 0.65–0.53 for women by 2016 (see Fig. 20.2).

Factors that led to this reduction are yet to be identified. Assessment of the mechanism and the size of impact of policies that are effective in reducing health disparities are expected to reduce disparities even further. Developments will occur based on unique Japanese efforts and those of other countries through trial and error. An example of such effort in Japan is the JAGES (Japan Gerontological Evaluation Study) initiative for universal health coverage and healthy aging. We described the lessons and key driving factors derived from 20 years of efforts of JAGES in a monograph [13].

Through these processes and efforts, it is expected that the goal and recommendations proposed by the WHO can be realized; that is, "Closing the gap in a generation: Health equity through action on the social determinants of health" [8].

References

1. OECD. Income distribution—poverty. Paris: OECD. Available at http://stats.oecd.org/Index. aspx?QueryId=9909&QueryType=View. Accessed 12 Jun 2011.
2. Kondo K, editor. Kenshō "Kenkō Kakusa Shakai": Kaigo Yobō ni Muketa Shakai Ekigakuteki Daikibo Chōsa. Tokyo: Igaku Shoin; 2007 (In Japanese). Health inequalities in Japan: an empirical study of the older people. Melbourne, VIC: Trans Pacific Press; 2010. (In English).
3. Abe Aya. Kodomo no Kenkō to Hinkon no Keiken. Kaneko Ryuichi: Kōrō Kagaku Kenkyūhi Hojokin (Tōkei Jōhō Sōgō Kenkyū Jigyō, H18—Tōkei—002) Paneru Chōsa (Jūdan Chōsa) ni Kan Suru Sōgōteki Bunseki Shisutemu no Kaihatsu Kenkyū. Heisei 19 Nendo. Sōkatsu Kenkyūhōkokusho. 2008; 205–216.
4. Centers for Disease Control and Prevention. CDC health disparities and inequalities report: United States, 2011. Morb Mortal Wkly Rep. 2011;60:9.
5. Hooper L, et al. Systematic review of long term effects of advice to reduce dietary salt in adults. BMJ. 2002;325:628.
6. Pennant M, et al. Community programs for the prevention of cardiovascular disease: a systematic review. Am J Epidemiol. 2010;172:501–16.
7. Ebrahim S, Taylor F, Ward K, Beswick A, Burke M, Davey Smith G. Multiple risk factor interventions for primary prevention of coronary heart disease. Cochrane Database Syst Rev. 2011; Issue 1. Art. No.: CD001561. https://doi.org/10.1002/14651858.CD001561.pub3
8. WHO. RESOUTIONS WHA62.14 Reducing health inequalities through action on the social determinants of health. Geneva: WHO; 2009. Available at http://apps.who.int/gb/ebwha/pdf_files/WHA62-REC1/WHA62_REC1-en-P3.pdf.
9. Commission on Social Determinants of Health. Closing the gap in a generation: Health equity through action on the social determinants of health. Geneva: World Health Organisation; 2008. Available at http://whqlibdoc.who.int/publications/2008/9789241563703_eng.pdf.
10. Bonita R, Beaglehole R, Kjellström T. Basic epidemiology 2nd edition. Geneva: World Health Organization; 2006. https://apps.who.int/iris/bitstream/handle/10665/43541/9241547073_eng.pdf;jsessionid=C9614237B6B47F3B58020677CE986292?sequence=1

11. World Health Organization (WHO). Adelaide Statement on Health in All Policies: moving towards a shared governance for health and well-being. Report from the International Meeting on Health in All Policies. Geneva: World Health Organization (WHO); 2010. Available at http://www.who.int/social_determinants/hiap_statement_who_sa_final.pdf.

12. Blas E, Kurup AS. Equity, social determinants and public health programmes. Geneva: World Health Organization (WHO); 2010. Available at https://apps.who.int/iris/bitstream/handle/10665/44289/9789241563970_eng.pdf?sequence=1&isAllowed=y.

13. Kondo K, Rosenberg M, editors. Advancing universal health coverage through knowledge translation for healthy ageing: lessons learnt from the Japan Gerontological Evaluation Study. Geneva: World Health Organization (WHO); 2018. Available at https://apps.who.int/iris/bitstream/handle/10665/279010/9789241514569-eng.pdf.

Open Access This chapter is licensed under the terms of the Creative Commons Attribution-NonCommercial-NoDerivatives 4.0 International License (http://creativecommons.org/licenses/by-nc-nd/4.0/), which permits any noncommercial use, sharing, distribution and reproduction in any medium or format, as long as you give appropriate credit to the original author(s) and the source, provide a link to the Creative Commons licence and indicate if you modified the licensed material. You do not have permission under this licence to share adapted material derived from this chapter or parts of it.

The images or other third party material in this chapter are included in the chapter's Creative Commons licence, unless indicated otherwise in a credit line to the material. If material is not included in the chapter's Creative Commons licence and your intended use is not permitted by statutory regulation or exceeds the permitted use, you will need to obtain permission directly from the copyright holder.

Appendix A: Recommendations

Assessing and Reducing Social Inequalities in Health in Japan

September 27, 2011
Science Council of Japan
Joint Basic Medicine Committee and Health and Life Science Committee
Public Health Science Commission
These recommendations are a publication of the summary of results of deliberations by the Public Health Science Commission that is a joint commission under the Basic Medicine Committee and Health and Life Science Committee of the Science Council of Japan.

Science Council of Japan Joint Basic Medicine Committee and Health and Life Science Committee Public Health Science Commission

© The Author(s) 2020
K. Kondo (ed.), *Social Determinants of Health in Non-communicable Diseases*,
Springer Series on Epidemiology and Public Health,
https://doi.org/10.1007/978-981-15-1831-7

Chairperson	Reiko Kishi	Second Group Member	Professor in the Graduate School of Medicine, Hokkaido University
Vice-Chairperson	Fumihiko Jitsunari	Liaison member	Vice President of Sanyo Gakuen University
Coordinator	Fumio Kobayashi	Liaison member	Professor in the Faculty of Medicine, Aichi Medical University
Coordinator	Yasuki Kobayashi	Liaison member	Professor in the Faculty of Medicine, Graduate School of Medicine, University of Tokyo
	Yoshiharu Aizawa	Liaison member	Vice President of Kitasato University
	Hirobumi Ohama	Liaison member	Chairperson of the Japanese Institute for Health Food Standards
	Katsuko Kanagawa	Liaison member	President of the Kobe City College of Nursing
	Norito Kawakami	Liaison member	Professor in the Faculty of Medicine, Graduate School of Medicine, University of Tokyo
	Michiko Konishi	Liaison member	President of the Gifu College of Nursing
	Teruichi Shimomitsu	Liaison member	Chairperson of the Department of Preventive Medicine and Public Health, Tokyo Medical University
	Hirofumi Takagi	Liaison member	Professor in the Department of Nursing, Graduate School of Medicine, Toho University
	Takehito Takano	Liaison member	Professor in the Graduate School, Tokyo Medical and Dental University
	Shinkan Tokudome	Liaison member	Chairperson of the National Institute of Health and Nutrition
	Tamie Nasu (nee Nakajima)	Liaison member	Professor in the Nagoya University Graduate School of Medicine
	Hiroshi Haga	Liaison member	Professor in the Graduate School of Gerontology, J. F. Oberlin University
	Seiji Yasumura	Liaison member	Professor in the School of Medicine, Fukushima Medical University
	Tatsuo Watanabe	Liaison member	Dean of Asahi Medical College Okayama Campus

Cooperation was received from the following individuals in preparing these recommendations and reference materials:

Kazuo Seiyama	Liaison member of the Science Council of Japan and Professor in the University of Tokyo Graduate School of Humanities and Sociology
Katsunori Kondo	Professor at Nihon Fukushi University

Hideki Hashimoto	Professor in the Faculty of Medicine, Graduate School of Medicine, University of Tokyo
Takashi Oshio	Professor at the Institute of Economic Research, Hitotsubashi University
Yoshiharu Fukuda	Professor in the Faculty of Medicine, Yamaguchi University
Naoki Kondo	Instructor in the Faculty of Medicine, University of Yamanashi

Abstract

Background for Preparing These Recommendations

Throughout history, health inequalities due to socioeconomic factors such as income, educational background and occupation (i.e. social inequalities in health) has been a major issue in public health. In recent years, public attention has been focusing on the increasing income gap in Japan, and there is concern about growing inequalities in socioeconomic status (SES). In addition to assessing issues in social inequalities in health in present day Japan and reconsidering healthcare, medical care and welfare in Japan overall from an inequalities viewpoint, the academic foundation needs strengthening to increase understanding of the current situation in such inequalities and reduce those inequalities. These recommendations are intended to provide an overview of the current research on social inequalities in health in Japan, lay out the challenges in determining the current situation of such inequalities and in making improvements and propose various measures for confronting those challenges.

Current Situation and Issues

Concerns related to social inequalities in health today can be roughly categorized into three groups: (1) With increasing prevalence of households in the poverty class or on public assistance, concerns that health problems are accumulating in the low-income population and that such families have poor access to the minimum, basic healthcare, medical care and welfare services, (2) Concerns of class-based disparities in health issues developing and growing in magnitude throughout society as a whole, not limited to the low-income or poverty class and (3) Concerns of health problems accumulating in socially disadvantaged individuals (such as the unemployed, disabled or homeless and foreign laborers) and the possibility that they are not receiving adequate healthcare, medical care and welfare services.

In the international sphere, the Social Determinants of Health (SDH) Committee of the World Health Organization (WHO) compiled a final report in 2008 in which it advocated the necessity of worldwide action to reduce health inequalities resulting from poverty and other socioeconomic factors. Measures to reduce social inequalities in health are important globally.

A research base on social inequalities in health is being built in Japan as well. Research has shown that those with low income and a low level of education tend to have poor subjective health and have a high prevalence of chronic illness and a high mortality rate. Some studies have also shown that poverty can affect health of children and their health later, in adulthood. Both physical and mental health are worse in those with jobs involving manual labor or operation of machinery than in those in managerial or executive positions, and in precarious workers (in non-standard employment, such as part-time and temporary work) than regular employees (in full-time, continuous work with one employer). Chronic disease morbidity and suicide rate are high in the unemployed population. Among older adults, disparities are seen in mortality, long-term care need, mental health and social activities depending on SES. Although social inequalities in access to health care may be smaller in Japan compared to other countries, reports have indicated that low income earners and precarious workers are hesitant to visit the doctor and have a lower rate of doctor visits.

These findings suggest that health problems are indeed accumulating in the low income and poverty class in Japan as well, and that health inequalities exist throughout all social strata. Precarious workers and others in a socially disadvantageous position may encounter problems in accessing health care services. Reducing social inequalities in health requires taking action where possible. Despite this, research findings on social inequalities in health are currently limited in number, quality and breadth, making it difficult to form an overall image of such inequalities in Japan. Further research is required on social inequalities in health in Japan. There is also a need for comprehensive and ongoing monitoring of social inequalities in health in Japan.

Issues in Japan concerning social inequalities in health can be summarized as:

1. Lack of a social inequalities in health perspective in healthcare, medical care and welfare policies and activities.
2. Inadequate systems/organizations for monitoring social inequalities in health in forming relevant policies.
3. Lack of a social inequalities in health perspective when training healthcare personnel.
4. Lack of public participation in actions to establish policies for correcting social inequalities in health.
5. Lack of research on social inequalities in health.

Recommendations

Consider Social Inequalities in Health in Healthcare, Medical Care and Welfare Policies

We recommend the government to clarify a social inequalities in health perspective for carrying out healthcare, medical care and welfare activities in Japan and appropriate response. A social inequalities in health perspective and relevant response must be clearly specified in Japan's health promoting strategies pursued by the Ministry of Health, Labour and Welfare (MHLW) and in occupational health and safety policies. By doing so, the government promotes incorporation of a response to social inequalities in health in regional healthcare plans of local governments and occupational health and safety activities of businesses. Academic societies may cooperate and provide assistance as groups of experts.

Development of Systems for Monitoring Social Inequalities in Health and Formulating Relevant Policies

We recommend the Cabinet, MHLW and other relevant government organizations to carry out chronological monitoring of social inequalities in health through analysis of existing government statistics and new explorations, and actively publish the results for the public. We also recommend establishing a new organization to link the results of social inequalities in health monitoring to the formulation of cross-Ministry policies aimed at reducing social inequalities in health. We also recommend the development and promotion of Health Impact Assessment (HIA) methodology, training of personnel in this methodology, and accumulation of experience and active utilization of the methodology, promoting its widespread use as a government tool for reducing social inequalities in health.

Incorporating a Social Inequalities in Health Perspective in the Training of Healthcare, Medical Care and Welfare Professionals

We recommend incorporating a social inequalities in health perspective in the training of healthcare, medical care and welfare professionals and their lifelong learning curriculum. The MHLW should add a social inequalities in health perspective to the training curriculum of healthcare, medical care and welfare professionals. In addition, the Ministry of Education, Culture, Sports, Science and Technology (MEXT) should further promote the establishment of graduate schools specializing in public health, incorporate social inequalities in health lessons in the curriculum and further promote relevant research in order to establish a research base for addressing social inequalities in health and develop advanced experts. Organizations for educating healthcare, medical care and welfare professionals may cooperate in this aim and academic societies may increase awareness of social inequalities in health in its members through lifelong learning, academic general assembly meetings and other opportunities.

Promoting Public Participation Initiatives to Address Social Inequalities in Health

We recommend the Cabinet or other government organization to establish a cross-Ministry round-table conference on social inequalities in health comprised of regular citizens, managers, labor representatives, healthcare, medical care and welfare professionals and representatives from relevant Ministries. Discussions from the conference should be referenced when determining national policies. In addition, opportunities should be created for providing accurate scientific information to the public, for examples through open symposiums and forums. Academic societies and private entities may cooperate in such endeavors from their unique positions.

Promoting Research on Social Inequalities in Health

We recommend stepping up interdisciplinary research on social inequalities in health. Academic societies may collaborate together to pursue interdisciplinary research on social inequalities in health.

Introduction

Heightening Interest in Social Inequalities in Health and Its History

Throughout history, health inequality due to socioeconomic factors such as income, educational background and occupation (i.e. social inequality in health) has been a major issue in public health. Japan has not been spared the growing income gap [1]. Children are increasingly likely to carry on the profession or social class of their parents and equality is being lost in education and job opportunities sought by individuals [2]. Concern is therefore growing that there is an increasing gap in health as well due to disparities in income and other aspects of socioeconomic status (SES).

Concerns about social inequalities in health are growing among not only public health experts and other healthcare and medical care professionals, but also in the general public [3].

In statistics from the mid-2000s, the relative poverty rate was 14.9% in Japan, fourth among OECD countries following Mexico (18.4%), Turkey (17.5%) and the United States (17.1%; Fig. A.1). The relative poverty rate in Japan increased from the 1980s to the 2000s, and was 15.7% in a 2007 survey [4] (Fig. A.2). The number of families on public assistance was the lowest in 1993, at 590,000, then grew across-the-board after that point, reaching 1.27 million in 2009 [5].

National and regional income gaps are assessed with a number of different indicators, and these indicators have been growing in Japan since the 1980s [1]. One of these indicators, the Gini coefficient, has continued growing on an equivalized initial income base, at 0.376 in 1995, 0.408 in 1998, 0.419 in 2001, 0.435 in 2004 and 0.454 in 2008 (Fig. A.3) [6]. The Gini coefficient based on equivalized disposable income (with taxes, social insurance premiums and social security benefits (cash benefits only) subtracted from the initial income) has remained roughly level since the year 2000, at 0.312 in 1995, 0.337 in 1998, 0.323 in 2001, 0.322 in 2004 and 0.327 in 2008. However, the Gini coefficient for disposable income is growing for certain groups such as the under 30 population [6]. An explanation for the minimal change in the Gini coefficient since 2000 may be that equivalized income of the general public has decreased, making it appear as if the Gini coefficient is also shrinking [7].

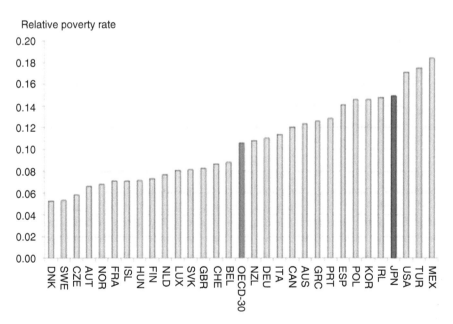

Fig. A.1 Country comparison of relative poverty rate (OECD countries in the mid-2000s). Japan is shown as JPN. (Source: OECD Growing Unequal? Income Distribution and Poverty in OECD Countries, 2008)

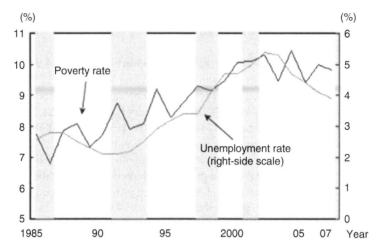

Fig. A.2 Annual change in relative poverty rate. (Taken from reference [9], Figure 3-2-8)
1. Estimates by the Cabinet Office of the Ministry of Health, Labour and Welfare's Comprehensive Survey of Living Conditions. Created based on the Ministry of Internal Affairs and Communications
2. The poverty rate is calculated as the ratio of individuals with an income level that is below the criteria (40% of the median), with the equivalized income derived by adjusting income by the square root of the number of units in the household as the income level for each individual
3. The poverty rate from the Comprehensive Survey of Living Conditions is calculated from estimates of the equivalized income per household individual. The annual income distribution is estimated based on the assumption of an even distribution of household income across each income class. Refer to Figure 3-2-3 remarks for the definition of "income"
4. The shadow zones are periods of economic recession. The most recent shadow continues until March 2009

Regarding labor income in Japan, while this measure has been increasing for those with an annual income of less than 3 million yen, it has been decreasing for those whose annual income exceeds 3 million yen (excluding those earning more than 15 million yen) [8]. The Gini coefficient for labor income has been rising steadily in Japan since 1987 (Fig. A.4). These values indicate that not only is income decreasing for laborers, but the income gap is also widening. A main cause of these trends reported in the 2009 Annual Report on the Japanese Economy and Public Finance is the spreading employment of precarious workers [9].

The public's attitude towards socioeconomic disparities is also changing. The proportion of the population that disagrees or strongly disagrees with the statement that "there are minimal inequalities in income and assets" has grown to over 50% since 1987, and a recent survey (in 2008) revealed that roughly half of the population disagrees or strongly disagrees with this statement [10] (Fig. A.5). A growing low-income population, widening income gap and resulting changes in public attitude create the background for increasing concern and interest in social inequalities in health in Japan.

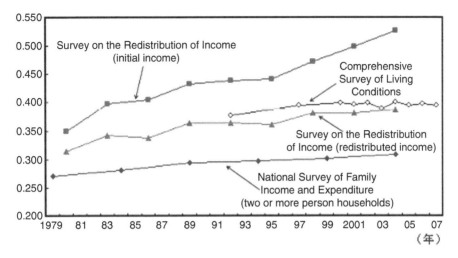

Fig. A.3 Annual change in disparity in household income (Gini coefficient). (Taken from reference [9], Figure 3-2-3)

1. Created based on the Ministry of Internal Affairs and Communications' National Survey of Family Income and Expenditure and the Ministry of Health, Labour and Welfare's Survey on the Redistribution of Income and Comprehensive Survey of Living Conditions

2. Annual earnings (National Survey of Family Income and Expenditure) includes workplace income, business revenue, side income, public pension benefits, income from agriculture, forestry and fisheries business and so forth, and is the amount prior to the subtraction of taxes

3. Annual income (Comprehensive Survey of Living Conditions) is the total of the earned income from January to December of each year (employees' income, business income, agriculture and livestock breeding income and industrial homework income), public pension benefits, property income, unemployment insurance benefits and other social security benefits, allowances, corporate and private pension benefits and any other type of income, and is the amount prior to the subtraction of taxes

4. Initial income (Survey on the Redistribution of Income) is the total of the employees' income, business income, agriculture and livestock breeding income, property income, industrial homework income and miscellaneous income as well as private benefits (the total of benefits such as allowances, corporate and private pension benefits and life insurance claims). Redistributed income (Survey on the Redistribution of Income) is the initial income minus taxes and social insurance premiums plus social security benefits (in-kind benefits)

Summary of Arguments on Social Inequalities in Health

The Science Council of Japan (SCJ) Joint Basic Medicine Committee and Health and Life Science Committee Public Health Science Commission has co-hosted two symposium today with the Japanese Society of Public Health (the 67th Japanese Society of Public Health (JSPH) Conference (Fukuoka) on November 6, 2008 entitled, "Public Health Challenges: A Stratified Society/Poverty and Public Health" and the 68th JSPH Conference (Nara) on October 21, 2009 entitled, "Social Inequality and Health: Towards Resolutions to Important Public Health Issues). During these symposiums, participants discussed the current state of social inequalities in health and actions to take as a group of experts. As a result, concern and

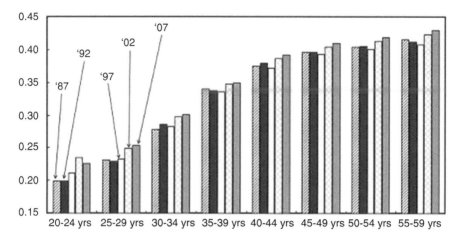

Fig. A.4 Annual change in Gini coefficient among employees by age group. The income gap is growing in all age groups. (Taken from reference [9], Figure 3-2-1)
1. Created based on the Ministry of Internal Affairs and Communications' Employment Status Survey. Employee excludes current students
2. "Labor income" is the annual pre-tax gross pay
3. The method for calculating the Gini coefficient is based on Ota (2005)
4. The income for each individual is the median of the division in which that individual's income falls. For example, for the 2–3 million yen division, the income is 2.5 million yen. For the first and last divisions, the income for the under 500,000 yen division is 250,000 yen, and for the 10 million yen or more group id 13.5 million yen. There are 11 divisions of age group in total

interest in social inequalities in health today can be roughly grouped into the following three topics (Fig. A.6):

1. With increasing prevalence of families in the poverty class or on public assistance, concerns that health problems are accumulating in the low-income population and that such families have poor access to the minimum healthcare, medical care and welfare services. For example, it is possible that low income earners avoid seeing the doctor because they cannot afford the co-pay amount. In particular, the global financial crisis and economic recession tended to place many citizens in financial difficulty. An urgent challenge is to determine how to maintain the health of low-income families in an environment of drastic socio-economic fluctuations.
2. As SES stratification progresses, concerns of class-based disparities in health issues developing and growing in magnitude throughout society as a whole, not limited to the low-income or poverty class. The concern is that those with a low level of education or low income have trouble using traditional healthcare, medical care and welfare services, such as health checkups and programs to prevent the need for long-term care.
3. Aside from aspects of SES such as level of education and income, concerns of health problems accumulating in socially disadvantaged individuals (such as

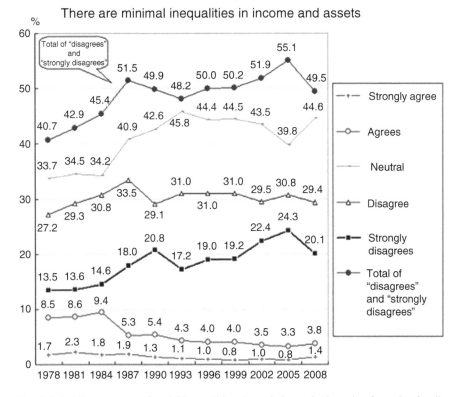

Fig. A.5 Public awareness of social inequalities: Annual change in the ratio of people who disagree or strongly disagree with the statement that "there are minimal inequalities in income and assets". (Taken from reference [10])

unemployed, homeless persons and foreign laborers) and that they are not receiving adequate healthcare, medical care and welfare services.

The World Health Organization (WHO) summarized a list of recommendations on "Social Determinants of Health" (in 1998 and then revised in 2003) [11, 12], and its Social Determinants of Health (SDH) Committee compiled a final report in 2008 [13]. In this report, it stated that poverty and other aspects of SES largely determined the state of health of individuals, and advocated the necessity of worldwide action to reduce health inequalities resulting from SDH. Social inequalities in health is being recognized as a critical issue in healthcare, medical care and welfare not only in Japan, but throughout the international sphere as well [14].

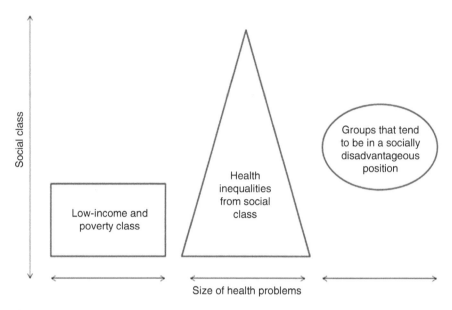

Fig. A.6 Three perspectives on social inequalities in health. Concerns are health problems in the low-income and poverty class, growing health inequalities from social class and an accumulation of health problems in groups that tend to be in a socially disadvantageous position

Past Recommendations by the SCJ and Stance for These Recommendations

In 2009, the SCJ released a set of recommendations entitled, "Creating policies for an inclusive society to combat economic crisis" [15]. These recommendations outline concrete proposals for the state of social security policies in the midst of the global financial crisis and economic recession.

In 2011, the SCJ released a set of recommendations entitled, "Rebuilding the system for labor/employment and health and safety: Towards enabling healthy and secure lifestyles for workers" [16], in which it proposed transforming policies and services to guarantee health and safety equally to all workers, including precarious workers and those in small and micro companies. A report entitled, "Health promotion for children in Japan" [17] emphasized the need to focus on child poverty and social disparities among children. The above recommendations and report are closely related to the present recommendations. However, no set of recommendations or report has yet been presented that focuses on a complete picture of social inequalities in health.

In addition to assessing the current state of social inequalities in health in present day Japan and reconsidering healthcare, medical care and welfare in Japan overall from an inequalities viewpoint, the academic foundation needs strengthening to increase understanding of the current situation in such inequalities and improve the situation. If aggressive actions are not taken immediately to confront issues in social inequalities in health, those inequalities may continue to grow unknowingly, without our understanding of the complete picture, eventually resulting in an even greater impact of such inequalities on the health of Japanese citizens and society as a whole.

In these recommendations, we outlined the current state of research on social inequalities in health in Japan according to each main subject, summarized the challenges in determining the current situation of such inequalities and in making improvements and propose various measures for confronting those challenges.

The Current State of Social Inequalities in Health

Educational Background, Income and Health

According to a recent review of the literature [18], studies have shown that inequalities in health are arising in Japan due to aspects of the socioeconomic background, such as level of education, income and occupation. Regarding associations between educational background and health, four regional correlation studies showed that areas with a large population of poorly educated individuals have a high all-cause mortality rate and suicide mortality rate. Five cross-sectional studies revealed a high mortality rate among those with a low level of education [19] (Fig. A.7), as well as a high prevalence of risk factors for cardiovascular diseases and subjective symptoms, a poor sense of well-being and fewer sleep hours. Two prospective cohort studies revealed higher all-cause mortality and stomach cancer morbidity among those with a low level of education. However, a cohort study on older adults showed longer life expectancy among the educationally impoverished.

Eleven reports have been published in Japan on earnings/income and health [18]. Of these, five ecological studies (regional correlation studies) showed that those living in low-income areas had a higher prevalence of stillbirth, malignant uterine and lung tumors, traumatic injuries and suicide [20] (Fig. A.8), and a shorter mean life expectancy. In addition, those living in municipalities with a low SES tended to avoid having physical checkups. A cross-sectional study showed that low income earners have poor self-rated health [21] (Table A.1) and quality of life, as well as a higher prevalence of unhealthy lifestyle habits such as smoking. Irrespective of the size of individual income, another study showed that simply living in an area with a wide income gap is associated with an increased health risk [22].

Comprehensive analysis (meta-analysis) of international research including studies from Japan revealed a higher mortality risk among those living in areas with wide income gaps [22]. It has been mentioned that socioeconomic disparities in health are smaller in Japan than in Western countries. That said, many of those studies were conducted before the recent global financial crisis. Claims have since been made that social inequalities in health due to socioeconomic factors may be growing in Japan [18, 23] (Fig. A.9).

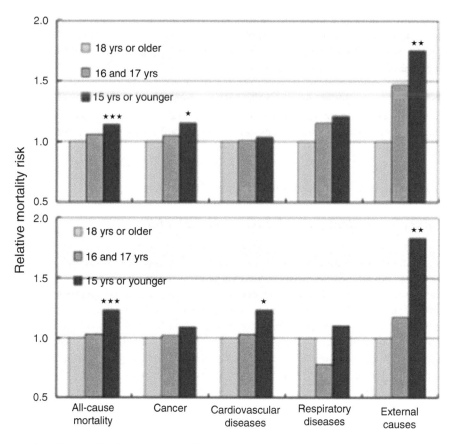

Fig. A.7 Relationship between level of final education and mortality in Japan. Final level of education is divided by age at graduation from last school. The relative risk shows how much higher the mortality rate is compared to high school equivalents (18 years or older) *p < 0.05, **p < 0.01, ***p < 0.001, adjusted for age, smoking status, drinking status and occupation. (Based on reference [19])

Social Inequalities and Health in Children

Children are raised by their families in their home and grow and develop while protected by society and the environment. During this phase, the foundation is built for developing lifelong health. Family, home and social environment may have various effects on children. In countries outside Japan, reports have claimed that household poverty and living in an area with a poor SES can affect children's health, and that SES can influence the prevalence of low birth weight and nutritional status of children during early childhood as well as their health later in life [24].

Japan is still lacking in research on social inequalities in health among children. A survey of the 23 wards of Tokyo revealed a higher number of caries in sixth graders in wards with a lower mean income [25]. A study using data from the Japanese

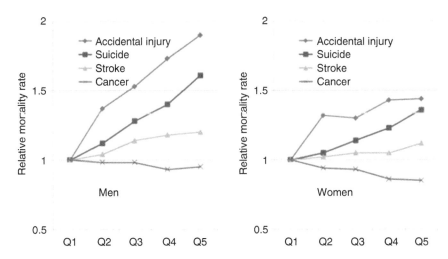

Fig. A.8 Relationship between regional SES and mortality rate in Japan. Municipalities are divided into five quintiles by socioeconomic index (Q1 is the highest and Q5 the lowest). Relative mortality rate shows how much higher the mortality rate is compared to Q1. (Based on reference [20])

General Social Surveys (JGSS) [7] indicated that children living in impoverished homes have a lower level of final education and a lower income in adulthood, as well as poorer subjective health. Another study showed that children who have lived in poverty between the ages of zero and four have a shorter stature, lower weight and higher number of hospitalizations by the age of 4 [26].

The SCJ Health and Life Science Committee Children's Health Commission compiled 56 issues in 16 categories of children's health in the modern era as well as relevant proposals and published this information in July 2010 in a report entitled, "Promoting health of children in Japan" [17]. The authors pointed to the importance of issues concerning social inequalities in health among children, stating that, "Although discussions are proceeding on child poverty and educational disparities among children, there are few reports giving evidence of associations between poverty and social disparities and children's health or measures to be taken.

However, cases are recently being reported in the news of children who cannot eat (are not being fed), children who are uninsured and children who cannot receive medical care, among others, and there have been some anecdotal reports based on regional characteristics." In this report [17], the authors gave the five points listed below to recommend that society as a whole to carry out measures to fight poverty and reduce inequalities so that children can lead safe, secure and healthy lives with a sense of hope.

(a) Change to policies with a perspective of reducing poverty and inequalities and develop and enhance the supportive social environment.
(b) Reduce inequalities by strengthening supportive socioeconomic and psychological factors such as social capital.

Table A.1 Prefectural-level mean income and income gap (Gini coefficient) in Japan and the impact of individual-level household income on poor subjective health of residents (relative risk)[a]

	Analysis on each variable	Analysis of all variables
Prefectural level		
Mean annual income of residents		
Low	1.33 (1.20–1.47)	0.79 (0.64–0.99)
Medium-low	1.15 (1.07–1.24)	0.85 (0.71–1.01)
Medium-high	1.15 (1.05–1.25)	0.93 (0.83–1.04)
High	1.00	1.00
Gini coefficient		
Small	1.00	1.00
Mdeium-small	1.00 (0.92–1.10)	0.99 (0.89–1.11)
Medium-high	1.07 (0.98–1.18)	1.02 (0.90–1.17)
High	1.14 (1.02–1.27)	1.13 (0.98–1.34)
Individual-level		
Annual equivalized household income		
Less than 1.50 million yen	1.93 (1.72–2.15)	1.54 (1.37–1.74)
1.50–1.99 million yen	1.48 (1.30–1.74)	1.30 (1.14–1.49)
2.00–2.49 million yen	1.38 (1.23–1.54)	1.24 (1.11–1.40)
2.50–2.99 million yen	1.23 (1.09–1.38)	1.23 (1.09–1.38)
3.00–3.99 million yen	1.05 (0.95–1.17)	1.08 (0.97–1.20)
4.00–4.99 million yen	1.01 (0.95–1.17)	1.04 (0.93–1.17)
5.00 million yen or more	1.00	1.00

Based on reference [21]

[a]Values are the relative risk that shows how much more a response of fair/poor is given for subjective health compared to controls (prefectures or individuals with a high mean income or prefectures with a small Gini coefficient). The numbers in the brackets are the 95% confidence interval. In analysis by variable, subjective health is poorer for prefectures with a low mean income and those with a low Gini coefficient and with individuals with a low household income. In analysis of all variables, subjective health is poorer in individuals with a low household income. All analyses are adjusted for age, marital status and health checkup visits.

(c) Empower schools and communities that are important supportive social environment factors for children's health.

(d) Educate people through school and social education to attain good health and rectify health inequalities.

(e) Promote life course epidemiology on health and socioeconomic and psychological rearing environment and publish important information.

Social Inequalities and Health in Workers

Seventeen reports have been published in Japan on occupational class and health [18]. These studies found that machine operators and manual laborers had poorer health [27] (Fig. A.10) and more disease risk factors than managerial staff and specialists. For

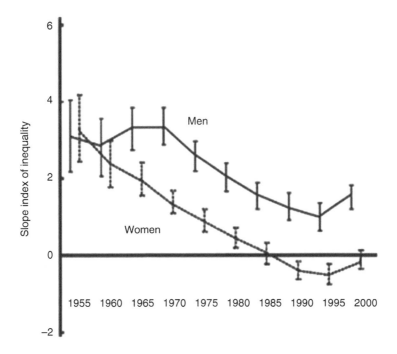

Fig. A.9 Annual changes in the relationship between mean income and mean life expectancy on a prefectural level in Japan. The vertical axis (slope index of inequality) shows the degree of correlation between mean income and mean life expectancy. More positive values represent stronger relationships between high income regions and longer life expectancy. The relationship between the two variables tended to weaken up to 1990, bottom out in 1995, then strengthen after that. Vertical bars show 95% confidence intervals. (Based on reference [23])

example, the studies consistently showed machine operators and manual laborers to have more sick days, more risk factors for cardiovascular diseases, poorer sleep quality and more occupational stress.

In the first half of the 1980s, roughly 15% of the working population consisted of precarious workers (e.g. part-time, fixed-term, temporary and contract workers)—a proportion that now exceeds 35% [16]. A 2009 survey with the mean income of male regular employees as 100 and that of female regular employees as approximately 70 put male and female precarious workers at only 57 and 42, respectively, showing an extremely large gap even for an OECD country. An overseas survey found precarious workers to have higher all-cause mortality and morbidity of occupational injuries than regular employees [28]. To date, almost no full-fledged studies or surveys have been conducted in Japan on the health of precarious workers [29]. However, recent studies have shown that precarious workers have a higher incidence of depression and anxiety than regular employees [30] (Fig. A.11), and that stress from an effort-reward imbalance has a larger effect on health (subjective symptoms) in fixed-term workers than permanent employees [31].

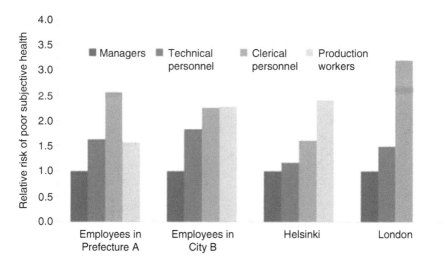

Fig. A.10 Relationship between job type and poor/fair subjective health among civil servants in Japan and other countries. Relative risk shows how much higher the proportion of those with poor/fair subjective health is in each job type with managers as 1. (Based on reference [27])

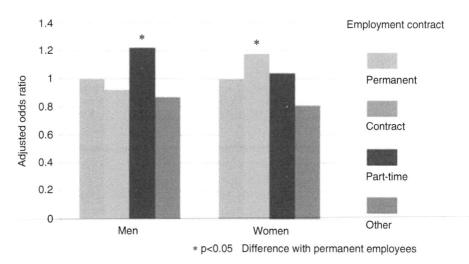

Fig. A.11 Frequency of psychological stress by type of employment contract in Japan. Odds ratio adjusted for basic attributes of how much higher the frequency of psychological stress is in contract/temporary workers and part-time workers with the frequency in permanent employees as 1. (Based on reference [30])

In particular, Japan must not ignore inter-generational (age-based) and gender-based differences in type of employment and working hours and the resulting effects on health status. The first job of over 50% of women is of a precarious employment. While the proportion of precarious workers among men is smaller than among women, there remains a high proportion who work long hours of 60 or more hours a week, especially in the 25–35 year age group. It has been suggested that there is a contrasting relationship between the increase in the working poor in precarious employment with an annual income of less than 2 million yen and regular (permanent) employees working long hours of overtime.

To rectify this situation, the Committee on Work/Employment Environment and the Lifestyle, Health and Safety of Workers that is a topic-specific committee under the SCJ released a set of recommendations entitled, "Rebuilding the system for labor/employment and health and safety: Towards enabling healthy and secure lifestyles for workers" [16] (described above). Ignoring major disparities in employment and labor conditions between generations and genders may impact not only health and safety, but also undermine the development potential (sustainability) of future society in Japan.

Twelve reports have been published in Japan on unemployment and health [18]. Ecological studies (regional correlation studies) have shown that areas with a high unemployment rate have a high all-cause mortality rate and suicide rate. Two cross-sectional studies also reported a high level of stress and prevalence of chronic diseases among the unemployed. A prospective cohort study showed unemployed individuals have a higher rate of death due to cerebrovascular disease. Moreover, the rate of suicides (per 100,000 people) in the unemployed population is estimated to be 184 among men and 34 among women, which is 4–6 times higher than the employed population (32 among men and 9 among women) [32].

Social Inequalities and Health in Older Adults

As physical functioning declines with aging, psychological and social health becomes even more important compared to other generations. In addition, the effects of physical, psychological and social factors from each stage of life accumulate, so that health inequalities increase even among the aged. Moreover, as the range of activities narrows with age, people become even more vulnerable to socioeconomic effects. In view of these characteristics, it is likely that socioeconomic status may generate health disparities among the older generation. The proportion of families with older adults receiving public assistance is growing. While the income gap among aged households is shrinking on account of income redistribution through social security and other benefits, it still remains wider than the gap among non-aged households [33]. This may be one reason for concern about social inequalities in health among older adults.

Research on social inequalities in health among older adults is scarce throughout the world. The Public Health Monitoring Report Committee of the Japanese Society of Public Health conducted a systematic search for literature on the relationship between socioeconomic factors and health in older adults in Japan and found five studies in English and nine in Japanese [34]. The studies showed SES-related disparities among older adults in Japan in mortality and the prevalence of major diseases (such as cancer, stroke and hypertension) [35], long-term care need and risk factors for long-term care need (such as falls, undernutrition and oral functioning), subjective health, depression and other mental health variables, social activities (such as reclusion, social participation, social support and abuse) and other aspects of health (Fig. A.12).

Also, socioeconomically-advantaged households have a higher capacity to care for older family members and may be providing better care in the days until death [36] (Fig. A.13). An overseas study showed that those with a low level of education and those with low income are more likely to develop dementia [37]. Such research has yet to be conducted in Japan.

Social Inequalities in Access to Medical Care

Japan has various social security systems, such as universal pension and healthcare (including long-term care), a special healthcare system for seniors and public assistance for low-income earners. As such, it may have smaller socioeconomic inequalities in access to health care than other countries. Nevertheless, a number of studies have shown that Japan is not spared from social disparities in access to health care. For example, one study showed that low income earners among those insured under a corporate health insurance association tended to have a lower

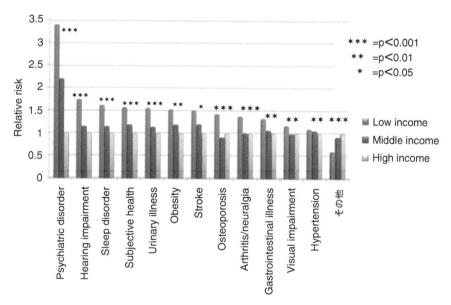

Fig. A.12 Relationship between income and prevalence of various illnesses in a survey of 15,302 older adults in Aichi Prefecture. The vertical axis shows how much higher the prevalence of illnesses is in low/middle income-earners compared to high-income earners. Income is assessed as annual equivalized income and divided into less than 1.6 million yen, 1.60–2.49 million yen and 2.5 million yen or more. (Based on reference [35])

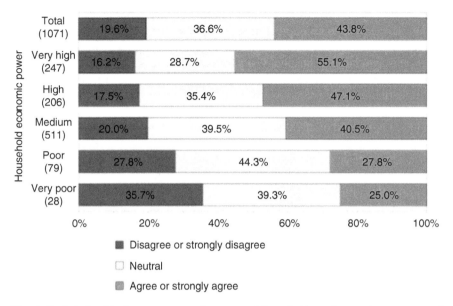

Fig. A.13 Relationship between economic power of households and nurses' assessment of whether or not the quality of end-of-life care was high. Re-tabulation of data from a home nursing station survey (secondary survey) to compare assessment by the nurses in charge of the quality of end-of-life care by economic power of the households. The proportion of cases with high quality care is higher among those with very high economic power. (Based on reference [36])

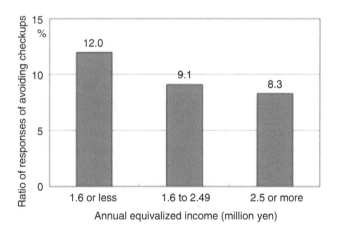

Fig. A.14 Ratio of responses of avoiding checkups in the past year in a survey of 15,302 older adults in Aichi Prefecture. The ratio of responses of avoiding checkups was higher among low-income earners than high-income earners. This trend remains even after adjusting for other basic attributes. Income is assessed as annual equivalized income and divided into less than 1.6 million yen, 1.60–2.49 million yen and 2.5 million yen or more. (Based on reference [35])

rate of visiting outpatient and dental clinics [38]. Another study showed that many older low-income earners have avoided visiting medical institutions for checkups [35] (Fig. A.14). While it cannot immediately be concluded that this represents avoidance of hospital visits for economic reasons, it does show a need for ongoing research on social disparities in access to health care in Japan.

Furthermore, many precarious workers are not enrolled in social insurance programs [39], which may hinder their access to healthcare. For example, a survey conducted at the end of 2008 on *Toshikoshi Haken Mura* (Dispatch Workers' New Year Village) established as an emergency shelter for precarious workers who lost their job and a place to live, determined that many people at the village found it difficult to visit medical institutions or discontinued treatment despite having subjective symptoms [40].

Health literacy, *i.e.* knowledge and understanding of insurance and healthcare, is important for voluntary visiting of doctor's offices and good communication with healthcare professionals to ensure receipt of high quality care. Those with a poor SES may have insufficient health literacy that results in problems accessing healthcare or in the quality of care received [13, 41]. A survey by a national organization in the United States found that socially disadvantaged groups such as minorities, low-income earners and educationally impoverished individuals tended to receive poorer quality of care including health guidance from doctors and routine checkups [42]. However, the relationship between SES and quality of care has yet to be examined in Japan.

Measures for Social Inequalities in Health

At the WHO World Health Assembly in 2009, WHO issued a resolution based on the final report of its Social Determinants of Health (SDH) Committee to recommend that member countries focus on SDH and pursue initiatives to close the health gap [14]. In particular, recommendations included improving lifestyle conditions in all stages of the life course from birth to old age, rectifying social inequalities themselves that generate the health gap, measuring health disparities and performing Health Impact Assessment (HIA) [43] on policies. At a national level, England [44], Sweden [45], South Korea and other countries set numerical targets for its government to reduce health disparities and are revising public health methods as attempts to reduce social inequalities in health through the government. In the United States as well, national research organizations are taking measures that include the publication of a National Healthcare Disparities Report [42].

As the background for the projects in these countries, a health gap is frequently observed between those of high social standing and those of low social standing who often have poorer health. Many studies have shown the latter to have poor access to healthcare and a high mortality rate, and have indicated that socioeconomic disparities play a role. Meanwhile, social inequalities in health is not considered a key government issue in Japan and almost no research has been conducted on improvement measures in the country.

Challenges Regarding Social Inequalities in Health in Japan

As described above, a research base on social inequalities in health is being built in Japan as well. These findings suggest that health problems are indeed accumulating in the low income and poverty classes in Japan as well, and that health inequalities exist throughout all social strata. Precarious workers and others in a socially disadvantageous position may encounter problems in accessing health care services.

Future research on social inequalities in health holds promise for a more thorough understanding of such inequalities and clarification of exactly how measures should proceed. However, considering the principle of equal health for all people in the WHO constitution [46] and the perspective of the right to health stipulated under Article 25 of the Japanese constitution, reducing social inequalities in health requires taking action right now where possible, with what research results are currently available.

Despite this, such research results are currently limited in number and quality. There is also a limit to the scope of social inequalities and health problems that can be covered. For example, discussions are still inconclusive about whether or not there are indeed social disparities in access to health care and availability of health care services in Japan. We still lack a complete picture of social inequalities in health. Further research is required on social inequalities in health in Japan from a variety of perspectives. There is also a need for comprehensive and ongoing monitoring of social inequalities in health in Japan.

Concrete issues in Japan concerning social inequalities in health can be summarized as follows.

Lack of a Social Inequalities in Health Perspective in Healthcare, Medical Care and Welfare Policies and Activities

At present, almost no regional healthcare activities are being conducted with a focus on social inequalities in health. In order to conduct community healthcare activities with such a focus, the first step required is to incorporate that perspective in healthcare, medical care and welfare policies. The Health Japan 21 campaign [http://www.kenkounippon21.gr.jp/index.html] that is a health promoting strategy being pursued by the Japanese government is centered on the concept of health promotion to form communities and environments that support the health building activities of individuals. No specific mention has been made in the campaign regarding health promotion that takes social inequalities in health into account.

The population approach that is another strategy of Health Japan 21 has been claimed to potentially increase social inequalities in health [47]. Starting with Health Japan 21, all of Japan's healthcare, medical care and welfare policies must incorporate an approach that focuses on social inequalities in health. In some regions, some prefectures have initiatives to address social inequalities in health in healthcare programs, but these are only carried out individually and are not part of the system of policies promoting local healthcare activities in Japan as a whole. Adding social inequalities in health perspectives and measures to the system of healthcare, medical care and welfare policies in Japan could help promote local healthcare activities that take such inequalities into account.

Clear statements on a social inequalities in health perspective and response should be noted in Japan's health building strategies and occupational health and safety policies being carried out by the MHLW. Regarding local healthcare activities of each municipality, the government should clarify that activities with a focus on social inequalities in health must be included in local healthcare activities as part of the basic agenda, that the role of public health centers and local governments in reducing inequalities should be clearly stated and that the departments in charge of local healthcare activities must cooperate with other departments involved in such activities as urban planning and industrial development to promote reducing inequalities from the side of social policies as well. Regarding occupational health and safety, the government should demand that workplaces provide all its workers in all types of employment conditions with the same industrial health services and promote the provision of fundamental industrial health services to those in socially disadvantageous positions, such as precarious workers and the unemployed.

Academic societies can assist by determining policies for reducing social inequalities in health and providing relevant information and education to healthcare, medical care and welfare specialists. They can also independently develop guidelines for healthcare, medical care and welfare services with a social inequalities in health perspective. Finally, they can provide support to enable professionals to carry out local health and welfare activities and industrial health activities with a social inequalities in health perspective.

Inadequate Systems for Monitoring Social Inequalities in Health in Forming Relevant Policies

Assessing the situation regarding health disparities due to socioeconomic factors is the first step in determining the extent to which socioeconomic disparities in health exist in Japan and which social inequality should be focused on as a priority. Social inequalities and their effects on health may vary greatly year-by-year depending on fluctuations in socioeconomic conditions. Existing government statistics must be utilized and social inequalities in health must be chronologically monitored in order to assess the situation and respond promptly.

The government (the Cabinet Office, MHLW) is making active efforts to publish indicators of health inequalities in the coming years. However, there is currently a lack of information being published on the actual circumstances surrounding social inequalities in health. By using existing government statistics and conducting new surveys as needed, the government can chronologically monitor social inequalities in health and clarify the situation on such inequalities in Japan. It is also preferable for the results of such activities to be actively made available to the public.

In particular, some considerations are being made in Japan for individuals with a low SES and others in a socially disadvantaged position to have better access to health care services, such as universal health insurance, medical assistance for families on public assistance and medical assistance and medical fee exemptions for persons with disabilities. Nevertheless, it is still possible that disparities exist in access to health care services among precarious workers and the uninsured, as well as other groups. The overall picture in Japan must be clarified, including the extent to which access to healthcare and welfare services is being obstructed in those who tend to be in a socially disadvantaged position, such as low income earners, those with a low level of education, homeless persons and foreign workers.

A government organization with advanced, integrated coordination function (or center function) must be established to conduct high level research and link findings to the formulation of government policies in order to undertake monitoring of social inequalities in health and promote measures to reduce such inequalities. At present, the administrative functions concerning social inequalities in health are dispersed among the Cabinet Office and various departments of the MHLW and there is no single organization that takes on a central, integrated role.

In England, the Department of Health (DH) developed a cross-Ministry action plan in 2003 as the primary government organization to take on the task of reducing social inequalities in health and has since been monitoring the progress of the action plan [44]. The DH also provides tools for assessing regional social inequalities in health. In the United States, the U.S. Department of Health and Human Services acknowledged the critical nature of dealing with social inequalities in health, and the Centers for Disease Control and Prevention (CDC) national research institutions began routine monitoring of inequalities across the nation [48]. An organization or center function needs to be established in Japan as well to conduct monitoring of social inequalities in health and form polices based on the results of monitoring to reduce inequalities.

In a set of recommendations for the 20th term entitled, "Use of government statistics and documents in fields of health and medical care: Establishment of a foundation for ensuring public health and safety" (August 8, 2008), the SCJ Joint Basic Medicine Committee and Health and Life Science Committee Public Health Science Commission called for the promotion of secondary use of government statistics and documents and their further development as well as development of a system to promote their use [49]. The aforementioned monitoring of social inequalities in health and system for developing policies are both included in these recommendations. However, it should be noted that no policies have yet been developed based on these recommendations.

Meanwhile, WHO recommends conducting Health Impact Assessment (HIA) to assess the effects of policies on health when developing and implementing social policies including those concerning the healthcare, medical care and welfare system for reducing social inequalities in health [14]. HIA is a combination of procedures and methods for predicting and assessing the effects of newly formed policies on health in order to optimize policies so that health benefits are maximized and adverse effects minimized. HIA has been developed mostly for use in environmental fields, but is currently applied to a number of fields such as employment, education and urban development, mainly in Europe, as a tool for forming national and local policies. HIA enables prediction of the effects individual policies will have on social inequalities in health. When policies are predicted to increase inequalities, they can be modified to reduce such an impact.

Despite such benefits, HIA is rarely carried out in Japan [50], and future challenges include providing HIA training, developing and spreading methodology and accumulating experience. Japan must develop and spread methodology, train professionals, accumulate experience and actively utilize HIA so that it can be performed when designing systems for health policies and social policies to include considerations of the impact of policies on health and especially on social inequalities in health. The government should commence engaging in discussions with the prospect of HIA eventually becoming a legal obligation when designing policy systems.

Lack of a Social Inequalities in Health Perspective When Training Healthcare Professionals

To carry out healthcare, medical care and welfare activities with a social inequalities in health perspective, it is necessary for healthcare, medical care and welfare professionals to understand such inequalities and carry out their duties with them in mind. Achieving this requires a social inequalities in health perspective to be included in educational programs and lifelong learning of healthcare, medical care and welfare professionals. However, there is currently no such perspective in the training curriculum of healthcare, medical care and welfare professionals. Neither is there a social inequalities in health perspective in lifelong learning of professionals. Moreover, there are no guidelines available for practicing healthcare, medical care and welfare with considerations for social inequalities in health. While there are some examples of information and learning opportunities on social inequalities in health being actively provided to members of academic societies through academic journals and conferences, as is the case with the JSPH [51], such cases are still rare.

In addition, in order to analyze social inequalities in health and recommend and develop healthcare, medical care and welfare services based on the results, healthcare, medical care and welfare professionals must raise the level of their expertise and interdisciplinary skills. From 2000, universities across Japan also began gradually establishing graduate courses specializing in training of public health professionals. At present, four graduate schools dedicated to public health have been established and public health courses have been added to existing master's programs in medical science in a number of graduate schools.

In October 2011, the SCJ Joint Basic Medicine Committee and Health and Life Science Committee Public Health Science Commission published recommendations entitled, "Utilization and enhancement of public health graduate schools in order to raise the level of public health in Japan" in which it called for the extension of graduate schools in public health and utilization of such schools [52]. Developing healthcare, medical care and welfare professionals who can respond to social inequalities in health requires provision of interdisciplinary education and dedicated public health graduate schools and other public health programs that include various academic fields related to social inequalities in health, such as economics, sociology, politics and public policy in order to cultivate the ability to respond to social inequalities in health and develop highly specialized professionals.

Academic societies may assist by including the current status of social inequalities in health and measures to combat inequalities in lifelong learning curriculum for healthcare, medical care and welfare professionals. They can also increase the awareness, knowledge and skills of society members through academic conferences and workshops. Educational institutions, including universities that train healthcare, medical care and welfare professionals, can give classes on social inequalities in health in their educational programs.

Lack of Public Participation Perspective in Initiatives to Address Social Inequalities in Health

The main stakeholders of social inequalities in health are the nation's citizens. Awareness of social inequalities in health is growing among the public as well. Discussions on which social inequalities in health are key issues, which ones can and cannot be tolerated and other points regarding their remediation are in fact discussions about the actual future of society in Japan. Despite this, there are limited opportunities for dispersing accurate, scientific information to the public on research findings and government strategies concerning social inequalities in health. There are currently no platforms for increasing understanding on social inequalities in health or carrying out dialogue on courses of action and priorities for government policies and the ideal future among the public, healthcare, medical care and welfare professionals (or relevant academic societies) and the government or for forming a public consensus.

There is a need for the government to establish a permanent cross-Ministry round-table conference (panel) on social inequalities in health comprised of regular citizens, managers, labor representatives, healthcare, medical care and welfare professionals and representatives from relevant Ministries. Such opportunities can be used for carrying out dialogues between a variety of individuals on social inequalities in health that can then be referenced when determining national policy strategies.

In addition, open symposiums and forums on social inequalities in health should be held periodically to create opportunities to provide the public with accurate, scientific information on the current state of such inequalities and strategies to improve the situation.

Academic societies and private organizations such as NPOs can assist by providing the public with information on social inequalities in health each from their own unique position in order to raise awareness on inequalities and have the public participate in initiatives to reduce them.

Lack of Research on Social Inequalities in Health

While research is progressing on social inequalities in health, the number of studies is still small compared to the breadth of topics, and the quality of such research is inadequate. Not enough studies have been conducted to clarify the psychological and biological factors mediating the relationship between health and SES including income and level of education. Similarly, few studies have been conducted with a focus on specific classes or groups, such as low-income earners, the unemployed, the homeless or foreign laborers. Almost no studies have been conducted on strategies to reduce social inequalities in health.

Research is needed to help clarify the overall situation regarding social inequalities in health in Japan and obtain guidelines for improving the situation. Such research should be pursued from all academic angles, including not only sociology and economics, but also medicine and public health science. Further progress in research on social inequalities in health may potentially increase our essential understanding of the mechanisms underlying such inequalities and aid in the recommendation of more concrete measures.

Recommendations

Consider Social Inequalities in Health in Healthcare, Medical Care and Welfare Policies

We recommend the government to clarify a social inequalities in health perspective for healthcare, medical care and welfare policies in Japan and appropriate response. A social inequalities in health perspective and relevant response must be clearly specified in Japan's health promoting strategies pursued by the Ministry of Health, Labour and Welfare (MHLW) and in occupational health and safety policies. By doing so, the government promotes incorporation of a response to social inequalities in health in regional healthcare plans of local governments and occupational health and safety activities of businesses. Academic societies may cooperate and provide assistance as groups of experts.

Development of Systems for Monitoring Social Inequalities in Health and Formulating Relevant Policies

We recommend the Cabinet, MHLW and other relevant government organizations to carry out chronological monitoring of social inequalities in health through analysis of existing government statistics and new explorations, and actively publish the results for the public. We also recommend establishing a new organization to link the results of social inequalities in health monitoring to the formulation of cross-Ministry policies aimed at reducing social inequalities in health. We also recommend the development and promotion of Health Impact Assessment (HIA) methodology, training of personnel in this methodology, and accumulation of experience and active utilization of the methodology, promoting its widespread use as a government tool for reducing social inequalities in health.

Incorporating a Social Inequalities in Health Perspective in the Training of Healthcare, Medical Care and Welfare Professionals

We recommend incorporating a social inequalities in health perspective in the training of healthcare, medical care and welfare professionals and their lifelong learning curriculum. The MHLW should add a social inequalities in health perspective to the training curriculum of healthcare, medical care and welfare professionals. In addition, the Ministry of Education, Culture, Sports, Science and Technology (MEXT) should further promote the establishment of graduate schools specializing in public health, incorporate social inequalities in health lessons in the curriculum and further promote relevant research in order to establish a research base for addressing social inequalities in health and develop advanced experts. Organizations for educating healthcare, medical care and welfare professionals may cooperate in this aim and academic societies may increase awareness of social inequalities in health in its members through lifelong learning, academic general assembly meetings and other opportunities.

Promoting Public Participation Initiatives to Address Social Inequalities in Health

We recommend the government to establish a cross-Ministry round-table conference on social inequalities in health comprised of regular citizens, managers, labor representatives, healthcare, medical care and welfare professionals and representatives from relevant Ministries. Discussions from the conference should be referenced when determining national policies. In addition, opportunities should be created for providing accurate scientific information to the public, for examples through open symposiums and forums. Academic societies and private entities may cooperate in such endeavors from their unique positions.

Promoting Research on Social Inequalities in Health

We recommend stepping up interdisciplinary research on social inequalities in health. Relevant ministries such as MEXT, MHLW, the Ministry of Internal Affairs and Communications, the Ministry of Land, Infrastructure, Transport and Tourism and the Ministry of Economy, Trade and Industry must each pursue research on social inequalities and health from the unique perspective of that organization. Academic societies may collaborate together to pursue interdisciplinary research on social inequalities in health.

Glossary

Equivalized income   The value obtained by dividing the disposable income of the household by the square root of the number of units in the household to adjust income for the number of household units.

Relative poverty rate   The definition for OECD countries is the proportion of citizens whose equivalized disposable income is below half the median of the equivalized disposable income for the entire nation.

Gini coefficient   An indicator that measures inequitable distribution of income in a society. It ranges from 0 to 1, with coefficients near 0 indicating the presence of small disparities and those near 1 indicating large disparities.

Regional correlation studies   One type of epidemiological study for analyzing the relationship between characteristics of multiple regions and health indicators based on municipalities or other geographical regions as units. Also referred to as ecological studies.

Health promotion   The 1986 Ottawa Charter for Health Promotion that was a new health strategy recommended by the World Health Organization (WHO) defines health promotion as "the process of enabling people to increase control over, and to improve, their health." Health promotion includes not only enhancing an individual's skills and abilities to improve health, but also activities to change the social environment and economic conditions in order to reduce the negative effects on public health and the health of individuals.

Population approach   The population approach is a method to reduce risks gradually among a large group of people by focusing on conferring tremendous benefits to the population in order to shift distributions across the entire population. It is often compared to the high-risk approach that is a preventive method in which individuals at high risk of diseases are targeted.

Health Impact Assessment (HIA)   HIA is a combination of procedures and methods for predicting and assessing the effects of newly formed policies on health in order to optimize policies so that health benefits are maximized and adverse effects minimized. HIA has been developed mostly for use in environmental fields, but is currently applied to a number of fields such as employment, education and urban development, mainly in Europe, as a tool for forming national and local policies.

School of Public Health   In Western countries, graduate education specializing in public health has been systematically implemented for many years to train a wide variety of public health experts. From 2000, universities across Japan also began establishing graduate courses specializing in training of public health professionals. The Kyoto University School of Public Health (professional graduate school) was established in 2000, the Kyushu University Department of Health Care Administration and Management, Graduate School of Medial Sciences (professional graduate school) in 2001, the University of Tokyo School of Public Health (professional graduate school) in 2007 and the Teikyo University, Graduate School of Public Health (professional graduate school) in 2011. In addition, other universities such as Osaka University and the University of Tsukuba established specialist public health courses in the existing medical science master's program in order to train public health specialists.

References

1. Tachibanaki T. Economic disparity in Japan: income and assets. Tokyo: Iwanami Shinsho; 1998.
2. Sato T. Japan as a society of inequality: goodbye all-middle class. Tokyo: Chuokoron-Shinsha; 2002.
3. Kondo K. Social determinants of health (1) Trends in social determinants of health and health inequalities. Jpn J Public Health. 2010;57(4):316–9.
4. Ministry of Health, Labour and Welfare. Publication of the relative poverty rate. Tokyo: Ministry of Health, Labour and Welfare; 2009.
5. Social Statistics Division, Statistics and Information Department, Minister's Secretariat, Ministry of Health, Labour and Welfare. 2009 Overview of results

of reported welfare policy cases. Tokyo: Ministry of Health, Labour and Welfare; 2010.

6. Ministry of Health, Labour and Welfare. Survey on income redistribution. Tokyo: Ministry of Health, Labour and Welfare; 2010.

7. Oshio T. Public welfare analysis of redistribution. Tokyo: Nippon Hyoron Sha; 2010.

8. Ministry of Health, Labour and Welfare. 2007 Employment status survey. Tokyo: Ministry of Health, Labour and Welfare; 2008.

9. Cabinet Office. Annual report on the Japanese Economy and Public Finance 2009 (Report to the Minister from the officer in charge of economic and fiscal policy): overcoming the crisis and vision for sustained recovery. Tokyo: Cabinet Office; 2009.

10. Cabinet Office. 2008 National survey on lifestyle preferences. Tokyo: Cabinet Office; 2009. Available at http://www2.ttcn.ne.jp/honkawa/4670.html. Accessed 17 Sept 2011.

11. Wilkinson RG, Marmot M, editors. Social determinants of health; the solid facts. Geneva: World Health Organization; 1998.

12. Wilkinson RG, Marmot M, editors. Social determinants of health; the solid facts. 2nd ed. Geneva: World Health Organization; 2003.

13. Commission on Social Determinants of Health. Closing the gap in a generation: health equity through action on the social determinants of health. Geneva: World Health Organisation; 2008.

14. WHO. RESOLUTIONS WHA62.14 Reducing health inequities through action on the social determinants of health. Geneva: WHO; 2009.

15. Science Council of Japan Sociology Committee and Economics Committee Joint Commission on Multifaceted Considerations for an Inclusive Society. Recommendations: creating policies for an inclusive society to combat economic crisis. Tokyo: Science Council of Japan; 2009.

16. Science Council of Japan Committee on Work/Employment Environment and the Lifestyle, Health and Safety of Workers. Recommendations: rebuilding the system for labor/employment and health and safety: towards enabling healthy and secure lifestyles for workers. Tokyo: Science Council of Japan; 2011.

17. Science Council of Japan Health and Life Science Committee Children's Health Commission. Report: Health promotion for children in Japan. Tokyo: Science Council of Japan; 2010.

18. Kagamimori S, Gaina A, Nasermoaddeli A. Socioeconomic status and health in the Japanese population. Soc Sci Med. 2009;68(12):2152–60.

19. Fujino Y, Tamakoshi A, Iso H, Inaba Y, Kubo T, Ide R, Ikeda A, Yoshimura T, JACC Study Group. A nationwide cohort study of educational background and major causes of death among the elderly population in Japan. Prev Med. 2005;40(4):444–51.

20. Fukuda Y, Nakamura K, Takano T. Cause-specific mortality differences across socioeconomic position of municipalities in Japan, 1973-1977 and 1993-1998: increased importance of injury and suicide in inequality for ages under 75. Int J Epidemiol. 2005;34(1):100–9.

21. Shibuya K, Hashimoto H, Yano E. Individual income, income distribution, and self rated health in Japan: cross sectional analysis of nationally representative sample. BMJ. 2002;324(7328):16–9.
22. Kondo N, Sembajwe G, Kawachi I, van Dam RM, Subramanian SV, Yamagata Z. Income inequality, mortality, and self rated health: meta-analysis of multilevel studies. BMJ. 2009;339:b4471. https://doi.org/10.1136/bmj.b4471.
23. Fukuda Y, Nakao H, Yahata Y, Imai H. Are health inequalities increasing in Japan? The trends of 1955 to 2000. Biosci Trends. 2007;1(1):38–42.
24. Public Health Monitoring Report Committee of the Japanese Society of Public Health. Public health monitoring. Jpn J Public Health. 2011;58(3):212–5.
25. Komamura K. Society with huge poverty. Kadokawa SS communications. Tokyo: Kodakawa SSC Shinsho; 2009.
26. Abe A. Children's experiences of health and poverty. Kaneko R. Health and Labour Sciences Research Grant (statistical information multidisciplinary research project, H18-tokei-002) Research and development on a comprehensive system for analyzing panel surveys (longitudinal research). 2007 Research Summary Report. 2008; 205–216.
27. Martikainen P, Lahelma E, Marmot M, Sekine M, Nishi N, Kagamimori S. A comparison of socioeconomic differences in physical functioning and perceived health among male and female employees in Britain, Finland and Japan. Soc Sci Med. 2004;59(6):1287–95.
28. Kivimäki M, Vahtera J, Virtanen M, Elovainio M, Pentti J, Ferrie JE. Temporary employment and risk of overall and cause-specific mortality. Am J Epidemiol. 2003;158(7):663–8.
29. Yano E. Precarious employment and health. Trends Sci. 2010;10:20–3.
30. Inoue A, Kawakami N, Tsuchiya M, Sakurai K, Hashimoto H. Association of occupation, employment contract, and company size with mental health in a national representative sample of employees in Japan. J Occup Health. 2010;52(4):227–40.
31. Inoue M, Tsurugano S, Nishikitani M, Yano E. Effort-reward imbalance and its association with health among permanent and fixed-term workers. Biopsychosoc Med. 2010;4:16.
32. Kaneko Y. Suicide prevention measures devised from statistical data. In: Motohashi Y, editor. Live: comprehensive lectures on suicide prevention measures. Akita Medical Library No. 1. Tokyo: Akita Sakigake Shimpo; 2009. p. 109–34.
33. Cabinet Office. 2008 white paper on national lifestyle. Tokyo: Cabinet Office; 2008.
34. Public Health Monitoring Report Committee of the Japanese Society of Public Health. Socioeconomic factors and health in older adults. Jpn J Public Health. 2011;58(7):564–8.
35. Murata C, Yamada T, Chen C-C, Ojima T, Hirai H, Kondo K. Barriers to health care among the elderly in Japan. Int J Environ Res Public Health. 2010;7(4):1330–41.

36. Sugimoto H, Kondo K, Higuchi K. Inequality in terminal care based on the household income level: from the nation-wide survey of older people receiving visiting nurse care. Jpn J Soc Welf. 2011;52(1):109–21.
37. Shirai K, Iso H, Kondo K. Social determinants of health (8) Dementia. Jpn J Public Health. 2010;57(11):1015–22.
38. Kawazoe N, Babazono A. Income effects in medical checkups of those insured under a corporate health insurance association. J Health Welf Stat. 2007;54(6):14–9.
39. Toda N. Social security and the increase in irregular employees. Reference. 2007;673:21–44.
40. Tsurugano S, Inoeu M, Nakatsubo N, Oi H, Yano E. Health status of precarious workers in "Toshikoshi Haken Mura (Dispatch Workers' New Year Village)". J Occup Health. 2009;51(2):15–8.
41. Sugimori H. Education inequality and health. In: Kawakami N, Kobayashi Y, Hashimoto H, editors. Social disparity and health: the perspective of social epidemiology. Tokyo: University of Tokyo Press; 2006. p. 105–26.
42. US Agency for Healthcare Research and Quality. 2009 National healthcare disparities report. Rockville, MD: Services USDoHaH; 2010.
43. World Health Organization (WHO). Health impact assessment. Geneva: WHO; 2004. Available at http://www.WHO.int/hia/en/. Accessed 17 Sept 2011.
44. Department of Health. Tackling health inequalities: a programme for action. London: Department of Health; 2003.
45. Hogstedt C, Lundgren B, Moberg H, Pettersson B, Ågren G. Background to the new Swedish public health policy. Scan J Public Health. 2004;32(Suppl. 64):6–17.
46. World Health Organization. Constitution of the World Health Organization. Geneva: WHO; 1948.
47. Fukuda Y. Does the population approach increase health inequality? Vulnerable population approach as an alternative strategy. Jpn J Hyg. 2008;63:735–8.
48. US Department of Health and Human Services, Centers for Disease Control and Prevention. CDC health disparities and inequalities report - United States, 2011. MMWR Morb Mortal Wkly Rep. 2011;60(Suppl):1–109.
49. Science Council of Japan Joint Basic Medicine Committee and Health and Life Science Committee Public Health Science Commission. Recommendations "Use of government statistics and documents in fields of health and medical care: establishment of a foundation for ensuring public health and safety". Tokyo: Science Council of Japan; 2008.
50. Fujino Y, Matsuda S. Basic concepts of health impact assessment and future initiatives in Japan. Jpn J Public Health. 2007;54(2):73–80.
51. Jitsunari F. Rebuilding a social foundation for protecting health, public health challenges and the role of academic societies. In: Kurumatani N, Jitsunari F, editors. Rebuilding a social foundation for protecting health: where are the leads? Tokyo: Japan Public Health Association; 2010. p. 57–76.
52. Science Council of Japan Joint Basic Medicine Committee and Health and Life Science Committee Public Health Science Commission. Recommendations

"Utilization and enhancement of public health graduate schools in order to raise the level of public health in Japan". Tokyo: Science Council of Japan; 2011.

Source

Recommendations, Assessing and Reducing Social Inequalities in Health in Japan, Science Council of Japan, Joint Basic Medicine Committee and Health and Life Science Committee

Public Health Science Commission, September 27, 2011

http://www.scj.go.jp/ja/info/kohyo/pdf/kohyo-21-t133-7e.pdf

Accessed date: June 10, 2019

Appendix B: Ministerial Notification No. 430 of the Ministry of Health, Labour and Welfare

Notice is hereby given under the provisions of Article 7, paragraph (4) of the Health Promotion Act (Act No. 103 of 2002) that, under the provisions of Article 7, paragraph (1) of this Act, the basic policies for comprehensive public health promotion (Ministerial Notification No. 195 of the Ministry of Health, Labour and Welfare of 2003) shall be completely revised as set out below, and the revisions shall be applicable from April 1, 2013.

Yoko Komiyama
Minister of Health, Labour and Welfare
July 10, 2012

A Basic Direction for Comprehensive Implementation of National Health Promotion

This direction, under the circumstance of aging population with falling birth rate and transition of disease structure of our nation in the twenty-first century, through improvement of lifestyle and social environment, aiming all citizens from infant to elderly to have hope and meaning for living while supporting each other, aiming to achieve a vibrant society with healthy and spiritually rich lives according to life stages (i.e. each stage of human life such as infancy, childhood, adolescence, adulthood, older ages and so on. The same applies hereinafter.), and therefore aiming social security system to become sustainable, declares basic matters for comprehensive implementation of national health promotion, and promotes "The second term of National Health Promotion Movement in the twenty first century (Health Japan 21 (the second term))" (hereinafter National Movement) from 2013 fiscal year to 2022 fiscal year.

© The Author(s) 2020
K. Kondo (ed.), *Social Determinants of Health in Non-communicable Diseases*,
Springer Series on Epidemiology and Public Health,
https://doi.org/10.1007/978-981-15-1831-7

Basic Goals for Implementation of National Health Promotion

Extension of Healthy Life Expectancy and Reduction of Health Disparities

Addressing issues associated with the rapid increase of the aging population and change of diseases structure, through prevention of life-style related diseases, and improvement and maintenance of functions to perform social life, we will extend healthy life expectancy (length of life that an individual lives without limitation in daily activities due to health problems).

Furthermore, through development of good social environment which supports health life at every life stage, we reduce health disparities (gap in health status between the groups, created by difference in community or socioeconomic status).

Prevention of Onset and Progression of Life-Style Related Diseases (Prevention of NCD)*

In order to prevent cancers, cardiovascular diseases, diabetes and chronic obstructive pulmonary disease (COPD), we will implement such programs focusing on primary prevention (i.e. preventing onset of life-style related diseases by improvement of life-style and promotion of health) as eating healthy diet and acquiring habitual exercise, and also implement programs aiming at prevention of progression of diseases, that is, onset of complications or worsening of symptoms.

*Cancer, cardiovascular disease, diabetes, and COPD are categorized as lifestyle-related diseases in Japan. Internationally, these four diseases are regarded as noncommunicable diseases (NCD), and the necessity to implement comprehensive program for prevention and control of NCD is stressed.

Maintenance and Improvement of Functions Necessary for Engaging in Social Life

In order for citizens to perform independent daily life, we will implement programs that would contribute to improvement and maintenance of mental and physical functions at every life stage from infancy to old age. In order to prevent or postpone life-style related diseases, we would implement programs for formulating healthy life-style from childhood. Moreover, we will implement "mental health programs" according to life stage, such as mental health issues for working generation.

Establishment of a Social Environment Where Health of Individuals Is Protected and Supported

As health of an individual is affected by such social environment as family, schools, the community, and workplaces, it is important to endeavor to develop environment which support and protect health of individuals as overall society, thus we would establish environment which comprehensively support people's health promotion movement by active involvement of the government as well as corporations and non-profit organizations.

Furthermore, by promoting mutual aid and social ties both in the community and occupational setting, this policy is intended to help organize a supportive and inclusive environment which protects health of all people, including those who find difficulty in ensuring comfortable life in time and spirit and those who are not interested in promoting health.

Improvement of Social Environment and Such Life-Style as Nutrition and Dietary Habits, Physical Activity and Exercise, Rest, Alcohol Drinking, Tobacco Smoking, and Oral Health

To accomplish the above four directions, it is important to improve nutrition and dietary habits, physical activity and exercise, rest, alcohol drinking, tobacco smoking, and oral health as basic factors related with promoting health of citizens. For the effective implementation of health promotion programs, it is crucial to segment the target populations based on life stage, gender and socioeconomic status, and to comprehend distinctive characteristics, needs, and health issues of each segment.

In addition, we specifically conduct measures to improve life-styles for the high-risk population of life-style related diseases and the young adults and middle-aged adults who will be the elderly during the period when proportion of elderly population becomes largest, and also reinforce health promotion among citizens through communities and workplaces, based on effect of social environment on health of citizens.

Items Relating to Targets in Public Health Promotion

Establishment and Evaluation of Targets

The national government shall set nationwide public health promotion targets and shall make these targets known to the public and to the many people involved in health, and shall continuously survey and analyze changes, etc. in health indices, and shall return the results of surveys and analyses to the public and to relevant personnel, in order to improve the awareness of relevant personnel and the general public and to support independent initiatives.

Also, in order to effectively promote public health promotion initiatives, in establishing specific targets, the national government shall have a shared awareness of the current status and issues, with information provided by the many people involved in health promotion, and shall select issues and shall establish specific targets that are based on scientific evidence and for which actual assessment is possible.

Furthermore, the specific targets shall generally be set with a span of 10 years, and the national government shall carry out systematic initiatives in order to achieve these targets. With regard to the targets that have been established, the national government shall continuously survey and analyze numerical changes, etc. relating to the main targets, and shall endeavor to appreciate differences in health and lifestyles among the various prefectures. Moreover, a midterm evaluation of all the targets shall be carried out 5 years after their establishment, and a final evaluation shall be carried out 10 years after their establishment, in order to appropriately evaluate the results of the various activities aimed at achieving the targets and reflect them in subsequent health promotion initiatives.

Approach to Establishment of Targets

The targets shall aim to prevent the onset or increase in severity of lifestyle-related diseases and maintain and improve the functions necessary for engaging in social life with the intention of extending healthy life expectancy and reducing health disparities, and they shall address improvement of lifestyles and provision of a social environment in order to achieve these objectives.

Extension of Healthy Life Expectancy and Reduction of Health Disparities

Extension of healthy life expectancy and reduction of health disparities are the ultimate objectives that should be realized in Japan through improvement of lifestyles and provision of a social environment. Specific targets shall be established according to Appended Table B.1, on the basis of the index of the average period with no impediment to everyday life. Also, the national government shall comprehensively promote measures against lifestyle-related disease and advance support initiatives in a range of fields, such as medicine and nursing care, toward the achievement of these targets.

Prevention of Onset and Progression of Lifestyle-Related Diseases

In addition to measures against cancer and cardiovascular disease, which are major causes of death in Japan, measures against diabetes, which has increasing numbers of patients and can cause serious complications, and against chronic obstructive pulmonary disease (COPD), which is predicted to become a rapidly increasing cause of death, are important issues in extending the healthy life expectancy of the people.

With respect to cancer, from a perspective of promoting comprehensive prevention, diagnosis, and treatment, the targets shall be to reduce the age-adjusted cancer death rate and, in particular, to increase the cancer screening rate in order to facilitate early detection.

With respect to cardiovascular disease, the targets shall be to improve hypertension and to reduce dyslipidemia, which are risk factors for the onset of cerebrovascular disease and ischemic heart disease, and to reduce the mortality rates of these diseases.

With respect to diabetes, the targets shall be to prevent onset in order to curtail the increase in the number of diabetic persons, and to prevent progression of the disease through appropriate control of blood glucose levels, a reduction in cessation of treatment, and a reduction in complications, etc.

With respect to COPD, the targets shall be to increase recognition that prevention is possible by stopping smoking since smoking is the major cause of COPD, and that early detection is important.

Specific targets relating to the above items are as shown in Appended Table B.2, and with the aim of achieving these targets, the national government will work to prevent onset and progression of these diseases by encouraging behavioral changes that are beneficial to health, such as appropriate diet, moderate exercise, stopping

Table B.1 Targets for achieving extension of healthy life expectancy and reduction of health disparities

Indicators	Current data	Target
1. Extension of healthy life expectancy (average period of time spent without limitation in daily activities)	Male 70.42 years Female 73.62 years (2010)	To extend healthy life expectancy more than the increase of life expectancy (2022)
2. Reduction of health disparities (gap among prefectures in average period of time spent without limitation in daily activities)	Male 2.79 years Female 2.95 years (2010)	Reduction in gap among prefectures (2022)

Note: To accomplish (1) above, not only the "average period of time spent without limitation," but "average period of time individuals consider themselves as healthy" should also be taken into account.

Furthermore, to accomplish (2), each prefecture should aim to extend their healthy life expectancy with the longest healthy life expectancy among all prefectures being the target.

smoking, etc., and by putting in place the social environment for them, and in addition, will promote a system of coordinated medical care and will work to implement specified health checkups and specified health guidance.

Maintenance and Improvement of Functions Necessary for Engaging in Social Life

As the birth rate decreases and the population ages, prevention of lifestyle-related diseases and maintaining the functions for engaging in social life even in old age are essential for extending healthy life expectancy.

In order to maintain the functions necessary for engaging in social life, mental health is as important as physical health. Maintaining mental health greatly influences the quality of life of the individual, and with the aim of building a society that supports healthy minds across all generations in order to prevent such social losses as suicide, the targets will be a reduction in the suicide rate, a decrease in severe depression or anxiety, an enhanced support environment in the workplace, and enhanced measures for coping with children's mental and physical problems.

Furthermore, promoting the health of expectant mothers and children is essential to supporting the health of the next generation, which will bear the burden of the future, and the targets will be to ensure acquisition of healthy lifestyles from childhood onward and an increase in the number of children with the ideal body weight.

Moreover, efforts that focus on the health of elderly people need to be strengthened in order to delay the reduction in function accompanying old age, and the targets will be to control the increase in the number of people making use of nursing care insurance services and to prevent cognitive decline and locomotive syndrome, and also to maintain favorable nutritional status, to increase the amount of physical activity, and to promote social participation, such as work.

The specific targets relating to the above items will be as shown in Appended Table B.3, and the national government will enhance measures for mental health, initiatives for sound health promotion among expectant mothers and children, and prevention or support initiatives relating to care.

Provision of Social Environment to Support and Protect Health

In order to provide social environment to support and protect health, it is essential for a range of such bodies as the people, companies, civil organizations, etc., to work voluntarily toward promoting health. As shown in Appended Table B.4, specific targets will be established with regard to strengthening the local links of mutual assistance within the community, increasing the proportion of people proactively involved in activities aiming to promote health, increasing the number of companies working on activities relating to promoting health and voluntarily giving out information, and increasing the number of bases for the activities of civil organizations that offer specialized assistance or consultations in familiar settings, and in addition,

Table B.2 Targets for the prevention of onset and progression of life-style related diseases

Indicators	Current data	Target
Cancer		
1. Reduction in age-adjusted mortality rate of cancer under age 75 (per 100,000)	84.3 (2010)	73.9 (2015)
2. Increase in participation rate of cancer screenings	Gastric cancer Male 36.6% Female 28.3% Lung cancer Male 26.4% Female 23.0% Colorectal cancer Male 28.1% Female 23.9% Cervical cancer Female 37.7% Breast cancer Female 39.1% (2010)	50% (40% for gastric, lung, and colorectal cancer) (2016)

Note: These rates represent individuals who are between 40 and 69 years old (for cervical cancer age of individuals is between 20 and 69 years).

Furthermore, breast and cervical cancer screening rates are percentage of women screened within the past 2 years.

Indicators	Current data	Target
Cardiovascular Disease		
1. Reduction in age-adjusted mortality rate of cerebrovascular disease (CVD) and ischemic heart disease (IHD) (per 100,000)	CVD Male 49.5 Female 26.9 IHD Male 36.9 Female 15.3 (2010)	CVD Male 41.6 Female 24.7 IHD Male 31.8 Female 13.7 (2022)
2. Improvement of hypertension (reduction in average systolic blood pressure)	Male 138 mmHg Female 133 mmHg (2010)	Male 134 mmHg Female 129 mmHg (2022)
3. Reduction in percentage of adults with dyslipidemia	Those with total cholesterol over 240 mg/dl Male 13.8% Female 22.0% Those with LDL cholesterol over 160 mg/dl Male 8.3% Female 11.7% (2010)	Those with total cholesterol over 240 mg/dl Male 10% Female 17% Those with LDL cholesterol over 160 mg/dl Male 6.2% Female 8.8% (2022)
4. Reduction in number of definite and at-risk people with metabolic syndrome	14,000,000 (2008)	25% less than 2008 (2015)
5. Increase in participation rates of specified health checkups and specified health guidance	Specified health checkups 41.3% Specified health guidance 12.3% (2009)	Will be set based on the second term of medical cost adjustment plan starting in 2013 (2017)
Diabetes		
1. Reduction in complications (number of patients newly introduced to dialysis due to diabetic nephropathy)	16,247 (2010)	15,000 (2022)

(continued)

Table B.2 (continued)

Indicators	Current data	Target
2. Increase in percentage of patients who continue treatment	63.7% (2010)	75% (2022)
3. Decrease in percentage of individuals with elevated blood glucose levels (HbA1c (NGSP) ≥ 8.4%)	1.2% (2009)	1.0% (2022)
4. Prevent increase in number of diabetic persons	8,900,000 (2007)	1,000,000 (2022)
5. Reduction in number of definite and at-risk people with metabolic syndrome	14,000,000 (2008)	25% less than 2008 (2015)
6. Increase in participation rates of specified health checkups and health guidance	Specified health checkups 41.3% Specified health guidance 12.3% (2009)	Will be set based on the second period of medical cost adjustment plan starting in 2013 (2017)
COPD		
1. Increase recognition of COPD	25% (2011)	80% (2022)

with the aim of reducing health disparities, targets will be established with regard to local governments understanding disparities in health status, which are issues at the regional level, and working on countermeasures.

The national government will work toward achieving these targets by disseminating information on the activities of companies and civil organizations, etc., working voluntarily on promoting health, and evaluating these activities in order to facilitate the motivation of the relevant companies, civil organizations, etc.

Improvement of Life-Style and Social Environment Relating to Nutrition and Dietary Habits, Physical Activity and Exercise, Rest, Alcohol, Smoking, and Dental and Oral Health

Targets relating to nutrition and dietary habits, physical activity and exercise, rest, alcohol, smoking, and dental and oral health will be shown in Appended Table B.5, and are based on the approaches for each of these items laid out in the following.

Nutrition and Dietary Habits

Nutrition and dietary habits are essential from the point of view of preventing life-style-related diseases, maintaining or improving functions necessary for engaging in social life, and improving quality of life. Targets will be established in relation to maintaining ideal body weight and appropriate diet, which are priority life stage issues and include targets relating to the health of the next generation and of elderly

Table B.3 Targets for maintenance and improvement of functions necessary for engaging in social life

Indicators	Current data	Target
Mental health		
1. Reduction in suicide rate (per 100,000)	23.4 (2010)	Will be set based on modified suicide prevention plan
2. Decrease in percentage of individuals who suffer from mood disorders or anxiety disorders	10.4% (2010)	9.4% (2022)
3. Increase in percentage of occupational settings where interventions for mental health are available	33.6% (2007)	100% (2020)
4. Increase in number of pediatricians and child psychiatrists per 100,000 children	Pediatricians: 94.4 (2010) Child psychiatrists: 10.6 (2009)	To increase (2014)
Children's health		
1. Increase in percentage of children who maintain healthy lifestyle (nutrition, dietary habits, physical activity)		
A. Increase in percentage of children who eat three meals a day	5th grade 89.4% (2010)	To reach 100% (2022)
B. Increase in percentage of children who exercise regularly	(Ref) Three times a week or more 5th grade Male 61.5% Female 35.9% (2010)	To increase (2022)
2. Increase in percentage of children with ideal body weight		
A. Reduction in percentage of low birth weight infants	9.6% (2010)	To reduce (2014)
B. Reduction in percentage of children who tend to be obese	5th graders who are overweight or obese (2011) Male 4.60% Female 3.39%	To reduce (2014)
Health of elderly people		
1. Restraint of the increase in Long-Term Care Insurance service users	4,520,000 (2012)	6,570,000 (2025)
2. Increase in identification rate of high-risk elderly with low cognitive function	0.9% (2009)	10% (2022)
3. Increase in percentage of individuals who know about locomotive syndrome	(Ref) 17.3% (2012)	80% (2022)
4. Restraint of the increase in undernourished elderly (BMI under 20)	17.4% (2010)	22% (2022)
5. Decrease number of elderly with back or foot pain (per 1000)	Male 218 Female 291 (2010)	Male 200 Female 260 (2022)

(continued)

Table B.3 (continued)

Indicators	Current data	Target
6. Promotion of social participation (employed or engaged in community activities)	(Ref) Percentage of those who are involved in any form of community activities Male 64.0% Female 55.1% (2008)	80% (2022)

Note: the target for 1 is set based on the results from the Outline basic and integrated Reform Plan for Social Welfare and Tax.

Table B.4 Targets for putting in place a social environment to support and protect health

Indicators	Current data	Target
1. Strengthening of community ties	(Ref) Percentage of those who consider that "There is a strong bond between the community and myself." 45.7% (2007)	65% (2022)
2. Increase in percentage of individuals who are involved in health promotion activities	(Ref) Percentage of those volunteering health or medical service 3.0% (2008)	25% (2022)
3. Increase in number of corporations that deal with health promotion and educational activities	420 (2012)	3000 (2022)
4. Increase in number of civilian organizations that offer accessible opportunities for health promotion support or counseling	(Ref) Number of Reported organizations 7134 (2012)	15,000 (2022)
5. Increase in number of local governments that make efforts to solve health disparity issues (number of prefectures that identify problems and have intervention programs for those in need)	11 (2012)	47 (2022)

people, and also with regard to reduction in salt content of food and nutritional and dietary control at specified food service facilities (facilities that provide meals to specified people in large numbers on a continuous basis. The same applies hereinafter.), in order to provide social environment foe health promotion.

The national government will work toward achieving these targets by setting standards and guidelines relating to healthy diet and nutrition, promoting people's movements relating to healthy diet through collaboration among relevant administrative organs, promoting dietary education, training human resources with specialized technical ability, and putting in place systems through cooperation between companies and civil organizations, etc.

Table B.5 Targets for improvement of everyday habits and social environment relating to nutrition and dietary habits, physical activity and exercise, rest, alcohol, smoking, and dental and oral health

Indicators	Current data	Target
Nutrition and dietary habits		
1. Increase in percentage of individuals maintaining ideal body weight (Reduction in percentage of obese individuals [BMI 25 and more] and underweight individuals [BMI less than 18.5])	Obese males in their 20s to 60s 31.2% Obese females in their 40s to 60s 22.2% Underweight females in their 20s 29.0% (2010)	Obese males in their 20s to 60s; 28% Obese females in their 40s to 60s; 19% Underweight females in their 20s 20% (2022)
2. Increase in percentage of individuals who consume appropriate quality and quantity of food		
A. Increase in percentage of individuals who eat balanced diet with staple food, main dish and side dish more than twice a day	68.1% (2011)	80% (2022)
B. Decrease in mean salt intake	10.6 g (2010)	8 g (2022)
C. Increase in consumption of vegetables and fruits	Mean daily intake of vegetables 282 g Individuals who consume fruit less than 100 g/day 61.4% (2010)	Mean daily intake of vegetables 350 g Individuals who consume fruit less than 100 g/day 30% (2022)
3. Increase in dining with family regularly (decrease in percentage of children who eat alone)	Breakfast Elementary school student 15.3% Junior high school student 33.7% Dinner Elementary school student 2.2% Junior high school student 6.0% (2010)	To decrease (2022)
4. Increase in number of corporations in food industry that supply food product low in salt and fat	Registered corporations 14 Registered restaurants 17,284 locations (2012)	Registered corporations 100 Registered restaurants 30,000 locations (2022)
5. Increase in percentage of specific food service facilities that plan, cook, and evaluate and improve nutritional content of menu based on the needs of clients	(Ref) Facilities with registered/non-registered dietitians 70.5% (2010)	80% (2022)

(continued)

Table B.5 (continued)

Indicators	Current data	Target
Physical activity and exercise		
1. Increase in daily number of steps	20–64 years old Male 7841 steps Female 6883 steps Over 65 years old Male 5628 steps Female 4584 steps (2010)	20–64 years old Male 9000 steps Female 8500 steps Over 65 years old Male 7000 steps Female 6000 steps (2022)
2. Increase in percentage of individuals who regularly exercise	20–64 years old Male 26.3% Female 22.9% Over 65 years old Male 47.6% Female 37.6% (2010)	20–64 years old Male 36% Female 33% Over 65 years old Male 58% Female 48% (2022)
3. Increase in number of local governments that offer community development and environment to promote physical activity	17 prefectures (2012)	47 prefectures (2022)
Rest		
1. Reduction in percentage of individuals who do not take rest through sufficient sleep	18.4% (2009)	15% (2022)
2. Reduction in percentage of employees who work 60 h or more per week	9.3% (2011)	5.0% (2020)
Alcohol drinking		
1. Reduction in percentage of individuals who consume alcohol over recommended limits (male >40 g, female >20 g/day)	Male 15.3% Female 7.5% (2010)	Male 13% Female 6.4% (2022)
2. Eradication of underage drinking	Third grade of junior high school Male 10.5% Female 11.7% Third grade of high school Male 21.7% Female 19.9% (2010)	0% (2022)
3. Eradication of alcohol consumption among pregnant women	8.7% (2010)	0% (2014)
Tobacco smoking		
1. Reduction in percentage of adult smoking rate (quit smoking among smokers who want to quit smoking)	19.5% (2010)	12% (2022)

(continued)

Table B.5 (continued)

Indicators	Current data	Target
2. Eradication of underage smoking	First grade of junior high school Male 1.6% Female 0.9% Third grade of high school Male 8.6% Female 3.8% (2010)	0% (2022)
3. Eradication of smoking during pregnancy	5.0% (2010)	0% (2014)
4. Reduction in percentage of individuals who are exposed to passive smoking at home, workplace, restaurants, governmental institutions, and medical institutions	Governmental institutions 16.9% Medical institutions 13.3% (2008) Workplace 64% (2011) Home 10.7% Restaurants 50.1% (2010)	Governmental institutions 0% Medical institutions 0% (2022) Workplace—no secondhand smoke (2020) Home 3% Restaurants 15% (2022)
Dental and oral health		
1. Maintenance and improvement of oral function (increase in percentage of individuals in their 60s with good mastication)	73.4% (2009)	80% (2022)
2. Prevention of tooth loss		
A. Increase in percentage of 80-year-old individuals with over 20 teeth remaining	25% (2005)	50% (2022)
B. Increase in percentage of 60-year-old individuals with over 24 teeth remaining	60.2% (2005)	70% (2022)
C. Increase in percentage of 40-year-old individuals with all teeth remaining	54.1% (2005)	75% (2022)
3. Decrease in percentage of individuals with periodontal disease		
A. Decrease in percentage of individuals in 20s with gingivitis	31.7% (2009)	25% (2022)
B. Decrease in percentage of individuals in 40s with progressive periodontitis	37.3% (2005)	25% (2022)
C. Decrease in percentage of individuals in 60s with progressive periodontitis	54.7% (2005)	45% (2022)
4. Increase in number of children without dental caries		
A. Increase in number of prefectures where over 80% of 3-year-old children have no dental caries	6 prefectures (2009)	23 prefectures (2022)
B. Increase in number of prefectures where 12-year-old children have less than 1 dmft (the mean decayed, missing, and filled teeth)	7 prefectures (2011)	28 prefectures (2022)
5. Increase in percentage of individuals who participated in dental check-up during the past year	34.1% (2009)	65% (2022)

Physical Activity and Exercise

Physical activity and exercise are essential from the point of view of preventing lifestyle-related diseases, maintaining or improving functions of social life, and improving quality of life. Targets will be established relating to making exercise habits entrenched and increasing the amount of physical activity, including targets relating to the health of the next generation and of elderly people, and will be established with regard to providing environment in which people can easily take on physical activity and exercise.

The national government will work toward achieving these targets by revising standards and guidelines for exercise for the purpose of health promotion and putting in place systems through cooperation between companies and civil organizations.

Rest

Rest is an important element in relation to quality of life, and having sufficient sleep in terms of both quality and quantity in daily life and maintaining the body and the mind through leisure are essential from the point of view of maintaining physical and mental health. Targets will be established relating to ensuring rest through sufficient sleep and to reducing the proportion of workers that work 60 h or more per week.

The national government will work toward achieving these targets by revising guidelines on sleep for health promotion.

Alcohol

Alcohol is not only a risk factor for health problems such as lifestyle-related diseases, various other physical diseases, and depression, it can also be a cause of social problems such as underage drinking and traffic accidents due to drunk driving. Targets will be established relating to reducing the number of people drinking quantities of alcohol that increase the risk of lifestyle-related disease onset and preventing underage drinking and drinking during pregnancy.

The national government will work toward achieving these targets by public awareness of correct information with regard to alcohol and by measures to prevent underage drinking, etc.

Smoking

Smoking is the largest preventable risk factor for non-communicable diseases (NCD) such as cancer, cardiovascular disease, diabetes, and COPD, and it is also a primary factor in the increase in low birth-weight infants, and passive smoking is a cause of various diseases, thus avoiding the health hazards of smoking is essential.

Targets will be established relating to reducing the rates of smoking among adults, underage smoking, smoking during pregnancy, and passive smoking.

The national government will work toward achieving these targets by measures to prevent passive smoking, help with quitting smoking for those who wish to quit, measures to prevent underage smoking, and education and public awareness on the health effects of tobacco and on quitting smoking.

Dental and Oral Health

Dental and oral health is essential for maintaining good food intake and articulation and, therefore, makes a huge contribution to quality of life. Targets will be established relating to prevention of periodontal disease, caries, and tooth loss, as well as maintenance and improvement of oral function, from the point of view of preventing disease in order to enable lifelong maintenance of healthy oral function.

The national government will work toward achieving these targets by public education relating to dental and oral hygiene and further promotion of the 80-20 Campaign (20 teeth at age 80 years).

Basic Items Relating to the Formulation of Prefectural Health Promotion Plans and Municipal Health Promotion Plans

Establishment and Evaluation of Health Promotion Plans

When formulating Prefectural Health Promotion Plans and Municipal Health Promotion Plans (hereinafter "Health Promotion Plans"), local governments need to select important tasks of their own accord using indices relating to the health of people in the local community such as vital statistics, data relating to medical care or long-term care, specified health checkup data, etc., and based on the current status of local social resources, etc., and need to establish targets for attaining these targets and periodically evaluate and revise these targets.

Prefectural governments shall take into consideration the nationwide health promotion targets established by the national government, and they shall formulate targets, based on regional circumstances, with respect to the representative national targets that are easy for local residents to understand, and in addition, they shall endeavor to understand differences in health and lifestyle among municipalities (including special wards; this applies hereinafter.) within the prefecture.

Municipal governments shall take into consideration the targets set by the national and prefectural governments, and they shall endeavor to set targets with an emphasis on the targets relating to specific types of implementation, projects, establishment of foundations, etc.

Points to Note When Formulating Plans

The following points need to be noted when Health Promotion Plans are formulated.

1. The prefectural government shall play a central role in formulating the Prefectural Health Promotion Plan from the point of view of promoting integrated initiatives by the municipal government, medical insurers, school health personnel, occupational health personnel, companies involved in health promotion, civil organizations, etc., and in strengthening cooperation between these relevant personnel. The prefectural government shall therefore make use of councils for the promotion of regional and occupational cooperation made up of Health Promotion Plans executive, personnel, medical institutions, representatives of companies, prefectural labor department personnel, and other relevant personnel, shall hold discussions regarding policy in order to define the divisions of roles between these relevant personnel and facilitate cooperation between them, and shall reflect the results of these discussions in the Prefectural Health Promotion Plan.

2. When the Prefectural Health Promotion Plan is formulated, consideration shall be given to harmonize between the Medical Care Plan that the prefectural government shall formulate as prescribed in Article 30-4 paragraph (1) of the Medical Care Act (Act No. 205 of 1948), the Prefectural Plan for Reasonable Medical Expenses prescribed in Article 9 paragraph (1) of the Act on Assurance of Medical Care for Elderly People (Act No. 80 of 1982), the Prefectural Insured Long-term Care Service Plan prescribed in Article 118 paragraph (1) of the Long-Term Care Insurance Act (Act No. 123 of 1997), the Prefectural Cancer Control Promotion Plan prescribed in Article 11 paragraph (1) of the Cancer Control Act (Act No. 98 of 2006), and other plans related to the Prefectural Health Promotion Plan, as well as the basic items prescribed in Article 12 paragraph (1) of the Act Concerning the Promotion of Dental and Oral Health (Act No. 95 of 2011) set by prefectural government.

   The prefectural government shall also support the formulation of the Municipal Health Promotion Plan and, as necessary, shall analyze individual municipalities and endeavor to establish targets within the Prefectural Health Promotion Plan that aim to correct regional disparities in health status.

3. Health care centers shall, as wide-area, specialized, and technical bases for local health, collect and analyze health information with the aim of reducing health disparities, etc. and provide this information to local residents and relevant personnel, and they shall also give support to municipal governments in the formulation of Municipal Health Promotion Plans according to regional circumstances.

4. When formulating the Municipal Health Promotion Plan, the municipal government shall cooperate with the prefectural government and healthcare centers, and, from the point of view of effective implementation of projects, shall aim for cooperation among health projects that it carries out in its capacity as a health insurer, such as integrated formulation of the Implementation Plan for Specified Health Checks, which it formulates as a health insurer as prescribed in Article 19 paragraph (1) of the Act on Assurance of Medical Care for Elderly People, and

the Municipal Health Promotion Plan, etc., and health promotion projects that it carries out in its capacity as a project executor, and shall also give consideration to harmony between the Municipal Health Promotion Plan and the Municipal Insured Long Term Care Service Plan prescribed in Article 117 paragraph (1) of the Long-Term Care Insurance Act and other plans relating to the Municipal Health Promotion Plan.

Furthermore, the municipality shall be mindful to position health promotion projects carried out on the basis of Article 17 and Article 19-2 of the Health Promotion Act (Act No. 103 of 2002) within the Municipal Health Promotion Plan.

5. Prefectural and municipal governments shall evaluate and revise the plans within a fixed period, taking into consideration the period of national government targets, and shall link them to continuous initiatives for health promotion among local residents. When carrying out these evaluations and revisions, as well as evaluating projects that they themselves have carried out, prefectural or municipal governments shall also evaluate the progress and achievements of initiatives by medical insurers, school health personnel, occupational health personnel, companies, etc. within the prefecture or municipality, and be mindful of reflecting these in subsequent initiatives, etc.

6. Prefectural and municipal governments shall be mindful to allow the independent participation of local residents in the establishment of health promotion targets, in the process until achievement of targets, and in the evaluation of targets, and to allow proactive reflection of their opinions in health promotion initiatives.

Basic Items Relating to Surveys of Public Health and Nutrition and Other Surveys or Research Relating to Health Promotion

Use of Surveys When Implementing Policy Relating to Health Promotion

The national government shall plan and efficiently carry out surveys of public health and nutrition, etc. in order to evaluate targets, etc. for advancing public health promotion. At the same time, the national government shall also advance surveys and research relating to improvement of the social environment, as well as improvement of lifestyle habits.

The national government, local governments, and independent administrative agencies shall analyze the current status of health promotion and evaluate policy relating to health promotion on the basis of information from national health and nutrition surveys, prefectural health and nutrition surveys, basic surveys of people's living, health checkups, health guidance, results of local cancer registration projects, different types of statistics relating to disease, etc., health insurance claims, and other information, etc. that has been collected. At this time, it is important that these bodies recognize the importance of ensuring strict enforcement of suitable handling of personal information and compliance with the Act on the Protection of Personal Information (Act No. 57 of 2003), the Act on the Protection of Personal Information Held by Administrative Organs (Act No. 58 of 2003), the Act on the Protection of Personal Information Held by Independent Administrative Agencies, etc. (Act No. 59 of 2003), the Statistics Act (Act No. 53 of 2007), and ordinances created by local governments based on the intent of Article 11 paragraph (1) of the Act on the Protection of Personal Information, etc., and also make full use of the results of the various surveys, etc. to efficiently implement policy relating to health promotion on a scientific basis.

Furthermore, these bodies shall proactively endeavor to publicize the information obtained from these surveys, etc.

Moreover, the national government and local governments shall endeavor to construct frameworks utilizing ICT (information and communications technology; the same applies hereinafter.) that allow health information such as the results of health checkups to be used by individuals and also allow collection and analysis of such information on a nationwide scale so that the people and relevant personnel can take effective steps with regard to lifestyle habits.

Implementation of Research Regarding Health Promotion

The national government, local governments, and independent administrative agencies, etc. shall implement research regarding the relationship between the social environment or lifestyle habits of the people and lifestyle-related diseases, and they shall provide accurate and sufficient information to the people and relevant personnel regarding the results of such research. Support also needs to be given to ensure that the outcomes of new research are linked to effective health promotion practices, such as by reflecting them in standards and guidelines relating to health promotion.

Basic Items Relating to Cooperation and Collaboration Among Personnel Implementing Health Promotion Projects

In order to effectively and continuously provide high quality health services, health personnel shall carry out through specified health checkups and specified health guidance, cancer screening, health checkups for workers, etc., and in order to ensure an adequate response when people change their residence, change their occupation, or retire, when health projects are executed, effective use must be made of existing organizations and mutual cooperation must be facilitated between health business personnel implementing joint projects, etc., with councils for the promotion of regional and occupational cooperation playing a central role.

As a specific method, policy relating to health will be implemented efficiently and effectively by measures that include sharing of individual health information between responsible organizations carrying out cancer screening, specified health checkups, and other checkups. Furthermore, with the aim of increasing the convenience of people undergoing checkups and achieving checkup rate targets, cancer screening, specified health checkups, and other checkups may be carried out at the same time, and campaigns may be carried out to improve the checkup rate through the participation of responsible organizations carrying out different types of checkups.

In addition to the above items, cooperation between health promotion project personnel involved in implementing health checkups will also depend on guidelines for health promotion project personnel relating to the implementation of health checkups, etc. established according to Article 9 paragraph (1) of the Health Promotion Act.

Items Relating to the Dissemination of Correct Awareness Relating to Diet, Exercise, Rest, Alcohol, Smoking, Maintenance of Dental Health, and Other Lifestyle

Basic Approach

Since changes in the awareness and behavior of the people are needed for health promotion, sufficient and accurate information must be provided to the people to support their proactive health promotion initiatives. Ways will therefore be devised to ensure that this provision of information in relation to lifestyle habits is based on scientific findings, is easy to understand, is easy to link to health promotion initiatives by the people, and is attractive, effective, and efficient. With this information provision, ways will also be devised to enhance recognition of the importance of the effects of the social environment of the family, nursery school, school, workplace, and community on lifestyle habits.

With the provision of information relating to health promotion, utilization of a variety of channels such as mass media including ICT, volunteer groups relating to health promotion, industry, school education, medical insurers, and health project health consultations, and giving effective encouragement that meets the characteristics of the target group by combining several methods are important. When information is provided, efforts shall be made to ensure that incorrect information or information that is inappropriate due to marked bias is not provided.

Furthermore, the national government, local governments, etc. shall work to formulate and disseminate guidelines relating to all areas of lifestyle habits.

Health Promotion Month, etc.

In order to further promote peoples' movements, September shall be designated Health Promotion Month, and the national government, local governments, companies, civil organizations, etc. shall carry out a variety of events, publicity, and other public awareness activities to enhance self-awareness among the people, and health promotion initiatives aiming to foment an environment of mutual support in health and fitness across society as a whole shall be further promoted.

In order to make the relevant initiatives more effective, a campaign for dietary improvement shall also be carried out in September.

When implementing Health Promotion Month and the campaign for dietary improvement (hereinafter "Health Promotion Month, etc."), efforts need to be made to establish tasks according to local conditions and devise ways to ensure the participation of as many local residents as possible, including those with little interest in health. As well as activities in the community, core events, etc. at nationwide level will also be implemented through mutual cooperation among the national government, local governments, companies, civil organizations, etc. in order to implement Health Promotion Month, etc. in a focused and effective manner.

Other Important Items Relating to Implementing Public Health Promotion

Effective Systems for Resolving Local Health Issues

It is desirable for institutions and groups related to health promotion to recognize the roles that they should each play, and, in order to resolve local health issues, for core implementation organizations comprising personnel from municipal health centers, healthcare centers, medical insurers, medical institution, pharmacies, local comprehensive support centers, educational institutions, the mass media, companies, volunteer groups, etc. to establish action plans centered on municipal health centers and healthcare centers and based on the various Health Promotion Plans to achieve each of the health promotion targets in the plans, and to aim for effective initiatives through measures to ensure cooperation among occupational categories, such as ensuring that the initiatives of the various institutions and bodies complement each other.

When local governments formulate Health Promotion Plans, etc., the national government also needs to give technical support through measures such as suggesting methods for the creation and analysis of databases of statistics and data, and prefectural governments need to give the same technical support to municipal governments.

Promoting Voluntary Initiatives and Cooperation Implemented by Diverse Responsible Bodies

Companies involved in health promotion services relating to nutrition, exercise, and rest, companies involved in the manufacture of health equipment, food-related companies, other companies involved in activities relating to health and fitness, and groups such as NGOs and NPOs need to carry out voluntary initiatives in order to further encourage peoples' efforts for health promotion, and information regarding these initiatives needs to be disseminated to the people. The national government and local governments need to provide incentives to increase the number of companies working to put in place the social environment for health and fitness by means such as acknowledging companies whose initiatives are outstanding among all the relevant initiatives and proactively publicizing these initiatives so that they are widely known by the public. As an initiative for health promotion, private companies that carry out health promotion services for the people could cooperate with responsible bodies and other relevant institutions that carry out health checkups and screening in order to provide recipients with effective and efficient health promotion services. The promotion of such initiatives will allow the development of a market for diverse, high quality health promotion services that meet the needs of recipients.

In the implementation of health promotion initiatives, the relevant administrative fields and the relevant administrative institutions also need to cooperate fully with respect to health and fitness measures, measures including health guidance in the fields of occupational health that take dietary education, maternal and child health, mental health, prevention of long-term care, and consideration during employment, measures relating to health promotion in the field of health, labor and welfare administration including measures implemented by health insurers, as well as school health measures, measures to create walking roads (paths such as promenades, etc. provided for people to walk along), etc., measures to facilitate use of the rich natural environment such as forests, etc., measures in the field of lifelong sports such as use of integrated local sports clubs, and cultivation of health-related industries, etc.

Human Resources Responsible for Health Promotion

In local governments, doctors, dentists, pharmacists, public health nurses, midwives, registered nurses, assistant nurses, registered dietitians, dietitians, dental hygienists, and other personnel shall be responsible for health guidance and consultations from local residents regarding lifestyle and habits overall, including nutrition and dietary habits, physical activity and exercise, rest, mental health and fitness, alcohol, smoking, and dental and oral health.

The national government and local governments shall endeavor to secure public health nurses, registered dietitians, etc. to implement policy relating to health promotion and improve their qualifications, to cooperate with exercise coaches working for health promotion, such as health and exercise trainers, and with general and sports physicians, and to create systems to support volunteer organizations and self-help groups, including those with members promoting dietary improvement, the spread of exercise, stopping smoking, etc.

For this, the national government will need to enhance training of these human resources with a focus on cultivating their capacity for comprehensive planning and adjustment and improving their qualifications as leaders, and prefectural governments will have to collaborate with relevant bodies including municipal governments, medical insurers, regional medical associations, dental associations, pharmacists' associations, Nursing association, and dieticians' associations, in order to enhance training based on the latest scientific findings, not only for local government staff but also for specialists involved in policy relating to regional and occupational health promotion.

Endeavors shall also be made to ensure mutual cooperation between local health personnel and school health personnel, etc. for public health promotion.

Source

The second term of National Health Promotion Movement in the twenty first century (Health Japan 21 (the second term)) https://www.mhlw.go.jp/file/06-Seisaku-jouhou-10900000-Kenkoukyoku/0000047330.pdf

Accessed date: June 10, 2019

Appendix C: Public Health Monitoring Report (1)

Suicide Prevention Strategies in Periods of Economic Fluctuation[1]

Public Health Monitoring Report Committee, Japanese Society of Public Health

The Public Health Monitoring Report Committee of the Japanese Society of Public Health is comprised of the following members: Noriaki Harada (Chairman), Fujio Kayama, Norito Kawakami*, Fumio Kobayashi, Takashi Sako, Shigeru Sokejima, Tomofumi Sone, Shoichiro Tsugane, Yuji Nozu, Hideki Hashimoto*, Toshihoki Hasegawa, Yutaka Motohashi*, Eiji Yano, Fumihiko Jitsunari (Chairman of the Board).

*Authors of the present report

Introduction

On February 8, 2010, the Japanese Society of Public Health (JSPH) submitted a report entitled, "Recommendations for suicide prevention strategies in periods of economic fluctuation" [1] to Mizuho Fukushima, the Cabinet Office Minister of State for Suicide Prevention Measures. Suicide is a preventable public health issue. In 2009, the number of suicides was 32,753 (National Police Agency Statistics, provisional figure for the end of December 2009), surpassing 30,000 people annually for the twelfth consecutive year since 1998. Japan has the eighth highest suicide rate in the world among countries for which such statistics are available.

The central and local governments as well as researchers and workers in the field of public health work to prevent suicide while fulfilling their unique roles, and

---

[1] May 15, 2010, Japanese Journal of Public Health Issue 57-5.

© The Author(s) 2020
K. Kondo (ed.), *Social Determinants of Health in Non-communicable Diseases*,
Springer Series on Epidemiology and Public Health,
https://doi.org/10.1007/978-981-15-1831-7

some regions have succeeded in lowering their suicide rate through local suicide prevention measures [2, 3]. Nevertheless, the suicide rate for Japan as a whole remains high, raising the need for further suicide prevention measures.

The central government launched a Regional Suicide Prevention Emergency Enhancement Fund Program in 2009 in which it promotes suicide prevention measures carried out by local governments. On November 27, 2009, it further launched the 100-day Suicide Prevention Plan to be carried out by an emergency suicide prevention strategy team aimed at increasing focus on suicide prevention strategies by the end of the calendar or fiscal year. However, achieving a drastic reduction in the number of suicides in Japan requires policies to be enhanced even further, ensuring that suicide prevention measures carried out by each municipality are enforced continuously and effectively.

The JSPH must also take an active stance in suicide prevention measures as a community of experts. A working group on the social determinants of health established within the JSPH Public Health Monitoring Report Committee contains a sub-working group concerned with suicide prevention. This group analyzed conditions from July 2009 to February 2010 and debated the best ways for Japan to effectively enforce suicide prevention measures. Measures for promoting suicide prevention were sorted along axes of urgency, feasibility, acceptability to the public, size of target, size of effect and fairness, and further classified as short-term or mid- to long-term based on the time framework. The result was the extraction of four key points: (1) recommendations of ways to collect statistics on and monitor suicide, (2) effective use of the Regional Suicide Prevention Emergency Enhancement Fund Program, (3) development of a vision for mid- to long-term suicide prevention measures, and (4) independent actions to be taken by the JSPH.

The following is an introduction to the main arguments surrounding the debate for each key point and a description of the background concerning the recommendations for suicide prevention strategy in periods of economic fluctuation that were proposed by the Public Health Monitoring Report Committee to the Board of Directors based on the above arguments and then published.

Short-Term Initiatives for Suicide Prevention Measures

Establishment of a Framework for Collecting Statistics on and Monitoring Suicide

For a local government to plan suicide prevention measures, the first necessary step is to assess the characteristics of that municipality and determine what angle would be the most effective for formulating measures. When actually implementing measures, it then becomes necessary to evaluate how effectively they are being carried out. When the Regional Suicide Prevention Emergency Enhancement Fund Program was launched in 2009, there was no clear framework provided by the central government for evaluating its effectiveness. Development of a common efficacy assessment framework that could be used nationwide would potentially facilitate more effective implementation of the program.

In particular, quantitative outcome measures for evaluating suicide prevention programs must be utilized alongside measures to assess the process of implementing those programs. While the key outcome indicator of suicide prevention measures is the suicide rate of the relevant region, suicide rate is an unstable indicator for regions with small populations and hence few suicides. Moreover, it gives no information on what angle should be taken for intervention and many years must pass before the effects are known. Alternatively, each municipality can independently investigate the factors related to suicide in local residents, but such findings can rarely be compared to those of other municipalities.

It would be useful to find an indicator that is related to suicide or could be used as an alternative indicator for suicide that could be surveyed in each region over time and used in cross-municipality comparisons. Findings from such comparisons could then be provided to local governments to enable the development of a framework for helping prevent local suicide that is essential for carrying out effective suicide prevention measures in the region concerned. From fall 2009, suicide statistics compiled by the National Police Agency ("Suicide Summary Document") have been published as suicide data for each precinct and provided to local governments. While the data includes information on background and motive for suicides, such information alone is insufficient for use in evaluating suicide prevention measures.

Meanwhile, the central government periodically conducts public statistical surveys such as the Comprehensive Survey of Living Conditions. One idea is to include questions on risk factors or intermediate indicators that are strongly linked to suicide in these surveys. For example, suicidal ideation [4], depression and anxiety [5], and mental health literacy [6, 7] are known factors related to suicide that are actually used in local suicide prevention measures as outcome indicators. Previous studies have suggested that a poor local community network and poor social support are linked to suicide [2, 5]. Including items on the quantity and quality of local social networks in such national surveys makes it possible to assess suicide prevention measures that are aimed at building local interpersonal relationships.

Characteristics of local social structure, such as trust, norms, and networks, that enrich interpersonal relationships are grouped under the term "social capital." A recent study comparing countries in Europe showed a negative correlation between social capital and suicide rate [8]. In Japan as well, social capital on a municipal level correlates negatively with depression in older adults [9], and programs to enhance social capital have been effective for preventing suicide [10]. Including these items in the Comprehensive Survey of Living Conditions and other surveys, presenting the results by prefecture or government-designated city and providing the findings to local governments could aid formulation of suicide prevention programs in those municipalities and enable evaluation of their efficacy.

Suicide Prevention Measures for the Unemployed

Although it is clear that there is a high suicide rate among those who are not employed (Ministry of Health, Labour and Welfare, Statistics by Demographic Occupation and Industry), this population includes those without work after retirement, and does not necessarily represent the situation of the unemployed who have lost their jobs. However, recent studies have suggested that the unemployed (i.e., who have lost their jobs) have more than double the suicide risk of the general population [11, 12]. For example, estimates by Kaneko [11] give a suicide rate (per 100,000 people) of 32 suicides among employed men versus 184.1 among unemployed men, and 8.9 among employed women versus 34.1 among unemployed women. Local suicide prevention measures until the present have not focused on the unemployed, and future initiatives should be considered that are aimed at preventing suicide among unemployed individuals.

One idea for a strategy to prevent suicide among the unemployed is to provide opportunities for health and other consultations at Hello Work, the Japanese government's employment service center for job seekers. Such opportunities could enable unemployed individuals to discuss and receive assistance for their mental health problems. The government has already established a One Stop Service for relocation, legal, health-related and other consultations at Hello Work under the scope of its 100-day Suicide Prevention Plan that is currently available. However, this service is only a provisional measure within the 100-day Suicide Prevention Plan that ended in March 2010 with no clear plans for continuation or financial backing. There was no independent budget during its operational phase either, and it was often run by local healthcare workers with limited frequency and consultation times. Under such conditions, it is impossible to say how well the One Stop Service functions as an effective health consultation program for preventing suicide.

An effective strategy would be for such consultation services to be closely linked to the healthcare and welfare system and local suicide measures in particular. One example could be to hold Safety Net worker conferences in each region that would enable effective sharing of information among healthcare workers and Hello Work staff, welfare workers, and others. However, no framework currently exists for collaborative implementation of the One Stop Service and local suicide prevention programs. Moreover, as employees providing health consultations through the One Stop Service should have some training on the subject, another important step would be to develop a training/human resources development system.

Another issue is that unemployment measures offered by Hello Work alone are insufficient. Unemployed individuals become ineligible for industrial health programs when they lose their jobs. In addition, they are only weakly connected to local healthcare systems. These factors make it difficult to provide them with healthcare services. A strategy to be considered would be to have companies provide thorough information on consultation services and systems that are available in the event of job loss. Revisions must also be made in the pension and health insurance system for irregular employees that are at high risk for becoming unemployed [13, 14].

Mid- to Long-Term Initiatives for Suicide Prevention Measures in Japan

The mid- to long-term goal of suicide prevention in Japan is to make the country more accommodating to a greater number of people. For example, when an individual who lost their job or failed in business commits suicide, their joint guarantor may lose everything, including their home and other livelihood infrastructure, to repay outstanding debts of the deceased. The joint guarantor system must be reconsidered and revised into one that does not allow financial bankruptcy to result in the loss of a place to live.

Furthermore, there appears to be a cultural climate in Japan that promotes a tendency among individuals who suffer social setbacks to feel that they cannot start anew, lose hope, and end up choosing death. This may be linked to suicide by those who have incurred social collapse. To make matters worse, individuals who have lost their social spending tend to be cast aside by those around them—a trend that also promotes suicide among socially wounded individuals. We must build a society that enables people who suffer financial and social setbacks to get back on their feet, find a new role and reason for living within the local community, secure at least the minimal living requirements and continue living.

This type of community development aligns with the recommendation of the Science Council of Japan to implement the recently established European-style social inclusion policy in Japan [15] and the government (Cabinet Office) enforcement of Policies on Cohesive Society aimed at creating a society with favorable living conditions. Over the long term, it would be preferable for suicide prevention strategies to be carried out under a nationwide people's movement as one part of social inclusion policies to ensure individuals with any type of disadvantage a place within the community.

Role of the JSPH

The JSPH is an academic group of Japan's most elite public health education researchers and an organization of specialized professionals directly involved in local and national suicide prevention measures. It therefore plays a large role in Japan's suicide prevention strategy.

Assertion of the JSPH Stance

The JSPH must recognize that suicide is a major public health concern in Japan and assert its stance as an organization. It must utilize its strengths to aid in effective implementation of suicide prevention measures and assist professionals in the field.

Effective Methods for Providing Information on and Evaluating the Efficacy of Suicide Prevention Measures

While it is the role of the government to develop a framework for evaluating the efficacy of the Regional Suicide Prevention Emergency Enhancement Fund Program, the JSPH can assist by examining and recommending frameworks for evaluating suicide prevention programs. In addition, the JSPH can assess national and local measures for suicide prevention, develop standardized procedures for effectively carrying out such measures, and recommend those procedures to local governments.

Contributing to Human Resources Development

The JSPH must actively strive to educate and train healthcare specialists involved in suicide prevention, and build a network of trained specialists. For example, it could develop a standardized program for training and educating suicide prevention personnel and provide courses for training lecturers and universal literature. The aim would differ from that of similar educational and training courses offered by the National Institute of Public Health, and the JSPH courses in literature would utilize the organization's strengths to offer the most effective contribution.

Support for the Bereaved

The grief felt by the bereaved who have lost a close relative to suicide is much more substantial than that felt when losing family members to other causes of death [16]. Moreover, local healthcare workers often do not have the means for supporting the bereaved after a suicide. The JSPH can help provide means for local health and welfare workers to support the bereaved by conducting surveys, collecting data on cases with a favorable outcome, and offering educational training courses.

Recommendations for Suicide Prevention Strategy in Periods of Economic Fluctuation

The JSPH recognizes the urgency of suicide as a public health concern in Japan and undertakes initiatives to prevent suicide that include suicide prevention research and evaluation of measures and strategies. It also provides education and training opportunities related to suicide prevention, such as the general assembly meeting. As an academic society, the JSPH recommends the following to the government for implementing suicide prevention strategies in Japan more effectively.

Recommendation 1. Nationwide Monitoring of Outcome Measures for Suicide Prevention Programs

Include universal indicators for evaluating the efficacy of suicide prevention programs in nationwide surveys carried out by the central government, and present the findings by municipality to enable their use by local governments in implementing suicide prevention programs. Specifically, assess mental health literacy, depression and anxiety, suicidal ideation, social support, social capital, and other indicators in the Comprehensive Survey of Living Conditions and other surveys, and make the findings available for use on a prefecture and government-designated city level.

Recommendation 2. Strengthen Measures to Prevent Suicide Among the Unemployed

Further strengthen the safety net for socially and financially supporting individuals suffering unfavorable socioeconomic conditions to prevent their suicide. In particular, assess the current usage of the One Stop Service at Hello Work for preventing suicide among unemployed individuals, revise the program for more effective implementation of suicide prevention measures, and devise methods for linking the program to local suicide prevention initiatives.

Recommendation 3. Build a Society that Accommodates a More Diverse Range of People

Achieving social inclusion to form communities capable of accommodating a diverse population with a wide range of disadvantages will help prevent suicide over the long term and facilitate suicide prevention measures. In particular, ensure a place to live for those in unfavorable socioeconomic conditions, increase the number of opportunities for such individuals to fulfill social roles in the community, raise awareness on the necessity for such actions and develop communities with a high level of trust, solidarity, and other elements of social capital.

The Suicide Prevention Sub-Working Group under the Social Determinants of Health Working Group is comprised of the following members: Norito Kawakami (professor in the Faculty of Medicine, Graduate School of Medicine, University of Tokyo), Katsunori Kondo (professor at Nihon Fukushi University), Hideki Hashimoto (professor in the Faculty of Medicine, Graduate School of Medicine, University of Tokyo), Teruaki Matsumoto (Director of the Shizuoka Mental Health and Welfare Center), Yutaka Motohashi (professor at the Akita University Graduate School of Medicine), and Keiko Sakurai (graduate student in the Faculty of Medicine, Graduate School of Medicine, University of Tokyo).

References

1. Japanese Society of Public Health. Recommendations for suicide prevention strategies in periods of economic fluctuation. Jpn J Public Health. 2010;57:71–2. (In Japanese).
2. Oyama H, Watanabe N, Ono Y, et al. Com-munity–based suicide prevention through group activity for the elderly successfully reduced the high suicide rate for females. Psychiatry Clin Neurosci. 2005;59:337–44.
3. Motohashi Y. Town with a reduced suicide rate: the Akita Prefecture Challenge. Tokyo: Iwanami Shoten; 2006. (In Japanese).
4. Ono Y, Awata S, Iida H, et al. A community intervention trial of multimodal suicide prevention program in Japan: a novel multimodal community intervention pro-gram to prevent suicide and suicide attempt in Japan, NOCOMIT–J. BMC Public Health. 2008;8:315.
5. Awata S, Seki T, Koizumi Y, et al. Factors associated with suicidal ideation in an elderly urban Japanese popu-lation: a community–based, cross–sectional study. Psychiatry Clin Neurosci. 2005;59:327–36.
6. Yaegashi Y, Kurosawa M, Sakata K, et al. Investigation of the impact of depression health education intervention in residents: regional intervention study on middle-aged residents of a suicide-prone region. Iwate J Public Health. 2006;17:44–52. (In Japanese).
7. Kaneko Y, Motohashi Y. Male gender and low education with poor mental health literacy: a population–based study. J Epidemiol. 2007;17:114–9.
8. Kelly BD, Davoren M, Mhaoláain AN, et al. Social capital and suicide in 11 European countries: an ecological analysis. Soc Psychiatry Psychiatr Epidemiol. 2009;44:971–7.
9. Matsumoto Y, Kaneko Y, Yamaji M. Social capital and suicide prevention. Akita J Public Health. 2005;3:21. (In Japanese).

10. Motohashi Y. Chapter 3: Suicide prevention measures in Japan. In: Motohashi Y, editor. STOP! suicide. Tokyo: Kaimeisha; 2006. p. 70–92. (In Japanese).

11. Kaneko Y. Suicide prevention measures devised from statistical data. In: Motohashi Y, editor. Live: comprehensive lectures on suicide prevention measures. Akita Medical Library No. 1. Akita: Akita Sakigake Shimpo; 2009. p. 109–34. (In Japanese).

12. Kawakami N. 1. Current state of suicide in Japan and the world. In: Takahashi Y, Takeshima T, editors. Current state of suicide prevention. Osaka: Nagai Shoten; 2009. p. 3–15. (In Japanese).

13. Toda N. Social security and the increase in irregular employees. Reference. 2007;673:21–44. (In Japanese).

14. Nishimura J. Conflicts regarding participation of non regular employees in the pension system. Res Soc Sec Over. 2007;158:30–44. (In Japanese).

15. Science Council of Japan. Recommendations: creating policies for an inclusive society to combat economic crisis. Tokyo: Science Council of Japan; 2009. Available at http://www.scj.go.jp/ja/info/kohyo/pdf/Kohyo–21–t79–1.pdf. Accessed 10 May 2010. (In Japanese).

16. Miyabayashi S, Yasuda J. A comparison of effects of four modes of death on health, depression and grief of the bereaved. Jpn J Public Health. 2008;55:139–46. (In Japanese).

Appendix D: Public Health Monitoring Report (3)

Children's Health and Social Inequality: The Impact of Low Birth Weight on Health[1]

Public Health Monitoring Report Committee, Japanese Society of Public Health

The Public Health Monitoring Report Committee of the Japanese Society of Public Health is comprised of the following members: (In alphabetical order after the Chairman) Noriaki Harada (Chairman), Fujio Kayama, Norito Kawakami*, Fumio Kobayashi, Takashi Sako, Shigeru Sokejima, Tomofumi Sone, Shoichiro Tsugane, Yuji Nozu, Hideki Hashimoto*, Toshihoki Hasegawa, Yutaka Motohashi, Eiji Yano, Fumihiko Jitsunari (Chairman of the Board).

*Authors of the present report

Epidemiology of Social Inequality and Children's Health

It is becoming widely accepted as a solid fact that socioeconomic factors such as income, academic background, and employment situation are strongly linked to health status [1]. Despite this, we lack a scientific understanding of the mechanisms underlying the correlation between socioeconomic disparity and health inequalities. Although research is underway on the mechanisms of health inequalities among adults, the next step is to carry out such studies on children who are likely quite vulnerable to the effects of socioeconomic conditions at home.

The characteristics of epidemiological studies on children are: (1) consideration is given to the impact of the environment before birth, including the fetal stage (with the "parent" as the environment of primary importance), and to the notion that this

---

[1] March 15, 2011, Japanese Journal of Public Health Issue 58-3.

© The Author(s) 2020
K. Kondo (ed.), *Social Determinants of Health in Non-communicable Diseases*,
Springer Series on Epidemiology and Public Health,
https://doi.org/10.1007/978-981-15-1831-7

environment is affected by external factors (such as socioeconomic and physical exposure), (2) the idea that investigations must cover not only the effects on growth and development, but also those of later environmental exposure on future illness and functioning, and, consequently, (3) concepts must utilize a life course approach or epigenetics approach [2, 3].

The life course approach is defined by Kuh and others as the study of the long-term effects of physical and social exposure in prenatal life, infancy, childhood, adolescence, and adulthood on the risk of adult diseases [4]. This approach is more than simply tracking individuals over a long period; it is a new epidemiological theoretical model that explicitly considers (1) the chronological ordering of events and (2) inter-relationships among those events (ibid pp8). For example, how do growth disturbances in utero caused by malnutrition of the mother or her smoking during pregnancy lead to the onset of cardiovascular diseases in adulthood because of rearing environment or lifestyle habits (such as their own smoking) later in life? The life course approach addresses this question using data collected from each life stage (prenatal life, infancy, adolescence, and adulthood) to gather experimental evidence.

The overly simplistic idea that gene sequences inherited from parents conclusively determine a child's later phenotypic expression has already been dismissed. Research on epigenetics has clearly shown that interactions with acquired environment result in diversification of genetic expression. In animal experiments, controlling transcription of certain genes (over or under transcription) during the critical period of prenatal life and infancy by altering the developmental environment has resulted in the expression of diversified phenotypes through mutual interaction with the developmental environment and lifestyle habits later in life. While interactions have been observed between a number of genes and lifestyle habits in humans as well, we have yet to discover exactly how the environment affects a child's development and future health on a gene expression level.

Effects of Health Inequalities in Children

Epidemiological studies in Western countries that apply the life course approach have focused on low birth weight as one mechanism for health inequality. The relationship between low birth weight and adult coronary heart disease, type 2 diabetes, central obesity, and other diseases is considered well-established evidence [5]. As to how the biological mechanism works, consider the example of diabetes. Existing in inferior conditions in utero could induce the expression of thrifty genes. Nutritional conditions after birth that are better than expected could then create a state of over nutrition in comparison. This type of concept is called the "fetal origins of adult disease" hypothesis [6, 7].

Some studies based on this hypothesis have indicated that those who were poorly developed at birth and caught up during adulthood have a significantly higher risk of diabetes. In a study not concerned with low birth weight, it was determined that height and leg length—thought to be markers for nutritional status in infancy—correlate with risk of brain hemorrhage [8].

It is not much of a stretch to imagine that low birth weight and nutritional status in infancy are affected by the socioeconomic variables to which the child and parents are exposed. Indeed, it has been reported that low birth weight infants are more prevalent in poorer regions and in regions with wide social gaps [9, 10]. Moreover, poverty, low level of education, and other socioeconomic factors are known to correlate with smoking and diet during pregnancy [11–13].

A longitudinal look at mean birth weight in Japan shows a drop of 180 g in both genders from 1980 to 2007, down to 3050 g from 3230 g in boys and down to 2960 g from 3140 g in girls [14]. Major reasons given for this drop are increasing prevalence of multiple births through progress in reproductive medicine and increased survival rate of premature infants [15]. Nevertheless, the possibility of an influence from maternal smoking cannot be dismissed [16, 17].

Recently, cases have been reported of developmental impairment in children resulting from environmental factors such as domestic violence and poverty. However, systematic investigations are lacking, and almost no comprehensive research has been conducted on the relationship between social inequalities and birth weight in Japan. A large-scale study to measure and analyze both regional-level social inequality and individual- and household-level variables (such as smoking, diet, and other lifestyle habits of parents, educational background and other socioeconomic factors, and growth and development records of children) could help elucidate the factors contributing to the increasing prevalence of low birth weight and the effects on children's health. Specifically, what is needed is an investigative scheme that focuses on collecting more comprehensive information than has been provided by previous cross-sectional epidemiological cohort studies and tracking individuals over time. This cannot be achieved by one researcher working alone.

Database for the Life Course Approach: Examples in Britain and the Situation in Japan

A prospective British National Birth Cohort Study carried out in the UK to track three cohorts of individuals born in 1946, 1958, and 1970 has generated numerous scientific findings [18–20]. A Millennium Cohort Study was also launched in the year 2000. These studies are funded by government or public organizations as large-scale projects and university organizations have established centers to oversee operations.

Variables measured include everything from birth weight and height obtained from birth records, later development assessed in checkups, grades in elementary school, choice of higher education schools, and even the socioeconomic status of the parents (e.g., employment, level of education, income, and lifestyle habits) at each time point. By combining objective and subjective, qualitative and quantitative measurement of health and socioeconomic status in both the children and their parents, comprehensive information is collected at numerous points in time over the long term, creating the possibility for analysis using the life course approach.

The Ministry of Health, Labour and Welfare in Japan also began a Longitudinal Study on Newborns in 2000 that is currently in progress and shows great potential [21]. This study differs from the British cohort studies in that it is carried out every year and thus offers quite dense observation data from the early stages of development. However, the study is limited by use of short questionnaires only, and thus lacks sufficient objective medical and epidemiological information. Moreover, variables on socioeconomic factors are limited to questions on the parents' income, employment status, and level of education. A further concern is that there are no clear plans for ongoing long-term surveys.

The Japanese Ministry of the Environment has launched the Japan Environment and Children's Study (JECS) [22], a large-scale prospective cohort study on newborns. The Ministry is investing an unprecedented large research fund in JECS and intends to track children over 13 years. Given that this study holds the potential for building a foundation for a full-scale life course approach, it is essential that findings from the Longitudinal Study on Newborns and other past studies are fully exploited.

At present, JECS is designed with a disproportionately strong emphasis on the impact of exposure to environmental chemicals. It is clear that a child's rearing environment that includes the household and community socioeconomic environment is a variable that affects health to an equal or greater extent than environmental chemicals. JECS should be designed carefully to allow its use to perform comprehensive measurements on variables that include socioeconomic environmental factors and to clarify the effects on children's developmental processes and the mechanisms through which such effects act.

The Japan Children's Study 2004–2009 [23] that was reported recently is a unique cohort study that includes experimental elements. The study may offer particularly valuable findings because of its focus on the developmental effects of interactions with parents from a developmental psychology perspective.

The Boyd Orr Cohort Study in the UK examines the cohort obtained by re-tracking individuals from historical data. Records on participants in a child diet and health survey conducted from 1937 to 1939 were retrieved in 1988 and follow-up of those individuals was re-initiated [24]. It is similar in design to the National Integrated Project for Prospective Observation of Noncommunicable Disease And its Trends in the Aged (NIPPON DATA) in Japan, but with children as the subjects and conducted over a longer interval. Given that Japan has already established a unique maternity health record book system, it is worth considering building a cohort by adding new surveys to these existing records.

When considering the effects of developmental conditions during childhood on health in adulthood, it is very difficult to determine causal relationships, because so many elements are intertwined—from early development conditions and genetic factors to acquired lifestyle habits. One unique method for overcoming this problem is the use of twin cohorts. By removing differences due to disparity in health status and developmental conditions in pairs of twins, shared variables (i.e., genetics and early developmental environment) are canceled out with a fixed effect model.

This method was initially used in economics, sociology and developmental psychology, but has come into use in the United States in recent years in epidemiological research on adult health [25, 26]. Projects are also underway in Japan, such as the Twin Research Association's cohort of alumni from the Secondary School attached to the Faculty of Education, University of Tokyo, and the Keio University Twin Research Center Tokyo Twin Cohort Project panel survey launched in 2006 [27], but none has been conducted in the field of social epidemiology.

Children's Health and Socioeconomic Policy

Through the above and other studies, the UK and other countries are amassing epidemiological facts on the effects of socioeconomic status in prenatal life, infancy and childhood on the health and growth of those children. Meanwhile, empirical studies to formulate policies for correcting socioeconomic disparities and evaluating the effects of those policies are advancing in the fields of sociology and economics, mostly in the United States. One study examined the effects of welfare and child support services for poor families on the lifestyle habits (including drug dependence) of the mothers [28].

Other studies have undertaken economic analysis of the effects of family income on children's school grades and employment [29, 30]. However, very few studies have measured and assessed children's health status from an epidemiological perspective. Methods to quantitatively measure health and use the results as outcome variables are advancing technologically in the field of epidemiology. Meanwhile, techniques for measuring policies and economic status are advancing in fields of economics, family sociology, and welfare policy, among others.

Despite such advances, the lack of technological collaboration between the former and the latter has resulted in limitations in both. In Japan, a law for providing a monthly child benefit allowance came into force in April 2010, but the conditions for its provision have bounced back and forth owing to political and economic factors. Empirical evidence is needed to determine exactly how such benefits affect children's health and development.

What is urgently needed right now is for the Japanese Society of Public Health (JSPH) and other academic societies to lead the development of a new large-scale cohort while collaborating with relevant economics and sociology societies, and to encourage all relevant parties to develop a scheme for addressing questions about children's health and socioeconomic inequality.

Conclusion

In this report, we discussed the concepts that are essential for taking on questions of socioeconomic inequality and children's health and the conditions needed for building up evidence. While it is already a solid fact that socioeconomic inequalities affect health, a lack of understanding of the mechanisms underlying this relationship makes it impossible to recommend concrete policies or empirically assess the impact of such policies. The most promising role for the JSPH and other academic societies in bridging the health gap among children is that of presenting scientific evidence.

- The JSPH and its members must strive to contribute to better health and development of children through new epidemiological and public health initiatives.
- To do so, the JSPH and its members must collect comprehensive, far-reaching, multilevel data (on individuals, families, and communities) for each stage of growth. The JSPH must collaborate with relevant academic societies and urgently request the establishment of a foundation for collaboration from the Ministry of Health, Labour and Welfare, Ministry of Education, Culture, Sports, Science and Technology, and other relevant ministries.
- The JSPH must build a scheme for scientific and timely assessment of the impact of various policies on children's health in a climate of ever-changing policies. Specifically, it must establish a monitoring organization as a permanent organization to recommend policies for eliminating social inequalities in children's health based on scientific evaluation.

Acknowledgments

This report was written as a Committee report based on *Jpn J Public Health* 2008; 55(5):344–349 by Takeo Fujiwara (refs. [2, 3]). In writing this report, we would like to express our appreciation to Dr. Takeo Fujiwara for providing essential literature and documents. The views in this report represent a consensus of the Japanese Society of Public Health Monitoring Report Committee and are not attributable to specific individuals.

References

1. World Health Organization European Office. Available at http://www.euro. who.int/document/e81384.pdf.
2. Fujiwara T. How parents as an environment in fetal and early periods of life alter genetic expression in children: the life course approach and epigenetics. Jpn J Public Health. 2008;55(5):344–9. (In Japanese).

3. Fujiwara T. Life-course approach for the prevention of adult diseases from fetal and early periods of life. J Natl Inst Public Health. 2007;56(2):35–43. (In Japanese).

4. Kuh D, Ben-Shlomo Y. A life course approach to chronic disease epidemiology. 2nd ed. Oxford: Oxford University Press; 2004. p. 3.

5. Lynch J, Smith GD. A life course approach to chronic disease epidemiology. Annu Rev Public Health. 2005;26:1–35.

6. Newsome CA, Shiell AW, Fall CH, et al. Is birth weight related to later glucose and insulin metabolism?—a systematic review. Diabet Med. 2003;20:339–48.

7. Baker DJ, Osmond C. Infant mortality, childhood nutrition, and ischaemic heart disease in England and Wales. Lancet. 1986;1:1077–81.

8. Song YM, Smith GD, Sung J. Adult height and cause specific mortality: a large prospective study of South Korean men. Am J Epidemiol. 2003;158:479–85.

9. Dibben C, Sigala M, MacFarlane A. Area deprivation, individual factors and low birth weight in England: is there evidence of an "area effect"? J Epidemiol Commun Health. 2006;60:1053–9.

10. Farley TA, Mason K, Rice J, et al. The relationship between the neighbourhood environment and adverse birth outcomes. Paediatr Perinat Epidemiol. 2006;20:188–200.

11. Watson PE, McDonald BW. Major influences on nutrient intake in pregnant New Zealand women. Matern Child Health J. 2009;13:695–706.

12. Rifas-Shiman SL, Rich-Edwards JW, Kleinman KP, et al. Dietary quality during pregnancy varies by maternal characteristics in Project Viva: a US cohort. J Am Diet Assoc. 2009;109:1004–11.

13. Motensen LH, Diderichsen F, Smith GD, et al. The social gradient in birthweight at term: quantification of the mediating role of maternal smoking and body mass index. Hum Reprod. 2009;24:2629–35.

14. Health Labour and Welfare Statistics Association. Trends in public health. Tokyo: Health Labour and Welfare Statistics Association; 2009.

15. Takimoto H, Yokoyama T, et al. Increase in low-birth-weight infants in Japan and associated risk factors, 1980-2000. J Obstet Gynecol Res. 2005;31(4):314–22.

16. Suzuki K, Tanaka T, et al. Is maternal smoking during early pregnancy a risk factor for all low birth weight infants? J Epidemiol. 2008;18(3):89–96.

17. Matsubara F, Kida M, Tamakoshi A, et al. Maternal active and passive smoking and fetal growth: a prospective study in Nagoya, Japan. J Epidemiol. 2000;10:335–43.

18. Wadsworth M, Kuh D, Richards M, Hardy R, Proàle C. The 1946 national birth cohort (MRC National Survey of Healthand Development). Int J Epidemiol. 2006;35:49–54.

19. Power C, Elliott J. Cohort profile: 1958 British birth cohort (National Child Development Study). Int J Epidemiol. 2006;35:34. https://doi.org/10.1093/ije/dyi183.

20. Individual data on the 1970 cohort of the British Child Cohort can be obtained by registering with the Economic and Social Data Service. Available at http://www.esds.ac.uk/findingData/bcs70.asp.

21. Ministry of Health, Labour and Welfare. Longitudinal study on newborns in the 21st Century. Tokyo: Ministry of Health, Labour and Welfare. Available at http://www.mhlw.go.jp/toukei/list/27-6.html.

22. Ministry of the Environment. Japan environment and children's study (JECS). Tokyo: Ministry of the Environment. Available at http://www.env.go.jp/chemi/ceh/intro/index.html.

23. Yamagata Z, Maeda T, Aneme T, Sadato N, Japan Children's Study Group. Overview of the Japan children's study 2004-2009; Cohort study of early childhood development. J Epidemiol. 2010;20(Suppl):397–403.

24. Gunnel D, Davey Smith DG, Frankel S, et al. Childhood leg length and adult mortality; follow up of the Carnegie (Boyd Orr) Survey of Diet and Health in Pre-War Britain. J Epidemiol Commun Health. 1998;52:142–52.

25. Fujiwara T, Kawachi I. Social capital and health: a study of adult twins in the United States. Am J Prev Med. 2008;35(2):139–44.

26. Fujiwara T, Kawachi I. Is education causally related to better health? A twin fixed effects study in the United States. Int J Epidemiol. 2009;38(5):1310–22.

27. Ando J, Nonaka K, Ozaki K, et al. The Tokyo Twin Cohort Project; overview and initial findings. Twin Res Hum Genet. 2006;9(6):817–26.

28. Knab J, Garginkel I, McLanahan S. The effects of welfare and child support policies on maternal health and well-being. In: Schoeni RF, House JS, Kaplan GA, Pollack H, editors. Making Americans healthier; social and economic policy as health policy. New York, NY: Russell Sage Foundation; 2008. p. 281–305.

29. Dahl G, Lochner L. The impact of family income on child achievement; evidence from the earned income tax credit. In: NBER working paper series no. 14599. Available at http://www.nber.org/papers/w14599.

30. Heckman JJ, Kruger AB. Inequality in America; what role for human capital policies? Cambridge, MA: MIT Press; 2003.

Appendix E: Public Health Monitoring Report (5)

Social Inequalities in Health Among Older Adults[1]

Public Health Monitoring Report Committee, Japanese Society of Public Health
The Japan Public Health Monitoring Report Committee is comprised of the following members: Noriaki Harada (Chairman), Fujio Kayama, Norito Kawakami*, Fumio Kobayashi, Takashi Sako, Shigeru Sokejima, Tomofumi Sone, Shoichiro Tsugane, Yuji Nozu, Hideki Hashimoto*, Toshihoki Hasegawa, Yutaka Motohashi, Eiji Yano, Fumihiko Jitsunari (Chairman of the Board).
*Authors of the present report

Introduction

As we accumulate findings on the impact of socioeconomic factors and other social factors on people's health, the need for a better understanding and application of those findings increases. The World Health Organization (WHO) compiled a summary on studies and recommendations concerning social determinants of health (SDH) [1–3] and is searching for measures to rectify social inequalities in health.

When compared to other groups, older adults show the following characteristics: (1) as physical functioning declines with aging, psychological and social health becomes even more important than for other generations; (2) the effects of physical, psychological, and social factors from each stage of life accumulate, so that health inequalities increase with aging; (3) as an individual's range of activities narrows with age, they become more vulnerable to the effects of the environment in which

---

[1] July 15, 2011, Japanese Journal of Public Health Issue 58-7.

© The Author(s) 2020
K. Kondo (ed.), *Social Determinants of Health in Non-communicable Diseases*,
Springer Series on Epidemiology and Public Health,
https://doi.org/10.1007/978-981-15-1831-7

they live. In view of these characteristics, it is likely that socioeconomic status and other social determinants may generate health disparities among the older generation.

Factors causing health inequalities and the process for their action may be more complex and intertwined in older adults than in other generations. Consequently, there is an even greater need to assess and establish measures for combating social inequalities in health in this age group, with a focus on the various healthcare, medical care, and welfare variables.

Japan has established a social security system for older adults that includes a universal pension and health insurance (medical care and long-term nursing care) coverage. Accordingly, it may boast smaller social inequalities in access of older adults to healthcare and medical care services than other countries. That said, few experimental studies have been conducted in Japan on this topic, and knowledge is lacking on the current state of social inequalities in health among older adults.

The proportion of families receiving public assistance, which often include older adults, is growing. Moreover, while the income gap among aged households is shrinking on account of income redistribution through social security and other benefits, it still remains wider than the gap among non-aged households (Cabinet Office 2008 White Paper on National Lifestyle). Given these facts, it is essential to assess health inequalities among older adults resulting from socioeconomic and other social factors, and to consider future strategies for public health activities including administrative policies to address these inequalities.

The working group on SHD established within the Japanese Society of Public Health (JSPH) Public Health Monitoring Report Committee contains a sub-working group concerned with older adults. This group reviewed the research findings in Japan to date on health inequalities among older adults caused by socioeconomic status. In addition, it held a meeting on September 28, 2010 to discuss ideas on social inequalities in health in the older population and continued to hold discussions thereafter. Based on those discussions, this report outlines the tasks for the Japanese government and academic societies to undertake to analyze the situation concerning social inequalities in health among older adults in Japan and to formulate measures to combat this issue.

Research on Social Inequalities in Health Among Older Adults and Current Policies

Current Research and Policies Overseas

As mentioned in the introduction, the WHO compiled a summary of past studies on SDH in 1998 [1] and a revised summary in 2003 [2]. In 2005, it established a Social Determinants of Health Committee that compiled a final report in 2008 [3]. In response, at the WHO World Health Assembly in 2009, member countries focused on SDH and issued a resolution to recommend pursuit of initiatives to close the health gap [4]. Recommendations included improving lifestyle conditions in all stages of the life course from birth to old age, rectifying social inequalities themselves that generate the health gap, measuring health disparities and performing Health Impact Assessment (HIA) on policies.

At a national level, England [5], Sweden [6], South Korea, and other countries have set numerical targets for its government to reduce health disparities and are revising public health methods. In the United States as well, national research organizations are taking measures that include the publication of a National Healthcare Disparities Report [7]. As the background for these overseas projects, a health gap is frequently observed between those of high social standing and those of low social standing who often have poorer health. Massive amounts of research have shown the latter to have poor access to healthcare and a high mortality rate, and have indicated that SDH play a role in those pathways.

However, few studies in other countries have focused on the older population. Moreover, government policies in response to the above are placed within policies to combat health inequalities among all citizens.

Current Research in Japan

Research on the importance of SDH in health inequalities has been conducted in Japan as well [8, 9]. However, this still includes very few studies on socioeconomic factors and health in older adults. The SDH working group searched literature databases [PubMed and the Japan Medical Abstracts Society (JAMAS) databases] for studies on socioeconomic factors and health in older adults in Japan using search keywords of {elderly OR older people} AND {health disparity OR health inequality OR socioeconomic factor} AND Japan and the equivalents in Japanese. The abstracts of the retrieved articles were read and those thought to be related to the above topic were selected, for a total of five studies in English and nine in Japanese. Most were regional correlation studies or individual-level cross-sectional studies, with very few cohort studies.

The studies showed disparities among older adults in Japan arising from socioeconomic status in mortality and major diseases (such as cancer, stroke [10], and hypertension [10]), long-term care need and risk factors for long-term care need (such as falls, undernutrition, and oral functioning), subjective health, depression [11] and other mental health variables, and social health (such as reclusion, social participation, social support, and abuse) [12, 13]. Regional socioeconomic inequalities assessed with Gini's coefficient have been shown to correlate with poorer health indicators in older adults by analysis of small regions such as old villages [14] or on a prefectural level [15].

The studies clearly show that socioeconomic status causes health inequalities in older populations in Japan. According to another report, socioeconomic status also causes inequalities in frequency of doctor visits and access to medical care among older adults. Even with universal healthcare coverage, low income individuals among the older population may be reluctant to visit doctors.

Other studies have also shown an association in older adults between health and social capital; that is, characteristics of the local community that include trust and mutual assistance [16–18].

Future Directions

As shown above, research is accumulating in Japan as well on SDH in older adults, and consideration must be given to socioeconomic factors in healthcare and welfare for the older population in Japan. In particular, to assess the state of social inequalities in health, Japan needs to (1) monitor health disparities arising from socioeconomic factors, (2) implement a HIA system to enable advance assessment of the effects of various social and health policies on health in older adults, (3) carry out research on SDH in older adults to determine the routes and mechanisms through which socioeconomic factors act on health, and (4) build a society that accommodates social participation across all generations.

The Importance of Monitoring Social Inequalities in Health Among Older Adults

As Japan has a social security system, it can be expected that socioeconomic disparities and the resulting social inequalities in health among older adults are somewhat moderate. However, certain groups such as low-income older adults may be particularly vulnerable to health disparities arising from an unfavorable socioeconomic status.

A system needs to be developed for periodic monitoring to ensure there are no income-related gaps among older adults in mortality, disease, activities of daily living and other health indicators, and in access to healthcare. This type of undertaking should be included in monitoring of social inequalities in health of citizens across all generations. As advised by the WHO, such monitoring should cover not only health indicators but also SDH that may affect such indicators.

Assessment of the Impact of Social and Health Policies on Health (HIA)

Health problems are common among older adults, and revision of the healthcare and welfare system may potentially have direct effects on health in the older population. When designing and implementing a system for health policies, the impact of such policies on health in older adults must be assessed ahead of time and taken into consideration. This was also recommended by the WHO for reducing social inequalities in health [19–21]. For example, Japan is considering abolishing its current medical care system for people aged 75 years and over and establishing a new system. When doing so, advance assessment is essential for predicting the impact of such a change on health and access to medical care in older adults, and especially those who have low incomes.

Monitoring will be needed after starting the new system as well; for example, to ensure low-income older adults are not inhibited from visiting the doctor. Health of older adults may also be affected by changes in or new establishment of social policies aside from those concerning health; for example, the abolishment of additional old age benefits in welfare aid. Accordingly, HIA should also be performed on these policies. HIA is rarely performed on social policies in Japan, and steps required for its application include training of human resources, spreading use of methodology, and accumulating research [21].

Directions for Research

Populations are graying across the globe and Japan already has the highest life expectancy in the world. In light of this fact, research on social inequalities in health and, more broadly, on SDH among older adults are fields in which Japan should certainly contribute. Compared to younger and middle-aged generations, gaps are larger in the older generation. Moreover, a selection bias exists because only the healthy survive (also called the survivor effect).

Longitudinal individual-level studies are needed to determine the size of health effects from social determinants accompanying aging that follow the life course, including old age. In addition, conducting analysis that takes the impact of regional environment into account would be aided by having a large-scale database that could be used for multilevel analysis. Such analysis could enable examination of associations with regional-level factors after controlling for individual-level factors.

There exist many more social determinants that may affect health in older adults in addition to socioeconomic status as discussed above. For example, whether an older person has means for transportation gives rise to disparity in access to healthcare and welfare services and may affect opportunities for social participation in seniors' clubs and other groups. Public health research could help examine these numerous social determinants.

The government has already accumulated large quantities of data that can be used to build a database for application in such research. Unfortunately, accessing the data from municipalities (insurers) is difficult owing to reasons such as the protection of personal information. Creating an environment that encourages understanding in and cooperation with academic investigations is one challenge to address in pursuing high-quality research.

Building a Society that Enables Social Participation by People of All Generations and Social Standings

Research to date has shown an association between social participation and favorable health status in older adults, and the effects are especially large on mental health and quality of life [22]. Social participation by older adults is affected by their situation, which includes everything from income to mobility, means of transportation, health foods, employment, medical and nursing care services, and social support, among others. Having older adults take on a role in society enables them to lead a healthy and happy life and helps build a rich community that supports the social participation and health of other residents.

This issue does not affect only older adults—it may be considered a challenge in and across all generations. Creating a society that accommodates social participation by all its individuals, regardless of age or social class, will surely improve health in the older population and reduce social disparities among older adults. This also equates to a harmonious society that accepts all manner of people; that is, social inclusion.

Recommendations to the Japanese Government

We make the following recommendations to the Japanese government based on scientific evidence on social inequalities in health among older adults, as shown by the research conducted to date, and on the conclusions derived from discussions among specialists.

Monitoring Social Inequalities in Health Among Older Adults Using Existing Databases

We recommend creating a usable database from currently available information to chronologically monitor and analyze SDH and disparities in health and access to medical care among older adults, by region and by social class. It would also be beneficial to create a database of information on long-term care insurance held by insurers by making the individuals anonymous with a trackable ID to protect their personal information. Using the ID, this database could then be combined with other health-related databases that are not related to long-term care insurance (such as information on health checkups and medical treatment fees and surveys on demographics).

When building the database, in consideration of the difficulty retrieving data from municipalities (insurers), the Ministry of Health, Labour and Welfare should send a message to relevant organizations stating that, "It is permissible to provide data to researchers after making it anonymous if used for appropriate policy assessment research approved by a research ethics committee, irrespective of the Personal Information Protection Law." Databases for monitoring should be publicly accessible to academic societies and researchers. In addition, an organization should be established to carry out monitoring and analyze the current situation and to perform risk assessments based on the monitoring results.

HIA on Social Policies Concerning Older Adults

We recommend performing HIA for older adults for all social policies that concern the older population and monitoring the effects of those policies. For example, a system is needed for advanced assessment of the impact on older adults, especially in the low-income class, to be conducted on policies that can be predicted to affect health in the older population, such as abolishment of the medical care system for people aged 75 years and over (geriatric care system) and establishment of a new system or the abolishment of additional old age benefits in welfare aid. The system should include post-hoc monitoring and a function that enables revision of social security systems as needed.

Building a Foundation for Research of SDH in Older Adults

We recommend creating an interdisciplinary academic field related to SDH in older adults in a broad sense by merging public health with other relevant academic fields. In addition, we recommend launching a large-scale, long-term, longitudinal research project to build a scientific knowledge base, and to train human resources. When doing so, increasing awareness and understanding in SDH among insurers, relevant organizations, and the public will be essential for accumulating high-quality data.

Creating a Goal of Developing a Society that Accommodates Social Participation by All Ages

To raise the level of well-being (health and happiness) in older adults, we must enable "ageless social participation," for social participation by all age groups, not limited to the one that is the focus of support. We must consider everyone as having a role in society and support that possibility. We therefore recommend striving to develop a society and communities that aim to accommodate social participation by individuals of all ages, including older adults. To create such an inclusive society, we recommend considering the social participation of all generations in all policies and projects.

Role of the JSPH

Health of older adults is an important public health issue in Japan as a country that is aging rapidly. The JSPH must strive to close social gaps in health among older adults based on the characteristics of such gaps and on research findings. Such an undertaking should be pursued within initiatives concerning social disparities in health throughout all generations and should also include considerations that are specific to the older population.

1. As an academic society, spread knowledge within and outside the society on the importance of SDH using various opportunities and take the steps necessary to have SHD monitored. Actively provide JSPH members with information on disparities in social determinants such as income, access and social participation in healthcare, medical care, and welfare services for older adults and build an environment that enables monitoring and promotes awareness of these problems in the daily activities of public health professionals.

   To enable monitoring and comparisons of disparities among and SDH in social classes, among regions, and among generations, formulate guidelines that include, for example, questions related to SHD that should be included in survey questionnaires. Urge municipalities to include a SDH perspective in their medical care and long-term care insurance program planning.

2. Urge the government to perform HIA before introducing important policies that may affect health in the older population, such as revisions in social security systems. In addition, recommend steps that are needed for monitoring the effects of those policies and provide assistance in the form of training human resources that can perform monitoring and developing a foundation that includes methodology and a database.

3. Improve the arrangement for accumulating and spreading awareness of findings related to social inequalities in health, and, more broadly, SDH, including in older adults. For example, position it as a separate session within academic general assembly meetings to take up academic society plans and build a research and literature database. Cooperate with other academic organizations and position SDH, social inequalities, gerontology, and longevity science as subjects/fields for interdisciplinary research in Grants-in-Aid for Scientific Research and other types of research grants. In addition, start preparations for carrying out a large-scale, long-term, longitudinal research project and take measures to promote the accumulation of interdisciplinary findings and methodology through interdisciplinary symposiums and book projects.

4. To build a society that accommodates social participation by people of all generations and classes, promote training for public health professionals that

incorporates concepts on SDH, and aid in the provision of effective services. For example, add this topic to training requirements for JSPH public health specialists and spread pioneering initiatives such as home guidance that incorporates SDH and social disadvantage in the JSPH Education and Lifelong Learning Committee through education and training.

The Social Determinants of Health Sub-Working Group under the Social Determinants of Health Working Group is comprised of the following members: Katsunori Kondo* (Nihon Fukushi University), Norito Kawakami* (Faculty of Medicine, Graduate School of Medicine, University of Tokyo), Hideki Hashimoto* (Faculty of Medicine, Graduate School of Medicine, University of Tokyo), Seiji Yasumura* (Fukushima Medical University), and Keiko Sakurai (Faculty of Medicine, Graduate School of Medicine, University of Tokyo).

*The individuals mainly responsible for writing this report.

References

1. Wilkinson RG, Marmot M, editors. Social determinants of health; the solid facts. Geneva: World Health Organization; 1998.
2. Wilkinson RG, Marmot M, editors. Social determinants of health; the solid facts. 2nd ed. Geneva: World Health Organization; 2003.
3. Commission on Social Determinants of Health. Closing the gap in a generation: health equity through action on the social determinants of health. Geneva: World Health Organisation; 2008.
4. WHO. RESOLUTIONS WHA62.14 Reducing health inequities through action on the social determinants of health. Geneva: WHO; 2009.
5. Department of Health. Tackling health inequalities: a programme for action. London: Department of Health; 2003.
6. Hogstedt C, Lundgren B, Moberg H, Pettersson B, Ågren G. Background to the new Swedish public health policy. Scan J Public Health. 2004;32(Suppl. 64):6–17.
7. Agency for Healthcare Research and Quality. 2009 national healthcare disparities report. Rockville, MD: Services USDoHaH; 2010.
8. Kagamimori S, Gaina A, Nasermoaddeli A. Socioeconomic status and health in the Japanese population. Soc Sci Med. 2009;68(12):2152–60.
9. Fukuda Y, Imai H. Review of research on social inequalities in health in Japan. J Natl Inst Public Health. 2007;56(2):56–62. (In Japanese).
10. Murata C, Yamada T, Chen C-C, Ojima T, Hirai H, Kondo K. Barriers to health care among the elderly in Japan. Int J Environ Res Public Health. 2010;7(4):1330–41.
11. Murata C, Kondo K, Hirai H, Ichida Y, Ojima T. Association between depression and socio-economic status among community-dwelling elderly in Japan:

the Aichi Gerontological Evaluation Study (AGES). Health Place. 2008;14(3):406–14.

12. Ikeda A, Iso H, Kawachi I, Yamagishi K, Inoue M, Tsugane S. Social support and stroke and coronary heart disease: the JPHC study cohorts II. Stroke. 2008;39(3):768–75.

13. Kondo K, editor. Evidence on a society with health inequality: large-scale social epidemiology survey for prevention of the need for long-term care. Tokyo: Igaku Shoin; 2007. (In Japanese).

14. Ichida Y, Kondo K, Hirai H, Hanibuchi T, Yoshikawa G, Murata C. Social capital, income inequality and self-rated health in Chita peninsula, Japan: a multilevel analysis of older people in 25 communities. Soc Sci Med. 2009;69(4):489–99.

15. Oshio T, Kobayashi M. Income inequality, area-level poverty, perceived aversion toinequality, and self-rated health in Japan. Soc Sci Med. 2009;69(3):317–26.

16. Aida J, Hanibuchi T, Nakade M, Hirai H, Osaka K, Kondo K. The different effects of vertical social capital and horizontal social capital on dental status: a multilevel analysis. Soc Sci Med. 2009;69(4):512–8.

17. Fujisawa Y, Hamano T, Takegawa S. Social capital and perceived health in Japan: an ecological and multi-level analysis. Soc Sci Med. 2009;69(4):500–5.

18. Kondo K, Hirai Y, Takeda T, Ichida Y, Aida J. Social capital and health. Behaviormetrika. 2010;37:27–37. (In Japanese).

19. World Health Organization (WHO). Health impact assessment. 2004. Available at http://www.who.int/hia/en/. Accessed 6 Jul.

20. Kemm J, Parry J, Palmer S, editors. Health impact assessment. Oxford: Oxford University Press; 2004.

21. Fujino Y, Matsuda S. Basic concepts of health impact assessment and future initiatives in Japan. Jpn J Public Health. 2007;54(2):73–80. (In Japanese).

22. Fujiwara Y, Sugihara Y, Shinkai S. Effects of volunteering on the mental and physical health of senior citizens: significance of senior-volunteering from the view point of community health and welfare. Jpn J Public Health. 2005;52(4):293–307. (In Japanese).

Appendix F: Public Health Monitoring Report (8)

Impact of Precarious Employment on Health[1]

Public Health Monitoring Report Committee, Japanese Society of Public Health

The 13th period Japan Public Health Monitoring Report Committee is comprised of the following members: Noriaki Harada (Chairman), Fujio Kayama, Norito Kawakami, Fumio Kobayashi, Takashi Sako, Shigeru Sokejima, Tomofumi Sone, Shoichiro Tsugane, Yuji Nozu, Hideki Hashimoto, Toshihoki Hasegawa, Yutaka Motohashi, Eiji Yano*, Fumihiko Jitsunari (Chairman of the Board).

*Authors of the present report

Background

Numerous legal cases concerning treatment and health issues of precarious workers (workers in nonstandard employment, such as part-time and temporary work) are accumulating. The suicide of a temporary worker at the Nikon Kumagaya Plant (Tokyo High Court, 2009); the physical abuse and harassment of a temporary worker at Yodobashi Camera (Tokyo High Court, 2006); the death from overwork of a 21-year-old part-time magazine editor (Osaka District Court, 2004): each of these cases had similar court rulings, which held the companies responsible. Were these health-damaging conditions for precarious workers simply the result of a select few workers happening to find employment at heartless workplaces?

In both Japan and abroad, precarious workers are encumbered with problems such as unstable employment, low wages, absent or limited benefits, and reduced rights [1]. Factors that may be associated with health problems arising from precarious

---

[1] October 15, 2011, Japanese Journal of Public Health Issue 58-10.

© The Author(s) 2020
K. Kondo (ed.), *Social Determinants of Health in Non-communicable Diseases*,
Springer Series on Epidemiology and Public Health,
https://doi.org/10.1007/978-981-15-1831-7

employment are the relationship between poverty and poor health, unstable employment and lack of benefits due to the short-term nature of contracts, a climate of treating labor as an object resulting from the indirect employment relationship, and division and discrimination among workers and in society in general associated with the above [2]. As for poverty, income gaps are known to affect mortality rate and mean life expectancy [3], and the increase in precarious employment is already recognized as one factor contributing to income gaps in Japan [4].

Accordingly, precarious employment should be investigated as one of the "causes of the causes" of social determinants of health [5]. In Japan, differences in type of employment not only result in income disparities [6], but also in a 2.5-fold disparity in lifetime earnings because wages do not increase with age [4, 7]. Such disparities may result in reluctance to get married or have children [8]. Should this situation continue, Japan may see a rise in problems concerning low-income older adults without family. Even more important than considering the current health of precarious workers may be to consider the future health of such workers.

The negative characteristics of precarious employment have only been investigated in fragments in the past. Precarious employment in the post-war Japan labor market has always been a controversial topic irrespective of strong or weak economy, because the employment of precarious workers is volatile and unstable [9]. From a health perspective, health issues have been examined in day workers [10] and migratory workers [11].

One reason for the lack of ongoing, active investigation of issues concerning precarious workers may be that such workers have traditionally been the minority in a society comprised mostly of workers with Japan's distinctive lifetime employment or regular employment (i.e., full-time, continuous work with one employer). Moreover, precarious employment, represented mostly by middle-aged women working part-time jobs, was considered a dependable side income for families. The need for social protection may have been undervalued as a result.

Precarious workers that were supposed to be in the minority now make up over 30% of the working population. According to means for 2010, Japan had 62.57 million employees, of which 54.63 million, or 87%, were employed by a company. Now, 17.55 million people, or 34.3% of all employees (excluding executives), are working under precarious employment conditions [12]. In Japan's Labor Force Survey, precarious employment is the classification used to label workplaces of those who indicated "part-time employee, temporary employee, contract employee, other" as type of employment. As the proportion of precarious workers who were previously in the minority rises with increasing diversification in type of employment, an emerging issue is that such individuals are not actually working in a care-free flexible working arrangement, but indeed are suffering problems in treatment.

If precarious employment and health were investigated as a public health concern, would the results actually show a relationship between differences in type of employment and health of workers? Is there a threat to health and safety in the workplace? Also, will being a society with diversified types of employment affect health, access to healthcare, social security related to future health and other factors in not only workers, but in all citizens? The following is a summary of the research findings and government response to date.

Impact of Precarious Employment on Health

Precarious Employment and Health of Workers

Findings from Research in Other Countries

Research is being carried out based on the hypothesis that precarious workers have poor health from working in an unstable employment situation. Among the review literature, a meta-analysis of differences in health status by type of employment found precarious workers to have poor mental health compared to regular employees (combined odds ratio: 1.25) [13]. A review of the literature on studies up to 2010 revealed that the areas in which physical health was suffering in precarious workers compared to regular employees were in mortality rate and some occupational injuries and accidents [14]. In particular, one cohort study showed that all-cause mortality and mortality from smoking-related and alcohol-related cancer was higher in male precarious workers [15].

Most studies on mental health status suggest that this status is poor in precarious workers. Indicators for measuring mental health include subjective indicators for assessing stress, objective indicators such as the General Health Questionnaire (GHQ), prescriptions for antidepressants, and the rate of attempted suicide. Many studies have shown poor mental health in precarious workers in all of these indicators. Despite this, precarious workers have fewer days off and absences from work compared to regular employees, and it is conceivable that such workers may be reluctant to take time off work for fear of losing their jobs [14]. Although it depends on the indicator and type of disease, findings from studies conducted in other countries generally suggest that precarious workers have poorer health than regular employees.

Research in Japan

Mental Health

Although such research is scarce, some studies have been reported on health of precarious workers compared to regular employees. As would be expected, the most commonly used outcome indicator is mental health. Looking only at studies carried out in Japan, most report poorer health in precarious workers than in regular employees. A study using the K6 scale for measuring anxiety and depression showed that part-time male workers and temporary female workers have a higher level of anxiety/depression compared to their counterparts in regular employment [16]. This is also backed by a study showing that part-time workers have less discretion regarding their job and receive less support from their boss and coworkers than regular employees [17]. Moreover, sense of coherence is gaining attention as a measure of stress-coping ability and was shown to be particularly low among precarious workers in manufacturing [18].

In examining stress, another study showed that precarious workers used an onsite company clinic more often than regular employees, raising the concern of presenteeism (attending work while sick) among precarious workers [19]. Regarding physical health, a large effort–reward imbalance has been linked to poor subjective health and obesity in fixed-term workers [20]. However, other studies have actually found precarious workers to have better mental health. One study showed female regular employees to have more pressure at work and job strain than precarious workers [21]. Studies and analyses befitting Japan's current situation need to be conducted; for example, to elucidate barriers for women in employment and overwork among regular employees.

Occupational Injuries

The vulnerable position of precarious workers can be seen from the occurrence of occupational injuries and receipt of workers' compensation benefits. According to statistics from the Ministry of Health, Labour and Welfare, there were 677 casualties requiring four or more days off work resulting from a work-related accident in 2004, the year that a ban was lifted on use of temporary workers in manufacturing, which rose eightfold to 5631 casualties in 2008 [22].

While the occurrence of work-related injury is on the decline for the entire labor force, it is on the rise for temporary workers [23]. Indeed, type of employment appears to play a role in not only occurrence of occupational injuries, but also in grant decisions (the decision to grant benefits) for workers' compensation insurance claims. The proportion of grant decisions for workers' compensation insurance claims in 2009 was 47% for regular employees and 14% for precarious workers for brain and heart diseases, and 28% for regular employees and 17% for precarious workers for mental illness and other illnesses [24]. These figures suggest that compensation after an occupational injury may also be affected by type of employment.

Lifestyle Habits

As for other indicators, conclusions on lifestyle habits are split between two studies. In one study, the proportion of complaints of fatigue and rates of alcohol consumption and skipping breakfast were higher among male fixed-term workers than retirement system workers [25]. However, a different study showed a higher proportion of those with five or more out of eight positive health habits among temporary and part-time workers than among regular employees [26]. The patterns therefore differ depending on the lifestyle habits examined. It is conceivable that current lifestyle habits will affect future health. Further studies are needed to clarify this point.

Social Security

The next point that is often addressed in public statistics is that of social security, including health insurance and unemployment insurance, that is essential for maintaining a healthy lifestyle. A breakdown by type of precarious employment gives a health insurance coverage rate of 68.9% for contract workers, 73.0% for fixed-term workers, 13.4% for temporary workers, and 38.5% for part-time workers. Differences were also seen in unemployment insurance coverage including accident and injury benefits, at 74.9% for contract workers, 15.0% for temporary workers, and 55.5% for part-time workers [27]. As to whether precarious workers have health insurance, many may be covered as a dependent of a family member. However, it is common nowadays for precarious workers to subsist solely on their own income.

Unemployment insurance is supposed to be eligible to those with 20 or more scheduled work hours a week or anticipated employment of 31 days or longer. Consideration is needed for workers that are not covered under this system. Lack of coverage by social security, including health insurance, and unemployment insurance, is certain to translate to limited access to healthcare services.

Most research carried out in Japan has used a cross-sectional paradigm. This may be because cross-sectional studies are simpler and easier to carry out than other types of studies and because frequent changing of jobs makes it difficult to track precarious workers. Cohort studies are needed to verify causal relationships.

Health Effects of Precarious Employment on Society

While it is clear that current health is worse in precarious workers than in regular employees, we must also consider the effects of precarious employment on society from a broader perspective. This includes investigating, for example, the effects on all workers of having a society that tolerates poor treatment of some of its workers, and of the impact of lifestyle habits on future health.

In one study, poor subjective health, rate of healthcare treatment, and prevalence of symptoms were monitored in workers over a 6-year period from 2001 to 2007 [28]. After controlling for age and other confounding variables, an increase in the rate of poor health was observed in both regular employees and precarious workers, possibly resulting from a period effect. This indicates that unfavorable changes in society, such as worsening employment conditions typified by precarious employment, are affecting the health of all workers, irrespective of type of employment. In particular, the finding that a position of tolerating precarious employment with poor treatment, as is the current situation in Japan, may itself worsen health should be taken very seriously.

Precarious employment in Japan is different from the nonregular employment seen in countries across Europe that enables a good work-life balance or from employment under conditions in which the rights of workers are protected. This type of society itself is liable to have a negative impact on health of all its members. Not only that, but current health management may influence future collective health. Normally, discussions are based on the premise that the ability of workers to work is positively correlated with good health. However, precarious workers, and especially temporary workers, reportedly have few opportunities for health checkups or workplace health management [29], which may affect their health in the future. It is easy to imagine that missing the window for early detection of abnormalities may affect workers over the long term, or in their old age. Even if workers are healthy in the present, holding workers responsible for their lack of opportunities to maintain their health is not a favorable choice for the future health of society as a whole.

Initiatives by Japan and International Organizations Concerning Health in Precarious Employment

Initiatives in Japan

Legal System and Government Actions

It must be remembered that the Labor Standards Law and the Industrial Safety and Health Law were originally intended to cover "all workers," and that eligibility was not to be based on type of employment. As such, all workers should be protected under the current legal system, irrespective of type of employment. Specifically, this includes such measures as health and safety education and obligation of attention to safety. Because such measures are not being enforced, the government sent out an official notice to take measures that address the current situation.

Individual cases are dealt with in a way that accommodates the diversification in type of employment. In addition, in an effort to carry out fundamental measures for dealing with the above issues, the Ministry of Health, Labour and Welfare established an advisory council in June 2011 to formulate a "Vision for Precarious Employment (tentative title)" as the principles underlying directions for measures needed to improve the job stability and treatment of precarious workers and ensure they are given fair treatment. Going forward, we must raise awareness on issues concerning the treatment of precarious workers, including the health of workers.

In particular, more consideration must be given to precarious workers in small business establishments that have been full of challenges up to now. There is no institutional obligation to appoint an industrial physician in workplaces with less than 50 employees. The result is that health issues are frequently arising in workers at small to mid-sized business establishments and independent businesses, even among regular employees. A breakdown by size of business shows a precarious employment rate of more than 35% among those with 1–29 employees. Research is needed to determine what approaches are taken for dealing with the health of precarious workers at small workplaces where interpersonal relationships are limited.

Academic Society Actions

The Committee on Work/Employment Environment and the Lifestyle, Health and Safety of Workers within the Science Council of Japan put together a list of recommendations in March 2011. These recommendations included developing laws for improving treatment of precarious workers and improving the system for ensuring good health and safety throughout the entire labor force [30]. The Study Group on Precarious Employment under the Japan Society for Occupational Health shares research findings and information and carries out educational activities. The Public Health Monitoring Report Committee under the JSPH focuses on precarious employment and other types of unstable employment. The academic world must continue making statements on how to protect the health of workers based on scientific evidence from research findings.

Trends Among International Organizations

Initiatives concerning precarious employment and other types of unstable employment are being encouraged in different countries by the International Labour Organization (ILO) and the World Health Organization (WHO).

In an aim to resolve employment issues in the twenty-first century, the ILO is working towards achieving its Decent Work Agenda (promoting decent work for all) that was proposed at the International Labor Conference (ILC) held in 1999. The ILO reaffirmed its position on social justice in employment at the 100th session of the ILC in 2011 as a fundamental concept in the ILO Constitution that was established in 1919. Two key principles of the Declaration of Philadelphia (1944) were "Labor is not a commodity" and "Poverty anywhere constitutes a danger to prosperity everywhere." These principles may be particularly important warnings to us in the present era. In addition to this conceptual perspective, Japan must once again enhance its efforts towards the ILO Promotional Framework for Occupational Safety and Health Convention (no. 187) that has been ratified and make considerations for proceeding towards conventions that have yet to be ratified, such as the Part-Time Work Convention (no. 175).

The WHO created a special-purpose Commission on Social Determinants of Health that was active from 2005 to 2008. In its final report that was based on support of findings from experimental studies on the health of precarious workers, as mentioned above, one of the commission's recommendations was Fair Employment in Decent Work. The commission recommended that governments resolve the issue of job instability among precarious workers through laws and policies [31]. The future thus holds promise for increasing measures to support the health of unstable workers around the globe.

Recommendations Concerning Health Effects of Precarious Employment

Precarious employment has been shown to affect health in workers and all of society. The health of precarious workers is being carefully examined by international organizations based on research findings that comprise scientific evidence. In light of this situation, we give the following recommendations for activities to be carried out in the field of public health to protect people from the impact of precarious employment on health.

1. Academic societies must strive to spread knowledge among individuals responsible for the health of workers and place pressure on the government and public administration to ensure possible measures are thoroughly carried out within the legal system and the realm of industrial hygiene activities.
2. Because research on the health effects of precarious employment in Japan is scarce, researchers must continue to build the research base. When doing so, care should be given to forming research plans that do not overlook the direction of causality, for example cohort studies, and consider methods for collecting data that take the difficulty of tracking precarious workers into account.
3. Researchers and academic societies must actively publish scientific evidence from research findings and share information with all stakeholders, including policymakers, company employers, those in charge of industrial hygiene, workers, and the general public. Accurate information should be provided in a format that anyone can understand and published using various easily accessible media outlets.
4. We must rectify the adverse effects on society as a whole in the present and the future that are caused by ignoring the suffering of health in precarious workers in Japan and tolerating discrimination of such workers. To achieve these objectives, we must have the citizens of Japan reconsider the ways of society. Under ordinary circumstances, a foundation would be built on changes in attitude and values of every citizen that form our society to achieve a consensus in society as a united group. Under the present circumstances, however, it is doubtful that major decisions in society are actually left to each and every citizen. Therefore, the government should move towards a consensus on a breakthrough in the current situation and create strategies for putting that consensus into action.
5. Health issues in precarious workers include problems that cannot be resolved solely from the perspective of work or health alone. Such problems include lack of education for students before entering the work force and insufficient employer funds for personnel expenses because of cost cutting. We can therefore predict that the manifold problems will not be resolved by each party acting on their own

towards a resolution. Working towards resolving health issues in precarious workers requires searching for clues for such a resolution from a wide perspective, not limited to the boundaries of fields such as healthcare and labor policy. To do so, representatives from the government, academic societies, and the financial and industrial sectors must hold multidisciplinary dialogues to help make strides towards resolutions.

In writing this report, we received support from Mariko Inoue (Graduate School of Public Health, Teikyo University). The views in this report represent a consensus of the Japanese Society of Public Health Monitoring Report Committee and are not attributable to specific individuals.

References

1. Benach J, Muntaner C, Santana V, editors. Employment conditions and health inequalities. Final report to the World Health Organization Commission on Social Determinants of Health. Employment Conditions Knowledge Network. Geneva: World Health Organization; 2007. p. 55–60.
2. Yano E. Part 5. Q&A on precarious employment and health of workers. In: Yano E, Inoue M, editors. Precarious employment and health of workers. Kawasaki: The Institute for Science of Labor; 2011. p. 308–37. (In Japanese).
3. Kawachi I. Inocome inequality and health. In: Berkman LF, Kawachi I, editors. Social epidemiology. New York, NY: Oxford University Press; 2000. p. 76–94.
4. Cabinet Office. White paper on the Japanese economy and public finance 2009. Tokyo: Nikkei Printing Inc.; 2009. p. 227–32. (In Japanese).
5. Marmot M. Introduction. In: Marmot M, Wilkinson RG, editors. Social determinants of health. 2nd ed. New York, NY: Oxford University Press; 2006. p. 1–5.
6. Ministry of Health, Labour and Welfare. White paper on the labour economy 2009. Tokyo: Nikkei Printing Inc.; 2009. p. 166–84. (In Japanese).
7. Ministry of Health, Labour and Welfare. Summary Report of basic survey on wage structure (Nationwide). Tokyo: Ministry of Health, Labour and Welfare; 2010. Available at http://www.mhlw.go.jp/toukei/itiran/roudou/chingin/kouzou/z2010/dl/koyou.pdf. Accessed 11 Jul 2011. (In Japanese).
8. Director General for Economic and Fiscal Management, Cabinet Office (Director-general for Policies on Cohesive Society). Survey report on marriage and family formation. Tokyo: Cabinet Office. Available at http://www8.cao.go.jp/shoushi/cyousa/cyousa22/marriage-family/pdf-zentai/hyoushi-mokuji.pdf. Accessed 11 Jul 2011. (In Japanese).
9. Inoue M. Part 3. Systems behind precarious employment. In: Yano E, Inoue M, editors. Precarious employment and health of workers. Kawasaki: The Institute for Science of Labor; 2011. p. 100–33. (In Japanese).

10. Kobayashi F, Watanabe T. Lifestyle and health of day workers: analysis of 5 years of health records. Jpn J Public Health. 1986;33:761–8. (In Japanese).
11. Temmyo Y. Changes in the migratory worker population in Japan and occupational injuries and diseases. J Sci Lab. 1981;57:21–8. (In Japanese).
12. Ministry of Internal Affairs and Communications. Labor force survey. Tokyo: Ministry of Internal Affairs and Communications. Available at http://www.stat.go.jp/data/roudou/sokuhou/4hanki/dt/index.htm. Accessed 11 Jul 2011.
13. Virtanen M, Kivimäki M, Joensuu M, et al. Temporary employment and health: review. Int J Epidemiol. 2005;34:610–22.
14. Inoue M, Nishikitani M, Tsurugano S, et al. The health of permanent workers and workers with precarious employment: a literature review. Sangyo Eiseigaku Zasshi. 2011;53:117–39. (In Japanese).
15. Kivimäki M, Vahtera J, Virtanen M, et al. Temporary employment and risk of overall and cause-specific mortality. Am J Epidemiol. 2003;158:663–8.
16. Inoue A, Kawakami N, Tsuchiya M, et al. Association of occupation, employment contract, and company size with mental health in a national representative sample of employees in Japan. J Occup Health. 2010;52:227–40.
17. Mizuno E, Sato T, Iwasaki M, et al. Work-related stress and mental health among Japanese employees: using the brief job stress questionnaire. Yamanashi Nurs J. 2008;6:31–6. (In Japanese).
18. Togari T, Yamazaki Y. The socioeconomic gradient of sense of coherence: from a representative sample survey of 4,800 Japanese people aged 20 to 40. Bull Soc Med. 2009;26:45–52. (In Japanese).
19. Inoue M, Tsurugano S, Yano E. Job stress and mental health of permanent and fixed-term workers measured by effort-reward imbalance model, depressive complaints, and clinic utilization. J Occup Health. 2011;53:93–101.
20. Inoue M, Tsurugano S, Nishikitani M, et al. Effort-reward imbalance and its association with health among permanent and fixed-term workers. Biopsychosoc Med. 2010;4:16.
21. Seto M, Morimoto K, Maruyama S. Work and family life of childrearing women workers in Japan: comparison of non-regular employees with short working hours, non-regular employees with long working hours, and regular employees. J Occup Health. 2006;48:183–91.
22. Industrial Safety and Health Department, Labour Standards Bureau, Ministry of Health, Labour and Welfare. Occurrence of fatal and serious accidents in 2009. Tokyo: Ministry of Health, Labour and Welfare. Available at http://www.mhlw.go.jp/stf/houdou/2r98520000006cdg.html. Accessed 11 Jul 2011. (In Japanese).
23. Watanabe M, Fukuda H, Tanaka S. The increasing of applicant of labor disaster insurance in dispatched workers in Japan. Juntendo University Faculty of Health Care and Nursing. J Health Care Nurs. 2011;7:1–9. (In Japanese).
24. Japan Occupational Safety and Health Resource Center. Workers' accident compensation for brain and heart diseases and mental illness. Saf Center News. 2010;7:20–1. (In Japanese).

25. Nakao M, Yano E. A comparative study of behavioural, physical and mental health status between term-limited and tenure-tracking employees in a population of Japanese male researchers. Public Health. 2006;120:373–9. (In Japanese).

26. Yang Y, Haruyama Y, Ichimura K. Relationship between employment status, lifestyle, and self-rated health at major educational institutions for female Japanese workers. Jpn J Health Hum Ecol. 2010;76:164–73. (In Japanese).

27. Ministry of Health, Labour and Welfare. General survey on diversified types of employment. Tokyo: Ministry of Health, Labour and Welfare. Available at http://www.e-stat.go.jp/SG1/estat/NewList.do?tid=000001021304. Accessed 11 Jul 2011. (In Japanese).

28. Tsurugano S, Nishikitani M. Part 4. Does precarious employment deteriorate health? Verification by data analysis. 1. Analysis of the comprehensive survey of living conditions. In: Yano E, Inoue M, editors. Precarious employment and health of workers. Kawasaki: The Institute for Science of Labor; 2011. p. 135–51. (In Japanese).

29. Tatsumi A. Current state of health management in temporary workers and future challenges. Job Stress Res. 2010;17:173–81. (In Japanese).

30. Science Council of Japan. Committee on Work/Employment Environment and the Lifestyle, Health and Safety of Workers. Rebuilding a system related to work/employment health and safety: ensuring health and well-being in workers. Tokyo: Science Council of Japan. Available at http://www.scj.go.jp/ja/info/kohyo/pdf/kohyo-21-t119-2.pdf. Accessed 11 Jul 2011. (In Japanese).

31. Commission on Social Determinants of Health (CSDH). Closing the gap in the generation. health equity through action on the social determinants of health. Final report of the CSDH. Geneva: World Health Organization; 2008. p. 76–83.

Index

© The Author(s) 2020
K. Kondo (ed.), *Social Determinants of Health in Non-communicable Diseases*,
Springer Series on Epidemiology and Public Health,
https://doi.org/10.1007/978-981-15-1831-7